THE LIBERALIZATION OF ELECTRICITY AND NATURAL GAS IN THE EUROPEAN UNION

EUROPEAN MONOGRAPHS

Editor-in-Chief Prof. Dr. K.J.M. Mortelmans

EUROPEAN MONOGRAPHS

The Liberalization of Electricity and Natural Gas in the European Union

Editor

Damien Geradin

KLUWER LAW INTERNATIONAL
THE HAGUE — LONDON — BOSTON

Published by:
Kluwer Law International
P.O. Box 85889, 2508 CN The Hague, The Netherlands
sales@kli.wkap.nl
http://www.kluwerlaw.com

Sold and Distributed in North, Central and South America by:
Kluwer Law International
101 Philip Drive, Norwell, MA 02061, USA
kluwerlaw@wkap.com

Sold and Distributed in all other countries by:
Kluwer Law International
Distribution Centre, P.O. Box 322, 3300 AH Dordrecht, The Netherlands

A C.I.P. Catalogue record for this book is available from the Library of Congress

Printed on acid-free paper.

Typeset by *Steve Lambley Information Design*, The Hague.

ISBN 90 411 1560 9
© 2001 Kluwer Law International

Kluwer Law International incorporates the publishing programmes
of Graham & Trotman Ltd, Kluwer Law and Taxation Publishers
and Martinus Nijhoff Publishers

TABLE OF CONTENTS

The Impact of Liberalization on Long-Term Energy Contracts —
Piet Jan Slot

II. TRANSMISSION AND TRADING

Network Access and Transmission and Distribution Pricing —
Dr. Wolfgang Fritz

Energy Trading in the EU: Commoditization of Electricity and the Emergence of Energy Exchanges — *Dr. Sabine Schulte-Beckhausen*

III. CONSUMER AND ENVIRONMENT PROTECTION

Consumers and Energy Liberalization — *Francis McGowan*

**The Interface between Electricity Liberalization and Environmental
Protection: The German Example —** *Anne Heinen*

IV. COUNTRY REPORTS

Belgium — *Dirk Vandermeersch*

France — *Nicolas Charbit*

Germany — *Dr. Achim-Rüdiger Börner*

Italy — *Gian Carlo Scarsi*

The Netherlands — *Martha Roggenkamp*

FOREWORD

The present volume reproduces the reports, often revised and updated, which were presented at the Conference on "The Liberalisation of the Electricity and Natural Gas Markets in the European Union" held in Brussels in March 2000. In addition, it contains several contributions written in the wake and as a result of the conference. This conference was organized in the framework of the *Pôle d'Attraction Interuniversitaire* (PAI) No. 36 (European Integration Law) granted by the Belgian Prime Minister's office to the University of Liège and the University of Ghent (1990-1996), later joined by the Free University of Brussels (1997-2001). Financial support was also provided by the "Regulation of Network Industries Project" at the University of Liège.

Special thanks are due to Benjamin Matagne, Anne Heinen and Lora Borissova, research assistants at the *Institut d'Etudes Juridiques Européennes* of the University of Liège, who played a central role in the organization of the above conference and in the production of the volume. Thanks also to Simon Neill who corrected the English of several papers.

Damien Geradin
September 2000

INTRODUCTION

The last decade has witnessed a major restructuring of the European electricity and natural gas markets in the European Union. For many years, such sectors were in most EU Member States dominated by public or private, generally vertically-integrated monopolies. Monopolies were often created or at least fostered by the Member States themselves. The theoretical justification for exclusive rights was the "natural monopoly" features of these industries. Monopoly privileges were also granted to the incumbent as the quid pro quo to perform a range of public service obligations.

Today, competition and liberalization are the buzzwords on the lips of all policy-makers and market players. In the early 1990s, some Member States, such as Sweden and the United Kingdom, initiated market opening reforms in the energy sector. For the remaining Member States, the liberalization process was triggered a few years later by the entry into force of Directive 96/92 on the internal market in electricity (the "electricity directive")[1] and Directive 98/30 on the internal market in natural gas (the "natural gas directive").[2] These directives provide that the market opening should initially be at least 26% of demand for electricity and 20% of demand for gas, but that these percentages would be gradually increased over a period of ten years. Interestingly, most Member States when transposing the directives into their national legislation went beyond the minimum opening requirements set by the Council and the European Parliament. In its March 2000 meeting in Lisbon, the European Council decided to accelerate the pace of liberalization in several network industries, including electricity and natural gas. It is expected that the Commission will soon propose measures to translate political will into regulatory commitments.

The energy markets are opening fast; however, liberalization is not something that can be achieved overnight. As pointed out in one of the papers in this volume, liberalization always involves a "process". This process starts with the lifting of the monopoly rights enjoyed by the incumbent. Nothing ensures, however, that the removal of monopoly rights will automatically lead to fully competitive markets.[3] An obvious obstacle in this regard

---

[1] Directive 96/92 of 19 December 1996 concerning the internal market in electricity, O.J. 1997, L 27/20. A copy of this directive is provided in the Annex.

[2] Directive 98/30 of 22 June 1998 concerning the internal market in natural gas, O.J. 1998, L 204/1. A copy of this directive is provided in the Annex.

[3] See generally, D. Geradin, "The Opening of State Monopolies to Competition: Main Issues of the Liberalization Process", in D. Geradin, Ed., *The Liberalization of State Monopolies in the European Union and Beyond*, Kluwer Law International, 2000, p. 182.

Damien Geradin (ed.), The Liberalization of Electricity and Natural Gas in the European Union, xvi–xx
©2001 Kluwer Law International. Printed in the Netherlands.

comes from the fact that the incumbent operator will usually remain dominant during the initial phase of the market opening process – because, for instance, it has a large market share or because it owns or controls essential network infrastructures. Thus, if one wishes liberalized markets to become competitive, it is essential to prevent abuses of market power through the application of competition rules and/or some form of *ex ante* regulation.

Besides creating competition, regulatory reforms in the energy sector must also further other objectives. One is to ensure the continuing performance of public service obligations which, as noted above, have traditionally been entrusted to the incumbents as a counterpart for their monopoly rights. Traditionally, these obligations have been funded through internal cross-subsidies (between profitable and loss-making market segments). Since cross-subsidies will no longer be tolerated in a competitive market, other forms of funding will need to be created. Another important objective is environmental protection. Air pollution and climate change are very serious ecological issues that require attention on the part of European policy-makers. The danger created by liberalization is that cheaper energy prices could very well translate into increased energy consumption and, thus, more pollution. A regulatory framework thus need to be adopted to ensure that the liberalization of energy markets does not aggravate the environmental problems created by energy use.

In the light of the above developments, the objective of this book is to take a closer look at the complex challenges raised by the liberalization of the electricity and natural gas markets in the European Union. The book is divided into four parts.

Part I comprises two papers examining the competition law issues generated by the liberalization of energy markets. The first paper (by Dr. Albers)[4] offers a panorama of such issues, whereas the second (by Professor Slot)[5] focuses on the compatibility of long-term energy contracts with EC competition law.

Dr. Albers identifies the four main competition law issues arising from the liberalizing process as: (i) the problems created by the continuing natural monopoly features of the transmission networks and the lack of capacity of interconnectors; (ii) the co-operation agreements and mergers between former monopolists; (iii) the various practices restricting the freedom of the consumer to choose their supplier; and (iv) the treatment of stranded costs as a form of State aid. These issues are complex, but also terribly important. For instance, refusal to grant access to the electricity grid or market consolidation through mergers and acquisitions could be used by incumbents as strategies to prevent market entry and consolidate their grip on the energy market. In this context, the challenge for the Commission will be to apply competition rules in a field where such rules have been ignored for a very long time.

Following the general overview provided by Dr. Albers, Professor Slot's paper concentrates on long-term supply contracts. Such contracts are widespread in the electricity and natural gas markets in particular due to the large capital investments that are involved.

---

[4] M. Albers, "Competition Law Issues Arising from the Liberalisation Process".

[5] P.J. Slot, "The Impact of Liberalisation on Long-Term Energy Contracts".

In a context of liberalization, the danger with such contracts is that they may bind customers to continue purchase their energy supplies from the incumbent for a very long period of time. Professor Slot's paper shows how the Commission has generally sought to reduce the length of the long-term contracts concluded between producers and customers. It also assesses the impact of the regulatory framework established by the electricity and natural gas directives on the validity of such contracts. Furthermore, Professor Slot examines the possible impact of the European Commission's reforms to modernize competition law on the application of competition rules to long-term contracts. The major elements of this reform are the new Block Exemption Regulation 2790/93 on vertical agreements, the Guidelines on horizontal agreement, and the White Paper on Modernization. As pointed out by the author, it is not clear whether this new approach to competition law enforcement relying heavily on national competition authorities and national courts will be appropriate in a sector where, as noted above, competition rules have been hardly applied in the past.

Part II of the book contains two papers dealing respectively with network access and pricing (paper by Dr. Fritz) [6] and energy trading (paper by Dr. Schulte-Beckhausen). [7]

In the first of these papers, Dr. Fritz, an engineer with a strong background in economics, provides an introduction to the technical issues and pricing principles of open access to energy transmission, with a special reference to the electricity sector. Electricity is a network industry. Producers need to have access to the electricity transport infrastructure in order to supply their customers. In a liberalized environment, a particular difficulty comes from the fact that the network infrastructure is both non-duplicable and generally controlled by the incumbent. Third party access (TPA) thus becomes a critical factor. Dr Fritz's paper explores how TPA operates in practice and discusses the various technical rules that have to be agreed on to make TPA work. His paper also examines the two main methods of calculating access charges (i.e., point-of-connection-based and transaction-based charges) and their consequences on competition.

Dr Schulte-Beckhausen's paper discusses the development of energy trading in a liberalized environment. After a brief description of the regulatory framework in which such trading takes place, this paper outlines the various types of physical contracts and financial tools that are currently used by market players. Physical contracts include long-term, spot and forward contracts. Financial tools, which do not include the physical delivery of electricity but only involve cash settlements, include swaps, options and futures. Dr. Schulte-Beckhausen explains that traders and customers use the different kinds of physical contracts and financial tools to compose their individual portfolio and that efficient portfolio management ensures an optimized mix of energy supplies according to the needs of the company. She also discusses the development of common market places, such as energy exchanges. The first energy exchanges were established in Scandinavia (Norway and

---

[6] W. Fritz, "Network Access and Transmission and Distribution Pricing".

[7] S. Schulte-Beckhausen, "Energy Trading in the EU: Commoditisation of Electricity and the Emergence of Energy Exchanges".

Finland), but they can now be found in several other European countries (e.g., the Dutch APX in Amsterdam or the Spanish OMEL in Madrid).

The two papers comprising Part III of the book examine the impact of energy liberalization on non-strictly economic objectives, such as consumer protection (paper by F. Mc Gowan)[8] and environmental protection (paper by A. Heinen).[9]

After a brief review of how "the consumer" has figured in the debate on liberalization, F. Mc Gowan's paper focuses on the actual impact of energy liberalization on consumers (based on the experience of UK regulatory reforms in the electricity and natural gas sectors). The paper looks at the impact on prices and other aspects of service, the role of the regulator and customer representation. The paper also looks at the impact of EU policies on consumers, in terms of the directives themselves, the overall EU energy policy and the overall approaches to consumer and competition policy. The paper then examines how utilities' responses to liberalization affect the consumer, taking into account such factors such as the "discovery" of the consumer triggered by competition and the consequences of the wave of corporate restructuring in the energy sector. F. Mc Gowan's paper then assesses the consumer's response to these changes, particularly in terms of the articulation of interests and the relationship to regulatory processes.

Anne Heinen's paper seeks to show that the liberalization process does not necessarily contradict the idea of sustainable development. However, sustainable development will only be achieved provided that a proper regulatory framework is adopted encouraging *inter alia* a reduction of fossil fuels and an increasing resort to renewable energies. Ms Heinen notes that whether such regulatory framework should be adopted at the EU level or at the level of the Member States is an open question. However, her discussion of the environmental statutes that were adopted by Chancellor Schröder's Red-Green coalition shows that unilateral measures raise complex legal issues of compatibility with the free trade provisions of the EC Treaty and are very difficult to implement due to strong political objections. In this context, collective action at the EU level to encourage sustainable development is a more effective approach.

Finally, Part IV contains four country reports analyzing the current state of liberalization in Belgium,[10] France,[11] Germany,[12] Italy,[13] and the Netherlands.[14] These reports show that there is a lot of diversity in the approaches chosen by the Member States to implement the electricity and natural gas directives. This is in great part due to the fact that the two

---

[8] F. Mc Gowan, "Consumers and Energy Liberalisation".

[9] A. Heinen, "The Interface between Electricity Liberalisation and Environmental Protection: The German Example".

[10] By D. Vandermeersch.

[11] By N. Charbit.

[12] By Dr. R.A. Börner.

[13] By G.C. Scarsi.

[14] By M. Roggenkamp.

liberalizing directives establish loose regulatory framework leaving a great deal of freedom to the Member States as to the means of liberalizing their market. It is open to question whether this approach inspired by the idea of subsidiarity is adequate to the task of creating an EU-wide energy market. The country reports also show that some Member States, such as Belgium and France, failed to implement the directives in due time. While in Belgium the delay in implementing the directives is in great part due to the complex institutional structure of the country, the French Government's extreme slowness to implement the directives seems to be motivated by the desire to protect as long as possible EdF and GdF, the two state-owned incumbents. This failure to implement within the deadlines set by the directives raised interesting legal questions, such as the direct effect of the provisions written in these instruments.

Damien Geradin

I. COMPETITION

Michael Albers

COMPETITION LAW ISSUES ARISING FROM THE LIBERALIZATION PROCESS

I. INTRODUCTION

The Community electricity markets are in the process of being opened up to competition. Since 19 February 1999 approximately 65% of the total demand for electricity in the EC has been liberalized. The gas markets will follow in August this year. The expectation is that around 80% of total EC demand for gas will then be liberalized. The "eligible" customers include the largest consumers of electricity and gas in the Community.[1] This creates powerful economic incentives for suppliers to compete. Such a degree of market opening is highly successful compared with the sceptical predictions made at the time of the adoption of the directives.

Respectively 1996[2] and 1998,[3] the Council decided that the electricity and gas markets should be liberalized initially to the level of at least 26% of demand for electricity and 20% of demand for gas, these percentages to gradually increase over a period of approximately 10 years, without fixing a date, for the markets to be fully liberalized. However, most Member States, have gone beyond the minimum liberalization thresholds set by the Council when implementing the Electricity Directive into national law.[4] It looks as if they will do the same for gas. These developments have attained a certain momentum. The European Council decided to use this momentum and agreed at the special meeting in Lisbon on 23/24 March 2000 "*to speed up liberalisation in areas such as gas, electricity, postal services and transport*".[5] The Commission may call for further market opening by proposing amendments to the existing electricity and gas directives to the European Council meeting in Stockholm in March 2001.[6]

The liberalization of an industry always involves a process. The process commences

---

[1] Eligible customers are those which are free first to choose among suppliers as defined by national law in accordance with the Community directives.

[2] Directive 96/92/EC of 19 December 1996 concerning the internal market in electricity, OJ No. L 27, 30 January 1997, p.20 (cited as ED in the text).

[3] Directive 98/30/EC of 22 June 1998 concerning the internal market in natural gas, OJ No. L 204, 21 July 1998, p.1.

[4] See *Second Report from the Commission to the Council and the European Parliament on the State of Liberalisation of the Energy Markets*, COM(1999) 198 final, 4 May 1999, p.5-11.

[5] See Press Release Lisbon (24 March 2000) – Nr:100/00.

[6] See *Communication from the Commission to the Council and the European Parliament on the recent progress with building the internal electricity market*, COM (2000) 297 final, 16 May 2000, p.11.

Damien Geradin (ed.), The Liberalization of Electricity and Natural Gas in the European Union, 3–17
©2001 Kluwer Law International. Printed in the Netherlands.

with the lifting of the monopoly rights of incumbent operators. This triggers the transformation of the industry. Monopolistic supply structures give way to competitive structures
and national markets grow into wider geographic markets which may eventually become
Community-wide while ensuring the continuity of national public service obligations.
The experience with the liberalization of the European telecommunications and the transport
industries is likely to be repeated with the European electricity and gas industries.

The transformation of industries with monopolistic structures triggers a number of
competition problems. This is due to the fact that former suppliers in monopoly positions
have an economic incentive to maintain their historic dominant position as long as possible.
The network monopoly, which is a particular feature of the electricity and gas industries,
is, for economic reasons, likely to remain a permanent monopoly in the foreseeable future.

The competition issues arising from liberalization are addressed by EC competition
law and policy. EC competition policy complements the Community's internal market
and energy policies. Whereas the latter have as their objective the abolition of legal obstacles,
EC competition policy has as its goal the removal of the remaining, mainly factual obstacles
to competition and the single market.

This article will deal with four competition law issues arising from the liberalization
process:
- firstly, problems related to the continuing network monopoly;
- secondly, cooperation agreements and mergers between former monopolists;
- thirdly, practices restricting consumers' choice of supplier; and
- fourthly, the treatment of stranded costs as a State aid.

It will conclude with a word on the cooperation of the Commission with the newly created
national regulatory authorities.

Since liberalization is more advanced in the electricity industry, the focus will be on
this industry at the current stage of the transformation process. Little can, at this stage, be
said about competition issues in gas markets because they have only been opened up in a
few Member States. However, this does not mean that none of the lessons learnt from the
first experiences in the electricity industry cannot also be applied to the gas industry which
will be opened up later this year.

II. NETWORK ISSUES

The most complex but also the most interesting competition law issues of the liberalization of the electricity industry arise from the continuing network monopoly. The electricity
industry is a network industry. The delivery of electricity to customers is effected via the
grid linking upstream supply with downstream consumers. The electricity grid shows
features of what economists call a "natural monopoly". The network is costly to establish
and embodies substantial fixed costs that determine economies of scale within the capacity

of a network. Hence the duplication of networks is normally not economical.[7]

This means in the terms of competition law that transmission system operators (TSOs) regularly enjoy a dominant position within the meaning of Article 82 of the EC Treaty within the geographical area covered by their grid. Electricity suppliers must, therefore, be provided with non-discriminatory access to the grid at fair prices in order to be able to compete effectively for customers.

Due to the vertical integration of power generation with grid operations in the European electricity industry there has never previously been a market for the provision of the transmission of electricity. Liberalization thus calls for the emergence of transmission services and the development of a transmission price.

A. Transmission Pricing

EC competition law does not prescribe a particular method for the calculation of prices. It only prohibits the imposition of unfair selling prices or other unfair trading conditions (Article 82(a) of the EC Treaty). Unfair prices are either predatory or excessive. EC competition law, thus, only sets the outer limits of permissible market conduct with regard to prices.

The issue of the calculation of transmission prices arose, for example, in Germany where industry Associations concluded a framework agreement setting out joint principles for the calculation of prices ("*Verbändevereinbarung*"). The associations were able to do so because Germany opted for the system of negotiated third-party-access to networks in implementing the Electricity Directive (Article 17 (1)). The first framework agreement was based on a price model which – in simplified terms – provided that the transmission of electrons should be calculated in a similar way to the transport of coal by train. Transmission prices are transaction-based. This means that a user of the network has to conclude a contract with the TSO each time a transmission is to take place. Furthermore, the price for the transmission depends, inter alia, on the distance between the location of the power plant (generation) and the location of the consumer (load). The distance component applied to all high-voltage transmissions in excess of 100 km.

The use of the distance component obviously renders the transmission of electricity over longer distances more costly. This has the effect of shielding power generation located in the vicinity of consumers against competition from more distant German or other Community suppliers.

In addition, the German Associations' agreement provided for the calculation of a weighted minimum distance in the case of multiple network generation and load points. This price component appears to give a competitive advantage to electricity suppliers with many power plants spread over a wider geographical area. It seems to operate to the benefit

---

[7] See *European Economy* (1999) No.4, "Liberalisation of Network Industries", p.21 (ed. European Commission).

of large incumbent producers. In contrast, smaller or foreign producers as well as newcomers with only one feed-in point would have to meet higher transmission prices and thus suffer a competitive disadvantage.[8]

Both distance components of the German *Verbändevereinbarung I* also raise doubts with regard to the underlying model for calculating the transmission price. Electrons do not travel like coal. They do not necessarily, as in the case of coal, follow the path laid out by the supply contract concluded between a supplier and his customer in the highly meshed networks of most Member States.

Meshed networks are characterized by the fact that there is not only one single line but several interconnected lines between generation and load. In addition, many generators feed in electricity at different points and consumers use electricity at even more points. Electrons move within the meshed network in accordance with the laws of physics. For instance, two transactions in opposite directions cancel each other out physically. There are also loop flows, i.e. electrons flow not only on the lines directly connecting the generation point with the load point, but also on other parallel running lines in accordance with the law of the least resistance.

For highly meshed networks the model of a lake probably represents the physical reality of transmission better that the model of the coal train. Generators are "pouring in" electrons and consumers are "drawing out" electrons like drops. The lake model may, therefore, also be more appropriate for designing a transmission tariff. If this is correct, the transaction-based approach of the German framework agreement as well as the use of the distance components may not be compatible with competition law.

According to the jurisprudence of the European Court of Justice a price is unfairly high within the meaning of Article 82 of the EC Treaty if it is excessive in relation to the economic value of the service provided.[9] The excess can be determined by making a comparison between the selling price and the cost of production.[10] A particular method for, or component of, the price calculation which lacks cost-reflectivity may thus be regarded as unfair within the meaning of Article 82 of the EC Treaty if it leads to excessive prices.

The original German framework agreement has been replaced in December 1999 by the so-called *Verbändevereinbarung II*. The new framework agreement now uses the lake model as a basis for price calculations. It provides for a non-transaction based tariff without any distance components within the newly introduced North and South German "trading zones".

The agreement proposes that German TSOs recover the network costs through simple connection charges from network users depending, *inter alia*, on the electricity they consume. The price a consumer has to pay for transmission does not alter with the change of the supplier within the same trading zone. Consumers can thus switch suppliers more

---

[8] See 1998 *Competition Policy Newsletter* No.3 (October) p.43-46.

[9] Case 26/75, *General Motors v. Commission*, (1975) E.C.R. 1367 §12.

[10] Case 27/76, *United Brands v. Commission*, (1978) E.C.R. 207 §255.

easily. This non-transaction based price will obviously foster competition among suppliers. It will also significantly facilitate the development of spot markets and power exchanges in Germany.

The competition issue of cost reflectiveness of transmission prices also arose in the Netherlands. This Member State introduced a non-transaction based tariff based on the lake model. However, consumers and producers share the total cost of transmitting electricity through the grid in the proportions 75% and 25% respectively. The dominant Dutch TSO intended to charge suppliers the same fee as domestic suppliers, i.e. 25%, for imports into the Netherlands as well as for transit transmissions of electricity through the Netherlands.

When it was consulted by the Dutch regulatory authority, the Commission replied that the Dutch TSO must only charge for import and transit transmissions to the extent that these cause extra costs on the lines interconnecting the Dutch grid with other grids in neighbouring Member States. In the emerging internal market for energy it is quite possible for electricity to be traded several times across national boundaries. This is particularly the case in Member States with a power exchange such as exists in the Netherlands. Care must be taken that foreign traders only pay import charges for electricity which is actually imported from another Member State. Only where electricity is imported for the first time into the Netherlands has the dominant TSO not already been paid the transmission charges. It is, however, for importers to prove the origin of the imported electricity.

B. Access to Interconnectors

Another important competition issue concerning the network monopoly is access to the grid and, more specifically, access to interconnectors. The electricity systems of most Member States are linked by interconnectors. These electricity lines which are sometimes submarine cables allow electricity to be transmitted across borders. They are essential elements of the trans-European electricity network, the existence of which is a pre-condition for the success of the internal electricity market.

Now that markets have been opened up suppliers and consumers can use interconnectors to import electricity from Member States with lower electricity prices. In those Member States that have a monopolistic supply structure, interconnectors will be the only source for competition for some time. Access to interconnectors is thus crucial for rendering liberalization effective for European consumers.

1. Allocation Methods

Access to interconnectors is becoming an issue for competition law because many of these cross-border lines lack sufficient capacity to carry all the electricity which producers, traders and large consumers, using their new market freedom, wish to import. TSOs are obliged to adapt their transmission system, and their interconnectors with other systems, to the new pattern of demand in the internal electricity market (Article 7(1) of the electricity directive). However, the enlargement and reinforcement of interconnection capacity takes time and in the meantime TSOs are exploring various methods to allocate the available transmission capacity whenever demand exceeds supply. The most frequently applied methods are pro-rata rationing and auctions. Pro-rata rationing means that all requested transactions are carried out but each transaction quantity is cut by the same percentage. No cuts occur in the case of an auction, however, only the highest bidders obtain the available capacity. Other allocation methods which seem to be applied in practice are "first-come-first-served" and merit order. Merit order means, for example, that the lowest bidder to a pool wins not only a supply contract but also transmission rights.

Again, competition law does not prescribe the implementation of a particular method for the allocation of transmission rights. It sets only the outer limits for dominant network operators within which they are free to use the method which suits best their particular situation.

This certainly holds true for the compatibility with the competition rules of pro-rata rationing. The Court has already dealt with this allocation method in a judgment concerning Article 82 of the EC Treaty. The case concerned a petrol company which cut supplies to an occasional customer during the 1974-1975 oil crisis. The Court can be interpreted as having approved pro-rata rationing in its decision, although it did not really have to take a position on the issue. The Court annulled the contested Commission decision on the ground that occasional and regular customers are not in an equivalent situation so the dominant firm could apply dissimilar conditions to each customer group.[11]

Pro-rata rationing is currently applied at several borders as well as to bottlenecks inside some Member States.[12] It seems to work in practice as long as demand does not exceed available capacity to a too large extent. If, however, demand exceeds free capacity more than 100 times, pro-rata rationing may lead to the allocation of so little capacity that the individual transaction loses its commercial value. This unfortunate result can be avoided by the use of auctions.

The compatibility of auctions with EC competition law is less clear. The Commission has intervened twice against tender procedures in telecommunications cases. Both cases concerned the first grant of a concession for the operation of a GSM network which would be the first competitor to the incumbent monopolist. The Commission was opposed to the use of auctions on the grounds that the payment of a lump sum would raise the cost of entry for the new entrant and create thus a competitive disadvantage vis-à-vis the state-

---

[11] Case 77/77, *BP v. Commission*, (1978) E.C.R. 1526-28.

[12] See, for example, BKartA, Decision of 30 August 1999, (2000) Wirtschaft und Wettbewerb DE-V 149.

owned telecommunications operator which did not pay an entry fee.[13] Both GSM cases are not easily comparable to the allocation of interconnector transmission rights. The GSM operators had to pay a fee for being the first new entrant into a telecommunications market. The fee for the allocation of electricity transmission rights will normally neither be of similar magnitude, nor will it be the price for market entry. It will only be the price for carrying out one or several supply contracts. Furthermore, very often there is no link between the TSO putting out the tender for transmission rights and the company holding a dominant position on the import market to which bidders request access. Where such links exist and the use of auctions becomes, therefore, more questionable, doubts as to the compatibility of the allocation method with EC competition law might be removed through ring fencing. This means that the proceeds of auctions are employed to reinforce the capacity of the interconnector with the aim of eliminating the bottleneck. This, of course, presupposes that such reinforcing is possible in the foreseeable future. The combination of auction with ring fencing may then create a prospect of market entry which may even have a disciplinary effect on the pricing behaviour of the dominant supplier on the downstream electricity market before the interconnector is actually reinforced.

The allocation method which might raise most doubts under the EC competition rules is arguably based on the "first-come-first-served" principle. This method can, under certain circumstances, favour former monopolists over new entrants, for instance, in a situation where the dominant firm concluded long-term reservation contracts before liberalization with the effect that new entrants are foreclosed from entering downstream electricity markets. The fourth allocation method mentioned, merit order, in contrast, would appear to be neutral from a competition point of view. This would seem at least to be true when it is combined with bidding into a pool.

The issue of allocating scarce transmission capacity might be better resolved by measures like redispatching of generation plants, countertrading or market splitting on either side of a bottleneck. The first measures would be taken by an independent TSO which is empowered to directly change the dispatching order of power plants connected to its grid in order to create overall electricity flows which remain within the limits of the network constraints or to engage in offsetting trading contracts through purchasing or selling electricity from generators or even consumers that are willing to increase or decrease generation or consumption. Market splitting normally requires a common spot-market and the possibility that there are different spot-market prices on either side of the bottleneck. Since electricity is likely to become more expensive in the area which is undersupplied, market participants are less interested in buying from this area and the flow over the bottleneck is reduced.[14]

---

[13] Commission, 1995 OJ L 280/49 – *Italy*, 1997 OJ L 76/19 – *Spain*; see also *Green Paper on radio spectrum policy*, COM (1998) 569, 9 December 1998 and Directive 97/13/EC of 10 April 1997 on a common framework for authorizations and individual licences in the field of telecommunication services, OJ No. L 117, 7 May 1997, p.15.

[14] See *Second Report to the Council and the European Parliament on Harmonisation Requirements*, COM(1999) 164 final, 16 April 1999, p.37.

The introduction of such measures requires, however, the adoption of legislation and, if they are to apply across national boundaries, Community directives or, at least, internationally binding agreements between Member States. It will take some time to achieve the harmonization of developed methods of capacity allocation. Until such harmonization is achieved EC competition law marks the outer limits of admissible methods. It provides a minimum level of harmonization of rules governing market conduct and thus a minimum level playing field for the internal electricity market.

2. Long-Term Reservation Contracts

Interconnectors very often become bottlenecks because of existing long-term reservation contracts concluded by former monopolists before liberalization. The assessment of reservation contracts under the EC competition rules depends on the particular circumstances of each case. Generalizations are difficult and risky. It may nevertheless be possible and helpful to distinguish between two extreme cases.

The first case would be a long-term contract which enables the TSO to make the construction of the interconnector at all commercially possible and viable. This is very often the case for submarine cables linking two national electricity systems for the first time. Since these interconnectors obviously increase competition, at least in the longer term, such long-term contracts will normally be compatible with the EC competition rules. The only issue arising in this context is, for how long are the contracting parties allowed to use the new line exclusively. In this regard the length of time required to ensure the parties a proper return on their investment is necessarily an essential factor to be taken into account.[15]

The Commission intervened in the case of a new interconnector where the TSO originally granted a power supplier priority rights for up to 100% of the available transmission capacity for 15 years. The reservation had been concluded some years before the adoption of the Electricity Directive and, therefore, had not been awarded in an open and transparent procedure. The network operator, who is solely responsible for the construction of the new interconnector, received funds from the European Community for the project. The Commission regarded the long-term reservation as excessive in terms both of capacity utilization and duration even when considering that it concerned a new submarine cable. After discussions with the competent national regulatory authority the parties informed the Commission of modifications of their agreement reducing the reserved capacity utilization to 50% for the duration of less than 6 years. This enabled the Commission to approve the modified agreement.

The other extreme case would be a contract through which two dominant suppliers reserve for themselves on a reciprocal exclusive basis the available transmission capacity

---

[15] Case T-374/94, T-375/94, T-384/94 and T-388/94, *ENS v. Commission*, (1998) E.C.R. II-3231 §230.

of an interconnector which is a simple connection point between two existing neighbouring grids for imports into their respective areas of supply. This agreement would appear to fall under Article 82 of the EC Treaty, in particular in situations where the most likely source of competition would be the supplier on the neighbouring geographic market. The contract reserving capacity might even be regarded as a vehicle to exclude potential competition among themselves, so that Article 81 of the EC Treaty may apply too.

All other cases of long-term reservation contracts will most probably fall in between these two extreme cases. This means that a refusal to grant access has to be objectively justified in a situation where the refusal has the effect of hindering competition in the downstream market for electricity.[16] If the TSO cannot validly justify the refusal, the requested transmission has to be carried out.

Transmission pricing and access to interconnectors are currently the most topical competition issues concerning networks. The continuing monopoly of the network poses a risk to the emergence of effective competition between electricity suppliers. Transmission tariffs must, therefore, be monitored closely in order to avoid excessive prices. In addition to excessive pricing, there is a risk of discriminatory conduct if a TSO is vertically integrated with an electricity supplier. It is an open question whether trade customs can successfully be developed to suppress the economic incentives derived from the vertical integration of transmission and generation. The stakes seem to be high. There may be a risk that supply competition remains limited to vertically integrated electricity companies because they alone can sustain a strategy of low electricity prices on the one hand and high transmission prices on the other. Complete "unbundling" might be the most appropriate means to remedy this competition issue as the experience of those Member States with economically independent TSOs suggests.[17]

III. COOPERATION AGREEMENTS AND MERGERS BETWEEN SUPPLIERS

There are other competition issues not linked to the network monopoly. The opening-up of electricity markets creates new opportunities for energy companies to grow. Some may regard it as a challenge which they can only meet in cooperation with other energy providers. Their customers may even contribute to this development in demanding single sourcing either for all their energy purchases or, at least, for all their purchases of a particular energy source in respect of all their business locations in the Community. Liberalization is thus leading to a re-structuring of the European energy industry through cooperation agreements and mergers. A similar increase of merger activity has been observed before in the European telecommunication and air transport industries.

---

[16] Case 85/76, *Hoffmann-La Roche v. Commission*, (1979) E.C.R. 461 §91.

[17] The TSO is an economically independent entity without supply interests in Finland, Sweden and UK.

A. Cooperation Agreements and Mergers between Electricity Suppliers

Cooperation agreements between electricity suppliers tend to be pro-competitive, if they allow these companies to enter the new electricity markets in order to trade at exchanges[18] or network services.[19] The same is true for joint ventures or mergers with the objective to enter into new geographic markets, in particular if these are highly concentrated.[20] Small suppliers (e.g. municipal companies) may also enter into cooperation agreements in order to better compete for large industrial customers.

Mergers and cooperation agreements between former monopolists that have become direct competitors as a result of market liberalization are more problematic. They raise the risk that the strong market positions of the parties will be consolidated in their former exclusive supply areas. The actual and future conditions for competition at the supply level will have to be assessed. The percentages of market opening, the degree of unbundling of TSOs (at the management, legal and ownership levels) and the actual conditions for and practice of third-party access (TPA) to the grid are important in this regard. Competing suppliers must have real opportunities to enter the supply territory of the merging or cooperating companies. If entry into the supply area of the former monopolists becomes less likely, the merger will most probably not be compatible with EC competition law.

Only one case has met difficulties with the Commission so far. EDF planned to form a joint venture with Louis Dreyfus that would be active in electricity trading. The French market had not been opened up at the time of the notification. The conditions and terms of TPA as well as the identity of eligible customers in France were not known. EDF would have been the only trader on the French market and thus would have been able to gain a competitive advantage over its competitors which were barred from entry. The Commission found that the joint venture would re-enforce its dominant position on the French electricity market under these conditions. The venture was subsequently cleared after EDF had undertaken that it would not offer trade services in France until the market is effectively open.[21]

---

[18] See for example Commission decisions 30 November 1999 – *Sydkraft/HEW* and 11.12.1998 – *DEO*; the full text of these decisions is available at: http://europa.eu.int/comm/dg04/index_en.htm.

[19] See for example Commission decision 3 February 2000 – *TXU/EDF London Investments*.

[20] See for example Commission decisions 15 October 1998 – *ENW/Eastern*, 30 September 1999 – *PreussenElektra/ EZH, Vattenfall/HEW*, 17 March 1998 – *EDF/Estag*, 25 May 1998 – *EDF/Graninge*, 27 January 1999 – *EDF/ London Electricity*, 19 July 1999 – *EDF/South Western Electricity*, 8 June 1995 – *EDF/Edison/ISE*, 5 January 2000 – *Fortum/Elektrizitätswerke Wesertal*, 7 February 2000 – *Electrabel/EPON*.

[21] Commission decision 28 September 1999 – *EDF/Dreyfus*.

B. Cooperation Agreements and Mergers between Electricity Suppliers and Other Energy Providers

There seems to be a trend towards the creation of companies selling electricity together with other energy ("multi-energy"). Companies with an established distribution network may see a competitive advantage in marketing electricity in addition to gas or other fuels. At the same time consumers with more complex energy requirements, in particular industrial customers, may wish to purchase all their energy from one single source.

Cooperation agreements as well as mergers between suppliers of different energy sources can again be pro-competitive if they lead to new operators entering the market. However, electricity is, at least potentially, substitutable with other energy sources used by households (cooking, heating, hot water) as well as by industrial operators (traction, heat). Although it is true that its substitutability is not perfect because it is very often more costly to use electricity and different equipment may be necessary, competition problems cannot be ruled out. It will depend on the particular circumstances of each individual case whether the cooperation or merger is compatible with EC competition law.[22]

Competition problems have arisen in the past when a dominant electricity producer intended to merge with a dominant gas importer and wholesaler. Gas is one of the energy sources from which electricity may be increasingly produced because of its economic and environmental advantages. It is expected that the growth of the gas market in the next decade will be driven to a considerable extent by the use of gas as a fuel for electricity generation.[23] A merger between a dominant electricity supplier and a dominant gas wholesaler may thus allow the electricity supplier to gain control over the most important source of competition in electricity generation. Competing electricity producers, who intend to enter a new geographic market on the basis of a gas-fired plant, may have to purchase the fuel from the incumbent dominant electricity supplier. Furthermore, the dominant electricity producer may be able to influence the choice of industrial consumers whether to engage in auto-production of electricity or to purchase from the incumbent. For these reasons the two merger cases of *Tractebel/Distrigaz* and *Neste/IVO* were initially opposed by the Commission. Both mergers were only approved after the parties had undertaken to divest their bulk gas sales business to a third party.[24]

---

[22] See for example Commission decision 20 January 1999 – *GDF/Bewag/Gasag*.

[23] *1999 Energy in Europe*, Special Issue December, "Economic Foundations for Energy Policy", p.27, 98 (ed. European Commission).

[24] See Commission decisions 1 September 1994 – *Tractebel/Distrigaz* (II) §47-49 and 2 June 1998 – *Neste/IVO* §47-61.

IV. SUPPLY CONTRACTS WITH CONSUMERS

A third category of competition law issues relates to supply contracts between electricity producers and their customers. These supply contracts have traditionally been long-term and if not, for an indefinite duration and exclusive. On competitive markets with sufficient liquidity such contracts are rather the exception than the rule as can already be observed on the electricity markets of Sweden and Great Britain which are more advanced in terms of liberalization than other markets. In order that liberalization process may advance, it is very important that eligible customers are really free to switch suppliers and are not bound by long-term supply contracts obliging them to take all their electricity from the former monopolist.

Exclusive purchasing commitments on a long-term basis are certainly not restrictive of competition as such, even if such contracts are frequently applied by suppliers. A dominant supplier has, however, a special responsibility not to impair emerging competition.[25] What may be neutral for competition for smaller market participants, may jeopardize competition, if applied by a dominant firm. Exclusive supply contracts on a long-term basis may create an obstacle for smaller competitors to expand their sales or for potential competitors to enter the market in question. A dominant firm is thus likely to abuse its market position within the meaning of Article 82 of the EC Treaty if it ties a substantial proportion of demand with an obligation to purchase on a long-term exclusive basis from the market leader.[26] Ties constitute an abuse irrespective of whether exclusivity is stipulated without further qualification or whether it is undertaken in consideration of the grant of a rebate.[27]

Dominant electricity suppliers will sometimes allow their customers to switch to another supplier if a competitor is able to offer more favourable terms and the dominant firm is not willing to match those terms ("English clause"). Such a clause has a discouraging effect on price competition because it creates price transparency for the dominant firm and allows it to react without lowering prices to a greater degree. Therefore, it infringes Article 82 of the EC Treaty and is prohibited.[28]

V. STRANDED COSTS

The fourth competition issue arising from the liberalization process to be mentioned here is the issue of stranded costs. Many electricity companies have given commitments or guarantees of operation to their governments which are not tenable under conditions of competitive markets. Examples of such commitments and guarantees are purchases of

---

[25] Case 322/81, *Michelin v. Commission*, (1983) E.C.R. 3461 §57.

[26] Case T-65/89, *BPB v. Commission*, (1993) E.C.R. II-389 §68.

[27] See *Hoffmann-La Roche*, §89 (footnote 16).

[28] See *Hoffmann-La Roche*, §107 (footnote 16).

electricity at a higher than average cost on a long-term basis or the construction of power plants in order to secure employment in structurally under-developed regions.

The Council recognized this problem and provided for a transitional regime which would allow the electricity companies concerned to obtain relief for their commitments or guarantees. The Electricity Directive provides that derogations from, for example, the obligation to grant third-party-access, could be given by the Commission (Article 24). Whereas two Member States notified and obtained temporary derogations from specific obligations of the Electricity Directive, eleven Member States did not wish to delay market opening in order to compensate for stranded costs and opted for the grant of financial assistance.

Aid given by a Member State or through State resources is subject to the Treaty rules on State aid. Financial compensation for stranded costs can endanger emerging competition on recently opened up markets and seriously distorts trade in the developing internal market. The Commission and the Member States agreed therefore that guidelines for the examination of State aid granted to electricity companies will be established and that all aid schemes will be scrutinized in accordance with these guidelines. Thus all financial measures of compensation will be assessed in a coherent and equitable fashion.

The guidelines will provide, *inter alia*, that the alleged stranded cost is a real cost and not only a risk. Furthermore, a causal link must exist between a stranded cost which will be compensated for by State aid and the opening up of electricity markets. Compensation for all turnover losses since February 1999, the date of the opening-up of the electricity markets, would not be acceptable. Furthermore, the actual amount of State aid must be fixed in view of actual price developments after liberalization. It cannot be fixed ex-ante. Payments may be effected beforehand. However, provision must be made for the return of payments, if price reductions are smaller than expected. A Member State, therefore, has to ensure that State aid is limited to the stranded costs actually incurred.

VI. COOPERATION BETWEEN THE COMMISSION AND NATIONAL COMPETITION AND REGULATORY AUTHORITIES

The Commission has exclusive power to monitor State aid. However, the Commission can also rely on national authorities in respect of other competition issues raised in connection with liberalized electricity markets. Most Member States have established a new regulatory authority which will monitor the market conduct of the electricity companies and in particular the access of third parties to the grid as required by the Electricity Directive (Article 20(3)). In addition, there is the existing network of national competition authorities. The Commission cooperates closely with the newly created regulatory authorities in order to bring to reality the new legal framework in the context of the liberalized electricity markets. The prime interlocutor will, however, continue to be the national competition authorities in accordance with the procedural regulations concerning the application of the

Community competition rules.[29]

Electricity regulators may have a significantly wider ambit to deal with issues of the industry than the Commission has under the Treaty. To the extent that there is an overlap between sectoral rules and the EC competition rules, both the Commission and the national authority are competent to deal with the case. Sector-specific rules do not exclude the application of the competition rules. This is also explicitly stated in Article 22 of the Electricity Directive. However, even where two sets of substantive rules apply in parallel and two authorities are in principle competent to deal with an issue, a duplication of proceedings will not necessarily occur.

It has been the long-standing policy of the Commission to encourage the decentralized application of the EC competition rules.[30] This includes the liberalized sectors of European industry such as the telecommunications sector for which the Commission issued a specific Notice on the application of the competition rules.[31] Similar rules as those spelled out in the telecommunications Notice are likely to apply to the energy sector. This means that the Commission will normally not intervene in areas where sector-specific regulation provides much more detailed rules or goes beyond the requirements of EC competition law. Since the new regulatory authorities have been especially created to resolve issues of third-party-access, the Commission will in principle leave the initiative to national authorities in this field.[32] The Commission will deal with cases having a particular political, economic or legal significance for the Community. Such cases are typically those affecting competition in a number of Member States, either where the case itself raises a cross-border issue or is of cross-border significance. In these cases the Commission has the task of ensuring a level playing field for all European electricity suppliers and consumers and thus provide for a minimum level of harmonization of rules governing market conduct. This division of tasks does not mean that the scope for the application of the Community competition rules to the electricity industry is limited. National regulatory authorities are under a duty to observe the EC competition rules whenever they intervene. They are obliged not to approve any practice or agreement contrary to the Treaty.[33]

---

[29] See Article 10 Reg. No. 17 and Art.19 Regulation (EEC) No. 4064/89 on the control of concentrations between undertakings.

[30] See Commission Notice on cooperation between national competition authorities and the Commission, OJ No. C 313, 15 October 1997, p.3 and Commission Notice on cooperation between national courts and the Commission, OJ No. C 39, 13 February 1993, p.6.

[31] See OJ No. C 265, 22 August 1998, p.2.

[32] The following cases are examples of action taken by national authorities in order to deal with third-party-access: BkartA (footnote 12); Decision of the Council of Administration of CNSE, case C.A.T.R. 1/99: *Hidrocantabrico Energia – Iberdrola*, 14 December 1999, full text of the decision is available at: http://www.chse.es; 1st Decision of the Dutch competition authority Nma, case 650/52 *Hydro Energy – SEP*, 26 August 1999, 2nd Decision of NMA in the same matter on 27 March 2000; available at: http://www.nma-org.nl.

[33] See Commission Notice on the application of the competition rules to access agreements in the telecommunications sector §13; case 66/86, *Ahmed Saeed v. Zentrale*, (1989) E.C.R. 851, §48.

VII. CONCLUSION

A number of competition law problems arise from the recent liberalization of the European electricity industry. This is mainly due to the previous monopolistic supply structure and the national orientation of the industry. EC competition law has a complementary function to the internal market and energy policy of the Community. It has as its goal the removal of legal, contractual and factual obstacles to effective competition and to the emergence of an internal electricity market:

– The electricity industry is a network industry. The monitoring of transmission pricing and third-party-access to the grid as well as to interconnectors is a priority for the Commission because of the gate-keeper function of the network for competition among electricity suppliers. Particular attention is paid to cross-border lines with scarce transmission capacity.

– Cooperation agreements and mergers between electricity companies can foster as well as restrict competition. The Commission is vigilant that combinations of former monopolists do not lead to the creation or reinforcement of dominant positions.

– Eligible customers must be free to switch to other suppliers in order to take advantage of liberalization. It is therefore the Commission's task to open up markets foreclosed through vertical restrictions such as long-term exclusive supply contracts.

– Member States may grant State aid to electricity companies as a compensation for stranded costs incurred by commitments given to governments before liberalization. However, aid must be strictly limited to compensation in order to avoid distortions of competition in the common market.

Except for State aid for which it is exclusively competent, the Commission tackles these competition issues in close cooperation with national competition and regulatory authorities.

Piet Jan Slot

THE IMPACT OF LIBERALIZATION ON LONG-TERM ENERGY CONTRACTS

I. INTRODUCTION

Long-term contracts (LTCs) are a widespread phenomenon in the electricity and gas markets. This is because in many instances large capital investments are involved. Historically the risks inherent in such large and long-term investments have often been offset by the granting of exclusive or special rights. Liberalization will necessarily change this. The essence of liberalization is the removal of exclusive and special rights. The forms of liberalization chosen by the EC are not crude measures of abolishing such rights without more ado. The political and legislative process in the EC has led to the adoption of two directives on the internal market for electricity and gas which introduce a gradual process of liberalization accompanied by special accommodating features which will be analyzed below in section III.[1] These features have an important impact on the legal and economic environment in which the assessment of long-term contracts will have to take place.

The context in which long-term contracts have to be assessed is undergoing further important changes as a result of the recent developments in the field of EC competition law. This major reshaping of the EC competition policy comprises vertical restraints,[2] the imminent and concomitant changes in the field of horizontal restraints[3] and last but not least the drastic changes proposed in the Commission's White Paper.[4] The relevant elements of these changes will be looked at in section IV of this contribution.

Although the issue of security of supply is clearly very important for the assessment of long-term contracts in the energy sector we will not discuss it in this contribution because we have done this extensively elsewhere.[5] It should also be stressed that, although the assessment of such contracts cannot be carried out at an abstract level, the actual evaluation will always have to take the concrete market situation into account. That is why we can

---

[1] Directive 96/92 on the internal market for electricity, OJ 1996, L 27/20; and Directive 98/30 on the internal market for natural gas, OJ 1998, L 204/1.

[2] Regulation 2790/99, OJ 1999, L 336/21.

[3] Drafts have been published in the OJ 2000, C 118/3.

[4] European Commission, "White Paper on Modernisation of the Rules implementing Articles 85 and 86 of the EC Treaty", OJ 1999, C 132/1.

[5] P.J. Slot, "Long Term Contracts (LTCs) from a National and EC Perspective", in L. Hancher, (ed.) *The European Energy Market: Reconciling Competition and Security of Supply*, ERA Trier 1995, Chapter 10.6.2.

Damien Geradin (ed.), The Liberalization of Electricity and Natural Gas in the European Union, 19–34
©2001 Kluwer Law International. Printed in the Netherlands.

only indicate the relevant elements for such an evaluation in this contribution.

We will make some final comments on the overall position of long–term contracts in the electricity and natural gas sector in section V. Before looking at these matters we will first take a closer look at the nature of long-term contracts and their compatibility with EC competition law.

II. LONG-TERM CONTRACTS IN THE ENERGY SECTOR [6]

It is useful to explore the nature of long-term contracts in the energy sector although it should be stressed from the outset that such contracts can take very diverse forms depending on the specific markets for which they are designed. Nevertheless, it is possible to get an idea of what sort of subjects are dealt with in such contracts by looking at a number of examples from the electricity and gas sectors.

Scottish Nuclear Ltd. concluded two long-term contracts with Hydro-Electric and Scottish Power. The contracts were originally concluded for a period of thirty years but were reduced to fifteen years at the instigation of the European Commission.[7] The contracts stipulated *inter alia* that Scottish Nuclear was not permitted to supply electricity to any other party without the consent of both Scottish Power and Hydro-Electric. Furthermore the buyers were under a take-or-pay (TOP) obligation: Scottish Power had to buy 74.9 per cent of Scottish Nuclear's production while Hydro-Electric had to buy 25.1 per cent. Both buyers bought electricity at the same, fixed price.

The contracts concluded between Electricidade de Portugal/Pego project,[8] REN/Turbogás[9] and ISAB Energy,[10] concerned the sale of the total production of a new electricity producer and a monopolist. The intended contract length was also reduced to fifteen years by the Commission in the case of Electricidade de Portugal/Pego project and REN/Turbogás instead of the initially intended twenty-eight and twenty-five years respectively. These contracts moreover contained a 'first-option' clause, allowing the generator to sell the capacity to third parties after a certain number (fifteen, in both cases) of years. In the case of ISAB Energy the Commission decided to submit the contract, initially concluded for twenty years, to re-examination after fifteen years.

The Belgian company Electrabel concluded contracts for the exclusive right to supply electricity to the so-called MIDC (mixed intercommunal distribution companies) for a

---

[6] This summary is based on the extensive treatment of this topic given in J. Faull and A. Nickpay, *The EC Law of Competition*, Oxford University Press, 1999, paragraph 10.61 *et seq.*

[7] Commission Decision 91/329 of 30 April 1991, IV/33.473-Scottish Nuclear, Nuclear Energy Agreement.

[8] Commission Decision of 29 May 1996 96/576/ECSC authorizing the granting of aid by Portugal to the coal industry in 1995 and 1996.

[9] OJ 1996 C118/7, (1996) 4 CMLR 881.

[10] OJ 1996 C138/3, (1996) 4 CMLR 889.

period of twenty to thirty years. After consultation with the European Commission this period was shortened to fifteen years and the exclusivity was also limited.[11]

The Dutch SEP and the Generation Companies set up a joint-venture agreement setting up the electricity generation and transmission system in the Netherlands. SEP was granted an exclusive right to import and export and the duration of the contract was for at least ten years.

The Almelo case is an example of a contract concluded between producers and the regional distributors.[12] In this case, the distribution of electricity is organized at the regional and local level. IJM was granted a non-exclusive concession to distribute electricity within the territory covered by that concession. Local distributors were prohibited from importing electricity while exclusive sales were granted to the regional distributor. The end-user, on his side, was required to enter into an exclusive purchasing obligation.

In the gas-sector, a distinction can be made between upstream and downstream long-term contracts. An example of such upstream long-term contracts is an agreement concluded between the Dutch government and the oil companies. This contract stipulates that all gas finds from the Groningen field intended for commercialization will be sold to Gasunie. Prices for such deliveries are determined by Gasunie's board after approval of the Minister of Economic Affairs. Gasunie also purchases gas from other operators of the smaller gas deposits located in the Netherlands or at Dutch offshore sites. The obligation to sell to Gasunie was incorporated in the concession for the exploration of oil and gas. Gasunie also imports substantial amounts of gas under TOP contracts from Norway and recently also from Russia.

Downstream long-term natural gas contracts exist for export markets and for the domestic market. Gasunie has concluded gas export contracts with Distrigaz (Belgium), Gaz de France, SNAM Italy, Ruhrgas and other German gas companies. These contracts typically provide for clauses detailing the total quantity of gas to be purchased during the contract period and the permissible range of take-off during the year with an indication of a minimum and a maximum. Some contracts contain TOP clauses.

Downstream long-term natural gas contracts for the domestic market can be further subdivided in the market for large industrial consumers and the sector which is supplied through the distribution companies. The latter type of contract covers the household sector and small industrial consumers. For the household sector which is supplied through the distribution companies, a framework agreement has been drafted which will be applied whenever individual distribution companies contract gas from the national provider. Such an agreement can, for example, provide that the national provider will serve the market for the larger industrial users, i.e. industries using more than 10 million m³. The contracts are concluded for a term of 15 years. The agreements for individual gas deliveries to the

---

[11] IP/97/351, 25 April 1997.

[12] Case C-392/92, *Gemeente Almelo v. Energiebedrijf IJsselmij*, (1994) E.C.R. I-1477; Commission decision 91/50, *IJsselmij*, OJ 1991, L 28/32.

smaller industrial consumers have been concluded for five years. They may be subject to specific general conditions. It should be noted that these contracts are now being revised in view of the recently liberalized market.

III. THE KEY FEATURES OF THE LIBERALIZATION PROCESS RELEVANT FOR LONG-TERM CONTRACTS

As a thorough discussion of the liberalization process in the electricity and natural gas sector would exceed the confines of this contribution, we will restrict ourselves to those elements of this process which are particularly relevant for the position of long-term contracts.[13]

The key liberalization measures in the area of electricity and natural gas are:

– Directive 96/92/EC of the European Parliament and the Council of 19 December 1996 concerning common rules for the internal market in electricity (the "Electricity Directive"). The directive had to be implemented before 19 February 1999, except for Belgium and Ireland which, according to Article 27, paragraph 2, had an additional year and Greece which has two additional years.
– Directive 98/30/EC of the European Parliament and the Council of 22 June 1998 concerning common rules for the internal market in natural gas (the "Gas Directive"). The directive had to be implemented before 10 August 2000.

Although the two directives mentioned contain the actual liberalization rules for the sectors we should also draw the attention to Directive 94/22/EC of the European Parliament and the Council of 30 May 1994 on the conditions for granting and using authorizations for the prospection, exploration and production of hydrocarbons (the upstream licensing directive).[14] The deadline for the implementation of this directive was 1 July 1995. This directive lays down rules for non-discriminatory access to the mining of oil and natural gas thus contributing to the liberalization process. The directive and national legislation implementing it have removed some obstacles to the market for oil and natural gas thereby enhancing the contestability of these markets. This will, of course, be relevant for the evaluation of long-term contracts.

There is another directive which should also be taken into account when discussing the liberalization of the energy markets and that is Directive 93/38/EC on public procurement by utilities.[15] Like the previous upstream licensing directive, Directive 93/38 will enhance

---

[13] I have given a more general analysis of the liberalization process in the energy sector (electricity and natural gas) in: D. Geradin (ed.) *The Liberalisation of State Monopolies in the European Union and Beyond*, Kluwer European Monographs No. 23, The Hague 2000, pp. 49-65.

[14] OJ 1994, L 164/3.

[15] Directive 93/38, OJ 1993, L 199/84, recently amended by Directive 98/4, OJ 1998, L 101/1, to incorporate the results of the Uruguay Round.

the competitive conditions on the markets.

The Commission has been following the implementation of the two directives on electricity and natural gas closely. It has produced two progress reports on the electricity directive and one the natural gas directive.[16] These documents provide useful information for our purposes.

The following elements of the directives and developments of the liberalization process may have an impact on the position of LTCs under EC competition law.

A. Public Service Obligations

The two directives on electricity and natural gas provide ample opportunity for Member States to lay down public service obligations (hereinafter "PSOs").[17] The obligations may relate to security, including security of supply, quality and price of supplies and to

---

[16] *Second report to the Council and the European Parliament on Harmonisation Requirements*, Directive 96/92/EC concerning common rules for the internal market in electricity, Brussels, November 1999, COM (1999). *Report to the Council and the European Parliament on Harmonisation Requirements*, Directive 98/30/EC concerning common rules for the internal market for natural gas, Brussels, 23 November 1999, COM (1999) 612.

[17] Article 3 of the "Electricity Directive": "1. Member States shall ensure, on the basis of their institutional organization and with due regard for the principle of subsidiarity, that, without prejudice to paragraph 2, electricity undertakings are operated in accordance with the principles of this Directive, with a view to achieving a competitive market in electricity, and shall not discriminate between these undertakings as regards either rights or obligations. The two approaches to system access referred to in Articles 17 and 18 must lead to equivalent economic results and hence to a directly comparable level of opening-up of markets and to a directly comparable degree of access to electricity markets.

2. Having full regard to the relevant provisions of the Treaty, in particular Article 90, Member States may impose on undertakings operating in the electricity sector, in the general economic interest, public service obligations which may relate to security, including security of supply, regularity, quality and price of supplies and to environmental protection. Such obligations must be clearly defined, transparent, non-discriminatory and verifiable; they, and any revision thereof, shall be published and notified to the Commission by Member States without delay. As a means of carrying out the abovementioned public service obligations, Member States which so wish may introduce the implementation of long-term planning.

3. Member States may decide not to apply the provisions of Articles 5, 6, 17, 18 and 21 insofar as the application of these provisions would obstruct the performance, in law or in fact, of the obligations imposed on electricity undertakings in the general economic interest and insofar as the development of trade would not be affected to such an extent as would be contrary to the interests of the Community. The interests of the Community include, *inter alia*, competition with regard to eligible customers in accordance with this Directive and Article 90 of the Treaty".

Article 10 of the "Electricity Directive": "1. Member States may impose on distribution companies an obligation to supply customers located in a given area. The tariff for such supplies may be regulated, for instance to ensure equal treatment of the customers concerned.

2. Member States shall designate or shall require undertakings which own or are responsible for distribution systems to designate a system operator to be responsible for operating, ensuring the maintenance of and, if necessary, developing the distribution system in a given area and its interconnectors with other systems.

3. Member States shall ensure that the system operator acts in accordance with Articles 11 and 12".

environmental protection. Such obligations must be clearly defined, transparent, non-discriminatory and verifiable. They and the revision thereof, shall be published. Article 3 of the directive also requires notification of PSOs to the Commission. It may be assumed that this will take place at the same time as the implementing legislation is notified to the EC Commission, in accordance with the obligation laid down in Article 27(1) of the Electricity and Article 29 of the Natural Gas Directive. Such PSOs are provided, for example, in Title 1 of the New French electricity Law.[18] Another example of such a PSO in the natural gas sector is the obligation for Gasunie to give preference in its buying policy to gas from indigenous small fields. This is a long established policy which serves to preserve the precious Groningen field which has special features in that it can easily accommodate differing load factors. The Groningen field can be used to vary supplies according to demand. It can also be used for storage.

There is as of yet no indication how the Commission will assess these PSOs and what criteria it will apply. Although Article 3(2) of the Electricity Directive does not say so, it must be assumed that Member States cannot implement PSOs prior to the Commission's approval. This raises the usual questions about the legal nature of the notification procedure in Community law in the context of Article 95, paragraphs 4 and 5 of the EC Treaty and Article 8 of Directive 83/189.[19] It should also be noted that the Member States may decide not to apply the key provisions of the directive: Articles 5 and 6 on the authorization of generation capacity, Articles 17 and 18 on access to the grid, and Article 21 on the construction of direct lines. This right is, however, according to the text of Article 3(3) of the directive, subject to the general obligations under Article 86 of the EC Treaty.

It is, therefore, useful to remember that the European Court of Justice (the "ECJ") has given a rather permissive interpretation of Article 86(2) in the electricity cases.[20] In these judgements the ECJ held that there is no absolute burden of proof for the Member States wanting to impose PSOs. It further held that the standard which has to be applied in this context is whether it is economically viable to operate the public service without the restriction. This interpretation has recently been confirmed in the Deutsche Post judgement.[21]

It should also be noted that specific obligations may be imposed on the basis of Article 8, paragraphs 3 and 4, of the Electricity Directive. These relate to the possibility to give priority to generation installations using renewables or CHP as well as using indigenous primary energy sources.

---

[18] *Journal Officiel* 112 du 14 mai 2000.

[19] See S. Weatherill, "Compulsory Notification of Draft Technical Regulations: the Contribution of Directive 83/189 to the Management of the Internal Market", (1996) 16 *Yearbook of European Law* 129.

[20] Cases C-157/94, *Commission v. Netherlands*; C-158/94, *Commission v. Italy*; C-159/94, *Commission v. France*; C-160/94, *Commission v. Spain*, (1997) E.C.R. I-5699, 5789, 5815, 5851. See also my annotation in 35 CMLRev. 1183-1203, 1998.

[21] Cases C-147 and 148/97, judgment of 10 February 2000.

B. Access to the Grid

The two directives both regulate access to the network. The fact that access, in whatever form – negotiated third party access (TPA), regulated TPA or the single buyer system – has to be secured, will in general lead to a presumption that markets will be more contestable. Hence, it will presumably lead to a situation where the incumbents will have less market power and, as a result, will no longer occupy dominant positions. Since a key element in the compatibility of long-term contracts with competition law is the degree of market power held by the parties, this would seem to lead to a presumption that such contracts might become more acceptable once liberalization is in full swing. The regulation of access to the grid should also be seen together with the ECJ's interpretation of the essential facilities doctrine in the Bronner judgement.[22] It will be recalled that this judgement restricted the use of the essential facilities doctrine to situations where there is no actual or potential substitute in existence for the service or the facility demanded. Although this judgement has generally been interpreted as restricting the use of the essential facilities doctrine, its actual application in the field of the electricity and natural gas sector would not seem to suffer greatly from this restrictive view since the conditions set in Bronner would normally seem to apply for these network-bound sectors.

C. Competition in Generation

Articles 4-6 of the Electricity Directive provide for competition in new generation capacity. This form of competition should also lead to more competitive markets. Note that Article 6(4) of Directive 96/92 states that consideration must be given to offers with long term guarantees. This provision seems to suggest that long-term contracts have to be considered as compatible with the competition rules.

D. Designation of System Operators

The rules relating to the designation of system operators in Articles 7-9 of the Electricity Directive aim at securing non-discriminatory and transparent dispatching of electricity by the different users of the system. This should be another factor leading to more competitive markets.

---

[22] Case C-7/97, *Bronner*, (1998) E.C.R. I-7791 at paragraph 41. See also the annotation by L. Hancher, 36 CMLRev. p. 1289-1307.

E. Freeing the Customers

The opening of the market by designating eligible consumers leads to more competitive markets. Articles 19 of Directive 96/92 and 18 of Directive 98/30 oblige Member States to open their markets by allowing eligible customers to freely source their supplies from a supplier of their choice. The quid pro quo of this right to choose the preferred supplier seems to be that eligible consumers can no longer automatically claim security of supply; they have to contract for that if they require it. The corollary will be that energy companies will not, or to a lesser extent, be able to claim the exemption of Article 86(2) of the EC Treaty. In this context, it is interesting to note the announcement made by Gasunie during the discussions in the Netherlands on the new Gas Bill implementing the gas directive, that the opening of the natural gas market will require it to abandon its policy of guaranteeing secured supplies.

F. Derogations

Article 25 of Directive 98/30 allows Member States to grant a temporary derogation from the obligation to give access in cases where a natural gas company would encounter serious difficulties as a result of prior TOP commitments.[23] Granting such derogation would, of course, lead to reduced competition. In implementing this article, the Dutch Gas Bill provides that the Director General of the Competition Authority, who is responsible for the implementation of the act, may upon request dispense with the obligation to negotiate access to the pipelines.

G. The Creation of National Regulatory Authorities (NRAs)

Although not strictly called for by the relevant directives, their implementation leads most Member States to establish national regulators. This is also encouraged by the Commission. Article 20 of the Electricity Directive requires Member States to take the necessary measures to enable independent producers and auto-producers to negotiate access. They shall also ensure that the parties negotiate in good faith. Article 21 obliges Member States to take similar measures securing access through direct lines. Similar provisions are contained in the Gas Directive in Articles 21 and 22.

The NRAs in the electricity and natural gas sectors have only recently been established. A clear picture of the importance of the role they can play in the development of the liberalization process can be gleaned by studying their role in the telecommunications

---

[23] See on this topic M. Brothwood, "The E.U. Gas Directive and Take or Pay Contracts", [1998] *O.G.L.T.R.* p. 318.

sector. The Commission's Fifth Report on the Implementation of the Telecommunications Regulatory Package summarises the role of NRAs in this sector as follows:

"There is a preliminary point which is worth reiterating. The NRAs are the rock on which full and uniform implementation of the regulatory package is built. They need a strongly supportive national framework to enable them to function effectively. This includes providing them with the necessary human and financial resources and the legal and political environment which will enable them to perform their pre-scribed tasks". [24]

As the Commission observes in its 1999 Communications Review[25] the role of the NRAs in the liberalization process has been vital and will continue to be vital. It also expresses concern about the functioning of the NRAs in several Member States:

"It is essential that they are properly resourced, truly independent, and seek actively to open their national markets to competition and innovation".[26]

The Commission expresses a concern that some NRAs are still insufficiently effective. It has four specific concerns:
— the independence of the NRA;
— the allocation of NRA responsibilities to different bodies should not lead to delays and duplication of decision-making;
— that there should be effective co-operation between NRAs and national competition authorities when both are involved in issues relating to telecommunications. NRAs should ensure that their decisions are compatible with Community competition law;
— that the decision-making procedures at national level should be transparent.

The Commission proposes to review the existing legal provisions with a view to accommodate the concerns listed above.

This rather extensive look at and evaluation of the NRAs in the telecommunications sector shows that the development of liberalization will be greatly dependent on the proper functioning of the NRAs. Such NRAs function in the relevant market is, therefore, of importance when assessing the compatibility of long-term contracts. This will be especially so in markets where the NRAs will actively supervise trade covered by long-term contracts. It is, however, too early to evaluate the role of the NRAs in the energy sector.

---

[24] COM (1999) 537 final.

[25] European Commission, "Towards a new framework for electronic communications infrastructure and associated services. The 1999 Communications Review" COM (1999) 539.

[26] At paragraph 4.8.2.

H. A New Definition of the Relevant Geographic Market?

One of the key questions is whether, as a result of the liberalization required by the directives, the relevant geographic markets will be extended. An example of this was the argument forwarded by the four electricity generators in the Netherlands when they sought to justify their merger plans. This merger would have created one generation company for all of the Netherlands. According to the four generators the relevant geographic market had to be viewed in the context of the liberalization and would, therefore, have to be defined as the Netherlands, Germany and Belgium.[27] The answer to this question will be greatly dependent on the possibilities for the development of cross-border trade. This is extensively discussed in the Commission's reports on the harmonization requirements for the electricity and the gas sectors referred to above. The Commission enumerates a number of obstacles for such cross-border trade. In the electricity sector it mentions the following obstacles:
- maximizing available transmission capacity;
- fair and non-discriminatory allocation of scarce transmission capacity;
- long-term reservation of transmission capacity;
- cross-border tarification and settlement.

On all these issues a lot of work needs to be done before cross-border trade can really take off. As is well known a forum of national regulators known as "The European Regulation Forum" meeting in Florence, is actively pursuing avenues to solve the problems. The First Report on harmonization requirements in the natural gas market lists the following problems:
- interoperability of gas networks;
- gas quality;
- odorization;
- network specifications;
- other requirements of the system;
- balancing regimes;
- capacity constraints; and
- tarification of transmission access.

These issues are also the subject of another group of experts, the "Gas Regulatory Forum", meeting in Madrid.

Without sufficient capacity and proper tarification and the removal of other obstacles the internal markets in electricity and gas will not come true and the result will be that the

---

[27] The merger plans were eventually abandoned because the parties could not reach an agreement on the question of stranded costs. Thus the Dutch Competition Authority was not in a position to comment on the proposed geographic market definition.

relevant markets for assessing the compatibility of long-term contracts will remain to be defined at the national level.

I. New Product Markets

Liberalization will also stimulate the development of new products/services. In both the electricity and the gas market new products and services are being introduced. In the electricity sector, contracts for different types of electricity depending on the hours of the day and the time of year, such as peak load contracts, are on the increase as are switch-off and back-up contracts. In the gas sector the former all-inclusive contracts are being divided into separate gas, storage and back-up contracts.

A further development which has already taken place is the move towards concentration in the utilities sector. There has been significant merger activity in the Member States of the EU. Such mergers are both of national nature as well as transnational nature. Many utilities deem it very important to gain a foothold in other markets. The concentration movement is to some extent accompanied, and sometimes preceded, by a move towards privatization. Central and regional governments are grappling with the question whether or not to allow local authorities to cash in on the liberalization boom by selling their shares in the electricity and gas utilities. At the same time the Commission is subjecting to close scrutiny government policies reserving to themselves "golden shares".

IV. THE RELEVANT RECENT CHANGES IN EC COMPETITION POLICY

Almost simultaneously with the liberalization movement, drastic changes in the EC competition policy are taking place and further changes are being planned. I refer first to the adoption of Regulation 2790/99 (i.e., the new block exemption for vertical agreements) and the related Guidelines.[28] As we will discuss, these new rules for vertical agreements embody important changes which may be relevant for long-term energy contracts especially since most long-term contracts are of a vertical nature. The second important change is the new proposals for block exemptions for horizontal agreements and the accompanying Guidelines.[29] The third change is the White Paper on modernization.[30]

---

[28] OJ 1999, L 336/21.

[29] A proposal to amend the R&D block exemption, the specialization agreements and the respective guidelines, drafts published in OJ 2000, C 118/3.

[30] OJ 1999, C 132/1. An excellent analysis of the impact of this proposal is given by the House of Lords Select Committee Report; *Reforming EC Competition Procedures*, HL 33, 2000.

A. The New Rules on Vertical Agreements

The most important amendment of the new style rules on vertical agreements is the threshold of the 30% market share of the participating undertakings below which the block exemption will apply.[31] Although long-term contracts in the energy sector will often involve companies with considerable market shares these new rules may nevertheless also become relevant for them. This will be all the more relevant as, with increasing liberalization, the market shares of the incumbents will decrease and/or the geographic markets will be defined more broadly.

The format of the block exemption is less formalistic than the exemptions it replaces. It provides for broad exemptions for vertical agreements that do not fall within the blacklist of Article 3. The latter includes such hardcore restrictions such as price fixing and territorial limitations. Article 4 excludes agreements with non-compete clauses. According to Article 1(b), a non-compete obligation means an obligation not to manufacture, purchase, sell or resell goods or services. It also includes, however, any obligation to purchase from the supplier or from an undertaking designated by the supplier more than 80% of the buyer's total purchases of the contract goods or services. Thus, regardless of the market share of the parties, contracts providing an obligation to purchase more than 80% of the total requirements cannot benefit from the block exemption. Exclusive supply obligations are defined in Article 1(c) as an obligation to sell only to one buyer inside the Community for the purpose of a specific use or resale. It is important to note that in case of an exclusive supply obligation Article 3(b) of the regulation specifies that it is the market share of the buyer that is relevant for the determination of the market share. Under the normal rules of the block exemption this is the market share of the supplier. An example of such an exclusive supply obligation is the contract between NAM and Gasunie in the Netherlands. According to this contract NAM can only sell to Gasunie.[32]

According to the text of Article 2(1), access agreements qualify as vertical agreements. However, it remains doubtful whether many access agreements in the electricity and gas sector will enjoy the benefits of the block exemption, as almost all owners of the network will have market shares higher than 30%.

It may be important to note that even though Article 4(c) of the regulation provides that the distributor may not be prohibited to sell outside the territory, this is, according to paragraph 44 of the Guidelines, allowed as otherwise the distributor would not be complying

---

[31] While writing this summary of the new rules on vertical agreements, I benefited greatly from the Article by Richard Wish: "Regulation 2790/99: The Commission's 'New Style' Block Exemption for Vertical Agreements" 37 CMLRev. (forthcoming).

[32] Although this contract may be beyond the protection of the block exemption this does not necessarily mean that it is incompatible with EC competition law. It may nevertheless qualify for an individual exemption and it may also benefit from the exemption of Article 86 (2). It should be noted that after liberalization the share of Gasunie on the Dutch market has dwindled rapidly. In the market for eligible customers, Gasunie's share is now reported to be below 80%.

with the specified criteria that make the system selective. This specification is important for long-term contracts between energy producers and distribution companies where the producers may wish to reserve certain markets for themselves.

Chapter VI of the Guidelines provides a framework for the analysis of individual exemptions in case the block exemption is not applicable. This is of particular relevance for the energy sector, since, as already pointed out, many agreements will involve undertakings with market share above the cap of 30%. Paragraphs 138 *et seq.* deal with vertical restraints which impose "single branding", i.e. arrangements whereby the purchaser in one way or another is led to purchase all his requirements only from one supplier. According to the Guidelines the possible competition risks are: "foreclosure of the market to competing suppliers and potential suppliers, facilitation of collusion between suppliers in case of cumulative use and, where the buyer is a retailer selling to final consumers, a loss of in-store inter-brand competition. All three have a direct impact on inter-brand competition."

Single branding is exempted when the supplier's share does not exceed 30% and subject to a limitation in time of 5 years for the non-compete obligation. The Guidelines provide guidance for market shares above 30% and time limits beyond 5 years. The Guidelines enumerate the following elements: the market share of the supplier and the market position of its competitors, entry barriers, countervailing power, the level of trade. The Guidelines specifically mention that English clauses will have the same effect as non-compete obligations. The two page long guidance may provide further useful indications for specific instances.

Furthermore, it should be noted, that since the amendment of Regulation 17 by Regulation 1216/99, it is no longer necessary for vertical agreements to be notified in order to get an individual exemption from the date of their enactment. There is, in the words of the Commission, no presumption that vertical agreements involving market shares above 30% are void. This has, of course, practical consequences. Except for agreements containing hard-core restrictions and clear instances of market foreclosure, there is no longer a need to notify.

B. The Proposed Rules for Horizontal Agreements

The actual proposals concern the revision of the block exemptions on R&D and specialization. Nevertheless, the accompanying Guidelines indicate that they are relevant as general guidance on the question what sort of horizontal agreements will be compatible with the EC competition rules. Paragraph 10 indicates that the Guidelines only cover agreements which potentially generate efficiency gains, i.e. agreements on R&D, production, purchasing, commercialization, standardization, and environmental agreements.

Paragraph 131 *et seq.* deal with commercialization agreements involving co-operation between competitors in the selling, distribution or promotion of their products. Such agreements may also cover the trade in electricity and gas. They may also be combined with joint production or joint purchasing. Such agreements will fall under the competition rules if the parties to the agreements are competitors. On the other hand, joint commercialization agreements can never be exempted if they enable the parties to eliminate competition in respect of a substantial part of the products in question.

C. The White Paper on Modernization

In essence the proposals contained in the White Paper will lead to giving up the Commission's monopoly in applying Article 81(3) of the EC Treaty and sharing this power with the national courts and competition authorities. They also provide for the elimination of notification for individual exemptions. The greater reliance on national courts and competition authorities will mean that there will be increased need for guidance on substantive issues. Thus, further Commission Notices and Guidelines on specific subjects such as long-term contracts will be needed.

The overall effect of these changes will be a less direct involvement of the Commission and more involvement of the national competition authorities and the courts. Combined with the less restrictive interpretation of Article 81(1) this will lead to a less interventionist policy. Although this policy shift is centred on the application of Article 81 it may nevertheless make competition policy as a whole, Articles 81, 82 and 86, less suitable for its engineering role in the network-bound sectors.

D. Further Elements to be taken into Account

The CFI's judgement in the *European Night Services* case,[33] contains a clear statement that the Commission, when considering the duration of an exemption, should indicate the reasons why exemptions for long-term contracts involve a period less than the full period necessary to enable the beneficiaries to ensure a proper return on the investment. This applies in particular when new major investments, substantial financial risks and the pooling of know-how by the participating undertakings are involved (paragraph 230 of the judgement). It should be recalled that in the past, the Commission has not been very forthcoming in this regard.[34] In *Pego,* the Commission reduced the exclusive supply contract term from 28 to 15 years, while accepting a "first option" for the remaining 13 years.

---

[33] T-374-375/94, T-384 and 388/94, (1998) E.C.R. II-3141.

[34] In this respect, see the *Pego* decision mentioned above in Section II.

V. LONG-TERM RESERVATION OF TRANSMISSION CAPACITY

The Commission's Second harmonization report on the internal market for electricity contains a section on the compatibility of long-term reservation of transmission capacity agreements with competition rules. The Commission notes that such contracts have the potential to exclude other market participants from using the interconnectors for their imports of electricity.[35] According to the Commission the problem becomes more sensitive when the Transmission System Operator is part of a vertically integrated company which itself benefits from a long-term electricity purchase or selling contract for which it claims the necessity of long-term capacity reservation. The starting point of an analysis of such arrangements is the question whether there is a need to reserve long-term capacity by virtue of supply or purchase contracts. In our view the Commission's analysis focuses too much on agreements relating to existing capacity. It would be more desirable to make a distinction between agreements for the construction of new capacity and agreements concerning existing capacity. In the case of the former, new capacity will be added to the system and should thus be favoured by allowing contracts needed for the financial support of the new construction. As long as there is such a justification, these contracts should in principle be allowed. Of course, the reservation should be subject to the well-known principles of Community law of necessity and proportionality. Agreements relating to existing capacity will in general be more difficult to justify as their financing has already been arranged. They may therefore be subjected to a more critical evaluation.

The Commission points to the fact that such agreements may frustrate the development of the internal market for electricity. It considers that the following parameters will be important for the analysis of the transmission market:
-   the share of the contracted capacity in relation to the relevant overall available interconnector capacity for imports;
-   the extent to which the capacity of the relevant interconnectors is reserved for exclusive use by one or several parties;
-   the extent to which the capacity is reserved long-term;
-   the duration of any such reservation;
-   whether there exists congestion;
-   the procedure adopted by the owner of the capacity when attributing it; and
-   the impact of a capacity constraint on the supply markets connected by the link. Particular attention will be paid, for example, to cases where an interconnector constitutes the sole available transmission opportunity towards any given market on which competition is already limited (for example, markets with a monopolistic supply structure).

---

[35] They may, of course, also restrict exports of electricity.

In the final analysis the compatibility of capacity reservation agreements will, of course, depend on all the relevant elements of the market in question.

VI. CONCLUSION

The effects of liberalization in the energy market on long-term contracts do not point in a single direction. On the one hand, it may be expected that as liberalization proceeds, more and more recourse will be made to such contracts because the guarantee provided by exclusive or special rights will have to be replaced by another instrument. On the other hand, the presumption of liberalization is that the geographic scope of the market will increase and hence the market share of the individual players will diminish. The latter is, of course, crucially dependent on the effective control of mergers. The latest developments in the energy markets in some Member States, the Netherlands in particular, have shown a dramatic increase in mergers and concentrations largely offsetting the advantages of liberalization. The liberalization process will certainly have the effect of making the application of the competition rules more likely. That in itself may well be an important effect. It should be recalled that under the previous regime of exclusive rights the application of the competition rules in the energy sector was not widespread.[36]

However, the recent changes and the forthcoming changes in EC competition policy raise serious questions whether the redesigned policy will be suitable to play its role. For the moment the newly established NRAs may fulfil a useful role in bringing about competition in the electricity and gas sector. In the longer run, however, it is generally assumed that competition policy should take over this function. It is doubtful whether the new system of competition policy relying heavily on the national competition authorities and national courts is suitable for that role.

In addition, long-term contracts will continue to be important in the liberalized market of the future although the context in which they function has undergone drastic changes.

---

[36] See my overview: "Energy and Competition", 31 CMLRev. 511-547, 1994.

II. Transmission and Trading

Dr.-Ing. Wolfgang Fritz

NETWORK ACCESS AND TRANSMISSION AND DISTRIBUTION PRICING

I. INTRODUCTION

One of the essential factors for the successful liberalization of electricity and gas markets is the availability for market operators of open access to the existing energy transport networks (i.e. third party access, TPA). This stems from the fact that the network sector is considered to be a natural monopoly, due to high investment costs, the impact on the environment, and other inherent characteristics of the equipment employed in the energy network. In contrast, the other areas of energy supply, such as production and sales, are considered to be well-suited to competition.

This paper provides a brief introduction to the technical issues and pricing principles relating to the provision of open access to energy networks, focusing exclusively on the electricity sector. However, the fundamental principles are also valid for the gas supply sector.

As is shown in figure 1, the value chain of electricity supply comprises mainly four steps. Two of them, transmission and distribution, represent the monopoly sector that requires TPA to be granted to network users by network operators. In vertically integrated electricity companies, these steps of the value chain must be strictly separated (or "unbundled") from the other activities of the companies at least in terms of separate accounting. This is to ensure that non-discriminatory TPA based on fair and verifiable terms is provided. Moreover, this sector continues to require some form of regulatory supervision and control in order to prevent abuses of their position by incumbent monopoly operators situation. Regulatory functions may be fulfilled by existing governmental bodies or by a sector-specific regulatory authority.

Since the generation and sales sectors, including electricity trading, are being more or less completely opened to competition, two interfaces between monopoly and non-monopoly sectors are created by the liberalization process. These interfaces require clear and non-discriminatory rules concerning technical and organizational procedures as well as financial compensation for network operators.

II. ELECTRICITY TRANSMISSION AND DISTRIBUTION

Before addressing the way TPA works in practice, it is helpful to have a look at the technical structure of today's electricity networks in Western Europe (figure 2). As a result of technical

Damien Geradin (ed.), The Liberalization of Electricity and Natural Gas in the European Union, 37–48
©2001 Kluwer Law International. Printed in the Netherlands.

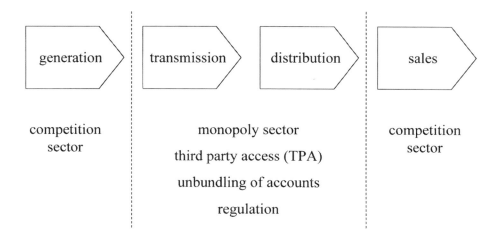

Figure 1. Value Chain of Electricity Supply

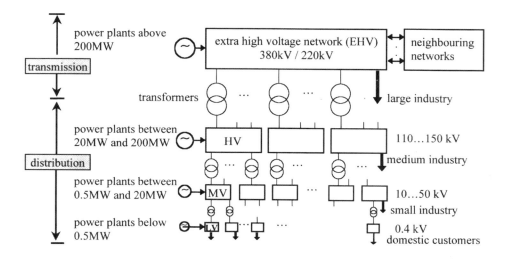

Figure 2. Technical Structure of Electricity Supply

and economic considerations, particularly concerning equipment costs and network losses, electricity networks are generally subdivided into different voltage levels which are vertically connected via transformers. The higher the operating voltage (given in kV = kilovolt) of a network level, the greater the power that can be transported and the lower the energy losses per unit of transported electricity; however, equipment costs are higher. Therefore power plants and consumers are connected to the different voltage levels depending upon their individual generation capacity or demand.

In Western Europe, electricity networks usually comprise four voltage levels. In the lower three levels, the single networks have only regional or even local extension, and they are not connected to each other. These networks are usually regarded as distribution networks because their main task is to distribute electricity coming from the upper voltage levels or from "decentralized" power plants to the consumers.

Only the networks at the highest voltage level ("extra high voltage") are connected Europe-wide to facilitate electricity transport over long distance from large power plants to the main centres of consumption. These networks are usually called transmission networks. Each operator of a transmission network (i.e., the transmission system operator, or "TSO") is responsible for a specific area that normally does not overlap with the areas of responsibility of other TSOs. There may be one or several TSOs in a country. In Germany, for example, there were eight TSOs at the beginning of 2000 (figure 3). It should be noted, however, that as a result of various mergers in the energy sector, this number is likely to drop.

1: Bayernwerk AG
2: Berliner Kraft- und Licht (Bewag)-AG
3: Energie Baden-Württemberg AG
4: Hamburgische Electricitäts-Werke AG
5: PreussenElektra AG
6: RWE Energie AG
7: VEAG Vereinigte Energiewerke AG
8: VEW ENERGIE AG

Figure 3. Transmission Systems in Germany (as at June 2000)

III. THIRD PARTY ACCESS TO ELECTRICITY NETWORKS

Before market liberalization, electricity supply was normally the task of vertically integrated utilities, owning transmission and/or distribution networks and supplying electricity to end consumers or other electricity companies within specific areas. The electricity procurement of each company was derived from its own generation capacity and/or purchases from direct pre-suppliers who were also operators at the next level up in the production chain. The opportunity to conduct relatively unrestricted electricity trading was the preserve of only a few companies that owned a part of the interconnected transmission system. In fact the international exchange of large volumes of electricity has been carried out for some considerable time. However this took place mainly between neighbouring companies, because transiting across third parties' networks required the "good will" of the affected TSOs.

An electricity customer in this "old world" used to have one supply contract with the local utility, as shown in figure 4. There was no opportunity to choose alternative suppliers, nor was there any need to conclude separate contracts for the delivery of electricity and the use of transmission and distribution networks. The price to be paid by the customer was therefore based on an aggregate of the costs of each segment of the value chain.

In contrast, in the "TPA world", customers need to conclude at least two separate contracts, one (or more) with a generator or trader for the delivery of electricity, and one with the operator responsible for the local network for use of the network. Similarly

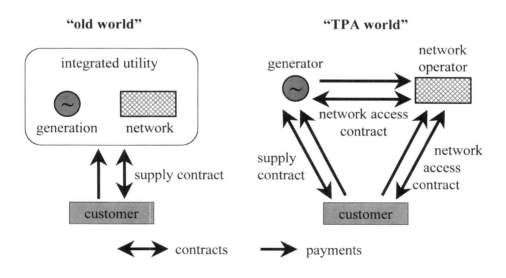

Figure 4. Contractual Relations for TPA

generators have to conclude contracts with network operators for network access. Strictly-speaking, it may be argued that generators and customers even need contracts with each and every network operator affected by a specific transport task. However, this raises practical difficulties; therefore, TPA rules must be developed such that a contract with the local network operator includes also the use of other networks. This requires the conclusion of contracts or agreements between the network operators.

As a consequence of the contractual separation of electricity delivery and network access, network users, i.e. generators and consumers, have to pay electricity prices and network charges separately. It should be mentioned that in order to simplify the supply arrangements for customers, the network access conditions and charges can – depending on the regulatory environment – be included in the electricity supply contracts and then be cleared between generators/traders and network operators. Customers would then only need one contract and receive only one bill for electricity supply, a situation similar to that which existed prior to the liberalization process.

An example of a TPA case is given in figure 5. The "old world" side shows two neighbouring utilities on the transmission level with interconnected networks. Each utility has to meet the total electricity demand of customers in the "own" supply area, i.e. 100 units in each area. In the example, each utility operates own generators to produce exactly this amount of electricity. In consequence, no power is exchanged across the tie lines between the two utilities.

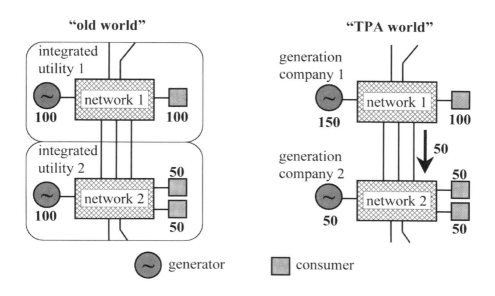

Figure 5. Example of TPA

It should be noted that in practice there would still be power flows on the tie-lines in a meshed interconnected transmission system even if generation and consumption were in perfect balance in each area. This is due to so-called "loop flows" that result from the fact that the network structure and the distribution of generation and consumption locations are not perfectly homogeneous throughout the system. However, this effect, as well as the unavoidable transport losses, is neglected here.

The right-hand side of figure 5 shows the situation under the TPA arrangements. The integrated utilities need to be unbundled at least with respect to their accounts. It is assumed here that the utilities are even split up into separate companies for electricity generation and network operation. This is more than the required degree of unbundling, but it represents the way of thinking that utilities should adopt even if they remain integrated.

Under TPA conditions, the generation companies are free to supply any customers inside or outside the area of the network they are connected to, and they are allowed to use any networks for their supply activities. The same is true for consumers: they are no longer obliged to choose a supplier in the local network area. It may for example happen, as shown in figure 5, that generation company 1 contracts a customer who was formerly supplied by utility 2. This requires of course that generator 1 has sufficient available generation capacity.

This change in the contractual relationship has a basic impact at a technical level on the generation situation: generator 1 has to increase generation to 150, while generator 2 must reduce generation to 50. In consequence, the power flow situation on the lines of the transmission system changes accordingly. In this simple example, the additional power flow of 50 units from generator 1 to one of the customers connected to network 2 could in fact be measured on the tie lines between the two networks.

On the other hand, the technical structure of the system does not change at all. The physical connections to the network used by generators and consumers remain the same, irrespective of the contractual relationship, and the total demand for electricity from consumers does not change either. Significant changes in the system structure may only occur in the medium- or long-term, when generators and electricity-intensive consumers begin to take account of the new arrangements in their decisions concerning the choice of location.

The situation shown in the example would of course increase the available generation capacity of generator 2 which would, as a consequence, seek new customers outside his traditional supply area to ensure that production capacity is fully utilized. Ultimately this may lead to a situation where contractual relations change completely, whereas the technical situation of generation and power flows remains more-or-less the same as before the introduction of TPA. This leads to the important conclusion that the contractual and the physical consequences brought about by TPA are not directly comparable, and the latter may be relatively insignificant.

IV. RULES FOR TPA

In order that TPA may work in practice, a number of rules on technical and economic aspects must be applied at different levels as shown in figure 6. The lowest and ultimately relevant level is the individual network access agreement between a network operator and a network user, i.e. generator or customer. If the parties are free to negotiate and agree the TPA conditions that will be applied for each individual contract, non-discriminatory access for all market actors would be difficult or even impossible to achieve. Therefore a framework of rules for TPA has to be developed at the national level, defining minimum requirements for the individual agreements and reflecting national regulatory policy.

To take an example, in Germany, the general regulatory policy is to provide TPA on the basis of individual negotiation between the contract partners and to let market players voluntarily agree on a framework of rules needed to achieve non-discriminatory TPA. Only where a voluntary agreement cannot be found or does not work satisfactorily for all market participants, the government may intervene by issuing an order on TPA rules. This, however, has not been necessary so far.

The various sectors of regulation in Germany are subject to sector-specific agreements. The agreement governing transmission and distribution pricing as well as power balancing and settlement has proved to be the most heavily discussed agreement. It has been concluded among the associations of electricity utilities and industrial power consumers and generators and is therefore called the "associations' agreement". At the beginning of the year 2000, a

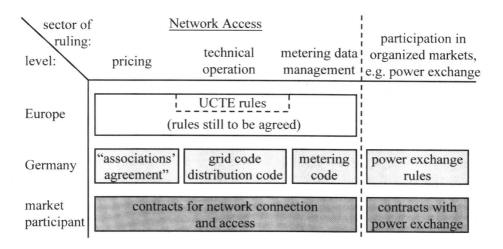

Figure 6. Necessary Rules for the Liberalized Market (Example: Germany)

second version of this agreement entered into force. The new agreement represents considerable progress over the initial version of May 1998, particularly in terms of the practical application of the rules and, thus, the facilitation of increased competition.

Technical and operational aspects of network connection and network use are addressed by the so-called grid code (for transmission networks) and distribution code (for distribution networks). The responsibilities and technical procedures relating to data management for metering are governed by a separate agreement called the metering code. In particular, these technical rules cover the following important issues:

- procedures for handling network access requests from market participants;
- network security assessment, identification of congestion, and allocation of scarce network capacity in case of congestion;
- details of power balancing, data management for metering and settlement;
- system coordination and ancillary services;
- technical criteria for connection to the network, including standards for network reliability and supply quality;
- terms of cooperation between network operators; and
- protocols for data exchange among network operators and between network operators and users.

The third level of regulation with respect to TPA is the European level, since national rules may not be compatible with each other and, therefore, they may create barriers to cross-border transactions within the Internal Market. This level is particularly difficult to handle because of the different degrees of market opening and the different regulatory policies of the Member States. Therefore the process of finding common rules for cross-border trading is still going on. The implementation of the first common approach to cross-border transmission pricing appears to be achievable by the end of 2000, but important technical aspects like congestion management still require considerable discussion and investigation.

In addition to rules on the technical and economic aspects of TPA, market liberalization requires rules on participation in organized markets, e.g. pool systems such as (so far) in the UK, or power exchanges such as Nordpool (Oslo), APX (Amsterdam), and others. Depending on the market organization in question, these rules can interfere to a certain extent with TPA rules. If, for example, a power exchange is given the responsibility to allocate scarce transmission capacity, as in the case of Nordpool, there is an important relationship between TPA and participation in the power exchange.

V. TRANSMISSION AND DISTRIBUTION PRICING

As indicated above, the development of an appropriate transmission and distribution pricing system is a crucial element of introducing TPA. There are different objectives to be fulfilled, some of which are highly contradictory:

- Network charges are of course intended to cover the cost-related to construction, maintenance and operation of the network equipment. On the other hand, in order to avoid inefficient network expansion and operation, they should include only that part of the total cost that is unavoidably necessary for the required level of supply quality. However, these costs are difficult to identify.
- Theoretically charges should reflect as precisely as possible the individual degree of network utilization of each network user. In practice, however, this is not feasible because charges that perfectly reflect cost would be too complicated to calculate. Apart from that, the assessment of what really reflects cost depends to a large extent on the individual point of view. A reasonable compromise between cost-reflectivity and practicality must therefore be found.
- Network charges should include adequate price signals to ensure efficient use of the networks. However, they should not be arbitrarily overloaded with politically motivated incentives.
- Charges should of course be non-discriminatory, i.e. equal for all market participants under equal conditions. They should be transparent and verifiable by market participants and regulators and they should be designed such that they promote competition.

The development of a network-pricing concept usually begins with an identification of the relevant cost elements. Each cost element can theoretically be reflected by separate charges, but for practicality reasons it is often more appropriate to reduce the number of charge elements. The main cost elements are:

- costs of the network infrastructure including investment, maintenance and operation costs;
- costs of energy required to cover network losses;
- costs of ancillary services that are necessary for the proper operation of the system and that are usually coordinated by the network operators. Such costs include frequency control and power balancing, voltage control, system coordination, fault management, etc.;
- costs of metering and settlement; and
- costs arising in the context of measures to avoid or to remove congestion and to allocate scarce network capacity.

In a second step, the identified costs have to be allocated to network users in accordance with their use of the network on an individual basis. There are many options to design the cost allocation principles in a reasonably cost-reflective and practical way. The most important decision to be taken is the selection of either point-of-connection-based or transaction-based cost allocation (figure 7):

− Charges related to the point of connection depend only on the characteristics of the network connection and the degree of network utilization of one single user, be it a generator or a consumer. They do not depend on the contractual supply relationship between the market participants. This has the great advantage that charges do not need to be modified each time a supplier or customer enters into a new supply contract.

− Naturally there are only a few parameters that can be used to differentiate such network charges. They are mainly related to the point of connection to the network, as indicated by the name of this concept. The most important parameter is the voltage level to which a network user is connected. Since there is no way to reflect in such charges the actual supply path between generator and consumer, charges are usually calculated such that they include contributions for all voltage levels from the level of connection of a network user up to the highest existing level, thus reflecting the value of the "option" to use the complete network.

− Additionally, charges can be differentiated according to the location or region of the connection to the network. This is mainly applied in order to provide incentives to

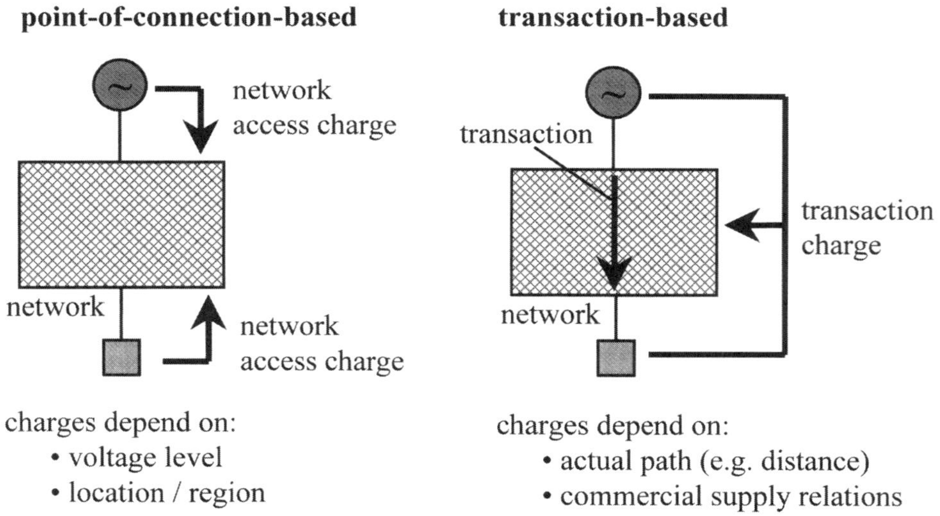

Figure 7. Basic Principles of Network Cost Allocation

generators to make efficient location choices from the network standpoint.

– Transaction-based charges are related to the characteristics of the individual electricity transaction between a supplier and a customer. They can depend, for example, on the voltage levels actually covered by the transaction path, or on the distance between the contract partners' network connection points. This implies however that charges have to be adapted each time the contractual relations change.

– It is often thought that transaction-based charges achieve better cost-reflectivity because they allow for the inclusion of more precise information on the individual's network utilization. This is however a highly controversial issue, mainly because networks are usually not designed to accommodate one specific transaction, but a great multitude of transactions that in total require much less network capacity than the sum of the single transactions would do. Therefore, it is a matter of dispute whether the characteristics of a single transaction actually reflect the cost drivers of network design and operation.

As regards national concepts for transmission and distribution pricing, it appears that most countries seem to opt sooner or later for point-of-connection-based charges, mainly because they are much easier to handle and to understand and because they help to avoid the problem described above concerning the cost-reflectivity of transaction-based parameters. Agreement on transmission pricing at the European level has not yet been found. One of the open issues is if costs allocated to the international network use should be allocated specifically to cross-border transactions, i.e. transaction-based, or rather to the totality of network users, i.e. point-of-connection-based.

Apart from this issue, there are a couple of further options for network pricing that can be used to best meet requirements:

– As already mentioned, charges can be split up into different charge elements. This is particularly useful to reflect those cost elements the degree of utilization of which is not in proportion with the user's overall network utilization. For example, the metering and settlement costs caused by a customer are usually not proportional to the customer's power and energy demand, but depend mainly on the type of metering equipment used.

– In the case of point-of-connection-based pricing in particular, the allocation of costs between suppliers and consumers must be defined. This aspect gains importance particularly if the allocation is not harmonized among the various network operators. If for example in the European context one country decided to allocate costs exclusively to generators while another country decided to charge only consumers, international competition would clearly be distorted.

– Charge elements can be related either to power (per kilowatt and year) or to energy (per kilowatt-hour) or both. They can be differentiated according to the location of the point of connection or to the time of network use, i.e. on the basis of different seasons or day and night time.

An example of a system of network charges as typically published by German network operators on the basis of the new associations' agreement is shown in table 1. These point-of-connection-based charges depend on the voltage level of a consumer's connection to the network, and on his annual utilization time. This is the quotient of maximum power and electricity demand within one year. The charges comprise a power-related and an energy-related component. There are no charges for generators because costs are completely allocated to consumers according to the agreement. The charges shown here include the costs of network infrastructure, network losses and ancillary services. Other cost elements like metering and settlement, reserve capacity, and balancing power are covered by separate charges that are not included in this table.

Table 1. Typical example of use-of-system charges of a German network operator (fictitious values)

Voltage level of connection to the network:	Annual utilization time			
	< 2500 h/a		≥ 2500 h/a	
	power rate €/kWa	energy rate ct/kWh	power rate €/kWa	energy rate ct/kWh
extra high voltage	3.00	0.75	18.00	0.10
incl. transformation	7.00	0.75	22.00	0.10
high voltage	5.00	1.30	35.00	0.20
incl. transformation	13.00	1.30	44.00	0.20
medium voltage	9.00	2.20	52.00	0.45
incl. transformation	22.00	2.20	67.00	0.45
low voltage	12.00	3.50	75.00	0.90

*Sabine Schulte-Beckhausen**

ENERGY TRADING IN THE EU: THE COMMODITIZATION OF ELECTRICITY AND THE EMERGENCE OF ENERGY EXCHANGES

I. INTRODUCTION

A. Electricity as a Commodity

In short, energy trading is the buying and selling of energy. Of course, buying and selling electricity was already possible in the old world of franchised service areas with clear boundaries. However, that cannot be seen as energy trading in today's terms, notwithstanding perhaps the long-established practice of exchanging power between interconnected companies at UCTE level.[1] In the old world market participants did not have freedom of choice, whereas under the new European framework companies as well as customers are, in principle, free to choose their supplier. Customer choice leads to energy trading. As a consequence, the product becomes a commodity that, as such, can be traded in a variety of ways. In the Anglo-American world this phenomenon is called commoditization.[2]

Before the liberalization of energy markets was being discussed at the European level, some authors argued that energy was a special good and thus fell neither under the rules of the Treaty concerning the free movement of goods, nor under the competition rules.[3] Under the new European and national framework it is evident that this view cannot be justified any longer. Indeed, the European Court of Justice stated very early, even before the proposal for the Electricity Directive was being discussed, that electricity was a commodity in

---

* Dr. Sabine Schulte-Beckhausen, Rechtsanwältin, is an expert with the Verband kommunaler Unternehmen e.V. (Association of Municipal Utilities) in Cologne. The considerations contained in this paper exclusively reflect the personal opinion of the author.

[1] UCTE = Union pour la coordination du transport d'électricité; until 1999 this association was responsible for co-ordinating the production of electricity within the European transmission grid, a task that also involved the exchange of electricity.

[2] See M. Haedicke, "Competitive-Based Contracts for the New Power Business", (1996) *Energy Law Journal*, Volume 17, No. 1, 103, 113.

[3] German authors relied upon the former cartel law according to which the energy sector was regarded as a specific sector governed by specific rules (the former paragraphs 103, 103a GWB), see for details Ludwig/ Odenthal/Schulte-Beckhausen, *Recht der Elektrizitäts-, Gas- und Wasserversorgung*, (1999), Vol. II, V. EGV, before Article 16 and 81-86, No. 3, 4.

Damien Geradin (ed.), The Liberalization of Electricity and Natural Gas in the European Union, 49–60
©2001 Kluwer Law International. Printed in the Netherlands.

terms of the rules of the EC Treaty on the free movement of goods and services.[4] Later, when the outlines of the Directive were already known, the Court confirmed this opinion.[5] Today, the experience gained from liberalized electricity systems shows that there can no longer be any doubt about qualifying electricity as a tradable good. The development of the energy markets has proved to overrule the existing legal framework.

B. Separation of Functions and New Players

Freedom of choice implies many new possibilities for all market participants. Companies can specialize in different activities: operation of the transmission and distribution systems, generation of energy and energy trading as well as marketing, sales and customer service. New market players then enter the electricity business as traders, brokers, aggregators and portfolio managers as well as independent system operators and service companies.

Energy trading in the proper sense refers exclusively to the wholesale market. This is another way of saying that companies that are active in trading are operating "business to business", which means doing business with power producers and other traders. As for the buying and selling of energy in relation to final customers, however, the term commonly used to designate this sector is the retail market. Consequently, the field of marketing, sales and customer services is not referred to as trading.

The separation of functions produces the necessary transparency in the market. In particular, the separation between the operation of the transmission grid and energy trading is a prerequisite for a transparent market place. This is due to the fact that the transmission grid functions as a common market place for electricity as a commodity. For this reason transparency is one of the guiding principles of the Electricity Directive.[6] In order to ensure transparency and non-discrimination, the Directive states that the transmission function of vertically integrated undertakings should be operated independently from the other activities "at least in management terms" (Article 7, paragraph 6). This does not imply a strict separation in terms of independent company organization. Thus, in countries that do not require organizational unbundling – for example in Germany – electricity companies on the high voltage level are still more or less vertically integrated. In other countries, for example in Sweden, the national energy legislation obliges undertakings to legally separate the operation of the system from trading activities.[7]

Once markets have been liberalized, however, the undertakings themselves see economic advantages in separating the above-mentioned functions. On the one hand, separation leads to cost transparency; on the other, it offers the possibility of transferring certain risks to

---

[4] Case C-7/68, *Commission v. Italy*, (Dec. 10, 1968), E.C.R. I-633, 642.

[5] Case C-393/92, *Almelo*, (April 27, 1994), E.C.R. I-1477.

[6] See preliminary considerations No. 25, 26, 30.

[7] See the Swedish Laws on Energy Trading and on Energy of January 1, 1996.

independent affiliated companies. With regard to energy trading activities, the risk argument is of great importance.

II. THE EUROPEAN FRAMEWORK ON ENERGY TRADING

A. EC Treaty

The EC Treaty rules on the free movement of goods, persons, services and capital form the basis for energy trading in Europe. In addition, the energy business is subject to EC competition law, in particular those provisions relating to cartels and market abuse. Moreover, the European rules governing services of general economic interest (Article 16, Article 86(2) of the Treaty, Article 3, paragraph 2 of the Electricity Directive) can affect the extent of energy trading in the EU. This is due to the fact that energy trading may be slowed down by national legislation imposing general economic interest obligations on undertakings operating in the electricity sector. On the basis of the principle of subsidiarity, the Directive offers the Member States a wide range of different solutions in this respect. For example, the new French law concerning the electricity sector contains important rules on public service obligations that lead to possible restrictions on activity.[8] Article 22, paragraph 3 of the French law requires as a public service obligation that supply contracts have a minimum duration of at least three years, in order to facilitate long-term planning of the electricity production. It is evident that this provision is compatible neither with the needs of energy traders nor with the needs of customers who want to make use of new power contracts.

Even in countries where the electricity market has been opened up 100%, for example Germany, energy trading remains partly restricted.[9] The new German energy law[10] contains a transitional provision (Article 4, transitional provisions, section 3) on the refusal to provide network access that aims at protecting a high level of power generation from lignite from the new Bundesländer. As a consequence of this clause the Eastern part of the German energy market is developing very slowly, despite complete liberalization.

---

[8] Loi No 2000-108 of February 8, 2000 relative à la modernisation et au développement du service public d'électricité (act concerning the modernization and the development of the public service in the electricity sector), *Journal Officiel de la République Française* of February 10, 2000, p. 2143.

[9] For an overview see S. Schulte-Beckhausen, "Stromhandel – Möglichkeiten und Grenzen im neuen europäischen und nationalen Ordnungsrahmen für Energie", (1999), *RdE (Recht der Energiewirtschaft)*, 51-59.

[10] Gesetz zur Neuregelung des Energiewirtschaftsrechts (Act revising energy industry legislation) of April 24, 1998, Bundesgesetzblatt 1998, Part I No. 23, April 28 1998, p. 730.

B. Electricity Directive

1. Elements of Market Opening

According to the preliminary considerations of the Electricity Directive (No. 1-3 and 5), the internal market for electricity will have to be established gradually. Thus, the philosophy of the Directive also envisages that energy trading evolves step by step. The Directive only lays down the general conditions that should assure the free movement of goods and services within the energy sector, but refrains from designing concrete market structures.

A competitive electricity market is to be ensured by the following elements: Member States are obliged to open their national electricity market, or at least a minimum share of it; and eligible customers are entitled to demand network access in order to participate in the free market, i.e. wholesale customers must be able to conclude contracts on the wholesale market and thus participate in energy trading. Furthermore, generation is freed up, leading to competitive energy prices. Players are also free to construct direct lines, which adds a supplementary element to competition. Finally, the transmission system has to be independent from generation and distribution services at least in management terms in order to ensure transparency of the market.

These general principles agreed at the European level provide for a general framework for energy trading. However, the importance of the subsidiarity principle, which is also enshrined in the Directive, means that the respective national solutions differ significantly. The shares of national markets subject to opening vary from a minimum share of roughly 30% (e.g. France, Belgium, Portugal) up to 100% (Germany, Great Britain, Sweden, Finland). In addition, the reciprocity clause is being applied in such a way as to prevent distributors and certain groups of customers from importing electricity, which obviously hampers trading. This situation leads to market distortions within the European wholesale electricity market.

2. Wholesale Customers

The Electricity Directive does not provide for specific rules on energy trading, nor does it define the rights and duties of traders. However, Article 2(8) stipulates that for the purposes of the Directive "wholesale customers shall mean any natural or legal persons, if the Member states recognize their existence, who purchase or sell electricity and who do not carry out transmission, generation or distribution functions inside or outside the system where they are established". Since the Directive does not oblige the Member States to separate the operation of the transmission grids from production and trading issues in legal terms, this definition remains largely theoretical. In practice, an important number of the new traders are subsidiaries of the incumbent energy utilities, which in many cases are still vertically integrated. Nevertheless, there are newcomers from the North American and Scandinavian energy markets who primarily operate as highly specialized trading companies within the definition of the Directive.

Some of the new national legislation, for example the Dutch law or the Spanish law, contain specific rules on trading or trading companies. On the grounds that the market in these countries is split into eligible customers on the one hand and captive customers on the other hand, a distinction is drawn between traders and concession holders, with the latter supplying energy to captive customers. Accordingly, the Dutch law[11] defines traders as organizational entities concerned with contracting agreements for the purchase and sale of electricity (paragraph 1, Article 1(h)). The Spanish law[12] states that traders are those legal entities, that, having access to transmission or distribution grids, have the function of selling electricity to eligible or other agents in the system (Article 9, No. 1(h)).

III. DEVELOPMENT OF PHYSICAL AND FINANCIAL MARKETS

A. New Types of Contracts

In the past, distribution companies as well as final customers used to conclude comprehensive supply contracts with one supplier who was responsible for meeting the total demand. Today, new types of contracts are being developed with regard to the duration and the timetable for performance. This marks a starting point for electricity trading and for the development of physical trading, i.e. the buying and selling of certain amounts of electricity for a clearly defined time period. The undertakings are differentiating their overall demand and entering into contractual relations with different suppliers.

In liberalized electricity markets different forms of contracts can be distinguished: long-term contracts, spot contracts and forward contracts (1). These transactions are to be performed on a physical basis. At the same time there are financial contracts such as swaps, futures and options which become important instruments to hedge price and market risks (2).

---

[11] Wet van 2 juli 1998, houdende regels met betrekking to de productie, het transport en de levering van electriciteit (Act of July 2, 1998 concerning rules on the production, the transport and the delivery of electricity).

[12] Ley 54/1997, de 27 Noviembre, del Sector Eléctrico (Act of 27 November 1997 on the Electricity Sector), Boletín oficial del Estado (BOE) of 28 November 1997.

Sabine Schulte-Beckhausen

1. Physical Contracts

Electricity is a homogenous product that can easily be standardized. In contrast to other commodities it cannot be stored. Thus, market forces need to be in balance at any particular time: the amount of electricity sold has to correspond to the amount bought. Because any imbalances have to be paid for, and that implies important cost risks depending on the price of the shortfall or excess, there is a strong economic incentive to keep supply and demand in constant equilibrium. However, supply and demand are not completely predictable, so there is a need for an open market place for daily or even hourly transactions, in other words for a spot market.

There are different definitions of the term spot market. According to the most common definition, a spot market refers to very short-term purchases and sales of energy, usually in a certain period of time (an hour or a day) for the following period.[13] Spot markets are usually organized on power exchanges. This enables the market participants to meet demand, as well as fulfil their responsibility to meet the balance of shortfalls in supply more easily and at the minimum cost. Transaction costs, in particular, can be reduced. In short, this is the reason why liberalized markets spawn spot markets, i.e. organized market places for very short time or real time transactions.

Apart from spot contracts, long-term transactions still play an important role in liberalized energy markets, though their role is changing. Spot contracts usually have a share of 20% of total supply on offer in these markets, whereas 80% of supply is still organized on the basis of long-term agreements. Nevertheless, it should be noted that in the past the contract term of traditional long-term contracts used to be up to 15 or 20 years, whereas today long-term contracts have a duration of one to five years. Long-term contracts within the portfolio of a modern electricity operator usually cover the base load demand.

A forward contract refers to the current energy price but stipulates that the performance of the obligation will take place in the future. It should be noted that forward contracts may be performed either by physical delivery or by financial payment. Long-term contracts and forward contracts are traded bilaterally, whereas short-term transactions are traded at the spot market on energy exchanges.

2. Financial Tools

A financial market is developing in parallel with the physical market. These kinds of contracts, which do not refer to the physical delivery of electricity but are performed by cash settlement, are called "contracts for differences" or derivatives. The experience of liberalized electricity systems shows that the financial market will only develop gradually after the physical trading has taken off.

---

[13] J. von Kistowski, "Stromhandel in den USA", (1998), *ET (Energiewirtschaftliche Tagesfragen)*, 81-85.

Market participants need these financial instruments to manage the risks arising from liberalization.[14] It is competition itself that drives the need to make use of the financial tools available. Electricity prices can be highly volatile; in some countries they fluctuate by as much as 40 – 50% per year. Thus the main objective is to hedge price risks, that means to protect profits in the physical market. In this respect hedging contracts are similar to price insurance contracts. They provide a degree of certainty for producers, utilities and customers by securing price deals over a period of six months up to two years.

However, these financial instruments can be used to pursue a quite different goal, namely speculation. Particularly in an early stage of liberalization speculative operations attract great interest, due to the fact that immature markets offer large arbitrage possibilities. Speculators try to profit by buying low and selling high, or vice versa, by for example taking a position in the futures market and hoping that the market moves in their favour. They play an important role in the market by adding liquidity. Whereas hedgers hold offsetting positions in the market for the physical commodity, speculators do not. In practice, neither producers nor customers are speculators.

Common types of financial tools in energy trading are swaps, options and futures.[15] Possible parties to a swap agreement are producers or traders on the one hand and traders or banks on the other hand. In principle, a swap follows this pattern: a producer, for example, wants to hedge the price risk of his electricity output for a period of six months, expecting a volatile price on the electricity market. He therefore concludes an agreement with a trader on a fixed electricity price for his production. This is a retail price the producer can live with. The partners agree to pay each other the price difference between the agreed fixed price and a price index that is floating. If the market price is lower than the agreed fixed price, the producer receives the difference from the trader; if the market price is higher he has to pay the difference to the hedging company. Payments are made at predetermined times, e.g. monthly. The producer hereby exchanges the opportunity to profit from increases in the market price of the product for insurance in the event the market price drops below the fixed price. This type of transaction can be of use to an energy purchaser as well: By taking the other side of the transaction and agreeing to pay a fixed price, he can utilize a swap to protect himself against price increases. It is important to see that in both cases the incentive for concluding such agreements is the difference between the price expectations of the partners.

A futures contract is a legally binding obligation for the holder of the contract to buy or sell a particular commodity at a specific price and location at a specific date in the future.

---

[14] For a comprehensive analysis see P. C. Fusaro, "Why use these financial tools?", *Energy Risk Management – Hedging Strategies and Instruments for the International Energy Markets*, New York 1998 (Editor: P.C. Fusaro), 1-7.

[15] P. C. Fusaro, "The ABCs of Energy Financial Instruments", *Energy Risk Management – Hedging Strategies and Instruments for the International Energy Markets*, New York 1998 (Editor: P.C. Fusaro), 9-35; M. Neuendorff, "Termingeschäfte auf Strom: Beschreibung der Spezifikationen und Verwendungsmöglichkeiten", (1996) *ZfE (Zeitschrift für Energiewirtschaft)*, 321-335.

In the case of electricity, a typical futures contract is brief and clearly fixes the contract volume in MWh, the delivery rate and period as well as the settlement details. Futures contracts are most widely used for hedging. Swaps and options are over-the-counter (OTC) negotiated contracts for differences, that means bilaterally negotiated, whereas futures are standardized contracts that are traded on power exchanges. A forward contract, too, can be settled in cash. In this case it is not used as a physical contract, but as a hedging instrument similar to the above-mentioned financial tools. Unlike futures contracts, they are not standardized but negotiated over the counter. When energy trading started on the Scandinavian power exchange Nord Pool, forward contracts were first settled physically, and later they changed into financial instruments.

Standardized trading of energy products started at the end of the seventies in the United States, with the first oil futures contracts being traded on the New York Mercantile Exchange (NYMEX) in 1978. The second energy product to be traded was a natural gas futures contract on the NYMEX in 1990. Later, the trading of electricity futures began in Norway in 1995 and one year later on the NYMEX as well. Today it seems that, of all the energy products, electricity shows the highest volatility. Thus electricity trading has become a highly attractive business in all liberalized markets worldwide.

B. Portfolio Management

Traders and customers use these different kinds of physical contracts and financial tools to compose their individual portfolio. Efficient portfolio management ensures an optimized mix of energy supplies according to the needs of the company. It is important to notice that energy trading always involves transactions on both the physical and the financial energy markets. The integration of physical contracts and financial tools within a comprehensive portfolio management strategy based on the undertaking's individual load forecast forms the basis of an efficient risk management strategy.[16]

Specifically, derivatives create both new opportunities and new challenges for companies. Properly employed, these instruments offer a new level of economic flexibility. However, in recently liberalized electricity markets they also give rise to legal issues never previously encountered, for example concerning security issues and guarantees.[17]

---

[16] Klaus-Michael Burger, "Risikomanagement beim Einsatz von Handels- und Finanzderivaten", (1998) *ET (Energiewirtschaftliche Tagesfragen)*, 126-130; A. Tillmann/F. Karbenn/R. Jaspert, "Konzeption und Umsetzung von Risikomanagementsystemen", *ET (Energiewirtschaftliche Tagesfragen)*, 378-382.

[17] See for the U.S. situation M. Haedicke, "Competitive-Based Contracts for the New Power Business", (1996) *Energy Law Journal*, Vol. 17, No. 1, 103,119.

C. New Contractual Systems

With the spread of short-term contracts, new contractual systems are being adopted. Following the pattern already set in the derivatives markets, traders are using so-called master agreements to define general terms and conditions, as well as transaction agreements to confirm specific deals. Recently, the European Federation of Energy Traders (EFET) published a standard form of contract for a general agreement to govern the mutual delivery of electricity as well as a form for the confirmation of individual contracts, referring either to fixed or to floating prices.

The general agreement governs the general terms and conditions for individual agreements regarding the delivery and acceptance of electricity. For example, it contains rules on guarantees and credit support, on non-performance due to Force Majeure and other reasons, on limitation of liability, on the term of the agreement and its termination and on confidentiality. On the basis of this general agreement the authorized traders of the parties conclude individual agreements via telephone, e-mail or fax by making use of the above-mentioned standard forms for the confirmation of individual contracts. These confirmation forms are very short: The buyer or seller merely has to fill in the details of the delivery schedule, the quality of delivery, the delivery point and the voltage level. In case the parties agree on a floating price, additional information concerning the price source, the calculation date, the calculation agent and the calculation method is required.

III. MARKET ORGANIZATION

A. Network Access and Independent System Operators

Non-discriminating conditions for the access to the system are the basis for a smooth-running electricity wholesale market. The Directive offers free choice between regulated third party access, negotiated access and the single buyer procedure. The experiences of liberalized energy markets in practice shows that regulated access to the high voltage system is the most appropriate way to ensure a functioning wholesale market. Furthermore, it is important to realise that trading may be hampered if the operation of the transmission system is not organized independently. Be that as it may, the European regulatory framework does not oblige the Member States to introduce such market structures. Thus, not all national systems have yet decided to establish independent system operators.

B. Energy Exchanges

In liberalized energy markets market participants feel the need to establish a common market place. Due to the fact that electricity is a homogenous product it can be traded via standardized contracts on energy exchanges. An energy exchange may offer different market places: a physical spot market, a forward and futures market as well as a balance power market. The energy price on each of these markets is determined by supply and demand.

An exchange maintains absolute neutrality toward the markets because its rules apply to both sides of a transaction. The exchange itself does not trade commodities, does not take positions in the market, and does not advise the participants on what positions to take. Instead, it provides a forum where members, on behalf of their customers or themselves, can trade standardized contracts in a safe, efficient and orderly manner.

From the point of view of the market participants an energy exchange brings numerous advantages. First, it functions as an open market place for all interested parties, thus it tends to attract a concentration of the liquidity in the market. At the same time, it ensures the transparency of electricity prices and guarantees anonymity of the participants in the power exchange. Finally, it offers clearing services to the customers and hedges the risk of liability and creditworthiness.

The first energy exchanges in Europe were established in Scandinavia (Norway and Finland). Today the Oslo-based Nord Pool covers the Norwegian, the Swedish, the Finnish as well as parts of the Danish power market. Nord Pool offers a spot market, a forward market and a balance market. The Dutch APX in Amsterdam, which started in spring 1999, offers a physical spot market, which is a day-ahead market. The Spanish OMEL in Madrid also started a physical spot market last year. In Germany, two energy exchanges will compete for market shares: the European Energy Exchange in Frankfurt (EEX) on the one hand and the Leipzig Power Exchange (LPX) on the other hand. LPX plans to start a physical spot market in June 2000. EEX is also likely to offer a spot market this year, despite its earlier announcements that it would start with a forward market. This is due to the fact that the German framework for network access, as laid down in the so-called Association Agreement, has been improved in order to make trading possible.[18]

Apart from power exchanges, price transparency may also be reached by independent price indices.[19] Examples in continental Europe are the Swiss Price Electricity Index (SWEP) and the Central European Power Index (CEPI). However, the problem of these index systems is that the participants in the index, and thus the traded volumes, are not transparent, which enables important market players to abuse their market power.

---

[18] See "Verbändevereinbarung II" (Association Agreement) of December 13, 1999, concluded by VDEW (Vereinigung deutscher Elektrizitätswerke e.V.), BDI (Bundesverband der Deutschen Industrie e.V.) and VIK (Verband der industriellen Energie- und Kraftwirtschaft e.V.).

[19] See VDEW – Vereinigung deutscher Elektrizitätswerke (editor), "Preisindices im Strommarkt – ihre Funktion, ihre Konstruktion und ihre praktischen Anwendungsmöglichkeiten", (3/2000) VDEW-Materialien M-06/2000.

C. Regulators

As far as energy trading is concerned, a regulatory regime needs in particular to deal with the terms and conditions of access to the transmission system. There is no liberalized energy market in the world without specific regulation in this field – except, that is, for Germany. However, it is likely that the completion of the internal electricity market will require the introduction of some minimum regulatory elements here at European level, at least as part of broader co-operation between the competent authorities of the Member States.

In its Second Report on harmonization requirements concerning the internal market on electricity, the European Commission states that cross-border trading is not yet working satisfactorily.[20] The problem of the "pancaking" arises, which refers to the accretion of network fees for different geographical areas. This is partly due to the different degrees of market opening, and partly to the regulation of network access and congestion management in the respective Member States. Consequently, the Commission has initiated a European discussion on how to organize cross-border electricity trading, as well as congestion management. Furthermore, the Commission has criticized the German model of dividing the market into two geographical trading zones on the grounds that it creates opportunities for abuse by the eight interconnected enterprises.

Within the so-called "Florence Process", the European Conference of Regulators is discussing possible solutions concerning the harmonization of different national network access systems. It is addressing two main subjects: on the one hand, cross-border network access tarification systems and, on the other, methods of congestion management. From the point of view of the energy traders, a non-transaction-based pan-European network access tariff should be the basic principle.[21] As far as congestion management is concerned, the traders insist that fair, non-discriminatory and market-related methods of capacity allocation at border interconnection points be developed as a matter of urgency, including the development of spot markets all over Europe.

Regulation seems to be less important for the business of energy trading as such. Most of the new national energy laws in the EU Member States do not stipulate specific requirements to traders planning to enter into the market. However, some of the rules already mentioned do refer to the trading activities of a company: The Swedish law, for instance, requires a strict unbundling of network operating and trading in legal terms. With regard to gradual market opening in Europe, most countries have adopted rules requiring a licence for supplying captive customers, whereas the supply of free customers by traders and other market players does not require any specific licence.

---

[20] *Second Report on Harmonisation Requirements* of April 16, 1999, COM (1999) 164, concerning Directive 96/92/EC concerning common rules for the internal market in electricity.

[21] See the recent position papers of EFET (European Federation of Energy Traders), available on the internet (http://www.efet.org).

IV. CONCLUSION

Recent market developments show that energy trading is developing very rapidly. Market pressures on energy prices are extremely strong. Nevertheless, some groups of market participants are able to benefit from the liberalized electricity market and from the new opportunities opening up in energy trading, whilst others are not. For example, German distribution companies suffer from the lack of transparency in wholesale market pricing and the lack of regulation of access to the transmission grids. We can clearly identify a gap between the existing European framework and the one that is needed to establish the preconditions for energy trading.

Nevertheless, it is important to bear in mind that the European internal electricity market is supposed to develop gradually and that the principle of subsidiarity has been accorded a key role in this process. We can therefore conclude that, on the one hand, neither the European framework nor the national rules of the Member States are yet ready to ensure the smooth running of energy trading in the internal market, i.e. with cross-border transactions and under non-discriminating conditions for all market participants. On the other hand, it is very likely that energy trading will soon evolve into a real European business sector to the benefit of all customers, hopefully integrating market participants from all the European countries and all levels of supply.

III. Consumer and Environment Protection

Francis McGowan

CONSUMERS AND ENERGY LIBERALIZATION

I. INTRODUCTION

This paper considers the impact of energy market liberalization on consumer protection. It does so by looking at how the position of consumers has changed as a result of greater competition in the electricity and gas sectors. What have been – or are likely to be – the economic effects, direct and indirect, for customers? How have the utilities themselves adapted their approach to customers? Are special measures to ensure consumer protection required in freer markets? How have consumer groups adapted to the new market structures? Does the European Commission give sufficient weight to consumer concerns? In addressing these questions, the paper is concerned primarily with the interests of small consumers, the traditional focus for "protection". However, in doing so, it is necessary to bear in mind that there are important distinctions to be drawn within this category (principally on the basis of their ability to exercise consumer choice in the energy market) and that developments in the energy markets as a whole – in particular what happens to larger consumers – impinge upon the domestic consumer. This latter aspect is significant in the case of EU energy liberalization as the market has not been completely liberalized. However, given the experience of liberalization overall – where the process seems to create its own momentum – and the declarations of governments themselves,[1] further market opening seems probable. Liberalization therefore is likely to affect all consumers directly as well as indirectly.

After a brief review of how "the consumer" has figured in the debate on liberalization, the paper focuses on the actual impact of energy market liberalization on consumers (based on the experience of more established domestic reforms, primarily on the UK). The paper looks at the impact on prices and other aspects of service, the role of the regulator and the nature of consumer representation. The paper then considers the effects of EU policies (actual and potential) on consumers, in terms of the directives themselves, the wider thrust of energy policy initiatives and the overall approaches to consumer and competition policy. The paper then shifts to examine how utilities' responses to liberalization affect consumers, taking into account such factors as the "discovery" of the consumer triggered by competition and the consequences of the wave of corporate restructuring in the energy sector. The consumer response to these changes is then assessed, particularly in terms of the articulation of interests and the relationship to regulatory processes.

---

[1] See for example the experience of other sectors such as air transport and telecommunications. Note also the commitments made by Heads of State at the Lisbon European Council, Presidency Conclusions, Lisbon 23 and 24 March 2000 (notwithstanding the reluctance of the French government to commit itself to a timetable for further reform, see *Financial Times*, 24 March 2000).

Damien Geradin (ed.), The Liberalization of Electricity and Natural Gas in the European Union, 63–79
©2001 Kluwer Law International. Printed in the Netherlands.

Francis McGowan

II. THE CONSUMER AT THE CORE OF THE LIBERALIZATION RATIONALE

To a very large extent, policies of liberalization have been rationalized on the basis of gains to the consumer resulting from more open markets. While other factors – most notably "competitiveness" – have been invoked as reasons to liberalize,[2] there has been a strong presumption that increased competition would benefit the consumer in the form of lower prices, better services and innovation. The underlying analysis justifying deregulation was one which sought to rebalance consumer and producer interests in favour of the former.[3] In the context of utility reform, this analysis included an exposé of the poor deal experienced by consumers under the ancien régime of "natural monopoly". It was argued that markets were organized and regulated according to the needs of the industry and its employees rather than to those of the consumer; instead of meeting the public or general interest, it was the private interests of producers that were primarily addressed. Reform was needed to deliver more benefits to consumers as well as to improve the functioning of markets.[4]

In the case of energy markets, the claims made for liberalization and against monopoly were perhaps less clear-cut than in other regulated industries. Defenders of the old status quo argued that the producer and consumer interests were addressed by monopoly, with consumers benefiting as a result of scale economies and low transaction costs.[5] Overall levels of efficiency were often high and regulatory or ownership factors actually ensured

---

[2] While liberalization was explicitly related to competitiveness in the Lisbon Summit communiqué, the link was also articulated in earlier Community milestones such as Cockfield and Delors' *White Papers*. See Commission of the European Communities, *Completing the Internal Market*, Brussels: Commission, 1985 and *Growth, Competitiveness, Employment: the Challenges and Ways Forward into the 21st Century*, Brussels: Commission, 1993.

[3] The arguments on competition and consumer benefits in electricity are also examined in Hunt, S and Shuttleworth, G, *Competition and Choice in Electricity*, Chichester: Wiley, 1996. On the gains for consumers (and producers) arising from deregulation more generally see Winston, C "Deregulation: Days of Reckoning for Microeconomists", *Journal of Economic Literature,* Vol 31 No 3, 1993. An account of the failings of the old system of energy regulation, as perceived by the regulatory authorities themselves, is given in California Public Utilities Commission, *California's Electric Services Industry: Perspectives on the Past, Strategies for the Future*, CPUC 1993.

[4] For an official statement of the virtues of reform see Moore, J. "The Success of Privatisation" in Kay, J and Mayer, C (eds) *Privatisation and Regulation – the UK Experience*, Oxford: Clarendon, 1986. On the possible tradeoffs and conflicts see Foster, C, *Privatisation, Public Ownership and the Control of Natural Monopoly*, Oxford: Blackwell, 1993 and Majone, G "Paradoxes of Privatisation and Deregulation" *Journal of European Public Policy*, Vol 1 No 1 1994. On the importance of competition to transforming utility performance, see Vickers, J and Yarrow, G, *Privatisation – an Economic Analysis*, MIT, 1988. On the difficulties of proving the relationship between competition and performance more generally, see Nickel, S "Competition and Corporate Performance" *Journal of Political Economy*, Vol 104, No 41, 1996.

[5] The advantages of the traditional system of integrated monopolies are discussed in Yarrow G, *Some Economic Issues Surrounding the Proposed Privatisation of Electricity Generation and Transmission*, London: Prima Europe, 1988. A robust defence, crafted by economists within EdF, was presented as the Eurelectric response to liberalization in 1991. "Organisation and Regulation of the Electricity Sector – A Response from the Continental Members of Eurelectric" 1991.

that the benefits of the regime were passed on to consumers. To the extent that there were shortcomings in performance and higher costs these were largely a result of the tendency of governments to use the industries as tools of fiscal, industrial, regional or social policy.[6] Leaving aside the impact of the balance of these technical gains and political losses upon consumers, it is probably true to say that, despite an extensive system of consumer representation, direct consumer input was relatively limited in determining government policies and corporate strategies in these sectors.[7] However it would be wrong to suggest that there was widespread consumer dissatisfaction with the performance of the energy utilities. Instead, the main advocates of change were the energy intensive industries who believed that they would gain from competitive energy markets.[8]

However even the strongest advocates of liberalization would admit that freer markets are not necessarily free of market failures and that consumers may still need protection.[9] Key concerns would include the risks of collusion and concentration and abuse of market power (competition policy concerns), the possibility of misselling as a result of inaccurate marketing techniques (information asymmetries) and a range of broader effects such as distributional impacts between different classes of customer (indeed the right to be supplied) and inadequate attention to the environment (negative externalities).[10] Note, however, that these concerns are not shared by all commentators to the same extent with opinions on the scope of regulation ranging from minimalist application of antitrust rules through to extensive intervention by regulatory authorities and/or the government.[11]

III. THE IMPACT OF ENERGY LIBERALIZATION ON CONSUMERS

Moving beyond principle, however, what have been the main effects of energy market liberalization upon consumers? The EU electricity and gas reforms have not been in force long enough for a meaningful assessing of their impact. Yet a number of member states

---

[6] See for example, Surrey, A J "Government and the Nationalised Industries" in Gretton, J and Harrisson, A (eds) *Energy 86, Policy Journals*, 1986 and McGowan, F "The Consequences of Competition", *Revue des Affaires Européennes*, No 2, 1994. For a sense of the issue beyond the UK see de Paoli, L "Electricity and the Single European Market", *Energy Studies Review*, Vol 1 No 3, 1989.

[7] Martin, J and Smith, G, *The Consumer Interest*, London, 1968.

[8] On the nature of disputes see McGowan, F, *The Struggle for Power in Europe*, RIIA 1993.

[9] See for example, Littlechild, S, *Privatisation Competition and Regulation*, IEA Occasional Paper No 110, 2000 and Kahn, A "Electric Deregulation: Defining and Ensuring Fair Competition", *Electricity Journal* 39, 1998.

[10] See for example Kay, J and Vickers, J "Regulatory Reform in Britain" Economic Policy, No 8, 1988; Noll, R "Economic Perspectives on the Politics of Regulation" in Schmalensee, R and Willig, R (eds) *Handbook of Industrial Organisation*, Vol 2. Amsterdam: Elsevier, 1989.

[11] On regulatory debates see Corry, D (ed) *Profiting from the utilities: new thinking on regulatory reform*, Institute for Public Policy Research, 1995 and Veljanowski, C, *The Future of Industry Regulation in the UK*, European Policy Forum, 1993.

have been engaged in reform for much longer periods – in some cases (such as the privatization and liberalization of the UK gas industry) since the 1980s. In this section we draw together some of the effects of national reforms and consider their relevance to the EU case. Our main focus is on the British energy market as this is both the longest established and most extensive liberalization[12] but we will also note some developments in other liberalized and non-liberalized markets.

The details of the liberalization and privatization in the British energy market have been well documented elsewhere,[13] but for the purposes of this chapter it is worth noting a few points. The process began in the early 1980s with attempts to introduce some competition in production and supply for both gas and electricity: neither measure was successful. Instead it was only with the privatization of the two industries (hitherto they had been publicly owned since the late 1940s) that the issue of competition was treated more effectively. In the case of the gas sector (where the incumbent supplier – British Gas – was privatized as a single entity) pressures for liberalization emerged rapidly, not least from the regulatory authority, the Office of Gas Supply (OFGAS). Along with the national antitrust bodies (the Office of Fair Trading and the Monopolies and Mergers Commission), the regulatory agency pushed for an improvement in the conditions under which competition was possible. A form of managed liberalization emerged in the late 1980s for industrial and commercial consumers, with domestic consumers being included from the mid 1990s on. They were already protected by a system of price control (a mechanism which remains in place despite the full liberalization of the market). In the case of electricity, the industry was vertically disintegrated as a part of privatization with the main generating company being split into three production companies and a transmission company. Competition was phased in over eight years with domestic consumers able to buy power from any supplier from 1998. As with gas this process was overseen by the industry regulator, the Office for Electricity Regulation (OFFER).

In both the gas and electricity cases, the regulatory agencies were charged with promoting competition (a primary objective of the regulator) as well as protecting the consumer (a secondary objective). Consumer protection was underpinned by a set of price controls for captive customers and monopoly services (such as transmission), using the RPI-X system, whereby prices were set in line with inflation minus an efficiency factor. The aim of this system was to ensure that consumers enjoyed real price reductions and that producers had an incentive to increase efficiency: if they did not reduce costs, their profits would fall; if they did they would be able to retain any savings beyond those necessary to fund the price

---

[12] On electricity it could be argued that Sweden and Norway leapfrogged the UK by rolling out full market liberalization much more quickly, see Midttun, A "(Mis) Understanding Change: Electricity Liberalisation in Norway and Sweden", in Kaijser, A and Hedin, M, *Nordic Energy Systems*, Canton: Science History Publications, 1995.

[13] See Helm, D, Kay, J and Thompson, D (eds) *The Market for Energy*, Oxford: Clarendon, 1989; Bishop, M, Kay, J and Mayer, C (eds) *Privatisation and Economic Performance*, Oxford, Clarendon 1994 and Surrey, A (ed) *The British Electricity Experiment*, London: Earthscan 1996.

reduction.[14] The regulators also devised a series of performance standards for such matters as supply disruption and fault repairs. The representation of consumers was handled differently in the two sectors. A Gas Consumers' Council was retained from the days of public ownership while its equivalent in the electricity sector was wound down and regional consultative committees incorporated into OFFER. General consumers' organizations such as the National Consumers' Council and the Consumers' Association kept a close eye on the two sectors. Large energy users were organized around a private lobbying organization, the Major Energy Users Council.

Initially, the growth of competition (and, of course, private ownership) made its biggest impact on the industry rather than consumers. Liberalization transformed the incentive structure faced by utilities, forcing a shift from cost plus behaviour to cost reducing behaviour; if new competitors entered the market offering lower priced energy, incumbents would have to adjust their cost structures to meet the new prices or lose market share. The main casualties of this process were the workforces in the utilities and supporting industries (notably the coal sector)[15] while the shorter time horizons of the industry also impacted upon capital-intensive investment projects as well as "overhead" functions such as research and development.[16] As we will see later there was also a redefinition of utilities' attitudes towards customers and a flurry of corporate restructuring. Effects on consumers have been more diffuse, though it is worth noting that where – as in the UK – privatization has been a part of the process of reform, the benefits of cost reduction have flowed as much (if not more) to the investors as to the consumers.[17]

In judging the impact of energy liberalization, the primary indicator of change has been that of price: whatever the broader effects of reform, most analysts (and consumers) want to know whether liberalization has brought about price reductions. Until 2000 (when energy prices as a whole rose on the back of increases in oil prices) there were cuts in prices for most groups of British consumers (big and small). In both electricity and gas markets, it is clear that commercial and industrial consumers have obtained lower energy prices over the 1990s: between 1990 and 1998, gas prices fell on average by 43% and electricity

---

[14] See Vickers, J and Yarrow, G "Privatising the Natural Monopolies" Public Policy Centre, 1985.

[15] See Department of Trade and Industry, Social Implications of Energy Liberalisation 2000. Gripaios, P and Munday, M "Regional Winners and Losers from Recent Trends in Utility Rationalisation" *Regional Studies* vol 33 No 8 2000.

[16] McGowan, F "The Consequences of Competition", *Revue des Affaires Européennes*, No 2, 1994.

[17] On utility strategies and their impacts on consumers see Graham, S "Liberalised Utilities, New Technologies and Urban Social Polarization" *European Urban and Regional Studies*, Vol 4, No 1, 2000 and Guy, S Graham, S and Marvin, S, "Splintering networks: The social, spatial, and environmental implications of the privatization and liberalization of utilities in Britain" in Coutard, O (ed) *The Governance of Large Technical Systems*, Routledge, 1999. On the split between consumers and investors see Yarrow, G "British electricity prices since privatization" *Studies in Regulation* No 1 Oxford: Regulatory Policy Institute, 1992 and National Consumer Council (NCC), *Paying the Price: a Consumer View of Water Gas Electricity and Telephone Regulation*, HMSO, London, 1993.

prices by 23.5% in real terms. The bulk of this decline took place in the second half of the decade as liberalization was extended across the whole of these markets (and as regulated prices for monopoly services such as transmission were also reduced).[18] Such average figures obscure the differences in price between different types of customer: unsurprisingly the bulk of the initial reductions was enjoyed by firms which were large enough to choose their supplier. The main exception to this trend was, ironically, the group of consumers which pushed for reform the hardest – the energy intensive large industrial users who in some cases saw their electricity prices rise. The reason for these increases is disputed: some analysts suggest that this was a result of the elimination of old cross subsidies to "strategic industries" under public ownership while the industries themselves claim that it is due to anticompetitive conduct by suppliers in the electricity pool.[19]

Domestic energy prices showed more modest reductions in price over the period. While there was a slight overall decline in the first half of the 1990s there were years in which prices rose due to vat and changes in the regulatory regime. Overall the level of was not greater than the long run reduction in energy prices.[20] Since 1994 the margin of price reductions has grown and over the decade as a whole prices fell by 15% for electricity and 17% for gas. The more limited price reduction seems to reflect the lack of liberalization in these market segments (with the reductions that did take place being largely attributable to regulatory rules) and the acceleration since the mid-90s coincides with liberalization (though even then some of the reduction has been generated by changes in regulation). Liberalization has had an effect: by the middle of 1999 approximately 4.5m. households had switched gas supply while 1.3m. had switched power supply. Most of these households would have been those who had most to gain from such a switch (even though in electricity the margins were very narrow).[21]

Of course, it is possible that such reductions were a feature of all energy markets in Europe. After all, the long run trend in energy prices has been downward. Put another way, comparing prices in markets where liberalization has taken place with prices in those where there has been little or no liberalization should reveal significant disparities. This appears to be the case in gas markets if we compare prices in the UK against those in other

---

[18] See Department of Trade and Industry, The Social Implications of Energy Liberalisation, DTI 2000 and Energy Report 1999. On the regulatory changes, both on price control and market liberalization see the annual reports of the regulators OFFER and OFGAS and OFGEM (2000), Press Release – Gas and electricity customers save almost £2 billion. PN58, 24/5/2000.

[19] See Holmes, P and McGowan, F "La Réforme des Services Publics au Royaume-Uni" *Sciences de la Société*, No 43, 1998.

[20] See Yarrow, G "British electricity prices since privatization" *Studies in Regulation* No 1 Oxford: Regulatory Policy Institute, 1992.

[21] Indeed the high cost of implementing liberalization for domestic customers has caused some to question its net benefits. See Green, R and McDougall, T "Competition in Electricity Supply: Will 1998 be Worth It" *Fiscal Studies* Vol 19 No 3, 1998 and Newbery, D "The UK Experience: Privatisation with Market Power" in Bergman *et al.*, *A European Market for Electricity?* CEPR Monitoring European Deregulation No 2, 1999.

member States. On a year-to-year basis UK energy prices for all classes of customer have been amongst the lowest in the EU, and the disparity has grown over time. The situation is very different in the case of electricity with UK prices often being closer to the EU average. It should be noted of course that for the last few years at least, the electricity data has included countries, such as the Nordic countries, where liberalization has also been introduced while in others there may have been political pressures to keep prices low.[22] Indeed, in the case of both fuels, one should note that, over time, some countries have seen dramatic oscillations in price and marked differences between classes of customer, reflecting particular policy choices or interventions rather than the degree of liberalization. While such events should serve as a caveat to any automatic equating of price changes and market structure, there does seem to be some basis for arguing that liberalization in the UK (and elsewhere?) may have contributed to lower prices in those countries than were experienced in the rest of the EU overall (even if the margin of difference is not very great).[23]

What of the broader effects of liberalization? As regards pricing, it is possible that increased competition may benefit some consumers but at the expense of others. Moreover, if prices become more cost reflective, previous cross subsidies between and within groups of consumers might be unravelled at the expense of the poor. In the case of the UK the distributional impact of liberalization is unclear. A number of commentators have highlighted how the gains have been skewed to the more affluent customers due to higher levels of usage and payment through direct banking while the poorest consumers are obliged to pay through expensive prepayment metering systems and are more at risk of disconnection.[24] The regulator and the government claims that the distribution effects have not been serious due to the survival of some price controls, the overall reduction in energy prices and macro-factors such as the improvements in the economy and in the housing stock (poor insulation is one of the major causes of high energy bills).[25]

---

[22] Though judging the overall effects is very difficult. See Midttun, *A European electricity systems in transition: a comparative analysis of policy and regulation in Western Europe*, Oxford: Elsevier Science, 1997 and Bergman, L and von der Fehr, N "The Nordic Experience: Diluting Market Power by Integrating Markets" in Bergman *et al.*, *A European Market for Electricity?* CEPR Monitoring European Deregulation No 2.

[23] See Department of Trade and Industry, *The Social Implications of Energy Liberalisation*, DTI 2000 and European Commission, *Opening up to choice: the single electricity market*, Luxembourg: OOPEC, 1999.

[24] National Consumer Council (NCC), *Paying the Price: a Consumer View of Water, Gas, Electricity and Telephone Regulation*, HMSO, London, 1993 and Graham, S "Liberalised Utilities, New Technologies and Urban Social Polarization" *European Urban and Regional Studies*, Vol 4, No 1, 2000 and Ernst, J (1994) Whose Utility Open University. For preliminary assessments of full liberalization, see Waddams Price, C and Hancock, R "Distributional Effects of Liberalising UK Residential Utility Markets" *Fiscal Studies*, Vol 19 No 3, 1998 and Young, A "Consumer Choice? Social Obligations, Cross Subsidies and Competition in the Privatised Utilities" *CMUR Research Paper 98/7*, 1998.

[25] Department of Trade and Industry, *The Social Implications of Energy Liberalisation*, DTI 2000 and Energy Report 1999. See also OFGEM, *Social Action Plan*, March 2000; OFGEM (2000), *Enhancing Social Obligations – Decision Document*, May 2000; OFGEM (2000), Press Release – Licence Changes Protect Disdvantaged Customers, PN 60, 25/5/2000.

The scenario of utilities abandoning "uneconomic" customers has not yet transpired, even if the formal rules on the obligation to supply are more ambiguous after reform.[26] There has also been more attention paid to the "fuel poor" in recent years by utilities, regulators and governments. A household is defined as being fuel poor if 10% or more of its income is spent on energy (the average expenditure is closer to 2-3%). One in five British households are judged to fit this category, mainly the unemployed, pensioners and those with poor housing conditions. While the problem is not a new one,[27] many expected it to deteriorate as a result of the changes in energy markets. Concern for the plight of such consumers increased as, in the wake of privatization, some utilities increased the rate of disconnection or required those customers unable to pay their bills to use prepayment meters. Partly in response to these developments – and as a result of extensive campaigning by consumer organizations and other advocacy groups – utilities, regulators and the government have given more attention to the problem. A variety of schemes have been designed to tackle the problem at both the customer and the utility level while changes in the regulatory regime have given greater attention to the socially disadvantaged.[28] How effective these policies will be in ensuring a degree of protection to the poorest consumers remains to be seen however as liberalization pressures intensify.[29]

The impact of liberalization on service quality is mixed, depending on which aspect of service is examined. The prospect of cost cutting pressures jeopardizing security of supply or other aspects of service delivery does not seem to have taken place: regulation has been effective in tackling any problems of performance by setting standards for utility performance.[30] It was, however, less effective at managing the effects of liberalization on the marketing of energy services: as markets were opened, there was a wave of misselling and

[26] Pollit, M "Issues in Electricity Market Integration and Liberalisation" in Bergman *et al., A European Market for Electricity?* CEPR Monitoring European Deregulation No 2, 1999. See also Foster, C, *Privatisation Public Ownership and Natural Monopoly*, Oxford: Blackwells, 1993.

[27] Berthoud,R, *Fuel debts and hardship: a review of the electricity and gas industries' code of practice Reports* 601 Policy Studies Institute 1981; "Electricity Consumers' Council, The code of practice on the payment of domestic electricity and gas bills: comments on its operations and interim suggestions for improvements" *Discussion paper 7*, 1980; Boardman, B (1991) *Fuel poverty: from cold homes to affordable warmth*, London: Belhaven.

[28] Consumers' Association, (1999) "Final Demand: Ending Fuel Poverty" August 1999. On one of the schemes see Markou, E "The Role of Fuel Direct in UK Competitive Energy Markets: Social Policy and Commercial Practice" *CMUR Research Paper 99/6* and Sharratt, D "Fuel Direct: Help or Hindrance? Users' Experiences" *CMUR Research Paper 99/5*. More generally see Department of Trade and Industry, *Energy Report 1999* and OFGEM, *Social Action Report*, 2000.

[29] Some commentators argue, however, that the high profile of the poverty issue may be obliging utilities to maintain cross subsidies, in the process limiting the scope of liberalization. Parmar, M, Waddams-Price, C and Waterson, M "Exercising Consumer Choice: Switching Gas Suppliers in the UK Residential Market" *CMUR Research Paper 1999*.

[30] See *OFGEM Annual Report* and Department of Trade and Industry, *The Social Implications of Energy Liberalisation*, DTI 2000.

other unfair practices.[31] The regulators have been active in tackling these problems since, however, and have also sought to make it easier to switch supplier.[32]

Indeed, it is clear that what benefits have been enjoyed by British consumers have been as much a function of the regulatory system as of liberalization. While competition has undoubtedly been an important factor in triggering many of the changes seen in the UK energy markets, it is important to recognize the role of active regulation in driving market changes. This is not only with regard to the pricing of monopoly services (such as transmission and distribution) and of supply in unliberalized markets, but also with regard to market conduct (particularly in policing anti-competitive behaviour). Many, however, have criticized the regulatory process for not being tough enough on utilities and for failing the consumer.[33]

The Labour government was elected in 1997 partly on the basis of its commitment to reform a system of regulation which it criticized as being too favourable to the industry at the expense of consumers. Along with a windfall tax on utility profits, its proposals for reform envisaged a refocusing of regulatory responsibilities and a reorganization of consumer interests.[34] As it has turned out, the changes have concentrated on the energy utilities rather than across the other privatized public services.[35] Along with a merging of the gas and electricity regulatory offices into a single organization, Office of Gas and Electricity Markets (OFGEM), the major change was the promotion of consumer interests to a primary regulatory objective, reinforcing this with a special commitment to the disadvantaged. As part of this shift in emphasis, the legislation also allows the government to issue statutory guidance to the regulator on social and environmental objectives, subject to consultation and normally in force for a full Parliament.[36]

What has also been notable has been the need for distinct and different consumer voices in the liberalization process. As noted, after privatization, the UK adopted a rather ad hoc approach to this matter, maintaining a separate consumer's council in the case of gas and rolling a consumer consultative function into the regulatory machinery in the case of

---

[31] Gas Consumers' Council, *Annual Report*, 1999.

[32] OFGEM (2000), *Marketing Gas and Electricity – Decision Document and Proposals on the Modification of Licence Conditions*, June 2000; OFGEM (2000), Press Release – Ofgem publishes plan for customer choice and value, PN26, 16/3/2000; OFGEM (2000), Press Release – Ofgem Makes Switching Easy, PN 59, 24/5/2000; OFGEM (2000), Press Release – Confidence Boost for Customers, PN 67, 21/6/2000.

[33] See Surrey, A (ed) *The British Electricity Experiment*, Earthscan 1994; Corry, D (ed) *Profiting from the utilities: new thinking on regulatory reform*, Institute for Public Policy Research, 1995 and *National Consumer Council Regulating the Public Utilities*, London: NCC, 1997.

[34] Department of Trade and Industry, "A Fair Deal for Consumers: Modernising the Framework for Utility Regulation" – *Green Paper*, HMSO, 1998.

[35] For details of the government's decision to narrow the scope for reforms of the energy utilities see *Financial Times*, 3 March 2000.

[36] These reforms have been criticized by advocates of a competition led regulatory regime. See Littlechild, S, "Privatisation, Competition and Regulation", *IEA Occasional Paper* No 110, 2000.

electricity. Neither was initially successful – the former closer to the industry than the regulator, the latter effectively neutered. The government's reforms have created a new consumer organization independent of the regulator.[37] The status of consumers is to be reinforced by the creation of a Gas and Electricity Consumers Council.[38] This new consumer council was expected to investigate consumer concerns, advise the regulator of consumer concerns, to act as a first step in addressing any complaints by consumers, if necessary referring to OFGEM (it does not have power to enforce) to provide information and advice to consumers and to gain access to information on their behalf. In order to minimize the risk of overlap and conflict between the new consumers' body and the regulator, a "concordat" signed in 2000 between the new regulatory and consumer organizations established how the two bodies would cooperate with each other and coordinate their activities.[39]

IV. THE IMPACT OF EU POLICIES ON CONSUMERS: SECTORAL AND HORIZONTAL ASPECTS

The reforms of energy regulation in the UK suggest that not all aspects of consumer interests were addressed. Of course, as we have noted elsewhere, there is no such thing as "the consumer interest" – the differences between different groups are as great as those between consumers and producers – yet the attempt to balance out the original objectives of privatization and liberalization with concerns for the weakest consumers indicates that the initial regulatory bargain was not properly conceived. Even so, one could argue that liberalization in the UK seems to have delivered benefits to many consumers, more so, perhaps than would have been the case without reform. Elsewhere in the EU, liberalization – mainly in the electricity sector and mainly in Northern Europe – also seems to have brought benefits albeit on a more modest scale. In all cases however it is clear that there are still problems with the markets with utilities continuing to enjoy substantial market power.[40] What is also notable is the way in which the institutional changes associated with reform have highlighted tensions between the industry, regulators, consumers and government. This has been particularly the case in Spain where the question of stranded costs –

---

[37] Department of Trade and Industry, *Public Consultation Paper on Consumer Councils*, 1998. In many cases it has been left to the national consumer organizations to voice criticisms of the regulatory process – see NCC, *Consumer Representation in the Public Utilities*, London, 1997.

[38] Robinson, A (2000) *GECC – A Consultation Document*. However it appears this change was not welcomed by the large industrial users, *Financial Times* 12 April 1999.

[39] See OFGEM Press Release – OFGEM and GECC: Joint Working Arrangements 2000.

[40] Riechmann, C and Schulz, W "Regulatory Reform in the Electricity Industry" in Galli, G and Pelkmans, J, *Regulatory Reform and Competitiveness in Europe – Vertical Issues*, London, Edward Elgar, 2000. Skytte, K "Market imperfections on the power markets in northern Europe: a survey paper" *Energy Policy* Vol 27, No 1, 1999.

and the burden these would place upon consumers – has ranged the regulator and consumer groups against the industry and government, and highlighted the need to keep the roles of these different actors distinct from one another.[41]

How relevant are these experiences for the EU reforms?[42] The first thing to note is that liberalization has often been associated with reorganizations of national industries, most notably privatizations.[43] While we might debate whether or not the logical consequence of EU liberalization (and of other EU policies) is a restructuring that inevitably includes a shift to the private sector, it is not a formal part of the EU liberalization process. Thus changes which have been accompanied (or, more accurately, constrained) by privatization may not emerge in the EU case. Even so we would expect that the extension of liberalization would bring about important changes in utility strategies and in prices and other aspects of consumer protection. However, in assessing these effects we should distinguish between the direct impact on consumers of the specific liberalization measures for electricity and gas on the one hand, and broader, "horizontal" EU policies on the other.

One might expect that the biggest "EU" impact on consumers would arise as a result of the specific sectoral liberalization measures. Certainly these have been amongst the most controversial measures proposed by the European Commission with agreement proving hard to achieve and only possible with many compromises and derogations. Estimates of a liberalized energy market have indicated that major savings are possible thanks to the effects of competition and the better use of infrastructure and reduced reserve requirements. One study prepared for the Commission indicates annual savings of 6.2-7.8 bn ecus by 2000 and of 14.4 – 18.8 bn ecus by 2010[44] though it does not explore the distribution of these gains. Given the nature of the EU reforms it is worth noting that some of these savings would accrue as a result of greater integration, regardless of integration. However, to the extent that a substantial element of the savings accrues from liberalization, the effects will depend on how the reforms are implemented nationally. It is clear that there are disparities in approach between member states. The most obvious dimension of this is with regard to the share of the market which is affected by the reforms. As we know the formal requirements of the legislation set a threshold of just over 25% rising to 33% by

---

[41] The dispute contributed to the resignation of the electricity regulator, see *El Pais*, April 1999. On the short-comings of the Spanish system see Arocena P, Kuhn, KU, and Regibeau P "Regulatory reform in the Spanish electricity industry: a missed opportunity for competition", *Energy Policy*, Vol 27, No 7, 1999; Regibeau, P "Regulatory Reform in the Spanish Electricity Industry" in Bergman *et al.*, *A European Market for Electricity?* CEPR Monitoring European Deregulation No 2, 1999.

[42] J Stern "The British gas market ten years after privatisation: a model or a warning to the rest of Europe" *Energy Policy*, Vol 25, No 4, 1997.

[43] On the diversity of national approaches to energy reform see Richard J. G. and Kahn, E (eds) *International comparisons of electricity regulation*, Cambridge: Cambridge University Press, 1996 and Bergman *et al.*, *A European Market for Electricity?* CEPR Monitoring European Deregulation No 2, 1999.

[44] Commission of the European Communities "Single Energy Market", *Single Market Review*, Subseries Two, Vol 10, Luxembourg: OOPEC, 1997.

2003. National responses to this have ranged from a strict translation of the threshold to the 100% opening of the market.[45] For those countries where market opening falls well short of full liberalization it is arguable that the benefits will be correspondingly limited; the experience of national liberalization reforms seems to suggest that it is only when a market segment becomes "contested" that significant reductions take place. What remains to be seen is whether these uncompetitive market segments may be used as a captive market which will be exploited to enhance market share in competitive market segments.

Within the overall liberalizing thrust of the directives, however, there are some important countervailing provisions which impinge upon consumers, namely those relating to public service obligations and transitional regimes (the details of the latter are covered elsewhere in the book). While, as noted in the introduction, consumer interests have been invoked by proponents of reform, many of those more sceptical or hostile towards liberalization have argued at least partly on the grounds that it will have adverse effects upon consumers.[46] In a sense the incorporation of these factors into the legislation reflected a perceived need to provide some "safeguards" for liberalization – for example by leaving open the option of uniform pricing within a region or country – and their presence in the rules reflects a recognition of the wider consequences of liberalization particularly for poorer consumers. Nonetheless, there have been some advocates of liberalization who have cautioned that such derogations could be abused, in the first instance to delay competition, in the latter to impose additional costs upon consumers.

As noted, however, the reforms themselves not only are limited in terms of the scope of the market affected but also have to be interpreted by member states. Indeed, a number of aspects of consumer protection will remain the concern of national authorities, subject to the subsidiarity principle. However, the provisions of the directives are not the only ways in which EU policies impact upon energy and gas consumers. In two related areas – competition and consumer policies – the EU can both set a framework and tackle specific issues which will have an impact upon consumers.

Competition policy: Competition policy has been a mainstay of consumer interests within the EU. Under recent Competition Commissioners there has been a consistency of purpose in ensuring the concerns of consumers are more fully addressed and a willingness to use competition policy both as a mechanism to bring about liberalization and as a regulatory mechanism within liberalized markets.[47] However, in both respects competition policy has been constrained by the need to take account of other interests, most notably those of the industries affected by liberalization. These concerns manifest themselves in the form of policy debates within the DG for Competition but are also apparent in the form of direct lobbying by firms and national governments and indeed other Commission officials

---

[45] European Commission, *Opening up to choice: the single electricity market*, Luxembourg: OOPEC, 1999

[46] CEEP/ETUC, European Public Services Charter, Brussels 1996.

[47] Brittan, L, *European competition policy: keeping the playing-field level*, London, Brasseys, 1992. See also the Commission's Annual Reports on Competition Policy, Luxembourg: OOPEC.

and Commissioners.[48] Like all EU policy making, competition policy works on the basis of compromise and the resolution of competing claims. In many instances there is not a single consumer interest to address, leaving open how this interest can be articulated and addressed vis-à-vis other interests in the EU economy. In the case of energy liberalization, the role of competition has been very important in both driving the policy and in determining how competitive energy markets should function. Amongst the issues highlighted by competition policy officials in dealing with energy markets are grid access, transmission pricing, capacity allocation, long term contracts, State aid and joint ventures and mergers. Most cases have concerned relations between producers but clearly they have important indirect effects upon consumers. Overall, however, it has adopted a relatively permissive approach towards conduct and structure in the energy sector, imposing only a few conditions on mergers and other ventures (see below). So far, it would seem that the Commission sees relatively little cause for concern over the way in which energy markets are being restructured and judges that consumers' interests are not being adversely affected. However, with the EU reforms not long in place and with many details of policy still to be resolved, the process of restructuring is likely to go further and present greater challenges for competition policy.

Consumer policy: Of course, it might be thought that the obvious area for considering the effects of liberalization upon consumers would be the context of EU Consumer Policy. Yet, until recently, the role of EU consumer policy in regard to utilities has been relatively underdeveloped.[49] While the responsibilities of the EU in the field of consumer policy have increased over time, particularly in the last ten years, the primary focus for that policy has been on matters of product and food safety. At the same time a wider consumer agenda, linked to the Single Market programme and (perhaps oddly) presented as issues of "citizenship" for many years, concentrated on details of freedom of movement and qualifications as well as the general impact of an internal market upon prices to the consumer. Both of these aspects figure in national debates, of course, but are normally accompanied by a social dimension of consumer protection – at the EU level, by contrast, this aspect was less visible.

For a time, therefore, the consumer interest in energy liberalization was primarily viewed in terms of gains from open markets rather than from a consumer protection perspective. More recently however DG for Health and Consumers has addressed the issue explicitly and has done so from the vantage point of "public service". Although, as noted, there exist specific derogations in the legislation on this issue – and similar exemptions and concessions exist in the rules for opening up other utility markets – the general principle of public service has figured in the last ten years as a distinct debate in the EU. Various groups – including some utilities, consumer organizations and trade unions – have sought to reassert

---

[48] McGowan, F "Competition Policy: Limits of the Regulatory State" in Wallace, H and Wallace, W (eds) *Policy Making in the European Union*, Oxford, Oxford University Press, 2000.

[49] BEUC (1999), Press Release – Consumer Policy and the Amsterdam Treaty, 99/13.

this as a principle in its own right. While entrenched in the traditional utility model, bundled up within the monopoly structure of the industry and ensured by either public ownership (most of Western Europe) or some form of regulation (US), its role is changed and perhaps challenged under liberalization. Market liberalization can be seen as both rendering more necessary some public service mechanisms as well as rendering it more difficult to obtain: opening markets up to competition will highlight the relative returns of supplying different classes of customers, prompting utilities to call into question the worth of supplying low volume unreliable customers unless an obligation is imposed upon them to do so. Yet the means for compensating such support are threatened by practical and legal constraints on cross-subsidy. For the proponents of public service, reinserting it as a core issue would make it possible to counterbalance what are perceived as the excesses or dangers of liberalization.

As a general rule the principle of public service is strongest in those countries where market liberalization has been most contentious.[50] Correspondingly some in those countries have sought to reinstate the idea at the EU level to mitigate what they regard as the possible adverse effects of liberalization, prompting the Commission in turn to set out its views on the matter.[51] Over the 1990s a campaign to incorporate the principle into EU rules was carried out, resulting in a rather weak provision in the Amsterdam Treaty.[52] However, it may be the incorporation of the issue onto the consumer policy agenda which may be of greater significance. The issue was picked up by the Consumer Consultative Committee and was placed on the Council Meeting of Consumer Ministers in November 1999.[53] While there have been proposals to strengthen the Treaty Provisions and possibly incorporate the principle into the Charter of Fundamental Rights of the European Union, there is equally significant opposition to such measures amongst many member States. If, however, the issue is "adopted" by a directorate – particularly if that directorate is responsible for consumer protection – then this could ensure that the matter receives greater concern in any future liberalization measures.

---

[50] See Flynn, L "Competition Policy and Public Services in EC Law after the Maastricht and Amsterdam Treaties" in O'Keeffe, D and Twomey, P (eds) *Legal issues of the Amsterdam Treaty: Treaty of Amsterdam*, Oxford: Hart, 1999.

[51] Commission of the European Communities, *Services of General Economic Interest in Europe*, Brussels: Commission of the European Communities, 1996.

[52] Ross, M "Article 16 EC and services of general interest: from derogation to obligation", *European Law Review*, Vol 25 No 1, 2000.

[53] Commission of the European Communities, *Elaborating the Universal Service Concept in the Services of General Interest – a Consumer Committee Position Paper*, 1999.

V. MARKET LIBERALIZATION AND UTILITY TRANSFORMATION – IMPACTS ON CONSUMERS

In this section we review how the changes wrought by liberalization are transforming the utilities and their relationships with consumers. We focus on two aspects – the "discovery" of the consumer and related adjustments in marketing and other strategies on the one hand and the indirect effects of corporate restructuring upon consumers on the other.

It is clear that one effect of liberalization has been a transformation of the corporate culture of utilities and to make them more aware of consumer concerns. Utilities either individually or collectively (in bodies such as Eurelectric or national associations) have been keen to display consumer-friendly credentials, adopting the language and the techniques of marketing and public relations to demonstrate their familiarity with, or willingness to emulate, other industries' "best practice" in consumer relations. The inevitable bench-marking exercises have taken place, highlighting both that the energy utilities are lagging behind other sectors in their treatment of the consumer and that there is considerable divergence amongst the utilities themselves. Comparisons with other industries may be of more than passing relevance as these sectors have begun to enter the market for retail customers (though not to the extent that was predicted).[54]

As a result of these exercises, utilities have embarked on widespread branding and marketing campaigns. The issue is perhaps most significant where utilities are reinventing themselves as multi-utilities and/or where they are seeking to enter new markets: establishing credibility in new territories or market niches is clearly an essential task. Moreover, there is some evidence that in seeking to capture market share utilities have become more responsive to the specific needs of consumers, developing a wider portfolio of services. This development is a double-edged sword in the domestic market; on the one hand it can open up innovative options such as "green power"; on the other it can create complexity and impose high search costs for households and other low volume customers. It remains to be seen where the balance will lie between the genuinely innovative and the cynically manipulative.

Perhaps the development which should be of more concern to the consumer is the restructuring on the producer side. Over the last ten years there has been an accelerating trend towards consolidation and cross border partnerships and acquisitions across the energy industries. These mergers and acquisitions might be regarded as part of a wider restructuring of European business – as the energy sector becomes "just another industry" so it will be subject to the same pressures for reorganization which are present in the rest of the EU economy. Whether or not this is the case there are some causes for concern. Are we moving from a situation where national champions cooperated with one another from their respective

---

[54] Unipede Press Release – "The Electricity Companies and their Customers: a WinWin relationship" Paris, Unipede, 1998. Eurelectric, "Best Practice Benchmaking of Retail Marketing and Customer Relationships", Brussels, 2000.

monopolies to one where we have a core of European champions competing against each other more aggressively (the US deregulation story) or just a process of consolidation and re-defining a modus vivendi amongst the monoliths of the EU energy sector (the European banking sector story)?[55]

The rationale for such mergers are fairly clear: to deal with increased market risk, to enhance competitiveness in supply, to be able to compete internationally, to reduce overhead costs and costs of capital. What of the consumer interest, however? Some indication of the effects on consumer interests of such consolidation (and also perhaps of the pattern of consolidation itself) can be gained from the UK experience. Over the second half of the 1990s the UK electricity industry was the target of a wave of takeover activity, most of it from foreign corporations. This phenomenon was a function both of the relatively open nature of the UK industry (operating on a more or less competitive basis and firmly in the private sector) and the "Anglo Saxon" style of corporate governance which prevails in the UK. In such an environment, claims of the strategic or special nature of the industry were dismissed as utility after utility was subject to acquisition. The bulk of the successful mergers were led by foreign utilities, raising few of the market concentration concerns which attended takeover attempts by local incumbents (though ironically attempts by British firms to enter their markets through acquisition have encountered considerable regulatory opposition).

What has been the impact of such acquisitions? A report by the British National Consumers' Council on the takeover wave raised a number of concerns not least those of the balance of benefits between consumers, companies and shareholders, the impact on regulatory scrutiny and the degree of transparency. It remains to be seen how far the mechanisms put in place by the UK regulator will be effective in assuaging such concerns. The direct effect on consumers' prices is hard to discern given the flurry of events and regulatory changes taking place in the sector. However, given the underlying reason for the takeovers – the healthy position of utilities – begs the question whether more could have been done for consumers in the years following privatization instead of making them more attractive to foreign investors.[56]

It is interesting to note that the European Commission has broadly backed the wave of European electricity and gas mergers. Where it has raised concerns it has not judged these to be sufficiently acute to impose conditions on the alliances. Whether this will continue to be the case (given ongoing investigations of utilities with overlapping market presences) seems unlikely. More generally, however, the Commission might want to identify how the consumer might benefit from such restructuring.[57]

---

[55] On restructuring in the European power industry see *Power in Europe*, London Financial Times Publishing.

[56] *National Consumers Council Electricity Takeovers – the Implications for Consumers*, London, NCC, 1997.

[57] Albers, M "Views and Expectations of Competition Developments in the EU Electricity Market", Unipede-Eurelectric Workshop, Brussels, 1999 and Tradacete Cocera, A "The Role of EC Competition Policy in the Liberalisation of EU Energy Markets" European Energy Millennium Forum, Brussels, 2000. See also the Commission's Annual Reports on Competition Policy.

The changes in the structure of EU energy utilities present a major challenge to small consumers. For the most part, larger energy consumers are better placed to cope with the changes and to defend their interests. As noted earlier, it was the energy intensive sectors which pushed for reform at the EU level. These companies have continued to lobby on energy liberalization whether as individual firms or in sectoral organizations (such as CEFIC). More generally, the bulk of European business will seek to maintain liberalization through Unice. In all these cases there are close ties back to national organizations and where the balance of policy lies will depend on how truly integrated European energy markets become.[58] Domestic energy consumers, by contrast, are relatively underrepresented. While bodies such as BEUC have tried to alert the Commission to some of the problems for small consumers arising out of liberalization, there is not yet a European lobby representing the interests of small consumers. Until there is, it may be that their interests will not be adequately represented.[59]

VI. CONCLUSION

This article has attempted to highlight some of the ways in which consumers will be affected by energy market liberalization and the implications of these developments for consumer protection. Drawing on national experiences and evolving debates at the EU level a few concluding points can be made.

The first point is that liberalization requires regulation to ensure that market power is not abused. This paper has not explored how far that regulation needs to be based at the EU level. Given the trends towards decentralization of regulation, the growing cooperation between national authorities and the lack of enthusiasm in both the Commission and member States for a Euro-Energy Regulator such a development may be neither necessary nor desirable. However, there must be an assumption that the Commission will be prepared to act as regulator of last resort. It is clear that for regulation to be effective consumer organizations need to be active in both the national and European settings.

There is no single consumer interest in such a complex policy area as energy liberalization. However there is a need for the diverse consumer concerns to be as united as possible across borders in order to ensure their interests are represented. In this respect the Commission's supported and extended. A major gap in the present array of representation, however, concerns the small energy consumer. As liberalization evolves and extends, it is vital that this interest is extensively involved at the EU level as well as the national level.

---

[58] Bartle, I "Transnational Interests in the European Union: Globalization and Changing Organization in Telecommunications and Electricity", *Journal of Common Market Studies*, Vol 37, No 3, 1999.

[59] Schweren, K *Advantages noticed or expectations from the small consumers since the liberalisation of the electricity sector* Paper to Unipede/Eurelectric Workshop, BEUC/56/99, 1999.

Anne Heinen

THE INTERFACE BETWEEN ELECTRICITY LIBERALIZATION AND ENVIRONMENTAL PROTECTION: THE GERMAN EXAMPLE [1]

I. INTRODUCTION

This paper seeks to show that the liberalization process in the electricity market does not necessarily contradict the idea of sustainable development. However, these two objectives of European energy policy do not go hand in hand by themselves. The electricity market must be regulated in order to achieve a balance. Whether this is possible at a national level or whether measures at the European level are to be preferred is an open question. In order to find an answer, we will have a look at the situation in Germany which is characterized by full liberalization[2] followed by several new environmental laws that have provoked objections raised by market participants, German politicians and the European Commission. In the author's view, the German laws in question probably do not violate European law. However, the conclusion of this analysis will be that a solution at the European level seems to be preferable. The reason is that in this way, the economic and political problems encountered by such a national solo initiative seem to be avoidable or at least more manageable. The paper will finish with a brief look at the probability of the introduction of new legal instruments at the EC level.

II. LIBERALIZATION AND SUSTAINABLE DEVELOPMENT: A BASIC CONTRADICTION?

A. Sustainable Development – A Big Challenge

Article 2 of the EU Treaty names as one of its basic objectives the promotion of balanced and sustainable development. In this context, the term "sustainable" means policies and

---

[1]   A longer version of this paper has been published under the title "*La libéralisation du marché de l'électricité et un développement soutenable: Deux objectifs contradictoires? – Une analyse exemplaire des conflits potentiels entre le droit allemand et le droit communautaire*" by Nomos Verlagsgesellschaft, Baden-Baden, 2000, No. 10, within the framework of the series "Kölner Miszellen zum Energierecht" edited by the Institute for Energy Law of the University of Cologne.

[2]   See the article of A.-R. Börner in this book.

Damien Geradin (ed.), The Liberalization of Electricity and Natural Gas in the European Union, 81–104
©2001 Kluwer Law International. Printed in the Netherlands.

strategies that attempt to achieve continuous economic and social progress which also respect the environment and do not put at risk the natural resources necessary for modern human life.[3]

Global phenomena such as climate change seriously threaten the ecological equilibrium of the whole planet.[4] Climate change will (also) lead to serious problems in the EU.[5] Some figures might help to understand why it is important to act in Europe. In the European Union, the production of electricity and heat contributes to almost one third of the increasing total emissions of CO_2.[6] Currently, the European Union is responsible for about 16 per cent of the global emissions of CO_2 which are linked to energy, whereas it only represents 6 per cent of the global population. Apart from the emissions of CO_2, coal-mines are an important source of CH_4 emissions.[7] In connection with the Kyoto Protocol on the United Nations Framework Convention on Climate Change of 11 December 1997, the EU and its Member States have committed themselves to reduce their greenhouse gas emissions by 8 per cent from now until 2008-2012 in comparison to the level of 1990.[8] In addition, one should not forget that fossil fuels are scarce, non-renewable raw materials which are necessary for many economic sectors.[9]

It is obvious that in the long run, the current consumption of energy is incompatible with sustainable development.[10] Energy policy is the key to such development. The challenge which has to be faced is to ensure that economic growth, efficient and safe energy supplies and environmental protection are compatible aims. The measures which seem to be necessary do not only include the promotion of energy efficiencies and savings,

---

[3] See European Commission, "Towards sustainability, Community program of policy and action in relation to the environment and sustainable development", OJ 1993 C 138/5 at 12.

[4] See the Preamble of the United Nations Framework Convention On Climate Change, http://www.unfccc.de/resource/ccsites/jordan/conven/text/preamble.htm.

[5] See Community Program, *supra* note 3, at 42.

[6] See European Commission, *Communication to the Council, the European Parliament, the Economic and Social Committee and the Committee of the Regions –The energy dimension of climate change*, COM (1997) 196 final, para. 34; European Commission, *Second Report to the Council and the European Parliament on harmonisation requirements, Directive 96/92/EC concerning common rules for the internal market in electricity*, COM (1999) 164 final, at 33.

[7] Commission Communication, *supra* note 6, para. 46.

[8] The EU has not yet ratified the protocol, but estimates that it will start the political proceedings for ratification after the 6th conference of the parties of the United Framework Convention on Climate Change in November 2000, See European Commission, *Communication to the Council and the European Parliament on EU policies and measures to reduce greenhouse gas emissions: towards a European Climate Change Programme (ECCP)*, COM (00) 88, at 1.

[9] See J.-P. Schneider, *Liberalisierung der Stromwirtschaft durch regulative Marktorganisation: Eine vergleichende Untersuchung zur Reform des britischen, US-amerikanischen, europäischen und deutschen Energierechts*, (Baden-Baden, 1999) at 142; D. Kuhnt, "Energie und Umweltschutz in europäischer Perspektive", *Deutsches Verwaltungsblatt* (1996), 1082.

[10] Commission Communication, *supra* note 6, para. 39.

but also an important reduction of the use of fossil fuels, a larger use of combined heat and power (hereafter, "CHP") and a change of the energy sources used for the production of electricity including an increasing use of renewable energies.[11]

In this context, nuclear energy plays an ambiguous role. On the one hand, it seems to be difficult to fight against climate change without reliance on this source of energy. On the other hand, nuclear energy implies security risks and thereby the danger of immense damages. In addition, the problem of what to do with radioactive waste has not been resolved yet.[12]

B. The Effects of Liberalization of the Electricity Market

It is questionable whether the achievement of sustainable development is possible within the framework of the liberalization of the electricity market which has been introduced by Directive 96/92/EC.[13]

On the one hand, the introduction of (more) competition leads to greater efficiency. From an environmental perspective, this is an advantage as this leads to economies of resources and to innovation.[14] This entails integrated offers of energy supply and saving measures in the sense of a real service culture as well as a promotion of renewable energies and CHP in order to gain and keep environmentally conscious clients.[15] In addition, new competitors whose production methods are more environmentally friendly get the chance to enter the market because of the liberalization process.[16]

On the other hand, greater competition leads to price cuts and thereby to increased energy consumption.[17] In Germany, for instance, prices have already fallen considerably,

---

[11] Commission Communication, *supra* note 6, para. 39, 55 and 57; Community Programme, *supra* note 3, at 12.

[12] See J.-P. Schneider, *supra* note 9, at 140; P. Badura, "Umweltschutz und Energiepolitik" in H.-W. Rengeling (ed.), *Handbuch zum europäischen und deutschen Umweltrecht, Band 2: Besonderes Umweltrecht* (Cologne-Berlin-Bonn-Munich, 1998), § 83, at 1184; L. Krämer, *E.C. Environmental Law,* 4th edition (London, 2000), at 269; G. Cappelle-Blanchard and S. Monjon, "L'industrie nucléaire en France", in M.-H. Labbé (ed.), *Le nucléaire à la croisée des chemins* (Paris, 1999), 27, at 41 and 45; G. Cappelle-Blanchard et S. Monjon, "Le nucléaire face aux defis économiques et environnementaux du XXIe siècle" in M.-H. Labbé, *op. cit.,* 55 at 62.

[13] Directive 96/92/EC of the European Parliament and of the Council concerning common rules for the internal market in electricity, OJ 1997 L 27/20.

[14] See I. Pernice, "Umweltschutz und Energiepolitik", *Recht der Energiewirtschaft* (1993), 45 at 51.

[15] See J.-P. Schneider, *supra* note 9, at 259.

[16] See H.D. Jarass, *Europäisches Energierecht: Bestand – Fortentwicklung – Umweltschutz* (Berlin, 1996), at 128.

[17] See J.-P. Schneider, *supra* note 9, at 369; W. Hoffmann-Riem and J.-P. Schneider, "Wettbewerbs- und umweltorientierte Re-Regulierung im Großhandels-Strommarkt" in W. Hoffmann-Riem and J.-P. Schneider (ed.), *Umweltpolitische Steuerung in einem liberalisierten Strommarkt* (Baden-Baden, 1995), 13 at 51.

especially as regards industrial clients.[18] Electricity at low prices seriously interferes with a policy that tries to achieve energy savings.[19] In addition, renewable energies are in general not competitive for the time being and this will not change in the medium-term.[20] Thus, since the low prices only concern traditional energy sources, renewable energies and CHP are not very attractive in a liberalized market.[21]

As a consequence and because of the necessity for sustainable development, the liberalized market needs to be completed by a regulatory framework,[22] including, for example, measures which counteract excessive consumption and which support greater efficiency through the use of CHP and renewable energies.[23]

C. The EC Regulatory Framework and the Particularity of the German Situation

We will now have a look at the way in which the EC tries to reconcile the electricity liberalization with the pursuit of sustainable development. Directive 96/92/EC[24] itself does not contain any mandatory prescriptions in favour of environmental protection. There are

---

[18] See C. Graf Hohenthal, "Strom aus der Steckdose", *Frankfurter Allgemeine Zeitung* of 3 February 2000, 10; R. Schäfer, "Deutsches und europäisches Energiewirtschaftsrecht", *Energiewirtschaftliche Tagesfragen* (1999), 553 at 559.

[19] See L. Krämer, *supra* note 12, at 270; K. Meßerschmidt, "Energieabgaben und Klimaschutz", *Recht der Energiewirtschaft* (1992), 182 at 184.

[20] See J. Grawe, "Umweltschutz und Energiepolitik", *Recht der Energiewirtschaft* (1993), 85 at 90.

[21] See L. Krämer, *supra* note 12, at 271; E. Baer, "Kraft-Wärme-Kopplung vor dem Ende?", *Zeitschrift für kommunale Wirtschaft* (February 1999), 3; E. Baer, P. Felwor, H. Kirchoff and G. Ziegelmann, "Ende oder Fortbestand der KWK-Fernwärmeversorgung", *Energiewirtschaftliche Tagesfragen* (1999), 324.

[22] See in this regard P. Badura, *supra* note 12, at 1165; G. Ott, "Energie – kein Thema?", *Recht der Energiewirtschaft* (1997), 128 at 132; E. Bohne, "Grundzüge einer wettbewerbs- und umweltorientierten Reform des energierechtlichen Ordnungsrahmens der Stromwirtschaft" in W. Hoffmann-Riem and J.-P. Schneider, *supra* note 17, 140 at 152-156.

[23] See J.-P. Schneider, *supra* note 9, at 259; A. Schaub, *Europäische Energiebinnenmarktpolitik und Umweltpolitik* (Baden-Baden, 1996), at 46.

[24] See *supra* note 13; for a general analysis of the Directive see R. Schäfer, *supra* note 18, 553; D. Geradin, "L'ouverture à la concurrence des entreprises de réseau – Analyse des principaux enjeux du processus de la libéralisation", *Cahiers de Droit Européen* (1-2/1999), 13 at 20-23; F. Lagondet, "Du dogme du marché intérieur à la négociation du service public – À propos de la directive électricité", *Europe* (May 1997), 4 ; A. Schaub and R. Dohms, "Der wettbewerbliche Binnenmarkt für Strom und Gas", *Die Aktiengesellschaft* (1998), 566; G. Britz, "Öffnung der Europäischen Strommärkte durch die Elektrizitätsbinnenmarktrichtlinie?", *Recht der Energiewirtschaft* (1997), 85; B. Rapp-Jung, "Die EU Richtlinie für Elektrizität im Spannungsfeld zwischen den Wettbewerbsregeln des Vertrags und den verbliebenen energiepolitischen Befugnissen der Mitgliedstaaten", *Recht der Energiewirtschaft* (1997), 133; for a general description of the transposition in Germany see M. Cronenberg, "Das neue Energiewirtschaftsrecht", *Recht der Energiewirtschaft* (1998), 85; B. Scholtka, "Die Entwicklung des Energierechts in den Jahren 1998 und 1999", *Neue juristische Wochenschrift* (2000), 548.

measures at the European level which financially support measures in favour of energy savings.[25] However, up to now, there does not seem to be a coherent and systematic approach.[26]

Anyhow, since no sweeping legal act has so far been adopted, the Member States are still competent to introduce measures in favour of sustainable development as regards the electricity market.[27] As a consequence, one good method to find an answer to the question at which level measures should ideally be taken seems to be an analysis of what happens at the national level. This article does not claim to discuss the measures taken, if any, in all the Member States. Only Germany is taken as an example for the following reasons. Firstly, the electricity market has already been fully liberalized.[28] Secondly, the "red-green" coalition government seeks to pursue ambitious environmental objectives in the energy field. Specifically, the government announced its intention to reinforce the efforts in favour of climate protection, to intensify the promotion of renewable energies, to create the framework conditions for a clear reduction of energy consumption and to leave behind nuclear energy as quickly as possible. [29]

III. THE RELEVANT LEGAL QUESTIONS AS REGARDS GERMANY

This part of the article discusses the compatibility of selected German laws with EC law. However, this rather narrow approach is only used as a method to find out whether national laws, such as for instance those recently adopted in Germany, can adequately achieve the objective of sustainable development despite the liberalization process (chapter IV).

In Germany, especially two fields deserve legal analysis as regards a possible violation of Community law: The ecotaxes and the regulatory measures taken in favour of renewable energies and CHP.[30]

---

[25] For a description see L. Krämer, *supra* note 12, at 227 and 270.

[26] L. Krämer, *supra* note 12, at 270.

[27] See A. Schaub, *supra* note 23, at 275.

[28] See *Gesetz zur Neuregelung des Energiewirtschaftsrechts* of 24 April 1998 ("Act on the New Regulation of The Energy Industries Law"), Bundesgesetzblatt 1998, part I, 730.

[29] "Koalitionsvereinbarung zwischen der SPD und Bündnis 90/Die Grünen vom 20. Oktober 1998: Deutschlands Weg ins 21. Jahrhundert", *Zeitschrift für Rechtspolitik* (1998), 485.

[30] The envisaged end of the use of nuclear energy in Germany, which is subject to a recently reached agreement, has also led to an important political and legal dispute, *inter alia*, about its compatibility with European law (See "Stoiber bittet Prodi um Rechtsprüfung", *Frankfurter Allgemeine Zeitung* of 9 February 2000, 2; "Stoiber: EU soll gegen Atomausstieg klagen", *Süddeutsche Zeitung* of 8 February 2000, 2; U. Di Fabio, *Der Ausstieg aus der wirtschaftlichen Nutzung der Kernenergie: Europarechtliche und verfassungsrechtliche Vorgaben*, (Cologne – Berlin – Bonn – Munich, 1999) at 46-48; P. Badura, *supra* note 12, at 1185; B. Rapp-Jung, *supra* note 24, at 134; B. Stüer et H. Spreen, "Ausstieg aus der Atomenergie – Das Beispiel Krümmel", *Natur und Recht* (1999), 16 at 23; K. Borgmann, *Rechtliche Möglichkeiten und Grenzen des Ausstiegs aus der Kernenergie* (Berlin, 1994) at 402-406; R. Steinberg, "EG-rechtliche Rahmenbedingungen der Atomrechtsreform",

A. The Ecotaxes

Before analysing the specific case of German ecotaxes, it has to be mentioned that, in general, the Commission is in favour of this kind of price-determining instruments. The reason is that they rely on market forces to achieve sustainable development. Thus, they induce economic behaviour which is at the same time environmentally friendly.[31] In fact, ecotaxes can neutralize the effects of low energy prices[32] by means of a simulation of an actual lack of resources.[33]

There are two systems of indirect taxation applicable to electricity. The first one is VAT which is largely harmonized at European level. The second is a number of taxes which are not harmonized at European level.[34] In its *proposal for a Council Directive restructuring the Community framework for the taxation of energy products*[35] the Commission proposes *inter alia* an enlargement of the scope of the harmonized taxation as regards electricity, but this is only a vague future perspective.[36]

Europäische Zeitschrift für Wirtschaftsrecht (1993), 497 at 498). At least from a legal perspective and as regards the question of a possible violation of European law, the dispute seems to be brought to an end by a letter written by the Commission President, Mr. Prodi, to the Prime Minister of the Land Bavaria, Mr. Stoiber (See http://europa.eu.int/rapid/start/cgi/guesten.ksh?p_action.gettxt=gt&d.../10/0/RAPID&lg=F; "Prodi schaltet sich in Streit um deutschen Atomausstieg ein", *Frankfurter Allgemeine Zeitung* of 20 April 2000, 1). The letter says that the Commission does not see any violation of Community law as regards the choice of energy sources itself. However, some arguments made in the political discussion are quite important in order to understand the difficulties in attempting to bring about a change in policy. The project of the German government has been severely criticized by the conservative opposition parties who cite as reasons the need to reduce the CO_2 emissions and the danger that Germany loses its competitiveness as an electricity producing country (See "Stoiber bittet Prodi um Rechtsprüfung", *Frankfurter Allgemeine Zeitung* of 9 February 2000, 2; http://www.bundestag.de/ns-search/aktuell/bp/99.../aaaDczryadbc344&NS-doc-offset=48). Another reason for this criticism is probably the fear of cheap electricity imports from other countries (See "Bundestag streitet über Atomausstieg", *Die Tageszeitung* of 24 March 2000, 7; A. Klemm, "Strom aus dem Ausland", *Europäische Zeitschrift für Wirtschaftsrecht* (2000), 69). Above all, this concerns France — which is the world's second largest producer of nuclear energy behind the United States and where this energy source is the most competitive one (See G. Cappelle-Blanchard et S. Monjon, *supra* note 12, at 35, 38 and 40) — since *EdF* intensively tries to gain a foothold in the German market (See C. Graf Hohenthal, *supra* note 18, at 10; "Stromkonzerne – Bewegt", *Die Zeit* of 6 April 2000, 31). However, another interesting question related to nuclear energy still is of practical importance. The financial reserves for the disposal and shutdown of nuclear power stations could be contrary to Community law (for a recent analysis see for instance G. Hermes, "Rückstellung für die Entsorgung und Stillegung von Kernkraftwerken und EG-Beihilferecht", *Zeitschrift für neues Energierecht* (1999), 156).

[31] Community Program, *supra* note 3, at 70-71.

[32] See I. Pernice, *supra* note 14, at 52.

[33] See K. Meßerschmidt, *supra* note 19, at 183.

[34] See Second Report, *supra* note 6, at 37.

[35] COM (97) 30 final.

[36] See *infra* p. 102.

In Germany, the Act Introducing the Ecological Tax Reform of 24 March 1999[37] entered into force on 1 April 1999. It does not only include an increase of the taxes on fuels and gas, but also a new electricity tax which is laid down in the Electricity Tax Act.[38] According to the federal government, the ecological tax reform shall encourage energy savings and the development of energetically more efficient products and technologies from an energy perspective.

1. A Violation of Article 90 (ex-Article 95) of the EC Treaty?

The German ecotax does not provide for a differentiation of the tax rates according to the degree of pollution like the Finnish tax law which has been subject to the ECJ's judgment in case *Outukumpu,*[39] but contains general tax exemptions under certain conditions. Nevertheless, some authors are of the opinion that certain provisions of the Electricity Tax Act violate Article 90 (ex-Article 95) of the EC Treaty.

Article 90, para. 1, of the Treaty provides that "no Member State shall impose, directly or indirectly, on the products of other Member States any internal taxation of any kind in excess of that imposed directly or indirectly on similar domestic products". According to para. 2 of the same Article "no Member State shall impose on the products of other Member States any internal taxation of such a nature as to afford indirect protection to other products."

For some observers, Article 9, para. 1, no. 1 of the Electricity Tax Act is a forbidden discrimination in the sense of Article 90 of the EC Treaty.[40] According to this provision, renewable energies can be exempted from the tax under certain conditions. Broadly speaking, one of these conditions is that the electricity originating from renewable energy sources is not mixed with electricity originating from non-renewable energy sources.[41] Obviously, this does not constitute a direct discrimination and it is even doubtful whether this can be regarded as an indirect discrimination.

If one took for granted that it was legally impossible or at least difficult to import electricity originating from renewable energy sources, we may consider that it may constitute indirect discrimination, but in this case it would not be the provisions in question that could possibly violate EC law, but the obstacle to imports itself.

---

[37] *Gesetz zum Einstieg in die ökologische Steuerreform,* Bundesgesetzblatt 1999 part I, 378; the Act has been modified by the *Gesetz zur Fortführung der ökologischen Steuerreform* ("Act on the Continuation of the Ecological Tax Reform") of 16 December 1999, Bundesgesetzblatt 1999, part I, 2432.

[38] *Stromsteuergesetz,* in German.

[39] Case C-213/96, *Outukumpu* [1998] E.C.R. I-1777.

[40] See H.-W. Arndt, *Stromsteuergesetz* (Heidelberg, 1999), at 17-19; M. Bongartz and S. Schröer-Schallenberg, "Die Stromsteuer – Verstoß gegen Gemeinschaftsrecht und nationales Verfassungsrecht?", *Deutsches Steuerrecht* (1999), 962 at 964-965.

[41] For details see J. Bloehs, "Verstößt das Erhebungsverfahren der deutschen Stromsteuer gegen EU-Recht?", *Betriebsberater* (1999), 1845 at 1846.

At least for technical and economic reasons, it is in all event unlikely that a lot of electricity originating from renewable energy sources is directly imported into Germany. Thus, the provision in question could constitute a hidden discrimination in the sense that, in practice, only German producers benefit from it. However, one should not forget that the ECJ accepts tax differentiations that are based on objective criteria under the condition that *these criteria* do not have a discriminating or protectionist effect, even if the taxes on imported products are higher.[42] The technical or economic reasons and not the tax provisions make imports difficult. The legislature has not established the particular technical characteristics of trade with electricity, that is to say the necessity of a network and the costs of installing an electricity line. Thus, a violation of Article 90 of the EC Treaty is not established.

The ECJ's judgment in *Outukumpu* fits perfectly well into this line of reasoning. There are substantial differences between the German Electricity Tax Act and the Finnish law which was subject to the judgment. According to the latter, a system of tax differentiation was only applicable to electricity produced in Finland whereas an average tax rate was applied to imported electricity. The ECJ, contrary to its Advocate General, considered this to constitute a violation of Article 90 of the EC Treaty although, once the electricity has entered the network, its origin and consequently its method of production cannot be determined anymore.

However, this does not mean that as a result of this judgment, all tax differentiations based on production methods are void. In *Outukumpu,* the Court highlighted that the Finnish law did not permit the undertaking carrying out the imports to demonstrate that the imported electricity had been produced in a specific way in order to benefit from the favourable tax rates applicable to domestic production.[43] *A contrario*, one can conclude that tax laws that permit electricity produced abroad to benefit from the differentiated system do not necessarily violate Article 90 of the EC Treaty. The reasoning of the ECJ in the discussed judgment therefore indicates that a system like the one introduced in Germany probably does not constitute a violation of Article 90 of the EC Treaty for the reason that Article 9, para. 1, no.1 of the Electricity Tax Act treats domestic and imported electricity in a similar fashion.[44]

It has also been advanced that the Electricity Tax Act contains a violation of Article 90 of the EC Treaty because of the distinction which is made between different taxpayers depending on the origin of the electricity.[45] According to Article 5, para. 2, of the Electricity

---

[42] See in particular Cases C-132/88 *Commission v. Greece* [1990] E.C.R. 89, para. 18-20; C-113/94 *Casarin* [1995] E.C.R. I-4203.

[43] Case *Outukumpu, supra* note 39, at para. 39.

[44] Another possible solution could be the introduction of (partial) refunds if the exporting undertaking proves the general percentage of the different energy sources from which its electricity originates. Obviously, this percentage has nothing to do with the composition of the electricity which crosses the border. However, in this way the aim of penalizing the energy production according to its degree of pollution could also be achieved.

[45] See J. Bloehs, *supra* note 41, at 1848-1849.

Tax Act, the distributor who delivers the electricity to the final consumer does in principle have to pay the tax. In case the electricity comes directly from abroad, then it is the consumer who has to pay the tax according to Article 7, para. 2, of the Electricity Tax Act. Since the obligation to file a tax return is a burden, one could argue that the consumer will generally prefer to buy electricity which is already on the German grid. This could be considered as indirect discrimination.[46] This reasoning reminds of the case-law regarding equal access to judicial protection guaranteed by the principle of non-discrimination according to Article 12 (ex-Article 6) of the EC Treaty.[47] According to this case-law, national provisions that require persons established in another Member State to furnish security for costs where they wish to bring legal proceedings violate Article 12 of the EC Treaty if persons from that Member State are not subject to such a requirement. Indeed, procedural rules are subject to the general principle of non-discrimination laid down by Article 12 of the EC Treaty in so far as they have an effect on intra-community trade. However, it is questionable whether the provisions at issue here really contain such discrimination. In fact, the consumers who are possibly affected by the procedural differentiation are not private persons who have difficulties to understand administrative forms, but generally sophisticated companies. One could maintain just the opposite by saying that it is much more difficult for a foreign distributor or producer than for an industrial customer in Germany to file a German tax return. As a consequence, interstate trade might well be impeded in a greater fashion if the taxpayer was the foreign market participant.

Thus, the objections raised against the Electricity Tax Act because of an alleged violation of Article 90 of the EC Treaty have to be taken seriously, but it is doubtful whether the ECJ would adopt the arguments described above.

2. The Rules on State Aid

We will now have a look at the European Commission's State aid decisions on the German tax laws. On 28 January 1999 and 26 February 1999, the German government notified several measures that form part of the Act Introducing the Ecological Tax Reform.[48] These provisions deal with (partial) exemptions of the new electricity tax in favour of the manufacturing industry, farms and forestry, the railway sector as well as the systems of CHP and bus companies, all of them in their capacity as final consignees.[49]

The provisions in favour of bus companies have not been considered as constituting

---

[46] See J. Bloehs, *supra* note 41, at 1848.

[47] See Cases C-43/95 *Data Delecta* [1996] E.C.R. I-4661; C-323/95 *Hayes* [1997] E.C.R. I-1711.

[48] Commission Decision of 3 May 1999, State Aids n° NN 47/99 – Germany, SG (99) D/3289, http://europa.eu.int/comm/sg/sgb/state_aids.

[49] For a first analysis of the case see W. Frenz, "Energiesteuer und Beihilfenverbot", *Europäische Zeitschrift für Wirtschaftsrecht* (1999), 616.

State aids in the sense of Article 87 (ex-Article 92) of the EC Treaty,[50] but there can be almost no doubt that the remaining exemptions constitute State aids according to Article 87 of the EC Treaty.

Article 87, para. 1, of the EC Treaty in principle prohibits "State aids" under the following conditions: There has to be (i) an aid which (ii) favours certain undertakings or the producers of certain goods, (iii) distorts or threatens to distort competition and (iv) is granted by a Member State or through State resources. In addition, (v) trade between Member States has to be affected.

The notion of aid has to be interpreted broadly. In principle, not only traditional forms of subsidies (such as, for instance, direct payments), but aids "in any form whatsoever" are prohibited. This does not only include positive acts, but also losses like measures that remit debts, for example tax exemptions.[51] The exemptions in question here are also applicable to certain sectors, i. e. limited groups of undertakings.[52]

The condition according to which the aid must at least threaten to distort competition also has to be interpreted broadly. Competition is distorted if the State intervention provokes an artificial change of certain production cost factors of the beneficiary undertaking and strengthens its position in comparison to other competitors.[53] Thus, a distortion of competition is a "natural" consequence of an aid and can almost be presumed unless there are exceptional circumstances.[54] Such circumstances are only conceivable as regards the systems of CHP. The latter participate in the electricity market which is characterized by a considerable amount of subsidies during decades, especially in favour of traditional energy sources.[55] It can be argued that because of the specific economic characteristics of the sector, it would be necessary to support weak competitors in order to establish real competition. If fixed sunk costs are high for potential new entrants, the latter may have to be supported in order to enable them to enter the market and thereby achieve a (more) competitive market structure.[56] However, at least in the past, the ECJ generally seemed to be reluctant to adopt this kind of reasoning[57] and the Commission has not referred to any

---

[50] The intra-community trade cannot be affected because the service in question does not entail any cross border aspect, but only concerns local traffic.

[51] Cases 173/73 *Italy v. Commission* [1974] E.C.R. 709, para. 33-35; C-387/92 *Banco Exterior de España* [1994] E.C.R. I-877, para. 13-14; European Commission, "Community Framework For Environmental Aids", OJ 1994, C 72/3, para. 1.5.3.

[52] See European Commission, *XXVIIth Report on Competition Policy (1997)* (Brussels-Luxembourg, 1998), para. 222; J.-P. Keppenne, *Guide des aides d'État en droit communautaire* (Brussels, 1999), at 24

[53] Case 730/79 *Philip Morris v. Commission* [1980] E.C.R. 2671, para. 11.

[54] See J. -P. Keppenne, *supra* note 52, at 120.

[55] See for example concerning coal European Commission, *XXVIIIth Report on Competition Policy (1998)*, (Brussels–Luxembourg, 1999), para. 236-241.

[56] See L. Muir, *The Liberalisation of Electricity in the European Union – An Economic Evaluation*, (Bruges, 1999) at 12-13.

[57] See – in the context of the application of Article 81 EC Treaty – joint cases 56/64 and 58/64 *Consten and Grundig v. Commission* [1966] E.C.R. 299 at 342.

such considerations in its decision.[58]

The condition of an influence on trade between Member States is also easily fulfilled. If financial aid granted by the State strengthens the position of an undertaking in comparison to other competing undertakings as regards interstate trade, the latter have to be seen as affected by the aid.[59] As regards CHP, one could have some difficulties to explain this, but, according to the Commission,[60] even the non-existence of intra-community trade in the concerned market does not have as its consequence that the analyzed condition is not fulfilled. If the national markets are closed because of their special characteristics, the aids should at least be controlled to the extent that they support this foreclosure.[61] Even the fact that the concerned undertaking does not export itself does not exclude that trade between Member States is affected. When a Member State grants aid to an undertaking the internal production can be supported or increased with the consequence that it is more difficult for undertakings established in other Member States to export into this country.[62]

Therefore, all the conditions of a State aid in the sense of Article 87, para. 1, of the EC Treaty are fulfilled.

In its decision, the Commission applied the exemptions contained in Article 87, para. 3, of the EC Treaty and came to the conclusion that the State aids in question are compatible with the common market.[63] As regards the manufacturing industry, the measures are considered to be justified because many undertakings could not bear the tax burden in the short term. A transitional exemption is therefore regarded as justified. As regards farms and forestry, the Commission also accepted the exemptions as being necessary in order to enable the undertakings concerned to adapt themselves to the new competitive conditions. In addition, the Commission considered the measure in favour of CHP to be compatible with the Common Market because of its generally favourable attitude towards this production method.[64] The measures in favour of the railway sector were also considered to be compatible with Article 3, para. 1, lit. b) of Regulation 1107/70.[65]

---

[58] *Supra* note 48.

[59] Case *Philip Morris v. Commission*, *supra* note 53, para. 11.

[60] European Commission, "Notice pursuant to Article 93 (2) of the EC Treaty to other Member States and interested parties concerning investment grants of the Land of Brandenburg for the preferential use of brown coal", OJ 1997 C 381/5 at 6.

[61] European Commission, *Decision of 2 October 1996 concerning aid granted by the French State to the audiovisual production company Société française de Production*, OJ 1997 L 95/19, para. VIII.

[62] Cases 102/87 *France v. Commission* [1988] E.C.R. 4067, para. 19; C-278/92, C-279/92 and C-280/92 *Spain v. Commission* [1994] E.C.R. I-4103, para. 40.

[63] *Supra* note 48.

[64] *Communication from the Commission on a Community strategy to promote combined heat and power (CHP) and to dismantle barriers to its development*, COM (1997) 514 final, para. 3.

[65] *Regulation (EEC) No. 1107/70 of the Council of 4 June 1970 on the granting of aids for transport by rail, road and inland waterway*, OJ 1970 L 130/1.

This decision has to be seen in the context of the Commission's general practice[66] as well as the Community guidelines on environmental State aids from 1994.[67] The Commission acknowledges that certain undertakings cannot immediately bear an additional tax burden resulting from the introduction of ecotaxes and that they need a temporary relief. Therefore, the Commission's practice has to be understood as an acceptance of State aids which are in principle undesirable, but which seem to be necessary in order to introduce ecotaxes at all.

In the case in question, the Commission maintained that the German government committed itself to re-submit the relevant measures to be authorized by the Commission within three years following notification if it did not notify beforehand the second step of the ecological tax reform. This was necessary because the Commission only accepts temporary measures and the provisions in question do not contain any time limits.[68]

Finally, the Commission took into account that the German system was compatible with its proposal for a Council Directive restructuring the Community framework of the taxation of energy products from 1997.[69]

It can be argued that the decision is contrary to the polluter-pays-principle laid down in Article 174 (ex-Article 130r), para. 2, of the EC Treaty pursuant to which the costs of pollution should be borne by the polluters and not by the public.[70] This is regrettable from an environmental perspective. However, it is understandable from a practical, political perspective. The Commission acknowledges that it can be temporarily necessary to offset losses in competitiveness of domestic undertakings vis-à-vis undertakings established in other countries.[71]

It is also interesting to note that the Commission did not pay any attention to the principle of proportionality although the Member States are not empowered to grant State aids which have as their effect a strengthening of the financial situation of the beneficiaries without being necessary in order to attain the aims foreseen by Article 87, para. 3, of the EC

---

[66] See European Commission, *XXIIth Report On Competition Policy (1992)* (Brussels–Luxembourg, 1993), para. 75 and 451; *XXVth Report On Competition Policy (1995)* (Brussels–Luxembourg, 1996), para. 206; Press Report IP/98/411 of 6 May 1998; Press Report IP/96/1129 of 4 December 1996, http://europa.eu.int/rapid/start/cgi/guesten.ksh?p_action.gettxt.../1129/0/AGED&1g=F .

[67] See *supra* note 51, para. 3.4; for a general analysis of the guidelines see J. H. Jans, "State Aid and Articles 92 and 93 of the EC Treaty: Does the Polluter Really Pay?", *European Environmental Law Review* (1995), 108; there will probably be new Community Guidelines soon, see *Commission Communication, supra* note 8, at 3; Press Report IP/00/676 of 28 June 2000; "Strengere Prüfung von einzelstaatlichen Umweltbeihilfen", *Frankfurter Allgemeine Zeitung* of 14 March 2000, 29; for a recent analysis of environmental State aids in general see D. Geradin, "EC competition law and environmental protection", Han Somsen (ed.) *Yearbook of European Environmental Law* (Vol. II, Oxford University Press, forthcoming 2001).

[68] See Guidelines, *supra* note 51, para. 3.4.

[69] *Supra* note 48.

[70] See D. Geradin, *supra* note 67.

[71] See D. Geradin, *supra* note 67.

Treaty.[72] As we have seen, the exemptions in question are only a "necessary evil". As a consequence, the principle of proportionality should be applied very strictly. The lack of severity of the Commission Decision could indicate that the necessity of tax exemptions is of a political rather than economic nature.

The Commission also approved the continuation of the ecological tax reform in Germany[73] according to the State aid rules.[74] The second stage essentially provides for progressive, annual increases of taxes on electricity and power fuels. Even after the increase of the electricity tax, the reduced tax rates are maintained. As a result, the value of the partial exemptions already notified beforehand increases although the beneficiaries have to pay higher taxes than before. In addition, after the increase of the electricity tax, the reduced tax rates are applicable to an increasing number of undertakings which thereby benefit from partial exemptions. The Commission decided not to raise any objections against the notified amendments of the German laws in question. On the whole, it thereby refers to the reasoning of its decision of April 1999.[75] This is a little bit surprising since the ecotaxes were already introduced at this time. Taking into account the general justification of tax exemptions one could come to the conclusion that the German government amended the new law because the negative effects of the introduction of ecotaxes on the domestic industry were more serious than had been expected. It could also be that the amendments are a reaction to political impediments caused by fears about cost disparities with other jurisdictions.[76] Apparently, this argument has not been advanced; at least the Commission does not refer to any such arguments.

3. Conclusion

The German ecotax system probably does not contain any violation of Article 90 EC of the Treaty. Nevertheless, the (partial) tax exemptions in favour of certain undertakings and sectors constitute State aids. Up to now, the Commission has considered them to be compatible with the Common Market. As we have seen, the Commission's reasoning is vulnerable to some extent. It is not certain that such exemptions will be accepted easily in the future.

---

[72] Cases *Philip Morris, supra* note 53, para. 17; 74/76 *Iannelli/Meroni* [1977] E.C.R. 557, para. 15.

[73] *Gesetz zur Fortführung der ökologischen Steuerreform, supra* note 37.

[74] See Press Report of the Commission IP/00/157 of 15 February 2000.

[75] See *supra* note 48.

[76] For an overview and analysis of explanations of governmental decisions reducing environmental standards see D. C. Esty and D. Geradin, "Environmental Protection and International Competitiveness – A Conceptual Framework", *Journal of World Trade* (1998) No. 3, 5.

B. The Access to the Grid, the Obligation to Purchase and the Fixed Prices of Electricity Originating from Renewable Energy Sources (and CHP)

A pending case[77] before the ECJ has provoked a very lively debate[78] over the compatibility of the German Act on the Intake of Electricity Originating from Renewable Energy into the Public Grid[79] (the "Electricity-Intake-Act") with EC law, especially as regards the rules on State aids and on the free movement of goods. The provisions in question of the Electricity-Intake-Act provide that the network operators have to accept a certain percentage of electricity originating from certain renewable energy sources and whose production sites are situated in their respective zones of responsibility. This electricity has to be purchased at rates whose calculation is prescribed by the law in question. This law has recently been replaced.[80] To be precise it has to be said that the obligation to purchase is not explicitly mentioned in the German law, but it is the logical consequence of the obligation to pay certain prices for electricity originating from renewable energy sources.

---

[77] See "Reference for a preliminary ruling by the *Landgericht* Kiel by order of that court of 13 October 1998 in the case of *Preussen Elektra Aktiengesellschaft* against *Schleswag Aktiengesellschaft*", OJ 1998 C 397/19; for the whole ordonnance see *Recht der Energiewirtschaft* (1999), 116. Advocate-General Jacobs has submitted his conclusions on the case on 26 October 2000, after the completion of this article.

[78] See H. Mengers, "Novellierungs- und Anpassungsmöglichkeiten des Stromeinspeisungsgesetzes (StrEG)", *Zeitschrift für neues Energierecht* (1998), 29; H. Falk, "Anmerkung zum Beschluß des LG Kiel vom 20. Oktober 1998 – (15 O 134/98)", *Zeitschrift für neues Energierecht* (1998), 50; S. P. Iro, "Die Vereinbarkeit des Stromeinspeisungsgesetzes mit dem EG-Vertrag", *Recht der Energiewirtschaft* (1998), 11; P. Salje, "Die Vereinbarkeit des Stromeinspeisungsgesetzes mit dem EG-Vertrag", *Recht der Internationalen Wirtschaft* (1998), 186; S. K. Richter, "Die Unvereinbarkeit des Stromeinspeisungsgesetzes mit europäischem Beihilferecht (Art. 92 EGV a. F./ Art. 87 EGV n. F.)", *Recht der Energiewirtschaft* (1999), 23; K. Ritgen, "Stromeinspeisungsgesetz und europäisches Beihilfenaufsichtsrecht", *Recht der Energiewirtschaft* (1999), 176; K. Gent, "Deutsches Stromeinspeisungsgesetz und Europäisches Wettbewerbsrecht", *Energiewirtschaftliche Tagesfragen* (1999), 854; D. Fouquet and I. Zenke, "Das Stromeinspeisungsgesetz auf dem europarechtlichen Prüfstand", *Zeitschrift für neues Energierecht* (1999), 61; H. Pünder, "Die Förderung alternativer Energiequellen durch das Stromeinspeisungsgesetz auf dem Prüfstand des europäischen Gemeinschaftsrechts", *Neue Zeitschrift für Verwaltungsrecht* (1999), 1059.

[79] Bundesgesetzblatt 1991 part I, 26, in the version of Article 3, point 2, of the *Gesetz zur Neuregelung des Energiewirtschaftsrechts* of 24 April 1998, *supra* note 28; as regards the problems that have to be faced by applying this Act see B. Herrmann, *Anwendungsprobleme des Stromeinspeisungsgesetzes* (Baden-Baden, 1996).

[80] It is now called *Erneuerbare-Energien-Gesetz* ("Renewable-Energies-Act"), Bundesgesetzblatt 2000, part I, 305; for a brief description see *infra* P. 28.

1. The Electricity Directive [81]

The question asked by the *Landgericht* Kiel[82] and most of the legal doctrine on the matter[83] do not say anything about the Directive 96/92/EC. In addition, they do not distinguish the access to the grid from the obligation to purchase and the price fixing. However, such a distinction seems to be preferable in order to be able to understand the legal problems at issue.

As regards access to the grid, Article 8, para. 3, and Article 11, para. 3, of the Directive seem to clearly authorize giving a preference to producers which exploit renewable energy sources. Nevertheless, it should not be disregarded that the two provisions are not part of Chapter VII which governs access to the grid. This does not necessarily mean that these articles are not relevant here. The rules on access to the grid bear strongly the mark of the negotiations.[84] The final version has been changed time and again. It is the result of a difficult compromise. Thus, one should probably not attach too much importance to the structure of the Directive. Rather, the content of each article should be analyzed carefully. Therefore, the provisions referred to above have to be understood as regulating access to the grid.[85] The priority access to the grid as prescribed by the Electricity-Intake-Act can thus be seen as being compatible with the Directive.

In contrast, the obligation to purchase electricity originating from certain renewable energy sources and the price fixing are not expressly authorized by the Directive. Article 3, para. 2, of the Directive does not reverse this conclusion since this provision explicitly says that the rules of primary law have to be entirely respected. However, one could advance as an argument that the obligation to purchase and the fixed prices are necessary conditions of a priority access because of the lack of competitiveness of renewable energy sources.[86] Without such provisions, the regulation of the market as authorized by the Directive would probably fail to have any practical impact. Obviously, such reasoning[87] is quite daring. Taking into account the severity which the ECJ showed in *Outukumpu*[88,89] it is unlikely that the Court would interpret the Directive in such a creative way. It is more likely that the ECJ would understand the provisions as giving priority access to electricity sold to final consumers. Such an interpretation does not go beyond the literal meaning of the text.

---

[81] *Supra* note 13.

[82] *Supra* note 77.

[83] *Supra* note 78; H. Mengers briefly names the relevant provisions.

[84] See F. Lagondet, *supra* note 24, at 5.

[85] See in this regard R. Lukes, "Richtlinienkonformität der Netzzugangsregelung im Neuregelungsgesetz", *Energiewirtschaftliche Tagesfragen* (1999), 80 at 82.

[86] See *supra* p. 3.

[87] Although this seems to be presumed by R. Kemper, *The power struggle: Liberalisation of the electricity market in the European Union* (Bruges, 1998), at 20.

[88] See *supra* note 39.

[89] See *supra* p. 7.

2. A Violation of Article 87, para. 1, of the EC Treaty?

As regards the obligation to purchase and the fixed prices, one of the hot issues is whether these constitute State aids within the meaning of Article 87, para. 1, of the EC Treaty. According to the Commission the answer must be positive. With regard to the predecessor of the German law in question which had been notified by the German Government[90] and a Danish law,[91] the Commission considered that obligations to purchase electricity originating from renewable energy sources at fixed prices constituted State aids. The Commission's reasoning was as follows: Even if the Government did not directly use its own budget in order to support producers that exploit renewable energy sources, the obligation to purchase would be equivalent to a tax on the distributor's revenues which would directly be disbursed in favour of producers exploiting renewable energy sources. In the author's opinion, this reasoning is not convincing.

Firstly, for Article 87 to apply, there has to be an aid, that means an economic advantage. The beneficiary undertakings would receive such an advantage if they could not obtain it under ordinary market conditions.[92] It has to be analyzed whether the reciprocal obligations or dispositions contain an inequality in favour of the undertakings in question.[93] Since it is impossible to store electricity, the advantage cannot be the producers' guarantee to get rid of the electricity as such, but above all the payment. As a consequence and in principle, the fixed prices and not the obligation to purchase have to be qualified as an economic advantage. The obligation to purchase reinforces this economic advantage because of its influence on the total amount which has to be paid. Therefore, it is an element of the overall economic advantage conferred.

According to Article 87, para. 1, the beneficiaries of such an advantage do not need to be individual undertakings, but can also be a whole economic sector.[94] This condition is easily satisfied as regards the producers exploiting renewable energy sources.

In addition, Article 87, para. 1, requires that the State aids are "granted by a Member State or through State resources". The Electricity-Intake-Act prescribes fixed prices and an obligation to purchase, hence an advantage which has been created by the German Federal State. It is doubtful whether this is sufficient.[95] If the aid in question was granted through State resources, there would be no doubt at all. Therefore, we will first have a look at this alternative. One could think that the German Government makes use of the State resources because the German State in a broad sense holds shares in some of the network

---

[90] European Commission, *XXth Report on Competition Policy (1990)* (Brussels–Luxembourg, 1991), para. 219.

[91] European Commission, *supra* note 52, para. 286.

[92] Case C-39/94 *SFEI* [1996] E.C.R. I-3547, para. 60.

[93] See J.-P. Keppenne, *supra* note 52, at 19.

[94] See J.-P. Keppenne, *supra* note 52, at 24.

[95] In the French and in the German version, the text of Article 87, para. 1, of the EC Treaty is much more ambiguous.

operators.[96] The fact that they are not held by the Federal State but by the municipalities does not exclude a possible use of State resources although the municipalities are entirely independent from the Federal State in this context. EC law does not make any distinction as regards the internal division of State power.[97] However, it is difficult to deduce from the fact that a part of the network operators are partially owned by State organisms that State resources are the source of the advantage in question. According to constant case-law[98] it is sufficient that the State has a decisive influence on the administration of the financial means in question.[99] However, the simple fact that some of the companies are possibly decisively influenced by local entities does not turn the resources of all the network operators into State resources. Even if the State had a decisive influence on some of the companies it would still be strange to talk about State aid because the only possible way to escape from the application of the State aid rules would be to impose the fixed prices only on those undertakings in which no public entity holds the majority of the shares. This would obviously be contrary to the principle of non-discrimination which is also applicable in purely national circumstances according to Article 3 of the German *Grundgesetz*.[100]

However, according to consistent case-law, the economic advantage must be financed by the State even when applying the first of the above-mentioned alternatives pursuant to which the aid must be "granted by a Member State".[101] This means that the aid has to be granted by the public budget.[102] In *Van Tiggele*[103] the ECJ has even established that the fixing of minimum prices (at the retail level) did not constitute an aid in the sense of Article 87, para. 1, of the EC Treaty because it was not granted by State resources.

As a consequence, consciously or not, the Commission and many of the legal authors who write about the pending case in question try to alter the case-law of the ECJ. The latter has been criticized before. In a more general context, some of the Advocate Generals[104]

---

[96] This is not mentioned by the *Landgericht* Kiel, *supra* note 77.

[97] See case *Germany v. Commission* [1987], E. C. R. 4013, para. 17.

[98] See Cases 82/77 *Van Tiggele* [1987] E.C.R. 25, para. 24-25; 67/85, 68/85 and 70/85 *Van der Kooy v. Commission* [1988] E.C.R. 219, para. 28; C-72/91 and C-/3/91 *Sloman Neptun* [1993] E.C.R. I-887, para. 19-21; C-189/91 *Kirsammer-Hack* [1993] E.C.R. I-6185, para. 17-18; C-52/97, C-53/97 and C-54/97 *Viscido e. a.* [1998] E.C.R. I-2629, para. 13.

[99] See case *Van der Kooy e.a. v. Commission* [1988], *supra* note 98, para. 36 and 37.

[100] "Basic Act", the German Constitution.

[101] See for example case *Viscido e.a.* [1998], *supra* note 98, para. 13.

[102] See J.-P. Keppenne, *supra* note 52, at 112.

[103] See *supra* note 98, para. 24-25.

[104] See Advocate General M. Verloren van Themaat in joint cases 213/81 to 215/81 *Norddeutsches Vieh- und Fleischkontor* [1982] E.C.R. 3583 at 3617; Advocate General M. Darmon in *Sloman Neptun, supra* note 98, para. 40-41; Advocate General M. Darmon in *Kirsammer-Hack, supra* note 98, para. 23-27.

and a considerable section of legal doctrine[105] consider that the conditions "aid granted by a Member State" and "state resources" are alternatives in a strict sense, which means that State aid does not necessarily need to be financed by the State. It is true that in some language versions, the meaning of the text of Article 87, para. 1, is not very clear. It is possible to understand it as providing that the aids have to be either stimulated or financed by the State. However, such an interpretation has as its consequence that the second so-called alternative does not make any sense at all. It is unconceivable that an aid is not stimulated by the State, but still financed by its resources. By contrast, an interpretation of the conjunction "or" as an "or at least", which is quite possible at least in the English, French and German versions, seems to be much more solid. The ECJ was right not to follow the opinions of some of its Advocate Generals.

3. A Violation of Article 81 (ex-Article 85) in Conjunction with Article 10 (ex-Article 5) of the EC Treaty?

The Commission seems to be of the opinion that the German law at issue violates Article 81 (ex-Article 85) in conjunction with Article 10 (ex-Article 5) of the EC Treaty.[106] According to the Commission, the Electricity Intake-Act constitutes an obstacle to the effectiveness of Article 81 of the EC Treaty. However, according to the ECJ, the principle of loyalty according to Article 10, read in conjunction with Article 81 of the EC Treaty, does not prohibit all State measures that could affect competition, but only those that impose, reinforce, simplify, favour or permit a violation of Article 81 of the EC Treaty by undertakings.[107] According to the Electricity-Intake-Act, by contrast, the undertakings do not have any discretion. The producers exploiting renewable energy sources are not even in a position in which they have the power to impose conditions on the network operators and the latter are surely not in favour of provisions such as those at issue. The law is not an incentive to a concerted business practice and does not replace an agreement within the meaning of Article 81 of the EC Treaty.

As a consequence, the Electricity-Intake-Act does not entail any violation of Article 81 in conjunction with Article 10 of the EC Treaty.

---

[105] See L. Hancher, T. Ottervanger and P. J. Slot, *EC State Aids*, 2nd edition (London, 1999) at 41; K. Bacon, "State Aids and General Measures", *Yearbook of European Law* (1997), 269; M. M. Slotboom, "State Aid in Community Law: A Broad or Narrow Definition?", *ELR* (1995), 289; B. J. Rodger, "State Aid – A Fully Level Playing Field?", *ECLR* (1999), 251.

[106] See D. Fouquet and I. Zenke, *supra* note 78, who declare to know the non-published position of the Commission in the pending case in question.

[107] See cases 229/83 *Leclerc v. Au blé vert* [1985] E.C.R. 1, para. 15-20; 231/81 *Cullet v. Leclerc* [1985] E.C.R. 305, para. 16-18; 311/85 *VVR v. Sociale Dienst van de Plaatselijke en Gewestelijke Overheidsdiensten («Vlaamse Reisbureaus»)* [1987] E.C.R. 3801, para. 10, 22-24; 136/86 *BNIC v. Aubert* [1987] E.C.R. 4789, para. 22-25; C-2/91 *Meng* [1993] E.C.R. I-5751, para. 14-22.

4. A Violation of Article 28 (ex-Article 30) of the EC Treaty?

Electricity is a good in the meaning of Article 28 (ex-Article 30) of the EC Treaty.[108] It is doubtful whether the Electricity-Intake-Act contains a measure having equivalent effect or not. According to the famous "*Dassonville* Formula",[109] Article 28 of the EC Treaty prohibits business regulations which are capable of directly or indirectly, actually or potentially, distorting intra-community trade.

In this context, it is essential to keep in mind that access to the grid and the obligation to purchase only concern the electricity produced in the zone of responsibility of the respective network operators and thus only cover electricity produced in Germany. Therefore, a possible consequence of the law at issue is that the network operators are unable to accept a certain percentage of electricity produced by other undertakings or at least coming from foreign grids. There would be no actual obstacle in case the capacities of the respective networks were already exhausted without taking electricity originating from renewable energy sources in Germany, but even in such circumstances, there would remain a potential obstacle to trade. The law in question is not conceived as a provisional measure. According to the ECJ, [110] even a very minor restrictive effect is sufficient. As a consequence, the obligation to purchase, including the priority access to the grid, is a formally discriminatory measure.

The fixed prices do not have any additional effect as regards the potential distortion of intra-community trade. There are no fixed prices without a simultaneous obligation to purchase. Therefore, the "special" case-law on price regulation does not need to be taken into consideration.[111] Only the obligation to purchase deserves a more profound analysis.

According to *Cassis de Dijon*,[112] obstacles to intra-community trade which result from different national regulations have to be accepted to the extent that these restrictions are necessary in order to satisfy mandatory requirements. Environmental protection is one of the mandatory requirements that have been acknowledged by the ECJ.[113] Therefore, the established discrimination could be justified. Nevertheless, it should not be forgotten that the ECJ claims that it does not apply *Cassis de Dijon* to distinctly applicable measures.[114]

---

[108] Case C-393/92 *Almelo* [1994] E.C.R. I-1477, para. 28.

[109] Case 8/74 *Procureur du Roi – Dassonville* [1974] E.C.R. 837, para. 5.

[110] See joint cases 177/82 and 178/82 *Van de Haar and Kaveka de Meern* [1984] E.C.R. 1797, para. 13.

[111] See in this regard U. Ehricke, "State Intervention and EEC Competition Law Opportunities and Limits of the European Court of Justice's Approach – a Critical Analysis of Four Key-Cases", *World Competition* (1990), 79; E. Paulis, "The Danis Case – Reconciling Statutory Price Controls with the Free Movement of Goods", *ECLR* (1980), 163.

[112] Case 120/78 *REWE v. Bundesmonopolverwaltung für Brandwein* [1979] E.C.R. 649, para. 8.

[113] See cases 302/86 *Commission v. Denmark* [1988] E.C.R. 4607, para. 9; 2/90 *Commission v. Belgium (Wallonian Waste)* [1992] E.C.R. I-4431, para. 29 and 32.

[114] See case C-21/88 *Du Pont de Nemours Italiana* [1990] E.C.R. 889, para. 14.

The measure at issue here is formally discriminatory. As a consequence, it does not seem to be possible to apply the reasoning of *Cassis de Dijon* at all.[115]

However, a more profound analysis of the famous *Wallonian Waste* case[116] could lead to a different conclusion. In this judgment, the ECJ applied *Cassis de Dijon* in order to justify a restriction of interstate trade which clearly discriminated against imports in the name of the particularity of waste and the principle according to which environmental damage should as a priority be rectified at its source.[117] With reference to the reasoning of the ECJ in this judgment, one can draw the conclusion that the particularity of electricity justifies an application of *Cassis de Dijon*. Articles 8 and 11 of Directive 96/92/EC[118] mention the responsibility of the network operators in the zones covered by them (para. 1) and the possibility to favour the producers of electricity originating from renewable energy sources (para. 3).[119] These provisions can be understood as a consequence of the particularity of electricity which is transported by means of a network. The construction of special lines for every producer would be economically absurd. Thus, the logical reference points of the regulation of access to the grid are the respective zones of responsibility of the network operators. In addition, this corresponds to the principle of Article 174 (ex-Article 130r), para. 2, of the EC Treaty evoked by the ECJ in *Wallonian Waste*. Therefore, one can argue that the specific nature of electricity itself prescribes a direct discrimination because the German government does not have the power to impose obligations on network operators established in other Member States. The explicit reasoning of the ECJ in *Wallonian Waste* is, therefore, applicable to the facts of the pending case at issue.

This conclusion shows the vulnerability of the ECJ's reasoning in *Wallonian Waste*.[120] One section of legal doctrine is of the opinion that it would be much more honest to explicitly apply *Cassis de Dijon* to distinctly applicable measures, in particular because there is no absolute need for such a distinction between mandatory requirements and the justifications laid down in Article 30 (ex-Article 36) of the EC Treaty.[121]

It still has to be seen whether the Electricity-Intake-Act also passes the proportionality test. When a Member State has a choice between different measures which can achieve the same aim, it has to choose the measure which leads to the free movement of goods being least affected.[122] The obligation to purchase can lead to increased use of electricity

---

[115] S. P. Iro, *supra* note 78, at 19; K. Gent, *supra* note 78, at 857; P. Salje, *supra* note 78, at 190.

[116] See *supra* note 113.

[117] See *supra* note 113, para. 30 and 34.

[118] See *supra* note 13.

[119] See already *supra* p. 18.

[120] See in this regard D. Geradin, "Trade and Environmental Protection: Community Harmonization and National Environmental Standards", *Yearbook of European Law* (1993), 151 at 160-161.

[121] See A. Schaub, *supra* note 23, at 172; A. Epiney, *Umweltrecht in der Europäischen Union* (Cologne – Berlin – Bonn – Munich, 1997), at 119.

[122] See case *Commission v. Denmark* [1988], *supra* note 113, para. 6.

originating from renewable energy sources. This has already been demonstrated by the real effect of the German law in question and the corresponding Danish law. It is not surprising that the figures about the installed capacities in the wind energy sector indicate the largest increases in Denmark and Germany.[123] In addition, for each kWh supplied to the grid, the new potential investors in renewable energy production sites receive the best remuneration in Germany.[124] However, this does not necessarily mean that the obligation to purchase is also necessary in the strict sense. It has been proposed that this was not the case because the fixed prices were too high.[125] It is doubtful whether this is true. As we have seen, it is the obligation to purchase and not the price fixing which constitutes a measure having equivalent effect. It has also been proposed that the application of Article 82 (ex-Article 86) of the EC Treaty — which prohibits the abusive exploitation of a dominant position – would be a less harmful intervention in the market.[126] This probably signifies the application of the "essential facilities" doctrine.[127] Producers of electricity originating from renewable energy sources could possibly claim a right of access to the network and reasonable payment for their products. This opinion is even more doubtful. Firstly, it is not conceivable how the electricity originating from renewable energy sources would be specifically supported by such an application of Article 82 in comparison to other kinds of electricity. Secondly, in contrast to the conclusions that one could draw from the ambiguous reasoning of the ECJ in *Commission v. Denmark*,[128] a section of legal opinion[129] is convinced that the Member States have the right to choose the level of protection they want. Indeed, the consideration expressed by the EC Treaty itself[130] could indicate that obstacles to the free movement of goods have to be accepted in order to achieve a very high level of protection. Therefore, it is not unlikely that the ECJ would consider Article 2 of the Electricity-Intake-Act to be compatible with the principle of proportionality.

As a consequence, the Electricity-Intake-Act probably does not violate Article 28.

---

[123] See European Commission, *Working Paper, Electricity From Renewable Energy Sources And The Internal Electricity Market,* SEC (99) 470 final, at 15.

[124] See European Commission, *supra* note 123, at 16.

[125] See S. K. Richter, *supra* note 78, at 29-31; P. Salje, *supra* note 78, at 190.

[126] See P. Salje, *supra* note 78, at 190.

[127] For more information about this doctrine see, for instance, J. Temple Lang, "Defining Legitimate Competition: Companies' Duties to Supply Competitors and Access to Essential Facilities", 18 *Fordham International Law Journal* (1994), 437.

[128] See *supra* note 113 para. 16-21; see in this regard D. Geradin, *supra* note 120, at 157-158.

[129] See L. Krämer, *supra* note 12, at 78-80; L. Krämer, "Environmental Protection and Article 30 EEC Treaty", *CMLR* (1993), 111 at 123-125.

[130] See Article 6, Article 95 (ex-Article 100a), para. 3, Article 174 (ex-Article 130r), para. 2, and Article 176 (ex-Article 130t) of the EC Treaty.

5. The Effects of the Electricity Tax Act on the Prices that have to be paid according to the Electricity-Intake-Act

The Commission has opened proceedings as regards the effects of the new electricity tax on the prices calculated according to the Electricity-Intake-Act. This procedure only concerns the increase of the fixed prices owing to the electricity tax. The tax is an element of the calculation of the prices as prescribed by the Electricity-Intake-Act. The Commission is of the opinion that the prices that have to be paid constitute State aids according to Article 87, para 1, of the EC Treaty.[131]

Since the Electricity-Intake-Act probably does not contain a violation of Article 87, para.1, it is even more unlikely that the effects of the Electricity Tax Act can be qualified as such. It is also rather unlikely that the Act constitutes a violation of Article 81 in conjunction with Article 10 of the EC Treaty or a violation of Article 28 of the EC Treaty.

6. Recent Developments in Germany

A new law on renewable energies,[132] which replaces the Electricity-Intake-Act, entered into force on 1 April 2000.[133] The objective of this law is to permit the pursuit of sustainable development in the energy sector by increasing the contribution of renewable energy sources to the electricity supplies. The most important differences between the Renewable-Energies-Act and the Electricity-Intake-Act are that the support of wind energy has declined whereas the prices that have to be paid for electricity originating from other renewable energy sources have increased. In addition, the prices are now fixed at a constant but declining rate. Before, only the calculation method was prescribed.[134] The responsibility of the respective network operators is now solely determined by the distance between the production site and the grid. Before, the national zones of responsibility were decisive. The Renewable-Energies-Act does not contain any limitation of the obligation to purchase according to the percentage of the electricity originating from renewable energy sources already taken, but, under certain conditions, the new obligation to enlarge the grid.

---

[131] Press Report IP/99/667 of 9 September 1999.

[132] See *supra* note 80.

[133] For first comments on this law see B. Nagel, "EU-Gemeinschaftsrecht und nationales Gestaltungsrecht – Entspricht das EEG den Vorgaben des Gemeinschaftsrechts?", *Zeitschrift für neues Energierecht* (2000), 3; V. Oschmann, "Gesetz für den Vorrang Erneuerbarer Energien (Erneuerbare-Energien-Gesetz – EEG) — Synoptische Gegenüberstellung des Stromeinspeisungsgesetzes 1998, des Gesetzentwurfs vom Dezember 1999 und des endgültigen Gesetzestextes", *Zeitschrift für neues Energierecht* (2000), 7; V. Oschmann, "Das Gesetz für den Vorrang Erneuerbarer Energien", *Energiewirtschaftliche Tagesfragen* (2000), 460.

[134] See *supra* p. 16.

In addition, on 18 May 2000, a new German law on CHP[135] entered into force.[136] This new law has as its objective the safeguard of existing and future installations of CHP. Subject to certain conditions, the law prescribes a mechanism of support which is comparable to the Electricity-Intake-Act and the Renewable-Energies-Act. The background to this measure is that CHP is a production method which is very much compatible with the idea of sustainable development[137] and that many CHP producers are in serious economic difficulties.

IV. CONCLUSION

From a legal standpoint, the result of the analysis of the problems posed in Germany shows that national policies in favour of sustainable development are probably still possible within the framework of the liberalization of the electricity market. Nevertheless, the description of the political background of the end of the exploitation of nuclear energy,[138] the tax exemptions,[139] and the position taken by the Commission as regards the Electricity-Intake-Act[140] show that it is difficult for a Member State to introduce such measures. One of the reasons is the fear of a loss of competitiveness in comparison to neighbouring countries.[141] The introduction of national taxes and laws that support certain production methods has as its consequence a different economic framework in each Member State. The discovery that diverging national legislations in favour of environmental protection within the European Union may threaten the unity of the Internal Market is not new.[142] In contrast to what one could think at first glance, a positive harmonization at the European level is thus preferable. However, a compromise that has as its result a high standard of environmental protection is difficult to achieve, also at this level.[143]

It is not a secret that during the last decade little progress has been made at Community level as regards the direct taxation of energy products.[144] It is not difficult to find out which European institution is responsible for the enormous delay. In its official declarations, the

---

[135] Kraft-Wärme-Kopplungs-Gesetz (Combined-Heat-And-Power-Act), Bundesgesetzblatt 2000, part I, 703.

[136] For a first analysis see B. Herrmann, "Das Kraft-Wärme-Kopplungsgesetz – Systematik, Anwendungsbereich und Grenzen", *Recht der Energiewirtschaft* (2000), 184.

[137] See already *supra* p. 81.

[138] See *supra* note 30.

[139] See *supra* p. 85.

[140] See *supra* pp. 85 and 87.

[141] See *supra* note 30.

[142] See D. Geradin, *supra* note 120, at 152.

[143] See D. Geradin, *supra* note 120, at 152.

[144] See for example European Commission, *Green Paper on green house gas emissions trading within the European Union,* COM (00) 87, 26.

Commission openly implores the Council to adopt its proposition.[145] Article 93 of the EC Treaty requires an unanimous decision and, as is well known, it is difficult to find an agreement between Member States where conflicting interests are involved.[146]

However, as regards other possible measures, the future perspectives are apparently not as bad from an environmental point of view. In a recent list of common and coordinated policies and measures about climate change,[147] the Commission proposed *inter alia* the following as regards energy supplies: access to the grid of decentralized electricity production, an increase in the share of renewable energy sources on the grid, increased use of cogeneration as well as energy efficiencies in the electricity distribution sector. A new directive has been proposed recently.[148] Its expected adoption will probably take place according to the procedure of Article 251 (ex-Article 189b) of the EC Treaty which only requires a qualified majority. Therefore, there is a distinct possibility that the directive will be adopted more quickly. However, the proposed directive leaves much autonomy to the Member States. Thus, dramatic changes at the European level seem to be unlikely within the foreseeable future.

---

[145] See Commission Communication, *supra* note 8, at 3.

[146] See for example E. Margallo González, *La fiscalidad ecológica y el mercado interior en la Unión Europea* (Barcelona, 1997) at 15 and 95.

[147] See Commission Communication, *supra* note 8, at 11.

[148] See European Commission, *Proposal for a directive of the European Parliament and of the Council on the promotion of electricity from renewable energy sources in the internal electricity market,* COM (00) 279 final.

IV. COUNTRY REPORTS

D. Vandermeersch

COUNTRY REPORT: BELGIUM*

I. INTRODUCTION

A. The Belgian Electricity and Gas Markets: Institutional Aspects

Due to the federal structure of the Kingdom of Belgium, the implementation in Belgium of Directive 96/92 on the internal market in electricity (the "Electricity Directive")[1] and of Directive 98/30 on the internal market in natural gas (the "Natural Gas Directive")[2] requires action by each of the federal and the three regional authorities.

While both the Electricity Directive and the Natural Gas Directive already have been the subject of federal implementation laws, adopted in 1999, at present, none of the regions has taken formal action to implement the directives in the areas of their competency. Moreover, the Federal Electricity Law and the Federal Gas Law require a series of implementing decrees in order for them to become fully effective or for their provisions to become fully operational.

As a result, Belgium has not met the implementation deadlines to which it is subject, *i.e.*, 19 February 2000 (the "Electricity Directive")[3] and 10 August 2000 (the "Natural Gas Directive").

B. The Belgian Electricity and Gas Markets: The Market Structure

The liberalization of the electricity and gas markets in Belgium will entail a radical departure from the way in which both markets were regulated (or not regulated) in the past.

In the electricity sector, private producers (now merged into one company, *i.e.*, Electrabel, which is controlled by the French Suez group) have traditionally been predominant. The public producer SPE accounts for less than 10% of capacity. Moreover, Electrabel and SPE jointly operate their capacity in the framework of the joint venture company CPTE. While production is predominantly privately owned, distribution is carried out under a

---

* This report is up to date to March 2000.

[1] OJ, 30 January 1997, No L 27/20.

[2] OJ, 21 July 1998, No L 204/1.

[3] Belgium benefited from an extra one-year extension of the implementation period (Article 27.2 Electricity Directive).

Damien Geradin (ed.), The Liberalization of Electricity and Natural Gas in the European Union, 107–121
©2001 Kluwer Law International. Printed in the Netherlands.

statutory monopoly of the municipalities.[4] Municipalities carry out their distribution tasks through associations, most often in a joint venture structure with Electrabel[5]. These associations of municipalities have as a rule entered into long-term exclusive supply arrangements with Electrabel. Following an intervention by the Competition Directorate General of the European Commission, the term of these exclusive supply arrangements has been reduced so that they now come to an end on 31 December 2011. In addition, the municipality associations may as of 31 December 2006, source up to 25% of their needs from third parties.[6] Through its intervention, the Commission sought to safeguard the opportunities provided by the Electricity Directive by preventing the foreclosure for an extended period of a significant part of the Belgian electricity market.

In the natural gas sector, one company, *i.e.*, Distrigas, which is also controlled by the Suez group, prior to the entry into force of the Federal Gas Law, benefited from a statutory monopoly on the transport and underground storage of natural gas.[7] Distribution, however, has been carried out by the municipalities.[8] Municipalities assume their distribution role through associations of municipalities, most often in the same joint venture structure with Electrabel as is used for the distribution of electricity.

C. The Belgian Electricity and Gas Markets: The Regulators

Although both the electricity and gas sectors have been subject to regulatory provisions at the federal level, granting certain competencies to the federal authorities – for instance, as regards price controls and approval of major infrastructure investments –, since the 1950s, an important role has been played by the Control Committee for Electricity and Gas ("CCEG"). This Committee is composed of representatives of the social partners.[9] In the framework of the CCEG, the social partners assume the role of "controlling entities", making recommendations (in particular as regards prices and price structures, use of energy sources) to the "controlled entities" (*i.e.*, the electricity and gas sectors).

---

[4]   Article 3, Law of 10 March 1925, BS, 25 April 1925. The monopoly concerns the distribution of electricity up to 1,000 kW. In Wallonia, this limit has been increased to 10,000 kW (Walloon decree of 29 November 1990, BS, 7 March 1991).

[5]   Pursuant to Articles 11 and 17 of the law of 22 December 1986 on associations of municipalities (BS, 26 June 1987), the representatives of the municipalities must have majority control of the management of the associations. However, the articles of association of the distribution joint venture associations grant considerable veto rights to Electrabel, thus giving Electrabel joint control over major operational matters.

[6]   See Commission Press Release IP/97/381, 25 April 1997, *27th Competition Report* (1997), 150.

[7]   Until 1983, Distrigas also enjoyed a statutory monopoly over the importation of natural gas in Belgium.

[8]   There is no express statutory provision granting the municipalities a monopoly over the distribution of natural gas. However, it is generally assumed that such a monopoly flows from the municipalities' exclusive right to regulate, e.g., the use of public land and roads.

[9]   The national employers' federation and the three national trade unions.

These recommendations are, as a practical matter, considered to be binding upon the controlled entities.[10] Significantly, the federal and regional governments are not members of the CCEG, although they are associated with its activities as observers. CCEG recommendations on maximum prices are reflected by (federal) ministerial decrees adopted pursuant to general price control legislation.

The liberalization required by the Electricity Directive and the Natural Gas Directive has caused the Federal Electricity Law and the Federal Gas Law to reduce the jurisdiction of the Control Committee to the non-liberalized (or "captive") segments of the electricity and gas markets. The liberalized segments will be subject to control and regulation by a new federal agency, the Commission for the Regulation of Electricity and Gas ("CREG"), which is to be independent from the government and the social partners.[11]

II. THE FEDERAL AND REGIONAL POWERS

Following the constitutional reforms of 1980/1988, responsibility for the energy sector has been split between the federal authorities, on the one hand, and the regional authorities (Flanders, Wallonia, Brussels),[12] on the other hand. Their respective competence is mutually exclusive: each authority is competent for matters falling within its substantive (and, in the case of the regions, geographic) jurisdiction. There is no federal pre-emption or priority right pursuant to which federal law would prevail over regional law in the areas regulated by the federal law.[13]

The division of energy competencies between the federal and the regional authorities may be summarized as follows.

A. Powers of the Regional Authorities

The jurisdiction of the regions extends to the "regional aspects" of energy policy, in particular, with respect to electricity and gas, the "distribution and local transport of electricity using lines of up to 70 kV" and "public gas distribution". Other areas of regional authority include renewable energy sources and rational energy use.

---

[10] Pursuant to an agreement dated 21 March 1995, between the controlling parties and the controlled entities, the latter agree to cooperate fully with the activities of the CCEG.

[11] It is expected that the regions will set up their own agencies, modelled upon the example of the CREG, to regulate and supervise activities within the jurisdiction of the regions, in particular distribution.

[12] Each of these regions has its own parliamentary assembly having law-making powers and an executive authority (referred to as the regional government).

[13] However, pursuant to Article 16, §3, of the Special Law of 8 August 1988, as amended, the federal State may take action with regard to a matter within a region's jurisdiction whenever the region concerned has failed to comply with an obligation of international or supranational law, such as EC law, and such failure has led to Belgium being condemned by a competent international court (e.g., the European Court of Justice).

B. Powers of the Federal Authorities

The federal State has jurisdiction over matters which "because of their technical and economic integration require uniform treatment at the national level", *i.e.*, matters such as "large facilities for transport", the "transport and production of energy", nuclear energy and the regulation of prices.

C. Issues

Commentators and federal/regional authorities disagree as to the respective scope of federal and regional jurisdiction in the area of energy regulation. For instance, the Flemish Government appears to take the position that federal jurisdiction is limited to the matters expressly listed in the Special Law of 8 August 1980, as amended, while all other matters would fall within the ambit of regional regulatory power. Some legal commentators have taken the opposite view. Similarly, according to the Flemish Government, any activity related to distribution or renewable energy would be for the regions to regulate.[14]

III. THE IMPLEMENTATION OF THE ELECTRICITY DIRECTIVE IN BELGIUM

A. Scope of Implementation and Entry into Force

The federal law of 29 April 1999 on the organization of the electricity market,[15] implements the Electricity Directive with regard to the areas covered by the directive that (according to the federal government) fall within the jurisdiction of the federal State. The Federal Electricity Law regulates the generation and transmission of electricity, electricity pricing and transmission tariffs, access to the transmission system and opening up of the electricity market to producers supplying electricity to, and users being supplied electricity by, the Belgian national transmission system.

Certain provisions of the law entered into effect on 2 June 1999.[16] These provisions generally concern institutional and regulatory issues, such as the provisions regarding the creation of the CREG and the provisions enabling the federal government to adopt implementing rules by way of royal decree. There are as yet no implementation measures

---

[14] This would mean, for instance, that electricity production units connected exclusively to the distribution network or using renewable energy sources would be within the (exclusive) jurisdiction of the regions.

[15] BS, 11 May 1999, 2nd Ed, p. 16264.

[16] Royal decree of 3 May 1999, BS, 2 June 1999.

adopted by the regions with regard to the areas covered by the directive that fall within the jurisdiction of the regional authorities.

B. The Generation of Electricity: The Production Permit

Belgium has opted for the construction of new generating capacity to be subject to the authorization procedure contemplated by Article 5 of the Electricity Directive. Prior to the adoption of the Federal Electricity Law, the creation of new generating capacity was subject to planning through a "national infrastructure plan" recommended by the CCEG to the electricity sector and approved by the federal government.

Under the new regime, the creation of new generation capacity[17] is subject to a permit granted by the federal energy minister, acting upon a proposal from the CREG.[18] The criteria for the granting of production permits are still to be determined by royal implementing decree. These criteria may include the imposition of public service obligations as to the regularity and quality of supplies and security of supply for ineligible customers.

The CREG is to prepare an "indicative plan" of the means of electricity production in Belgium. The plan, which is subject to approval by the federal energy minister, must estimate the evolution of demand and the generation capacity needs that are expected from that demand. In addition, the plan is to contain guidelines for the choice of primary energy sources. These guidelines should take into account the need to diversify energy sources and to stimulate the use of renewable primary energy. The plan is to also assess the need for (and the costs of) public service obligations in the field of production.

Finally, the Federal Electricity Law empowers the federal government to adopt, by way of royal decree, "market organizational" measures that would ensure a defined level of off-take at a minimum price of electricity produced from renewable energy sources.[19]

C. The Opening up of the Market: Eligible Customers

Pursuant to the Federal Electricity Law, customers established in Belgium are eligible to conclude contracts for the supply of electricity and to have access to the transmission

---

[17] The generation capacity provisions of the Federal Electricity Law apparently apply to all forms of generation capacity without distinction. As noted, some regional authorities take the position that only nuclear capacity and capacity that is technically and economically integrated, so as to require uniform regulation at the national level, is within federal jurisdiction. As a result, all production capacity using renewable energy or connected to a distribution network or local transportation network at or below 70 kV would be subject to regional regulation.

[18] Federal Electricity Law, Article 4. The federal government may, acting by royal decree, exempt small installations from the permit requirement.

[19] Federal Electricity Law, Article 7. The Federal Electricity Law defines "renewable energy sources" as all energy sources other than fossil fuels and nuclear energy, such as water, wind, solar, biomass and waste.

system if they annually consume more than 100 GWh on a consumption per site basis (including auto-production). Distribution companies are eligible for the volumes necessary for them to be able to supply consumers that are eligible within their distribution network.[20] As of 1 January 2007, distribution companies will be fully eligible.

The 100 GWh final customer threshold is to be lowered in the future by royal decree designating other categories of final customers connected to the transmission system that will become eligible. This decree will take into account the degree of market opening in the other EU Member States and should eventually lead to all such customers becoming eligible by 31 December 2006.

As of the 19 February 2000 implementation deadline set by the Electricity Directive, the necessary royal and ministerial implementing decrees (*e.g.*, designating the TSO and setting the technical rules for connection to and operation of the transmission system) and CREG decisions (*e.g.*, approving the transmission tariffs) were not in place. The current network owner CPTE, however, took the initiative of opening its network for the supply of customers consuming at least 100 GWh per year and per location. CPTE published on the Internet its negotiation procedures as well as its general terms and conditions for access to its network, including its transmission tariffs.[21] Under these rules and procedures, the electricity supplier and its customer must designate a joint representative who will, on behalf of the parties, enter into a network connection agreement and a network access agreement with CPTE.

D. Access to the Transmission System

1. The National Transmission System

Belgium has opted for its transmission system to be operated as one national system by a single system operator. This reflects the current situation in which the Belgian transmission system is operated by the private company CPTE, which is a joint venture grouping Electrabel and the public sector producers.

The Federal Electricity Law defines the transmission system as the national electricity transmission network, encompassing the aboveground and underground lines and installations intended for the transport of electricity (a) country to country, (b) to producers' direct customers in Belgium and/or (c) to distribution companies in Belgium. The transmission system also includes the interconnectors to other systems.

As noted above, for Belgian institutional purposes (*i.e.*, the dividing line between federal

---

[20] It is up to the regional authorities to determine the eligibility criteria for consumers connected to the distribution networks.

and regional jurisdiction), the distinction between transmission and local transportation/ distribution is crucial. Distribution systems (which are within the jurisdiction of the regions) are defined in the Federal Electricity Law as all systems having a voltage of 70 kV or less *and* used for the transport of electricity to regional or local customers.[22]

2. *The Transmission System Operator*

Designation. The transmission system operator ("TSO") will be designated by the federal energy minister after having received a proposal from one or more system owners who own a part of the transmission network covering at least 75% of the national territory and at least 66% of the territory of each region.[23] The TSO is designated for a renewable term of 20 years.

Independence and impartiality. The TSO must be set up as a separate company. It must not become involved in any activity of production or sale of electricity (except where required by its system coordination duties) nor may the TSO hold shares in electricity producers, distributors or traders or render services on the electricity market. To ensure the independence and impartiality of the TSO, the federal government is empowered to adopt by royal decree "corporate governance" requirements applicable to the TSO. These requirements were determined by royal decree on 3 May 1999.[24] For instance, the majority of the members of the board of the TSO must be non-executive directors and at least one-third of its members must be independent, *i.e.*, having no relationship with the TSO, any producer (other than an auto producer), network owner, distributor, intermediary or "dominating" shareholder of the TSO.[25] The independent directors must have the majority in a special corporate governance committee charged with examining any conflicts of interests between the TSO and a dominating shareholder and nominating candidate independent directors to the shareholders.

---

[21] www.cpte.be.

[22] This implies that a line, by virtue of having a voltage of 70 kV or less, will not necessarily be considered a line subject to exclusive regional jurisdiction. In order to fall within regional jurisdiction, the line must also be used for the supply of regional or local customers. As a result, the 70 kV (or less) lines currently operated by CPTE that are part of the transmission network (e.g., in cities) would arguably be considered to be part of the national transmission system and, therefore, subject to federal regulation. The regional authorities (such as the Flemish Government), however, take a voltage-only approach and consider that all lines at or below 70 kV are exclusively within regional jurisdiction, irrespective of the use of the line. This position is bound to lead to operational problems unless the TSO is also designated by the regional authorities as the "distribution" system operator for the lines concerned and regional DSO designation criteria are compatible with the federal TSO designation criteria.

[23] If no such proposal is made by the network owners, the TSO is designated upon a proposal made by the CREG.

[24] BS, 2 June 1999.

[25] A 10% share ownership in the TSO would already confer the status of "dominating" shareholder.

Transmission development plan. The TSO is required to establish a rolling seven-year development plan for the transmission network. The development plan must provide an estimate of the need for new transmission capacity and set forth the investments the TSO agrees to undertake to satisfy this need. The development plan is subject to approval by the federal energy minister. In the event that the CREG determines that the planned investments are insufficient to satisfy expected needs, the minister may require the TSO to amend the plan.

3. Rules and Tariffs for Connection to and Use of the Transmission System

The technical rules for connection to the system, the operational rules for the dispatching of generating installations, including the priority to be given to generators using renewable energy sources or producing combined heat and power, are still to be determined by royal decree.

The TSO's tariffs for connection to and use of the transmission network are subject to approval by the CREG on an annual basis. These tariffs must be based on a number of principles, including:

- tariffs are to be non-discriminatory and transparent;
- tariffs are to be set by reference to costs;
- tariffs are to ensure the TSO an equitable return on investment and the financing of the long-term development of the network; and
- tariffs are to distinguish between the use of the network, ancillary services and levies to cover public service obligations and stranded costs.

The application of the transmission tariff rules may be extended to the connection and use of distribution networks. Such extension requires a royal decree and prior consultation of the regional governments.

4. Regulated Third-Party Access

Eligible customers and producers have a right of access to the transmission system on the basis of the published tariffs. The TSO may refuse access in two circumstances:

- lack of capacity; or
- the applicant does not satisfy the technical rules for connection to or use of the system.

As an exception to regulated access, parties must negotiate commercial terms for access to the system "in good faith" as regards the transit of electricity in accordance with EC

Directive 90/547. In addition, negotiated access will apply (as an option) in the case of transport of large volumes (as defined by royal decree).

E. Direct Lines

Prior to the Federal Electricity Law, in Belgium there were no direct lines connecting producers and customers not connected to the transmission network. The construction of a direct line is subject to prior permit from the federal energy minister acting upon a proposal from the CREG. A permit may be granted where the line is intended to allow a Belgian producer or intermediary to supply its branches, subsidiaries and eligible customers. It may also be granted so as to allow producers and traders in other EU Member States to supply eligible customers in Belgium.

The criteria for the licensing of direct lines are to be determined in a royal implementing decree. This decree may subject the granting of a permit to the condition that access to the transmission network was refused or that no offer was made to use the distribution network under "reasonable economic or technical conditions".

F. The Regulation of Electricity Prices

The system of official price controls (maximum prices set by the federal minister for the economy acting upon a recommendation by the CCEG) remains unchanged as regards the electricity prices that may be charged to ineligible final customers (the so-called "captive market"). These maximum prices must apply uniformly to deliveries anywhere in the country (irrespective of the region of delivery).

As regards the supply of electricity to eligible final customers, the minister *may* set maximum prices, acting upon a recommendation from the CREG.

Maximum prices set by the minister (whether for the captive segment or the liberalized segment of the market) must aim to prevent cross-subsidization between categories of customers and to ensure that a fair share of the benefits of market liberalization accrue to private and professional users (in particular the small and medium-sized enterprises) by way of price reductions.

The federal government, acting by way of royal decree, is empowered to set minimum prices for the purchase of electricity generated through combined heat and power production, for resale to ineligible customers.

G. Public Service Obligations

The Federal Electricity Law empowers the federal government to impose, by way of royal decree, public service obligations upon producers, intermediaries and the TSO, in particular as regards the regularity and quality of supplies and the supply of ineligible customers.[26] In that connection, derogations may be granted from the provisions regulating the authorization of new generating capacity, the access to the transmission system and the construction of direct lines.

In addition, a special fund may be created to be financed through special levies on transmission tariffs or other levies payable by energy users or market operators.[27] The fund is to contribute to the financing of the cost of the public service obligations (provided such cost would impose an inequitable burden on the company concerned) or the stranded costs accepted by the European Commission.

H. Unbundling of Accounts

As noted, the Federal Electricity Law requires the TSO to be set up as a separate legal entity. In addition, the law requires the unbundling of the internal accounts of the TSO, the distribution system operators, the producers, the distributors and the intermediaries that are vertically or horizontally integrated. In addition, the financial statements must disclose all significant transactions with related companies and contain separate balance sheets and profit & loss accounts for the production, transmission and distribution activities as well as for any activities outside the electricity sector.[28]

I. Protection against Abusive Behaviour

One of the statutory tasks of the CREG is to cooperate with the Competition Service set up under Belgium's Competition Law,[29] in the framework of any competition case brought concerning the electricity sector.

In addition, the CREG is empowered to enjoin (subject to financial penalties) any person or company to comply with any provision of the Federal Electricity Law or its implementing decrees.

---

[26] Federal Electricity Law, Article 21.

[27] The royal decree that would create such a fund shall need to be confirmed by an act of Parliament within six months of its adoption.

[28] The CREG may, however, grant derogation from this publication requirement where the disclosure would be prejudicial to the competitive position of the company concerned.

[29] Law of 5 August 1991, on the protection of economic competition.

Finally, Belgian companies occupying a "strong position" on the Belgian energy market[30] must ensure that their internal decision-making processes include appropriate mechanisms aimed at preventing conflicts of interest with affiliated companies from leading to decisions or strategies that would harm the interests of consumers or the proper performance of public service obligations. The CREG may issue recommendations to the company concerned to clarify the implications of this requirement.

IV. THE IMPLEMENTATION OF THE NATURAL GAS DIRECTIVE IN BELGIUM

A. Scope of Implementation and Entry into Force

A second federal law of 29 April 1999, on the organization of the gas market,[31] implements the Natural Gas Directive with regard to those areas covered by the directive that fall within federal jurisdiction. The Federal Gas Law regulates the construction and operation of gas transmission facilities, the supply of gas, access to the transmission system and the opening of that system to suppliers and eligible customers.

A limited number of provisions of the law entered into effect on 15 June 1999,[32] *i.e.*, the provisions dealing with the tasks of the CREG concerning the gas sector, the crisis provisions, the conflicts of interest rules and the provisions regulating the "golden share" owned by the Belgian State in Distrigas.[33]

As yet no implementation measures have been adopted by the regions with respect to the matters covered by the directive that fall within the jurisdiction of the regional authorities.

---

[30] A 25% market share of the electricity market (or the relevant segment thereof) creates a presumption of such market power.

[31] BS, 11 May 1999, 2nd Ed., p. 16278. The law of 29 April 1999 amends a pre-existing law of 12 April 1965, which, as amended, is herein referred to as the "Federal Gas Law".

[32] Royal decree of 3 May 1999, BS, 15 June 1999.

[33] Pursuant to a royal decree of 16 June 1994, the one share held by the State in Distrigas confers certain special rights on the State. For instance, the State may object to a decision by Distrigas management to divest itself of certain key assets. The European Commission has objected that these special rights violate the EC Treaty provisions on the freedom of establishment to the extent that their exercise is not made subject to objective and transparent criteria. As a result, according to the Commission, there is no assurance that the Belgian State will not make use of its special rights in a manner that would discriminate against companies from other EU Member States, e.g., potential investors in Distrigas. The Federal Gas Law now calls for the adoption of a royal decree setting forth appropriate criteria for the exercise by the State of its special rights. The same applies to the golden share held by the State in the Nationale Maatschappij der Pijpleidingen, the national gas pipeline company.

B. The Construction and Operation of Gas Facilities: The Transmission Permit

The Federal Gas Law subjects the construction and operation of gas transmission facilities (*i.e.*, all pipelines, including direct lines and upstream facilities, storage facilities, LNG facilities, buildings and equipment) to the issuance of a prior permit granted by the federal energy minister if such facilities are used or intended for certain forms of supply as defined in Article 2, paragraph 1, of the Federal Gas Law.

Article 2, paragraph 1, of the Federal Gas Law lists the types of uses or intended uses that will bring gas transmission facilities within the scope of the federal permit requirement. Among the more significant of such uses are:
- the supply of gas distribution companies;
- the supply of final customers consuming on a permanent and consumption-site basis at least 1 million m^3 of gas per year;
- the transit through Belgium (without distribution or delivery in Belgium) of gas; and
- the supply of a final customer to which the local distribution company delivers insufficient quantities in accordance with the general conditions of the relevant delivery agreement.

By implication, other forms of gas transport are deemed to fall within the scope of gas distribution (and hence subject to the jurisdiction of the regions), which is generally defined as the supply of gas via local pipeline networks to customers established in the territory of one or more municipalities.

The federal permit requirement also applies to the construction and operation of direct lines.[34] A permit will be granted only if no offer is made to use the interconnected system at "reasonable economic and technical conditions".

Transmission companies must maintain and develop their facilities under economically acceptable conditions and with due regard to the environment. They must not discriminate between system users or classes of system users, in particular in favour of related companies. The federal energy minister is empowered to enjoin transmission companies to construct such connections or to make such improvements as he deems appropriate, provided they are economically justified or a customer undertakes to bear the additional cost involved.

C. The Supply of Natural Gas: The Supply Permit

The regular supply of natural gas to Belgian customers consuming on a permanent and consumption site basis at least 1 million m^3 of gas per year and to Belgian distribution

---

[34] Direct lines are defined as all gas transmission (as distinguished from distribution) lines that are not part of the interconnected system.

companies is subject to supply permit granted by the federal energy minister.[35] This federal permit requirement does not apply to supplies made by distribution companies within their respective networks. The criteria governing the granting of supply permits are to be determined by royal decree.

D. The Opening up of the Market: Eligible Customers

The Federal Gas Law designates as eligible customers:
– customers established outside Belgium who by virtue of the law of another EU Member State are entitled to enter into contracts for the supply of natural gas with a supplier of their choice;
– customers established in Belgium as follows:[36]
– *producers of electricity*, for the quantities of natural gas needed for electricity generation;[37]
– *final customers connected to a transmission system and consuming at least* 25 million m[3] natural gas on a consumption-site basis (this threshold is reduced to 15 million m[3] as of 10 August 2003 and to 5 million m[3] as of 1 October 2006; as of 10 October 2010, all final customers connected to a transmission network will be fully eligible);
– *distribution companies*, for the quantities of natural gas used by the customers designated (by the regional authorities) as eligible within the distribution network, provided that distribution companies shall as of 1 October 2006, in addition, be eligible for 33% of the balance of their requirements and become fully eligible as of 1 October 2010.

E. Access to the Transmission Systems

Belgium has opted for the system of negotiated access to transmission systems. Eligible customers and (as concerns supplies to eligible customers) holders of supply permits have access to each transmission network on the basis of agreements freely negotiated with the relevant transmission company. The parties must negotiate access to the network in good faith.

---

[35] Article 15/3 Federal Gas Law.

[36] The first phase of the market opening (through 10 August 2003) is expected to represent approximately 47% of natural gas consumption in Belgium.

[37] By royal decree, combined heat and power producers and auto-producers may until 1 October 2000 be made eligible only if their consumption exceeds a minimum quantity to be determined in the decree (subject to a maximum of 5 million m[3] per year per production unit).

The transmission companies are required to publish annually their main commercial conditions for the use of their network. A code of conduct regulating access to the transmission networks is to be determined by royal decree. The transmission companies may refuse access to their network in one of the following circumstances:
- insufficient capacity;
- the requested access would prevent the proper performance by the transmission company of its public service obligations; or
- the requested access would cause economic and financial difficulties for the transmission company due to take-or-pay contracts concluded by it prior to 1 January 1998.

Each refusal of access must be justified and, when based on the take-or-pay difficulties, must be authorized by the CREG.[38]

F. The Regulation of Natural Gas Prices

The system of official price controls (recommendations by the CCEG; maximum prices set by the federal minister for the economy) remains unchanged as regards the natural gas prices that may be charged to ineligible final customers (the so-called "captive market"). As regards the supply of natural gas to eligible final customers, the minister *may* set maximum prices, acting upon the recommendation of the CREG.

Maximum prices set by the minister must aim to prevent cross-subsidization between categories of customer and to ensure that a fair share of the benefits of market liberalization accrue to private and professional users (in particular the small and medium-sized enterprises) by way of price reductions.

G. Public Service Obligations

The Federal Gas Law empowers the federal government to impose, by way of royal decree, public service obligations upon the holders of transmission permits as regards the investments to be made for the benefit of ineligible customers, to the extent such investments are economically justified.

Similarly, public service obligations may be imposed upon the holders of supply permits as regards the regularity and quality of the supply of natural gas and as regards the supply of the distribution companies[39] and other customers, to the extent they are ineligible. As a

---

[38] Any such authorization shall cease as of 1 October 2006.

[39] Pursuant to Article 181 of the law of 8 August 1980, on budgetary proposals 1979-1980, the distribution companies must bear the cost incurred by the gas companies on account of their public service obligations as regards the supply of the distribution companies.

result, public service obligations as regards the security of supply may be imposed only to the extent necessary to protect the supply of the "captive" market. In the event of an overall supply crisis, the government must make use of the crisis provision in Article 23 of the Federal Gas Law, pursuant to which protective measures (including temporary derogations from the provisions of the Federal Gas Law) may be taken by royal decree.

H. Unbundling of Accounts

The Federal Gas Law requires gas companies[40] set up under Belgian law, which are vertically or horizontally integrated, to unbundle their internal accounts as regards their gas transmission, distribution and storage actives, as well as regards their activities outside the gas sector. The financial statements must disclose all significant transactions with related companies. However, separate balance sheets and profit & loss accounts for each activity are not required to be disclosed (but must be prepared internally).[41]

I. Protection Against Abusive Behaviour

The Federal Gas Law contains provisions on the protection against abusive behaviour, similar to those in the Federal Electricity Law.

---

[40] The term is defined to include all entities producing, transporting, distributing, supplying, buying and/or storing gas, with the exception of final customers.

[41] The CREG has access to the gas companies' internal accounting records.

*Nicolas Charbit**

COUNTRY REPORT: FRANCE

I. INTRODUCTION: THE CONTEXT OF FRENCH IMPLEMENTATION

A. Implementation Discussed and Postponed: Law no. 2000-108 of 10 February 2000 relating to the Modernization and Development of the Public Electricity Service

Once again, the French legislator was behind time in the implementation of a Community Directive. Even though a White Paper was published early 1998, allowing the Competition Council[1] and the Economic and Social Council[2] to give their opinion, it was not until 14 December 1998 that the Bill, relating to the modernization and development of the public electricity sector was circulated. The Parliament voted on a first version of the Bill on 2 March 1999. The Bill was finally passed on 10 February 2000, nearly one year after the EC deadline set up by the Directive 96/92/EC (the "Electricity Directive"), in the form of Law no. 2000-108 relating to the modernization and development of the public electricity service (the "Electricity Law").

However, the effects of this delay were limited, as EDF and the public authorities involved understood that the flaws in the text risked creating a legal lacuna detrimental to the legal validity of agreements. In fact, it has been suggested that there was a risk of direct applicability of the Electricity Directive,[3] and even before any implementation or transitional measure had been adopted, the first major contract had been signed by Unisor with a competitor of EDF. Furthermore, in order to deal with one of the aspects of this risk, a System Access Bureau was created at the beginning of March 1999 to ensure the transmission of electricity bought by eligible consumers from a supplier other than EDF.[4]

---

* *Avocat to the Paris Court of appeal;* author of "The Public Sector and Competition Law", *LGDJ-Joly,* 1999; "Electricity in Europe, Compared Implementation of the EC 96/92 Directive of 15 March 1999", *Gazette européenne du Palais,* 12 June 1999 and "Third Party Access in the Energy Sector", *Oil and Gas Law Review,* 1995/1. The author's views in this article represent his own views and do not bind any other person or entity.

[1] See Cons. Conc., Opinion No. 98-A-05, 28 April 1998, *BOCCRF,* 16 July 1998, p. 383.

[2] See Cons. Eco. Soc., *"The future regulation of the French electricity market",* sessions of 12 and 13 May 1998.

[3] See particularly, A.-M. Frison Roche, in *Le Monde,* 28 February 1999; *La Tribune,* 3 March 1999; *Le Figaro,* 3 March 1999; see *infra* C.

[4] See *Les Echos,* 12 March 1999.

Damien Geradin (ed.), The Liberalization of Electricity and Natural Gas in the European Union, 123–153
©2001 Kluwer Law International. Printed in the Netherlands.

B. Improved Implementation? The Gas Bill

Directive 98/30/EC of 22 June 1998 concerning the common rules applying to the internal natural gas market (the "Gas Directive") should have been implemented in the national legislation of each of the Member States of the European Union by 10 August 2000 at the latest. As of 1st June 2000, France had still not implemented the Gas Directive in its domestic legislation, but the legislative process has, to a great extent, already started.[5] First, the French Government published a White Paper on 18 June 1999 entitled "*Towards the Future Organisation of the French Gas Industry*", containing the blueprint of the French Bill.[6] Then it put MP Nicole Bricq in charge of consulting the parties involved in the implementation of the Directive; Mme Bricq presented her findings on 28 October 1999.[7] She particularly stressed that, from the point of view of opening the market to competition, *Gaz de France* (GDF) should have its role developed in downstream services and upstream supplies, through investments and acquisitions which could be financed by opening up its capital to partners like *Electricité de France* (EDF) and the national petroleum operator, whilst maintaining the State as majority shareholder. The above findings were referred to in a report by the Economic and Social Council, presented on 27 October 1999, highlighting the need for GDF to form industrial and financial alliances, preferably with EDF and *TotalFina*.[8]

Finally, as a last step in this preliminary legislative process, the Council of Ministers adopted a bill relating to the modernization of the natural gas public service and the development of gas companies which was transmitted to Parliament on 17 May 2000 (below the "Gas Bill"). In this Gas Bill, the French Government opted for minimal liberalization of the market in compliance with the minimum threshold of the Gas Directive for the opening up of the market to competition.

The major French gas operators recently united in order to form the Industrial Union of Private Gas Industries (*Union professionnelle des industries privées du gaz, UPRIGAZ*). The aim of this union is the protection of the interests of private operators, particularly as against public powers. The members are *Suez Lyonnaise des Eaux* and its subsidiary company *Elyo*, *Elf Aquitaine Gaz*, *TotalFina*, *Dalkia* (subsidiary of *Vivendi*) and *Gaz du Sud-Ouest* (70% of their shares are held by Elf and 30% by GDF). The scene was then set for industrial lobbying to take place at Parliament.

---

[5] See S. Wormser, "Structure of the gas market and implementation of the Gas Directive in France", *JCPE*, 17 February 2000.

[6] Secretary of State to Industry, DGEMP, "Vers la future organisation gazière française" *(White Paper)*, 18 June 1999.

[7] N. Bricq, Report to the Prime Minister, "Mission de réflexion et de concertation sur la transposition de la directive européenne sur le marché intérieur du gaz", 27 October 1999.

[8] Cons. Eco. And Soc., "Opinion relating to the future regulation of the French Gas Industry", 26-27 October 1999.

C. Direct Applicability of the Electricity and Gas Directives

The French delay in implementing the Electricity Directive unsettled the French electricity sector. Some believed that this delay revealed a protectionist attitude on the part of the State and its incumbent and they threatened to directly invoke the Electricity Directive in order to benefit, even prior to any implementation, from the EC liberalizing measures. This issue, now resolved by the passing of the Electricity Law, continues to generate particular interest with respect to the delay in the implementation of the Gas Directive in France and in some other Member States of the Union.

In order to ensure the "useful effect" of Community law, the European Court of Justice (ECJ), in certain circumstances, has allowed individuals to directly invoke the provisions of a directive that has not yet been implemented. In fact it is not legitimate for a State that fails to implement a directive within the stipulated time limits, to take advantage of its own failure and to thereby challenge rights conferred by Community law on individuals. Likewise, this theory allows individuals to directly invoke the directive when that directive has not been correctly implemented in national law; thus, national implementation only "exhausts" a Community directive insofar as such implementation is effected properly.

The capacity to directly invoke directives is however limited by a series of conditions. First of all a directive can only have direct applicability after the expiry of its implementation deadline.[9] Thereafter, some of its provisions may have direct applicability and others may not.[10] In addition, only specific and unconditional provisions of the directive can be directly invoked by individuals.[11]

Finally, direct applicability of a directive exists only by way of vertical effect, that is to say, by an individual taking action against a State; a directive that is not implemented cannot be invoked by one individual against another; in other words, there is no direct horizontal effect as between individuals.[12] The ECJ developed a wide interpretation of the term "State"; a directive with direct applicability can therefore be invoked against bodies or entities that are subject to the authority or control of the State.[13]

With regard to these criteria, the first step is to ascertain which provisions are likely to have direct applicability; in fact the requirement that these provisions be specific and unconditional, demands that such assessment be made on a case-by-case basis. Article 19 of the Electricity Directive seems to establish in a specific and unconditional manner the beneficiaries of the sector liberalization. Indeed, even if this provision gives Member States the freedom to stipulate which clients on their territory will have the capacity to enter into supply contracts, it provides, *inter alia*, that such end-users consuming over 100 GW/h/year

---

[9]   ECJ, *Ratti*, 5 April 1979, ECR p. 1645.

[10] ECJ, *Becker*, 19 January 1982, ECR p.72.

[11] ECJ, *Francovich*, 19 November 1991, ECR p. 5357.

[12] ECJ, *Marshall*, 2 August 1993, ECR p. 436.

[13] ECJ, *Foster*, 12 July 1990, ECR p. 3343.

(on a consumption site basis and including auto-production) are to fall within this category. Therefore, every operator that meets the minimum eligibility criteria specifically outlined in the Electricity Directive appears to benefit from the system set up by the said Directive. The possibility of determining the beneficiaries of a directive with a significant degree of certainty has been considered to be typical of a directly applicable provision.[14] The same reasoning also applies with respect to Article 20.

It is more difficult to determine whether the Electricity Directive may be invoked with respect to the access provisions (Articles 16, 17 and 18). Firstly, it may be considered that the Electricity Directive laid down some of the rules aiming to provide eligible clients with system access and that, therefore, it confers on clients deemed to be eligible a right of access to the system. However, it may be contended that the Electricity Directive allows a Member State the discretion to choose among the various types of access (negotiated access or single buyer, see Article 16) and that, therefore, it cannot have direct applicability with regard to these access provisions. However, the ECJ has held that the fact that a directive allows the States the freedom to choose among various options for the purpose of achieving a specific result, in no way prevents an individual from invoking rights conferred on him in a sufficiently specific manner.[15]

However, a more fundamental objection to the unconditional nature of the access right seems to exist in Article 3 which provides that "The Member States may decide not to apply the provisions (particularly those relating to negotiated access, to the sole buyer or to the direct lines) insofar as the application of these provisions would obstruct the performance, in law or in fact, of the obligations imposed on the electricity undertakings in the general economic interest and insofar as the development of trade would not be affected to such an extent as would be contrary to the interests of the Community". This issue remains unresolved.

Assuming that the direct applicability of Article 19 or any other provision of the Electricity Directive could have been established, the second issue relates to whether EDF may be likened to the State. The *Foster* case[16] supports an affirmative response. According to this decision, unconditional and sufficiently specific provisions of a directive may be invoked by any person against bodies or entities that are subject to the authority or control of the State or that have exorbitant powers in comparison with powers that are derived from rules that govern the relations of private individuals. In that case, the ECJ held that the directive was applicable against a body which, irrespective of its legal form, was commissioned by a public authority to provide, under the control of the said public authority, a service in the public interest and which had been endowed, for this purpose, with powers that were exorbitant when compared with the rules governing relations among private individuals. According to this decision, regarding direct applicability, EDF (an industrially

---

[14] ECJ, *Francovich*.

[15] ECJ, *Francovich*.

[16] ECJ, *Foster*.

and commercially public body created by the Act of 8 April 1946 and the monopolist provider of electricity production, transmission and distribution) should be treated in the same way as the French State.

Thus, it is likely that operators would have been able to invoke successfully the direct applicability of certain provisions of the Electricity Directive. This preliminary analysis is supported by the attitude of EDF itself. In fact, without even waiting for the passing of the Electricity Law, EDF had created a System Access Bureau for eligible consumers. The said Bureau, under the authority of EDF's delegate André Merlin, is in charge of regulating the transmission of electricity purchased by eligible undertakings from a supplier other than EDF.[17] Likewise, it is noted that EDF itself, in the recitals of its new contracts for the provision of electricity, expressly recognized the direct applicability of Articles 19 and 20 of the Electricity Directive. Thus, any issue relating to the direct applicability of the Gas Directive should be resolved along the lines of the precedent of the Electricity Directive.

II. ENERGY AS A PUBLIC SERVICE

A. The Public Energy Service Obligations are Broadly Defined

The Electricity and Gas Directives set out in a similar way the obligations of the public energy services in each of their Articles 2 and 3: i) security of installations and supplies; ii) regularity; iii) quality; iv) price; v) environmental protection and vi) social cohesion. This provision goes beyond the principles stated in the cases *Municipality of Almelo* and *Commission/France*, thus illustrating the broad French approach of the Electricity and Gas Directives. Such an approach raises the issue of the freedom of Member States to set up public service obligations in the context of EC harmonization directives.

---

[17] According to the letter of appointment sent by Mr. François Roussely, EDF Chairman, to Mr. André Merlin, the latter is temporarily in charge of "negotiations with authorised third parties or their agents as to technical specifications regarding connection to and use of the transmission system, as well as billing methods"; further, he is required to "set up a system safeguarding the confidentiality of commercially sensitive information". The transmission costs shall be billed in accordance with a public tariff, annexed to the letter of appointment which takes into account not only capacity but also the length of time of system use.

1. The Wide Approach to Energy Public Service Obligations

1.1. THE ELECTRICITY LAW: FROM "LONG-TERM PLANNING" TO "PLURIANNUAL PROGRAMMING"

France is unique in that the "public electricity service" is defined particularly broadly. Thus, under Article 1 of the Electricity Law, the public electricity service aims, in the public interest, to ensure the supply of electricity throughout the national territory (paragraph 1).

Within the framework of the energy policy, the French public electricity service contributes to the independence and security of supply, the fight against air pollution and the greenhouse effect, the optimal management and development of national resources, the stabilization of energy demands, the competitiveness of economic activity and the making of technological choices for the future as to the rational use of energy (paragraph 2).

This public service contributes to social cohesion (supplying electricity to non-eligible customers through the equalization of tariffs, supplying electricity to all eligible customers unable to find a supplier), as well as to defence and public safety (paragraph 3).

Pursuant to Article 2-I, the mission of a balanced electricity supply aims to achieve the objectives defined in the pluriannual programming of the production investments as decided by the Minister for Economy and to ensure supply to all areas that are not interconnected to the national system (the DOM-TOM).

The pluriannual programming of production investments constitutes the most significant of these particularly detailed provisions concerning public service missions. This provision is based on the Electricity Directive concept of long-term planning. We will see below how this concept is employed in the context of funding the cost of public service.

1.2. THE GAS BILL

Articles 1, 2 and 3 of the Gas Bill appear to be similar to the Electricity Law provisions in that they provide a variety of public service obligations, going beyond the Gas Directive: national supply of natural gas, rational development of services, environmental protection, rational use of energy, competitiveness of economic activity, social cohesion, balanced development of the territory, research, technological progress, etc.

The issue raised by these generous provisions, characteristic of the typical French public service notion, relates to the scope of freedom that the Member States have, within the framework of the Directives studied, to determine certain public service obligations.

2. The Scope of Freedom of Member States, within the Framework of the Electricity and Gas Directives, to Determine Public Service Obligations

In theory, EC law recognises the sovereignty of Member States to determine the nature and extent of public service obligations and duties that the States intend to entrust to certain companies or undertakings. Thus, in its Communication on services of general interest, the Commission emphasized the freedom of Member States to determine obligations in the public interest and to grant the special or exclusive rights that are necessary to ensure that such obligations are fulfilled.[18] Furthermore, the ECJ acknowledged that Member States have "wide discretion to regulate certain matters taking into account socio-cultural factors".[19]

2.1. CAN MEMBER STATES ADD TO THE PUBLIC SERVICE OBLIGATIONS ENUMERATED BY THE DIRECTIVES?

In the case of directives creating a common policy, the freedom of Member States to define public service obligations is limited by the Directives: the creation of a common policy leads to Community harmonization. Thus, Article 100 A of the Treaty (now Article 95), which constitutes the legal basis of the Electricity and Gas Directives, authorises the Commission to proceed to the harmonization of legal, regulatory and administrative provisions of the Member States.

The ECJ has, on numerous occasions, referred to the exhaustion of national competence to enact new or additional measures that are in conflict with a directive.[20] In particular, the competence to create measures intended to protect the public interest – relevant here – appears entirely exhausted in the case where a directive has expressly provided for derogation or safeguard clauses.[21]

The limited character of Article 3.2 is confirmed by recital 13 of the Electricity Directive: "For certain Member States, the imposition of public service obligations may be necessary to ensure security of supply and consumer and environmental protection, which, in their view, free competition, left to itself, cannot necessarily guarantee". This recital is identical to recital 12 of the Gas Directive.

---

[18] EC Communication on services of general interest in Europe, OJ 281/3, 26 09 1996, point 16. For a commentary, see D. Simon and F. Lagondet, "La Communication de la Commission sur les services d'intérêt général en Europe", *Europe*, January 1997, p. 4; for the opinion of the DG IV of the Commission: see J. -L. Bundia, "Services d'intérêt général en Europe et politique communautaire de concurrence", *Competition policy newsletter*, Vol. 2 No. 3, Autumn/Winter 1996, p. 14 and 41.

[19] ECJ, Case C-275/92, *Schindler*, ECR 1994, p. I-1039, point 61; Case T-106/95, *FFSA*, ECR 1997, p. II 229, point 99; Case T-32/93, *Ladbroke II*, ECR 1994, p. II 1015, point 37. The issues examined by the ECJ in these cases concern sectors as diverse as telecommunications, public postal services and horse betting.

[20] ECJ, Case 65/75, *Tasca*, ECR 1976, p. 291; Case 5/77, *Denkavit*, ECR 1977, p. 155.

[21] ECJ, Case 227/82, *Van Bennekom*, ECR 1983, p.3883.

However, these Directives do not eliminate entirely the margin for manoeuvre of the Member States. The Electricity Directive contains several provisions intended to provide greater freedom to the States (such as the designation of eligible clients, Article 19.4; temporary security measures, Article 23; costs incurred, Article 24, etc.). This is the same in the case of the Gas Directive (concerning permits to build or operate natural gas installations, gas mains and equipment, Article 3.3 together with Article 4; refusing system access where there is a lack of capacity or where access hinders the performance of public service obligations, Article 17; applications for derogations relating to *take or pay* contracts, Article 25, etc.). The presence of these derogations or stand still provisions suggests that the States lack the freedom to add on any new derogation provisions.

The practice of the Commission in sectorial liberalization directives, also confirms the exhaustion of a State's right to enact new provisions. Thus, a directive of 15 December 1997 defines the purpose of universal service in the postal sector.[22] This definition restricted the States from being able to redefine such a universal service. This is unequivocally emphasized in the Communication interpreting this directive which states that the service in respect of which the Member States may reserve special or exclusive rights to themselves, insofar as that is necessary for the maintenance of universal service, is harmonized by the postal services Directive.[23]

Thus, it is doubtful that Member States have the capacity to add further obligations to the public service obligations defined by the Electricity and Gas Directives. In any case, "public service obligations" going beyond the provisions of these Directives appear to be, in themselves, contrary to these Directives.

2.2. CAN NEW PUBLIC SERVICE OBLIGATIONS BE ADDED TO THOSE PROVIDED BY THE ELECTRICITY AND GAS DIRECTIVES?

In spite of the above Community restriction justified by the principle of harmonization, the French provisions seem to include public service obligations which are not provided for at all in the Directives.

No trace can be found in the Electricity and Gas Directives of some French public missions based on "the fulfilment of the objectives of pluriannual programming". This term is said to implement the notion of long-term planning provided in similar terms by Article 3.2 in each of the two Directives. However, as such programming cannot be provided without taking account of the economic interests of the public body over which the Minister exercises his authority, one may speculate as to whether the Electricity Law does not set up the programming of EDF. Such an interpretation of the concept of long-term

---

[22] Directive 97/67/EC of 15 December 1997, OJ L 15/14, 21 January 1998, article 3.

[23] "Communication on the application of competition rules in the postal sector", OJ C 39/2, 6 February 1998, point 8.2.

programming by the Minister was not provided by the EC legislature.

Further, the Electricity Law adds to the public service obligations restrictively authorized by the Electricity Directive numerous other obligations such as "competitiveness in economic activity", "optimal management of national resources", "development of technological options of the future" (Article 1, paragraph 2), "economic efficacy" (Article 1, paragraph 4), and "balanced development" (Article 2.I).

These obligations, presented as "public service obligations" and authorized by the Electricity Directive, must be interpreted in accordance with the requirement found in the Directive for a clear, transparent and non-discriminatory definition of public service obligations (Article 3.2).

Expressions such as "balanced development" or "optimal management of national resources" do not appear to be sufficiently clear. There is a risk that such ambiguity in definition may remove all transparency from the said expressions, and new operators may have to carry over the costs of the traditional operator leading to the possible conclusion that this is discriminatory. The obligation of "competitiveness in economic activity" is faced with the same criticism. It may be argued that the Electricity Law aims to finance the development and the competitive strength of the traditional operator.[24]

But, most of all, Community law is opposed to all legislation the aim of which is to protect strictly economic national interests.[25] The above provisions in the Electricity Law clearly appear to have the aim of encouraging the protection of national economic interests. This is particularly the case with the concept of "competitiveness in economic activity".

The same applies with respect to the Gas Directive. One would hope that the French legislator, sensitive to the criticisms of the Commission and neighbouring States, will adopt terms that are less protectionist and more compliant with EC law. The strategic aspect of these criticisms appears when turning to the issue of financing such public service obligations.

B. Generous Means of Finance

The Electricity public service fund, as with the Gas public service fund, were not provided for by the Electricity and Gas Directives. The requirement to make contributions to the Electricity and Gas Public Service Funds (1) gives rise to questions as to the lawfulness of the existence and operation of such funds (2).

---

[24] The EDF Chairman, Mr. Roussely, thus stated before the Exchange Commission: "EDF has a certain number of advantages related to its public service missions and its strong competitive position.... EDF must be given the means to be as prosperous in the competitive market as it was in a monopoly" (speech of 13 January 1999, *Bataille Report*, T. 1, p. 56)

[25] ECJ, Case 352/85, *Bond*, ECR p. 1988, p. 2085; Case C-17/92, *FEDICINE*, ECR 1993, p. I 2239.

1. Contribution to Public Service Funds

1.1. ELECTRICITY PUBLIC SERVICE AND ELECTRICITY EQUALIZATION FUNDS

The Electricity public service fund was created by Article 5-I of the Electricity Law. The purpose of the Fund is the sharing of the costs of public service obligations that are payable by all electricity producers. Although public service obligations are defined in a manner that is particularly wide, as seen above, the expenses related to such missions are specifically enumerated and limited: i) to the over costs which may result from contracts resulting from calls for tenders or from EDF's obligation to purchase the production of an installation implementing sophisticated techniques in terms of energy efficiency (such as cogeneration, the use of waste, the use of regenerated energy); ii) to production over costs in areas not interconnected to the continental metropolitan system (the case of the overseas departments and territories of France); and iii) to research and development over costs necessary to increase the transmission capacities of electric lines.

It will be noted that, as with the telecommunications sector, the Electricity Public Service Fund is funded by contributions that are due and payable by all operators, producers, suppliers, distributors, auto-producers beyond a specific production threshold, and even end-users that are electricity importers. Thus, producers are in the special position of being beneficiaries of the Fund as operators involved in certain public service missions and contributors to the Fund. The calculation of such contribution is made on a *pro rata* basis in accordance with the kW/h delivered to the end-user. But there is no doubt that EDF will be the main beneficiary of the Fund.

Finally, the funding of the public service costs is shared with the Electricity Equalization Fund that had been created by the Nationalisation Act of 8 April 1946.[26] The main purpose of this Fund is the spreading of costs incurred by the distribution organizations (and not the production undertakings). Further, this Fund contributes, with respect to social cohesion, to the social scheme created in favour of lower income groups and for town and country planning (Article 5-II), as is done in similar terms by the scheme used in the gas sector.

1.2. THE GAS EQUALIZATION FUND

As with the Electricity equalization fund, Article 33 of the 8 April 1946 Act on the nationalization of electricity and gas also created a fund for gas equalization. It is this Fund, never used before, which has been resuscitated in order to finance the expenses of some public service missions as defined by the Gas Bill.

---

[26] Article 33 of Act No. 46-628 dated 8 April 1946 on the nationalization of electricity and gas.

The singularity of the Gas Bill is to limit contributions to the cost of public service obligations solely to the task of supplying natural gas. These costs include contributions towards town and country planning and to the scheme set up in favour of lower income groups and underprivileged persons (Article 5).

Thus, the contribution of gas operators to public gas services appears limited, in comparison with the Electricity Law. As suggested by the State Secretary for Industry, this might be explained by the fact that certain public service costs have a natural counterpart in the exclusive rights of the distribution monopoly that GDF and the non-nationalized distributors continue to benefit from.[27]

However, in spite of this formal limitation, no provision of the Gas Bill allows an evaluation of the actual costs which are to be imposed on these operators.[28]

2. The Legal Basis for, and the Lawfulness of, Operator Contributions to the Electricity and Gas Service Funds

2.1. THE ANTI-COMPETITIVE CHARACTER OF PUBLIC SERVICE FUNDS

The equalization system relating to public service costs appears to be based on a mechanism supported by French law as well as by Community law. One may however question the validity of contributions to such funds by new operators, especially since these contributions are being made for the benefit of the incumbents. The new competitors should be the ones benefiting from the deregulation intended by the EC liberalization legislation and, conversely, the incumbent, having already benefited from revenues because of its monopoly position, should allow some ground to these competitors, in order to stimulate innovation, quality of service, and last but not least, competitive prices for consumers.

This theoretical presupposition clearly appears in the asymmetrical regulation of a number of liberalized sectors in Europe and elsewhere. Asymmetrical regulation means the differentiation of costs and regulatory constraints incurred by the former monopoly and the new entrants in favour of the said new entrants: new operators have the benefit of reduced regulation which aims at balancing the disparity between them and the incumbent benefiting from a market share and market forces automatically placing it in a dominant

---

[27] White Paper, p. 24.

[28] Thus, the White Paper provided that "The implementation of the Directive must allow room for the continuation of the public service. It is up to the public authorities to ensure the economic balance of the implementation of public service missions and to ensure, if necessary, the setting up of mechanisms for the financing of these obligations, on the basis of a precise definition of the said obligations and a rigorous evaluation of their cost", p. 24.

position right from the outset of the deregulation process.[29] Public service funds imposing a contribution on new entrants seem to overlook this principle of differentiation of constraints. Thus, the creation of such funds may appear to be potentially restrictive in the new competition environment created by the Directives.[30]

The organization of transport sectors appears to support this point of view. In the air transport sector, where EC Regulation 2408/92 expressly provides for the imposition of certain public service obligations and the possibility of sharing these obligations, the Air transport equalization fund is funded solely by passengers by means of a tax paid on each ticket, and not by the airlines themselves. This is the same in respect of the ground transport sector, even though the principle governing this fund is different: if the contributors are not the direct users but the States and their public service undertakings, or the licensees of the public services, the only beneficiaries of the fund are the undertakings that carry out transport by rail, road and navigable routes.

In contrast, besides the case of transport, the other deregulated sectors that have been studied seem to favour contributions to liberalization costs being made by new operators, for the benefit of former monopolies. This is the case, on the basis of various terms and conditions, with postal services, telecommunications and energy. However, a substantial difference distinguishes the latter of these three sectors: the Electricity and Gas public service funds are not authorized by any Community provision. One may therefore question whether they have been lawfully established.

2.2. NO LEGAL BASIS FOR THE ENERGY PUBLIC SERVICE FUNDS

Unlike the telecommunications sector, there is no foundation in the Gas and Electricity Directives for the Electricity public service fund or the Gas public service fund. The Electricity Law expressly provides that the expenses incurred in performing the public service obligations assigned to producers are spread between all of them, as well as distributors, importers and end users. This provision of the Law was hotly debated by MPs. The Gas Bill provides for a similar system whilst significantly limiting the scope thereof; thus, at this stage, the criticism relating to this aspect of the implementation of the Electricity Directive may not be aimed at the Gas Bill.

Where a directive is silent, one must take into account the purpose of the directive if one is to establish the validity of setting up such financing. The principle of useful effect of EC law requires that the choice of the implementation instrument be dictated by a concern

---

[29] See for example, the telecommunications sector where interconnection tariffs of powerful operators are oriented on cost, whereas the principle of free determination of such prices is applied for other operators.

[30] Regarding the telecommunications universal service fund, certain commentators did not fail to emphasize that such a solution amounted to causing "the competitors of France Télécom to contribute to the financing of the public operator through the fund", J. Chevallier, "La nouvelle réforme des télécommunications: ruptures, continuités", *RFDA* 1996, p. 909.

to ensure the full and proper operation of a directive.[31] Thus, according to the ECJ, it is incumbent on Member States to choose, in the framework of the freedom allowed to them by Article 189 of the Treaty,[32] the most appropriate forms and means with a view to ensuring the proper operation of directives, taking into account the purpose of such directives.[33] In other words, the instruments of implementation must ensure that the result sought by the directive is fully achieved.[34]

In the context studied here, in order to respect the principle of useful effect, the objectives sought by the Electricity Directive must be clearly identified by reference to its preamble and parliamentary debates. According to Recital 7 of the Directive, the first beneficiaries of the liberalization of the electricity sector are industrial operators, final consumers and producers.[35] Moreover, Recital 18 emphasises that the implementation "will have an impact on the activities [of undertakings entrusted with the operation of services of general economic interest] ".[36] Finally, in the mind of the "Community legislature",[37] as well as the French legislature, there is no doubt that the primary objective of the opening up to competition is to promote a drop in prices for eligible consumers.[38]

The aim of the Electricity Law appears to run counter to that. EDF's Chairman himself

---

[31] The principle of "effet utile" arises from Article 10 (former Article 5) of the EC Treaty which provides that Member States take all appropriate measures, whether general or particular, to ensure fulfilment of the obligations arising out of this Treaty or resulting from action taken by the institutions of the Community. The ECJ held that Article 10 constitutes for Member States a general obligation to ensure the full effect of Community law; see D. Simon, *La Directive européenne*, Dalloz, Connaissance du droit: 1997, p. 42.

[32] Article 249 (former Article 189(3)) of the Treaty provides that a directive shall be binding as to the result to be achieved, upon each Member State to which it is addressed, but shall leave to the national authorities the choice of form and methods.

[33] ECJ, Case 48/75, *Royer*, 8 April 1976, Rec. p. 497.

[34] More generally, the competence left to Member States as to the form and methods depends always on the result that the Council or the Commission wishes to bring about. In other words, according to Professor D. Simon, the freedom of the national authorities is only a monitored freedom, the use of which is measured in relation to the need for effective fulfilment of the objectives of the Community directive; D. Simon, *La Directive européenne, op. cit.*, p. 40; in this context see ECJ, Case 38/77, *Enka*, 23 November 1977, ECR p. 2212; ECJ, Case 102/79, *Commission/Belgium*, 6 May 1980, ECR p. 1473, sp. p. 1485.

[35] Refer to Recital 7 of the Electricity Directive.

[36] Recital 18 of the Electricity Directive.

[37] "…These benefits are mostly seen from the consumers' point of view… However, liberalisation opens up new horizons for industry, too. Generators and suppliers have no longer to think in regional or national dimension… It is a primary task of Community competition policy to assist suppliers who wish to take advantage of the new possibilities and serve new customers when they encounter difficulties in their business expansion. The Commission will monitor that supply markets remain open for new entrants, now that monopoly rights are abolished." M. Albers, "View and expectations on the Competition Developments in the EU Electricity Market", Conference UNIPEDE/EURELECTRIC, Brussels, 24-25 March 1999, (Mr. Albers is the Head of the Energy Unit of the European Commission's Directorate General for Competition).

[38] Mr. Borotra himself, MP and negotiator of the Electricity Directive, emphasized during the discussions before the Parliament, that in multiplying the constraints on new producers, there was a risk of incompatibility with the Directive and the case-law of the ECJ; see 28 January 1999, *Rapport Bataille*, T. 1, p. 97.

did not hesitate to announce at the time of the parliamentary debates that "EDF has a certain number of advantages connected with public service obligations and its strong competitive position ... EDF must be given the means to be as prosperous in the competitive context as it was in the monopoly".[39] Likewise, the State Secretary for Industry, asserted that: "The introduction of competition should not be carried out to the detriment of the traditional operator of public service obligations...".[40] Therefore, even if the Electricity Law does not appear to seek to favour the former monopoly, it appears to protect it as much as possible. The requirement of a contribution to the Fund from all electricity operators is based on the presupposition that all operators are in a similar position, whereas one may question whether the underlying principle of any opening up of the market should not be the recognition of the different position between new competitors and the incumbent.

In conclusion, the imposition of public service costs on new operators – in respect of which the Electricity Law failed to stipulate the method of calculation and, therefore, failed to limit the amount thereof – may be of such nature as to compromise the deregulation of the market. In fact, the financing by new operators (together with EDF but mainly for and on its behalf), in terms of net contribution, of various public service obligations may substantially limit the financial capacity of these operators and, therefore, restrict their capacity to offer attractive prices to eligible clients, contrary to the true aim of the Electricity Directive.

III. THE LIMITED OPENING UP OF THE MARKET

A. Eligible Customers as First Beneficiaries of the Liberalization

1. The Eligibility of Electricity Customers

At the beginning of the year 2000, there were no less than 440 eligible clients who benefited from the opening up to competition, including Eurodif, Péchiney, Elf Atochem, Usinor-Sacilor, Solvay, SNCF, etc. The Electricity Law contains a specific provision for owners of railway networks meeting certain technical connection specifications. Thus, *Réseau Ferré de France* (RFF) is authorized to obtain electricity supplies competitively and to transfer such electricity to the SNCF (Article 22 II, paragraph 3).

---

[39] Hearing of 13 January 1999, *Rapport Bataille*, T. 1, p. 56-58.

[40] Hearing of 9 December 1998, *Rapport Bataille*, T. 1, p. 54.

1.1. THE ELIGIBILITY THRESHOLDS SET UP BY THE ELECTRICITY DIRECTIVE

Pursuant to Article 19 of the Electricity Directive, all end users consuming at least 100 GW/h per annum (on a consumption site basis and including auto-production) are eligible consumers and they may, therefore, purchase their electricity from producers of their choice.

It is up to the Member States to determine the selection criteria of other eligible clients, so that the opening of the market to competition is at least equal to the percentage determined at EC level. This must progressively increase over a period of six years, leading to an opening up from 26.48% in 1999[41] to 33% in 2003. Member States may go beyond the rules set forth in the Electricity Directive and adopt a greater opening of their respective markets; this is the case particularly with Italy, Germany and Belgium. The list of criteria chosen must be submitted to the Commission for publication in the OJ, no later than 31 January of each year. The Commission may request that such criteria be amended "insofar as they distort competition and adversely affect trade in a manner which is at variance with the common interest".

The deregulation process should normally lead to a comparable level of national market deregulation. However, in order to avoid the possibility of a frontier disequilibrium among Member States having chosen different degrees of liberalization, Article 19(5) of the Electricity Directive provides that an eligible client may from its State of origin freely purchase electricity from producers set up in another Member State, if it meets the eligibility conditions in such other State, that State not being able to refuse access to its transmission system. If the client fails to meet the eligibility conditions in one of the two Member States, the Commission may, taking into account the situation of the market and the common interest, compel the refusing party to supply the electricity in question at the request of the Member State on the territory of which the eligible client is established.[42]

1.2. THE ELECTRICITY LAW AND THE DECREE OF 29 MAY 2000: ELIGIBILITY BASED ON INDUSTRIAL SITE

According to the Electricity Law, the definition of eligible clients, authorized to conclude electricity purchase contracts with a supplier other than EDF, is to be set up by a decree to be adopted after consultation of the Conseil d'Etat (the highest administrative jurisdiction and advisory body to the government in matters of legislation), with the objective of respecting the degree of Community deregulation determined by the European Commission each year (Article 22-I).

Parliamentary debates led to the rejection of an amendment introducing the possibility

---

[41] OJ C 334/16, 31 October 1998.

[42] See Cons. conc., "Electricity Notice", op. cit., p. 383.

of adjusting the "per site" criterion by considering the electricity consumption structure in the intermediary consumption of each industrial sector. The Competition Council had emphasized that this could have produced the effect of disadvantaging French undertakings *vis-à-vis* their competitors in Member States that may have chosen a much greater sectorial opening, as well as favouring the sectors in which undertakings are consolidated into large industrial sites.

The Eligibility Decree was adopted on 29 May 2000. The purpose of this Decree is to set the eligibility thresholds and to set up the procedure determining eligibility and the conditions for the application of the eligibility thresholds in accordance with the annual electricity consumption. The Decree adopts the notion of "establishment", for the definition of the term "site", an establishment being identified by its SIRET registration number in the register held by the National Institute for Statistics and Economics (INSEE, Article 1). Such a definition of the "site" is similar to the one referred to by the European Commission for the purpose of annual calculation of the average share of Community electricity market. In compliance with the requirements of the Electricity Directive and the Electricity Law, Article 3 of the decree sets the eligibility threshold at 16 GWh (the draft Decree provided a threshold of 15 GWh).

Eligibility should be acquired for a period of two years (Article 1). This provision should guarantee industry with just sufficient visibility for the negotiation of supply contracts (the draft Decree provided for a period of three years).

2. The Eligibility of Gas Customers

2.1. A STEP BY STEP OPENING PROVIDED BY THE GAS DIRECTIVE

Eligible customers are allowed to choose freely their supplier of natural gas. The Gas Directive provides that end-users consuming more than 25M m^3 of gas per year and per site must be eligible by 10 August 2000 (Article 18.2). This threshold will be set at 15 Mm^3 at 10 August 2003 and at 5 Mm^3 at 10 August 2008 (Article 18.6). Each Member State must define eligible customers so as to ensure that the total gas consumption of such eligible customers is at least 20% of national gas consumption in August 2000, 28% in 2003 and 33% in 2008 (Article 18.4).

The continuous process established by the Directive takes into account the legitimate interests of Take or Pay operators who have concluded long-term agreements.

2.2. The Minimum Implementation Threshold in the Gas Bill

Article 6 of the Gas Bill provides that an end-user of natural gas, whose on-site annual consumption is greater than the threshold fixed by a decree to be taken after consultation of the *Conseil d'Etat,* is an eligible client with respect to such site. This threshold is defined in a manner allowing an opening of the national natural gas market of at least 20% as of 10 August 2000. It may not be greater than 25 million cubic metres.

The eligibility threshold should be decreased no later than 10 August 2003, then no later than 10 August 2008, in such a way as to allow liberalization of the national natural gas market that is at least equal to 28% and to 33% respectively. It may not be greater than 15 million cubic metres as of 10 August 2003 and 5 million cubic metres as of 10 August 2008.

Moreover, under the same provision, an eligible customer shall be any person producing electricity from natural gas, within the limits of its consumption of natural gas used for the production of electricity from a given site (provided that the same producer's installation does not have the benefit of a contract for electric energy which falls within the obligation to purchase under Article 10 of the Electricity Law or which falls within Article 50 of the same Law). Such customer is eligible with respect to the entire consumption of natural gas from that site, to the extent that its annual consumption of natural gas for the production of electricity is above a certain percentage of its total annual consumption from the said site set by governmental decree.

Finally, distributors that actually supply all customers located in their servicing zone are recognized as eligible clients, when the volume of natural gas that they purchase is greater than the threshold mentioned above.

B. Electricity Production

1. The Electricity Directive: The Choice Between Authorization and Tendering Procedures

Under Article 4 of the Electricity Directive, Member States may choose between a system of authorizations and/or a system of calling for tenders for the construction of new generating capacity. Article 5 of the Directive governs the authorization regime: the criteria proposed by the Member States may relate to the safety and security of electric systems, installations and equipment, environmental protection, choice of sites, use of public property, energy efficiency, nature of primary sources, specific attributes of the applicant (technical, economic and financial capacities). This regime applies automatically to independent producers.

Article 6 applies to calls for tenders: the procedure is based on a bi-annual provisional inventory drawn up by the transmission operator or any other competent authority. The procedure is identical to that of EC public procurement directives. The criteria that may be adopted are the same as those listed above. The identical criteria adopted by the Directive for both these procedures allow factors such as the nature of primary energy sources or the needs of public service obligations to be taken into account.

The conditions for the grant of the authorization or the award of the contract must be objective, transparent and non-discriminatory; the procedures must be public, and negative decisions must be reasoned. Member States must appoint an independent body for production, transmission and distribution that will be responsible for the setting up of review and follow-up of tender.

2. A Clear Preference for the Authorization Procedure in the Electricity Law

The Electricity Law formally adopts both systems relating to authorization and tenders (Articles 6, 7 and 8), while at the same time preferring the first of these options. In fact, it is only when production capacities fail to meet the objectives of pluriannual investment programming (and according to the parliamentary debates, "particularly those concerning the techniques of production and geographical localisation of installations") that the Minister of Energy may call for tenders, on the advice of the transmission system operator. The Minister appoints successful candidates according to the opinion of the Electricity Commission.

The preference for the authorization procedure is in line with the Competition Council opinion which emphasized the dynamic effect of this procedure compelling authorized producers to search for markets for the electricity produced, in contrast to EDF's purchase obligation under existing specific tenderings.

The local authorities, as well as their undertakings, semi-public (*sociétés d'économie mixte*) or public institutions, benefit from special treatment to the extent that (for and within the limits of the requirements of non-eligible clients located on their territory), they may operate new hydro-electric installations located on their territory with a capacity of less than 8000 kWh (Article 11-I). However, these authorities may produce electricity without any limitation on capacity, from new installations using renewable energy or waste, or any new installations for cogeneration or regeneration of energy intended for heating networks.

The only condition is that such installation must lead to energy savings or reduction of atmospheric pollution; but this proviso appears easy to satisfy in light of the very nature of these installations. This provision constitutes a compromise with the demands of the largest local authorities that wanted to be recognized as one single consumer, taking into account electricity consumption by public buildings and of public lighting, in order to benefit from the eligibility conditions.[43]

IV. THE CONTINUATION OF MONOPOLIES AS REGARDS SYSTEM ACCESS

A. Maintaining the Management Monopoly of Electricity Transmission Systems

1. The Transmission System Operator

1.1. A KEY FUNCTION IN THE ELECTRICITY DIRECTIVE

Article 7 of the Directive allows Member States to choose either to appoint a transmission system operator, or to require of the owners of the system(s) that they appoint an operator. Pursuant to Articles 7 and 8 of the Directive, the system operator is in charge of the fulfilment of three objectives: i) to provide interconnection and to ensure that the systems are properly maintained; ii) to balance supply and demand "in real time", given the inability to store electricity; iii) to bring about the transmission of energy of independent producers and foreign suppliers to their customers and the energy of auto-producers to their own companies and subsidiaries.

Article 7.6 of the Directive provides that "unless the transmission system is already independent from generation and distribution activities the system operator, shall be independent at least in management terms from other activities not relating to the transmission system". Article 8.1 of the Directive specifies moreover that the transmission system operator is "responsible for dispatching the generating installations in its area and for determining the use of interconnectors with other systems".

1.2. THE FRENCH SYSTEM ACCESS BUREAU AND THE DRAFT DECREE

The Electricity Law establishes EDF as the operator of the public electricity transmission system (Article 12(1)). EDF's obligations, defined in Article 14, are based on both the

---

[43] See Amorce/Energie Cités, "Loi électricité: Collectivités territoriales, Energies renouvelables", 3 June 1998.

provisions of the Directive and the public service principles as provided for in Articles 1 and 2. The EDF-TSO director is appointed, following a nomination proposed by the EDF chairman, by the Minister of Energy after receiving the advice of the Electricity Commission (Article 12(3)).

The provisions of the Electricity Law aim to confer on the operator the degree of independence as intended by the Directive. Thus, in addition to maintaining management independence *vis-à-vis* other EDF activities, it has the obligation, pursuant to Article 8.2 of the Directive, to provide in a non-discriminatory manner the dispatching of various generating installations and importation sources taking into account the order of economic precedence and technical constraints on the system (Article 15 II). In order to ensure that commercially sensitive information within the system operator's knowledge remains confidential, a fine of 100 000 FRF is provided (Article 16, MPs rejected the proposal to refer to the provisions of Article 226-13 NCPC (French New Penal Code) providing for stricter criminal liability). A draft decree dated 9 February 2000 stipulates what kind of information (held by public transmission and distribution system operators) would, if communicated, infringe competition rules.

As mentioned in the introduction, a System Access Bureau was created at the beginning of March 1999 prior to the passing of the Electricity Law to ensure the transmission of electricity purchased by eligible customers from a supplier other than EDF. The Bureau's task is to negotiate, with authorized third parties or their agents, technical conditions relating to connection and transmission system use, billing, and further to ensure the confidentiality of commercially sensitive information.[44] Transmission costs are billed according to a public tariff scale taking into account the market forces in play and the periods of system use. This Access Bureau thus foreshadows the future French regime applicable to transmission. It will be up to the Regulation Commission to propose to the competent Ministers tariffs for use of the transmission system (Article 36-I.1°).

2. The Distribution System Operator Regime

2.1. THE DSO'S LIABILITY FOR DEVELOPMENT AND INTERCONNECTION

The Directive provides for the appointment of a system operator, responsible for the development of a distribution system and interconnection with other systems. Such operator must ensure system security and must refrain from any discrimination, particularly in favour of its own subsidiaries or shareholders (Article 11).

---

[44] Letter of appointment from the EDF Chairman to Mr. A. Merlin, head of the System Access Bureau, see *Le Figaro*, 3 March 1999.

2.2. THE CONTINUATION OF THE FRENCH DISTRIBUTION SYSTEM

Electricity distribution in France will remain governed by the licensing regime under the Electricity Law: the local bodies and their undertakings remain the licensing authorities of the public electricity distributor (Article 17). EDF and 140 independent distributors are appointed as operators of public electricity distribution systems (Article 18). They are subject to the same non-discrimination and confidentiality obligations as the transmission system operator (Article 20, see also the draft Decree dated 9 February 2000 cited above). The Regulation Commission proposes tariffs to the competent Ministers for the use of distribution systems (Article 36-I.1°).

B. No Monopoly for the Management of Gas Transmission Systems

Pursuant to Article 6 of the Gas Bill, an eligible customer is authorized to purchase natural gas from an authorized supplier; an eligible customer therefore has access rights to infra-structures for the transmission and distribution of natural gas and to installations for natural liquefied gas.

1. Licences for the Transmission and Supply of Natural Gas and Access Rights

The Gas Bill, following the Gas Directive, sets up a licensing system for the transmission and supply of natural gas (Article 7, authorized supplier, and Articles 20-24, transmission operator). The granting criteria relate to technical and financial capacities, compliance with public service and security obligations. These provisions must be set forth by decree.

Article 8 of the Gas Bill provides access rights to infrastructure for the transmission and distribution of natural gas and to natural liquefied gas installations, by any operator operating such infrastructure and installations, for the purpose of ensuring the supply of natural gas to eligible clients as well as the performance of exportation contracts (1°), and the performance of contracts relating to the transit of natural gas through large transmission systems (2°).

Moreover, for the purpose of avoiding differentiated treatment between the system operator and the users of these works and installations, Article 8.2(2) prohibits discrimination in any contract entered into by these persons. This provision appears to aim specifically at preventing the substantial risk of discrimination between users with no connection to an integrated industry such as GDF and users that have some connection to such an industry.

2. The Mixed Negotiated Access System

To ensure access to the transmission system on the basis of objective, transparent and non-discriminatory criteria, Article 10 specifies that general conditions of sale must be sufficiently detailed so as to indicate the main elements necessary to meet user demands.

An examination of Article 10 suggests that the Bill tends to put into place a hybrid system of negotiated access. On the one hand, this provision provides standard general conditions of sale which appear to cover the main items that are appropriate in meeting user requirements. But on the other hand, the last paragraph of Article 10 may give rise to confusion; this article provides that the publication of the conditions of sale is no obstacle to the drafting of specific contractual conditions when these are required. Such specific conditions are to be communicated to the Electricity and Gas Regulation Commission which may oppose them. The Gas Bill used to provide that this Commission could require the incorporation of corresponding prices in the scales and of the specific conditions of sale in the adjustment account. It is still unclear whether only the specific contractual conditions will be negotiable or whether this article brings a certain negotiation margin to the whole system. It will be up to the implementation instruments to clarify this important point.

Insofar as the setting of transmission prices is concerned, these must be non-discriminatory, fair, clear and transparent, as specified by Article 10. Moreover, they must detail what service was rendered and the corresponding costs. Tariff conditions shall be set forth in a decree to be adopted by the Regulation Commission.

Currently, pursuant to decree no. 90-1029 dated 20 November 1990 which regulates the price of gas sold from public transmission or distribution systems, the price of gas is determined and developed, on a weighted average, taking into account variables of construction, maintenance and renovation costs of transmission installations, distribution and storage, costs of supply in gas and operation costs of transmission, distribution and storage equipment. The procedure provided by the decree stipulates that bodies that transmit or distribute gas sold from public systems must file with the Minister for Economy their price lists set according to rules set forth by decree. The system provided by decree no. 90-1029 is maintained and reinforced by Article 10 of the Gas Bill.

In order to maintain the confidentiality of commercially sensitive information obtained from third parties in the framework of the negotiation or transmission of system access, Article 13 provides that the transmission company shall designate a department that shall be responsible for the management of the system, installation or storage that it operates. This department must maintain the confidentiality of information capable of contravening the rules relating to free and fair competition and non-discrimination. The type of information that is confidential is set by decree.

3. The Regime Governing the Operation of Transmission Systems

Finally, Article 26 governs the operation of transmission systems, that is in particular the nomination regime as well as that of system balancing. It provides that any transmission or distribution operator of natural gas, and any operation of a natural liquefied gas installation, is responsible for the maintenance and development of infrastructure in order to allow connection and access in non-discriminatory conditions, as well as interconnection with other infrastructures. The operator must at all times ensure the equilibrium of gas flow on its system. It must, therefore, ensure the availability and the implementation of services necessary for the continuing operation of the system. It is up to this operator to measure the flow.

The comparison with the operation of foreign systems, particularly Anglo-Saxon systems, suggests that these provisions are inadequate in themselves to ensure the proper daily management of the system. Drawing from the British and U.S. experiences, the system may be improved by the adoption of a code of practice.

A decree may be proposed in the future for the purpose of establishing a legal framework for the drafting of a code of practice regarding system access, along the lines of, among other things, the British *Offshore Infrastructure Code of Practice* adopted in January 1996. Such a code would define for transmission companies, including vertically integrated companies, and users of transmission systems, including third party access applicants, certain rules of practice regarding access and use of the system, in particular insofar as transmission tariffs and technical and commercial conditions are concerned.

All transmission tariffs governed by this code should be non-discriminatory, fair and transparent. They should include a fair and reasonable profit margin for the remuneration of capital invested by the transmission company with a view to ensuring optimal system development in the long-term. Moreover, the transmission company should provide an unbundled invoice showing each item of its services in the framework of a transmission contract.

Insofar as technical specifications are concerned, the code would specify technical specifications for access to its system by a transmission company which must fulfil the criteria for third party access (including criteria relating to pressure, conditions for the maintenance of system equilibrium and system configuration…), as well as the physical specificities of the gas that is ordered.

Finally, insofar as the conditions of sale are concerned, such a code would specify the main conditions of sale that the transmission company would have to publish in respect of each year of use of its system. These conditions would have to include, among other things, a transmission tariff structure, a description of services, the term of the transmission contract and the financial guarantees that must be supplied.

V. THE REGULATOR

A. The Necessity for an Independent Regulator in the Electricity and Gas Directives

The Electricity Directive refers to two aspects of regulation: the regulatory function and the monitoring function to ensure proper functioning of the market. The Member States must set forth criteria and authorization procedures relating to new producers (Articles 5 and 6), objective and non-discriminatory standards for system connection (Article 7.2), approve the criteria for tenders made by generating installations (Article 8.2) and must determine the criteria for the granting of direct lines (Article 21).

Member States must moreover guarantee the maintenance by integrated companies of separate accounts (Article 14), ensure the monitoring of the system operator (Articles 11 and 12) and take the necessary measures to ensure access of independent producers to the system. The Directive provides for the appointment of independent bodies to carry out the follow-up and monitoring of the calls for tenders (Article 6.4), and for the settlement of contractual disputes. Article 20 provides in fact that "Member States shall designate a competent authority, which must be independent of the parties, to settle disputes relating to the contracts and negotiations in question. In particular, this authority must settle disputes concerning contracts, negotiations and refusal of access or refusal to purchase". Further, the Directive provides that in the case of a cross-border dispute, the competent authority to settle the dispute shall be that of the jurisdiction of the operator that refuses the use of or access to the system and that recourse to such authority shall be "without prejudice to the exercise of rights of appeal under Community law".

It is further stipulated in Article 22 of the Electricity Directive, that "Member States shall create appropriate and efficient mechanisms for regulation, control and transparency so as to avoid any abuse of dominant position, in particular to the detriment of consumers, and any predatory behaviour. These mechanisms take account of the provisions of the Treaty, and more particularly Article 86 thereof ".

Articles 21 and 22 of the Gas Directive similarly provide that Member States must set up an independent authority to monitor the functioning of the market and to settle disputes inherent in a market that is open to competition; that is, disputes relating to system access, monitoring of conditions of sale and separate accounting of integrated companies and the issuing of opinions concerning the authorizations granted and the performance of obligations of public service.

B. A New French Administrative Body

1. *The* Commission de Régulation de l'Electricité *(CRE)*

1.1. SIX MEMBERS … AND A *COMMISSAIRE DU GOUVERNEMENT*

The Law sets up an Electricity Commission composed of six members appointed for a term of six years only, which as the Competition Council stressed, is an independent authority.[45] Three members, one of whom is the Chairman, are appointed by decree, the *Présidents* of the two chambers of the Parliament and of the Economic and Social Council each appointing a member (Article 28). A *Commissaire du gouvernement* appointed by the Minister of Energy is in charge of communicating to the Commission the views of the Government. He attends sessions but has to be absent during deliberations, and can have his questions registered on the agenda of the Commission (Article 29). The budget of the Commission, which is proposed by itself to the Minister of Energy, is registered in the State budget (Article 30).

1.2. KEY TASKS

One of the main functions of the Commission is its participation in the setting of transmission tariffs, the determination of public service expenses (Article 36), and the settlement of disputes relating to transmission and distribution system access (Article 38). When a dispute is referred to it by an operator, the Commission has to render a decision within a period of three to six months (initially thirty days was provided); it may, however, decide to adopt interlocutory measures. Along the lines of the regime applicable to independent administrative authorities, any decision may be the subject of an appeal before the *Cour d'appel* of Paris. In order to ensure close co-operation with the Competition Council, the Chairman of the Commission may refer the case to its counterpart and when it has knowledge of restrictive practices; conversely, the latter must communicate to the former any case falling within the scope of his competence (Article 39).[46]

Finally, the Commission may automatically or upon the request of the relevant Minister or any relevant person, set temporary prohibitions on system access and fines to a level of

---

[45] See Cons. conc., "Electricity Notice", p. 392.

[46] On the limited competence of this Commission, see the criticism of a senior civil servant, *Le Figaro*, 12 March 1999.

3% to 5% of turnover, against the operator of a generating installation or the operator of the transmission or distribution system (Article 40). The fact of operating an installation, or constructing a direct line, without authorization, or of obstructing agents of the Commission in the exercise of their functions is punishable by criminal sanctions.

A draft decree dated 9 February 2000 sets forth provisions that are useful for the organization and proper functioning of the Commission, in particular those provisions that relate to the adoption of internal regulation and the powers of the Chairman. These provisions are common to independent administrative authorities. The purpose of another key draft decree is to set forth the procedure for the settlement of disputes concerning access and the rules relating to penalties.

2. *A Common Regulator: the* Commission de l'Electricité … et du Gaz *(CREG)*

The Gas Bill reproduces the provisions of the Electricity Law insofar as the body of the Commission and its main functions are concerned (opinion on the conditions of sale of use of a transmission or distribution system, on the sale tariffs of natural gas to non-eligible clients and on the transfer tariffs of natural gas to distribution operators for volumes intended for non-eligible customers… Articles 16 to 19). The CREG shall receive communication of contracts and agreements on access to transmission and distribution works and natural liquefied gas installations. The Gas Bill extended the competence of this body in order to comply with the specific nature of the legislation and the regulation of the gas sector, in particular relating to the requirement to grant temporary derogation from the system access requirements (Article 17).

VI. ENERGY CONTRACTS

A. The Fate of Existing Contracts

1. Eligible Customers' Purchase Contracts

The question of the fate of electricity purchase contracts of eligible customers led to lengthy debate. In fact, pursuant to Article 47 of the Electricity Bill, a possibility was provided for the termination of such contracts in progress by eligible customers and by … EDF! Parliamentary criticism, however, has led to the review of this article. The Gas Bill directly benefited from these debates since the provisions in respect of termination of gas contracts were aligned with the electricity regime.

This principle of reciprocity of the right to terminate was criticized on the basis of the Electricity Directive and Community competition provisions. Such reciprocity would have given EDF, in practice, the means to restrict the freedom of eligible customers to terminate contracts. Such a provision would have had the effect of placing the traditional EDF operator, once again, in a dominant position for many years, having the capacity to abuse its position by the simple exercise of its termination right. Previous established case law of the ECJ would have prohibited such practices.[47]

Moreover, Article 47(3) of the Bill provided that termination or review in the framework of Article 47 may give rise to indemnities payable by one or the other of the parties. Thus, Article 47(3) could have led to the customer having to pay the cost for EDF of the application of the Directive to his contract. This singularity which appeared to be contrary to the provisions of the Directive with regard to the principles of "effet utile", absence of abuse and of judicial security, was simply deleted from the final draft of Article 47 (now Article 49).

It will be noted that these provisions would have constituted a precedent in the implementation of the Electricity Directive in the EC Member States. There appears to be no comparable provisions in Belgium, Germany, Great Britain, Italy or Spain. The Belgian Act, the German Act and the Italian Decree contain no provision relating to existing sale contracts between the traditional operators and eligible customers: the fate of the existing agreements is governed by the general law on contract. The comparison with the Italian and British position provides a wealth of experience. In fact, in Italy, ENEL attempted to impose new long-term contracts for a period of three years containing significant quantitative reductions. These contracts further contained a provision according to which ENEL had the right of first refusal in the case of a better offer from a third party producer at the expiry of the contract. Thus, these clients were under the obligation to communicate to ENEL any commercial offer from competitors, and ENEL could still renew such contracts. Following the joint intervention of the national competition authority and the electricity regulatory authority, ENEL terminated these contracts. In Great Britain, following the opening of the market, it was provided that the existing contracts in force prior to 1st April 1990 could be the subject of a termination taking effect on 30 June 1990 at the initiative of customers in order to gain the benefit of the new conditions. These provisions authorizing early termination were intended to stimulate competition. It does not appear that these terminations gave rise to any indemnity whatsoever.

In the face of such criticism, the French Parliament adopted the principle of the termination of existing contracts that may be triggered by the exercise of rights granted by virtue of eligibility criteria. The new Article 49 provides as follows: "Whilst an eligible

---

[47] Case 27/76, *United Brands*, 14 February 1978, point 182. This is established case law; see, among other things, *Polaroid/SSI Europe*, *XIII Competition report*, point 157; Case 6-7/73, *Commercial Solvents*, ECR 1974, p. 223; Case 22/72, *Hugin*, ECR 1979, p. 1869.

customer exercises, in respect of a given site as such is defined in Article 22 of this Act, the rights granted by section III of this same article, the existing contracts concerning the supply of this site by Electricité de France or the non-nationalised distributors mentioned in article 23 of the aforementioned Act no. 46-628 of 8 April 1946 are automatically terminated."

Insofar as gas is concerned, the Preamble to the Gas Bill provided in a way similar to that of the Electricity Act, in Article 6.IV, for the automatic termination of existing contracts for a given site. However, an important difference is that this text limits this right to termination of contracts concluded prior to the operation of the future Act. It is thus the risk of bad faith in the use of the termination right of eligible gas consumers that is limited.

2. The Gas Take or Pay Contracts

2.1. THE EXISTENCE OF TOP CONTRACTS MAY JUSTIFY REFUSALS TO ACCESS

For the purposes of preventing any disturbance of the gas market related to the existence of take or pay contracts, Article 17 of the Gas Directive provides a derogation mechanism allowing natural gas companies to refuse third party access to the system when they are undergoing serious financial or economic difficulties related to the performance of such contracts.[48]

When a company considers that it is aware of such difficulties, it may apply to the Member State or to the regulatory authority. Such an application may be presented prior to or after the refusal of access to the system, stating its grounds and providing evidence in support thereof, containing the necessary information concerning the nature of the problem, the seriousness of the problem and the efforts the company has made to resolve the problem. The difficulties concerning these contracts concluded prior to the entry into force of the Directive may not be taken into account as long as the gas sales do not fall below the level of minimum demand guarantees appearing in the take or pay gas purchase contracts, or that the pertinent purchase of gas may be adapted or further still that the company may find alternative markets (Article 25 of the Gas Directive).

The regulatory authority and the Commission must take into account eight criteria in order to grant, refuse or amend the derogation. These refer in particular to the dates of signature and the conditions of the contract, as well as the efforts made to improve the situation and to what extent, at the time of signature of the take or pay contracts, the company could have foreseen the serious difficulties linked to the entry into force of the Directive.

---

[48] In relation to this point refer to, B. Mator, O. Ribot, "The French market of gas upon the hour of competition", *LPA*, 22 November 1999, No. 232, p. 13.

It has been observed that the Gas Directive is not very precise and that in practice difficulties related to the interpretation of provisions governing this mechanism could soon appear, in particular with regard to the precise definition of financial difficulties, today still left to the unfettered assessment of the natural gas company seeking the derogation. Likewise, there is no way of determining whether the criteria for the assessment of the application for a derogation provided by the Directive are cumulative.[49] The Gas Bill specifically addresses these criticisms.

2.2. THE TOP EXCEPTION IN THE GAS BILL

Any transmission operator benefiting from a supply authorization or any distribution operator, to the extent that he is threatened by serious economic and financial difficulties due to the existence of TOP contracts and to the extent that the unfavourable evolution of its markets could not be foreseen at the time the TOP undertakings were given, may seek a temporary derogation from the Electricity and Gas Regulation Commission (Article 9).

The derogation is delivered for a period of no more than one year. The derogation decision is published and it defines the conditions under which the beneficiary is authorized to refuse to conclude a contract of access to the gas transmission system that it operates. Such derogation may be renewed in the same conditions.

The criteria for the grant of the derogation are objective, non-discriminatory and may be based only on: 1°) technical reasons linked to the necessity of gas infrastructures, 2°) priority to be given to infrastructures used for public service obligations, 3°) other criteria to be set by the CREG. The CREG will have to take into account: 1°) the necessity to ensure security of supply and to meet public service obligations which are incumbent on the applicant; 2°) the position of the applicant and the state of competition on the natural gas market; 3°) the seriousness of economic and financial difficulties threatening the applicant or its clients, as well as the measures taken by the applicant with a view to find alternative markets for the supply of natural gas that it purchases; 4°) the date of adoption of the contractual undertakings mentioned in the 1st paragraph and the conditions of adoption of these undertakings in the case of evolution of the applicant's markets.

B. The New Contracts: Minimum Term for Electricity Contracts

To conclude, we will examine the most astonishing provision of the French Act implementing the Electricity Directive. Article 22-III, 2nd final paragraph, states that: "…The contractual framework within which the supply of electricity is performed may not be for a period less than three years in the interests of the efficacy of the pluriannual

---

[49] Refer to B. Mator, O. Ribot, *op. cit.*, p. 15.

programming of production investments, public service functions and in compliance with the principle of mutability of contracts". This provision, maintained in spite of a rigorous parliamentary debate, is the subject of various doubts from a legal point of view. The European Commission is scrutinizing the issue.

1. The Minimum Term Appears to be Contrary to the Objective that Operators be free to enter into Contractual Relations

This minimum term of three years appears contrary to the objective that operators be free to enter into contractual relations in a competitive market, as stipulated by recital 9 of the Electricity Directive: "Whereas, in the internal market, electricity undertakings must be able to operate, without prejudice to compliance with public service obligations, with a view to achieving a competitive market in electricity".

As emphasized by the MP who had rejected an amendment imposing a period of eight years (!), the minimum term seriously restrains the freedom of eligible clients to contract, as well as the freedom of independent suppliers. It was expressly justified by its authors by the intention to limit "the freedom for large clients to choose their electricity supplier".[50] The legislative intention is clearly, therefore, to limit the freedom to contract of certain companies within the competitive market. In contrast, this three-year period allows, in practice, the traditional operator to preserve the eligible clientele that may have wished to have contracted with competitors and to avoid the necessity of having to formulate its offer to respond in a timely manner the requirements of its customers.

The European Commission has, on various occasions, been opposed to the conclusion of long-term supply contracts and the adoption of provisions tending to limit the freedom of eligible customers. Thus, M. Alexander Schaub, Director General of the DG in charge of competition, announced the opening of an inquiry into agreements between German operators on electricity tariffs (*Verbändevereinbarung*), particularly due to the fact that these agreements "tend to limit development of short-term supply".[51] Likewise, M. Michael Albers, head of the unit in charge of energy at the same DG, discussing the various contractual practices likely to have the effect of reducing the freedom of eligible customers to choose their suppliers, indicated that the Commission would examine carefully the exclusivity and penalty clauses. The purpose of this examination is to prohibit "all provisions imposed by a dominant operator for the purpose of preventing a consumer from changing a producer".[52]

These statements, relating to trade agreements and commercial contracts, directly apply

---

[50] Id, p. 1759.

[51] Refer to *Europolitique*, No. 289, 10 March 1999.

[52] M. Albers, "View and Expectations on the Competition Developments in the EU Electricity Market", Conference UNIPEDE/EURELECTRIC, Brussels, 24-25 March 1999.

to the Electricity Law which imposes a contract term which has the effect of restraining the freedom of choice of eligible customers. The entirety of these official statements, repeated on several occasions and at various levels of the Community institution, emphasises that the Commission intends to make short-term supply contracts possible and suggests that it is prepared to challenge any provision tending to restrain this freedom of the consumers.

2. The Minimum Term is Contrary to the Objective of a Comparable Degree of Access to Electricity Markets

Moreover, the minimum term is in conflict with the principle of uniform application of the Electricity Directive in the various EC Member States and is contrary to the objective of a comparable degree of access to electricity markets as stipulated by recital 12: "Whatever the nature of the prevailing market organisation, access to the system must be open in accordance with this Directive and must lead to equivalent economical results in the States, and, hence, to a directly comparable level of opening-up of markets and to a degree directly comparable degree of access to electricity markets".

The Electricity Law impinges on the freedom of contract of sector operators, which reduces to the same extent the degree of access to the market. The Belgian, Italian and British acts contain no provision as to the minimum term of supply contracts. Only Spain limited the minimum term of offers of contracts to one year. But, beyond the fact that such period is much shorter than the French term, it is observed that Spain has surpassed the minimum thresholds of eligibility and adopted in a limited way the practice of purchase for re-sale. Finally, even though in Germany there was no minimum period of contracts, the European Commission has looked into the question of the period of supply contracts. The dominant producers have in fact tried to impose long-term contracts, in return for the grant of discounts and a clause of first refusal. The DG in charge of competition, therefore, instigated an enquiry into these contracts which "reduce not only the freedom of choice of the consumer but also dissuade newcomers from entering the market".[53]

In practice, it will be observed that this provision of the Electricity Law is already violated by the operators who conclude standard contracts of three years, with the period of application of such contracts freely negotiated. Such an interpretation of the text could result from statements made by the Secretary of State for Industry who maintained that: "The period, the price, the quantities, … do not arise out of the contractual framework but must be left to negotiation".[54]Even if, from the point of view of the French text, such a practice could be considered to be contrary to the Law, it appears in any case to be authorized by Community law which takes precedence.

---

[53] Refer to *Europolitique*, No. 289, 10 March 1999.

[54] Debates AN, 3rd session of 18 February 1999, JO AN, p. 1760.

Dr. Achim-Rüdiger Börner

COUNTRY REPORT: GERMANY

I. INTRODUCTION

Due to the size of the German economy, its energy markets represent an essential element of the EU energy sector. The annual final energy consumption[1] in Germany amounts to almost 9,500 petajoules.[2] 485 million metric tons of hard coal equivalent are traded, transformed and distributed many times before being finally consumed.[3]

Broadly speaking, the energy markets in Germany are not regulated. Besides environmental laws, laws for the protection of the workforce and other public interest regulations, there is no regulation of the markets for crude oil and refinery products, lignite, coal, uranium, nuclear fuels and their reconditioning, biomass, etc. There are limited sector-specific regulatory regimes dealing with natural gas[4] and electricity distribution[5].

As a consequence, one third of the final physical consumption of energy (i.e., the share represented by electricity and gas) is subject to specific regulation.[6] However, one should not forget that the regulation of the markets for final consumption has a considerable impact on the upstream markets.

II. THE LIBERALIZATION OF THE ELECTRICITY AND GAS MARKETS

Historically, the electricity and gas markets have been subject to specific rules because of the natural monopoly features of the energy networks. In April 1998, most of these special rules have been abolished by the German legislator which claims to have completely abandoned the system of closed areas of supply and to have fully liberalized the electricity and gas markets. From a legal standpoint, there are practically no remaining barriers

---

[1] See the reply of the German government to a question asked by one of the opposition parties, "Energy Policy for the 21st Century", Printed Materials of the German Bundestag 14/2656 of 2 February 2000.

[2] This represents 324 billion metric tons of hard coal equivalent (MTCE); one MTCE equals 29.3 petajoules.

[3] H.-W. Schiffer, "Deutscher Energiemarkt '99", *Energiewirtschaftliche Tagesfragen* (2000), 114.

[4] The annual domestic availability amounts to 1,010.5 billion kWh and the final consumption adds up to 932 billion kWh; See H.-W. Schiffer, *supra* note 3, at 122-124.

[5] The annual domestic availability amounts to 554.3 billion kWh and adds up to a net consumption of 488.7 billion kWh; see H.-W. Schiffer, *supra* note 3, at 124.

[6] According to rough calculations – after taking out some 125 billion kWh of gas used for power production, the volume of final consumption of electricity and gas amounts to about 1.3000 billion kWh which represents about 165 million MTCE. This has to be compared with the total final energy consumption which equals 485 million MTCE.

Damien Geradin (ed.), The Liberalization of Electricity and Natural Gas in the European Union, 155–167
©2001 Kluwer Law International. Printed in the Netherlands.

preventing competition, not even the partial protection that is allowed by the EC Directives. Basically, there has not even been a transitional regime facilitating the move towards the new competitive environment.

The electricity and gas markets are now fully open to competition and remain subject only to the general rules of antitrust law.[7] It is not surprising that this approach has been criticized. Some experts believe that persisting particularities of these markets are not taken into account and that, as a result, at least some traditional market participants suffer excessively.[8]

The effects of the liberalization are particularly obvious concerning the electricity market which has evolved with an extraordinary speed. Since April 1998 there have been a remarkable number of entries on the market and a full-scale price war, as a result of which prices have declined by 30 percent or even more in most market segments. Even before the entry into force of the new Act on the New Regulation of the Law on the Energy Industry[9] and before the emergence of specific rules for power wheeling, the immense force of the expected changes became clear. Already in the beginning of 1998, retailers and industrial clients began to negotiate new electricity supply contracts and to re-negotiate old ones with existing suppliers and new market entrants. The market participants even agreed on industry standards for power wheeling in order to achieve a framework for the orderly management of energy resources and of the networks, as well as to facilitate the conclusion and implementation of wheeling contracts.[10] Although liberalization of the market did not start for individual consumers and small enterprises before summer 1999, some of the latter already began to form themselves into groups with the intention of creating enough market power at the demand level to be able to achieve favourable terms when negotiating with more powerful market participants. As regards individual consumers and small enterprises, the liberalization process created difficulties in the beginning since there was no equipment installed for measuring the rate of individual consumption and the installation of such equipment is too expensive.[11]

The future will show for how long the general tendency towards declining prices will continue and which kinds of measures the legislator will have to take in order to protect

---

[7] For a general description of the German system see K. Pritzsche, A. Meier, U. Wetzel and T. Diercks, "Germany", in: R. Tudway (ed.), *Energy Laws and Regulation in the European Union* (London, June 2000), 3001. For an overview of the new developments see B. Kunth and G. Wiedemann, "Country Reports: Germany", *Journal of Energy & Natural Resources Law* (London, passim); R. Schäfer, "Deutsches und europäisches Energierecht", *Energiewirtschaftliche Tagesfragen* (1999), 553.

[8] For references see literature in note 7.

[9] Gesetz zur Neuregelung des Energiewirtschaftsrechts of 24 April 1998, Bundesgesetzblatt 1998, Part I, 730.

[10] See *infra*, notes 52 and 53.

[11] A.-R. Börner, "Aspekte zum Wettbewerb um Tarifkunden in der Stromwirtschaft", *Versorgungswirtschaft* (1999), 225.

public interest objectives, such as environmental protection and climate change control.[12] The new laws on renewable energies[13] and cogeneration[14] show that free competition does not necessarily lead to welfare-enhancing results.[15]

III. EVOLUTION OF THE REGULATORY FRAMEWORK

The term "liberalization" describes a process. Without knowing the situation before and after it takes place, its meaning cannot be understood. Therefore, it is necessary to describe not only the new regulatory framework, but also the former legal situation. Hence, the present Part will be divided into three sections successively discussing the "old" model, the "transitional" period, and the "new" model created by the adoption of the new Act on the New Regulation of the Law on Energy Industry.

A. The "Old" Model

The former Energy Business Act[16] had as its purpose the availability of cheap and safe energy. Its basic aims were to exclude harmful competition[17] and to compensate for the lack of usual market forces by a system of close supervision of the industry.[18] With the intention of excluding harmful competition, the creation of closed territories of exclusive supply was permitted. In order to understand the former system it is necessary to know that the legislator believed that whatever the framework, producers and distributors would act in an entrepreneurial manner. In order to achieve fair prices, the market was, however,

---

[12] For some critical remarks, see A.-R. Börner, "Die Strom- und Gasversorgung im XII. Hauptgutachten der Monopolkommission", *Zeitschrift für öffentliche und gemeinwirtschaftliche Unternehmen* (1999), 231.

[13] Erneuerbare-Energien-Gesetz (Renewable-Energies-Act), Bundesgesetzblatt 2000, part I, 305.

[14] Kraft-Wärme-Kopplungs-Gesetz (Cogeneration-Act), Bundesgesetzblatt 2000, part I, 703.

[15] See the article of A. Heinen in this book.

[16] Gesetz zur Förderung der Energiewirtschaft (Energiewirtschaftsgesetz) of 13 December 1935, Reichsgesetzblatt 1935, Part I, 1451, in the version of 19 December 1977, Bundesgesetzblatt 1977, Part I, 2750; see also the Energiesicherungsgesetz (Energy Safeguard Act) of 21 December 1974, Bundesgesetzblatt 1974, Part I, 3681, in the version of 29 December 1979, Bundesgesetzblatt 1979, Part I, 2305; 2. Durchführungsverordnung (Second Implementing Decree Of The Energy Safeguard Act, which is about technical safety) of 14 January 1987, Bundesgesetzblatt 1987, Part I, 146; the following Articles of the new Energy Business Act constitute the transposition of the Electricity Directive: Article 4 (the operation of the electricity network), Articles 5 to 8 (third party access), Article 9 (Unbundling of accounts, financial statements), Article 13 (use of public ways).

[17] See the preamble of the old Energy Business Act which underlines the importance of the energy industry as a basis of general welfare and emphasizes the need to prevent economically harmful effects of competition, to achieve a reasonable balance by means of interconnection of networks and to achieve low prices and safe supply.

[18] See Articles 3, 4, 5, 8 to 9 and 13 of the old Energy Business Act, which went beyond the new law.

administered by public authorities. Monopolistic prices would, indeed, be to the detriment of the public. Conversely, prices lower than costs would jeopardize the security of supply. The regime of cost-based prices was used to discourage price inflation caused by unreasonable expenditures.

In the old model, the industry was partially exempted from the general competition rules of the Antitrust Act by several special provisions of that Act.[19]

First, the Antitrust Act permitted a system of concession contracts. This system was and still is a German particularity. The German meaning of the term "concession" differs from its equivalent in English or French law. Its underlying idea is that an undertaking supplies electricity and gas in specific territories, thereby exercising its own rights and freedoms. The right to conclude sales contracts with final consumers does not need to be conferred by public authorities. The latter do not even have an exclusive right of their own which they could transfer. However, the municipalities are the owners of the municipal roads and thus able to grant the easement to use their roads for the construction and operation of electricity lines and gas pipes. When granting the easement, the municipalities act under civil law rather than public law, according to the prevailing opinion.[20] As compensation for the grant of the easement, the municipality receives a payment. Normally, a one-off payment or regular payments in correlation to the intensity of the disturbance caused by the easement would be sufficient in terms of compensation for the rights of way for lines. The municipalities may, however, also ask for a participation fee. The law permits regular payments of certain maximum amounts per energy unit taken by final consumers.[21] This payment is calculated as compensation for the transfer of property rights and such compensation is called a "concession fee". The municipalities' income due to concession fees still amounts to about 6 billion Deutsche Marks. This figure shows that the fees contribute significantly to the financing of the tasks of general interest with which the municipalities are entrusted.

Second, the Antitrust Act also provided for special provisions granting permission to conclude agreements on horizontal and vertical restraints of competition as regards electricity and gas.

As a counter-balance to the above exceptions of the general antitrust law, free competition was maintained in certain markets such as, for example, in the market for heating energy.

---

[19] Articles 103 ff. of the Gesetz gegen Wettbewerbsbeschränkungen (GWB – Act Against Restrictions of Competition); the old Antitrust Act and its five major amendments have been published as follows: Bundesgesetzblatt 1957, part I, 1081; Bundesgesetzblatt 1965, part I, 1363; Bundesgesetzblatt 1973, Part I, 917; Bundesgesetzblatt 1976, part I, 1697; Bundesgesetzblatt 1980, part I, 485; Bundesgesetzblatt 1989, Part I, 2486.

[20] See for example B. Scholtka, *Das Konzessionsabgabenrecht in der Elektrizitäts- und Gaswirtschaft*, Veröffentlichungen des Instituts für Energierecht an der Universität zu Köln, (Baden-Baden, 1999) at 30.

[21] See Verordnung über Konzessionsabgaben für Strom und Gas (KAV – Regulation on Concession Fees for Electricity and Gas) of 9 January 1992, Bundesgesetzblatt 1992, Part I, 12, 407 in the version of 22 July 1999, Bundesgesetzblatt 1999, Part I, 1669.

The provisions on merger control were also applied very strictly to all transactions between monopoly producers. Moreover, the contractual conditions and prices of electricity[22] and gas[23] for small consumers were regulated. After World War II, ceiling prices for gas were no longer fixed due to the existence of effective competition between natural gas and other energies.

This legal regime supported an industrial structure which achieved the goal of security of supply of electricity and gas in Germany for more than fifty years, in spite of enormous challenges such as the reconstruction of the country, the various changes of the availability and prices of different primary energy sources (for instance, coal, crude oil, nuclear power) and the German reunification. As regards the electricity industry,[24] the system supported about 1000 enterprises, including twelve transmission companies, up to forty regional distributors and more than 950 local distributors (a fair number of which are at the same time significant electricity producers), joint production companies, independent power producers, and industrial auto-producers. As regards the gas industry,[25] the system provided support for about 700 companies, including three to four domestic producers, seventeen gas-trading companies and about 680 local distributors.

The system above was subject to gradual adjustment in order to allow competition for the acquisition of exclusive territories and to intensify fringe competition. During the last few years, observers became more and more suspicious about the effectiveness of the old system. In particular, this system was suspected to have become inflexible. In view of global and intensified competition in other economic sectors, it was no longer perceived as an adequate and cost-effective framework for the electricity market.

---

[22] See Verordnung über Allgemeine Bedingungen für die Elektrizitätsversorgung von Tarifkunden (AVBEltV – Regulation On The General Terms And Conditions Of Electricity Supply To Tariff Customers) of 21 June 1979, Bundesgesetzblatt 1979, Part I, 684, as amended on 25 September 1990, Bundesgesetzblatt 1990, Part I, 2106; Bundestarifordnung Elektrizität (BTOElt – Federal Tariff Order On Electricity) of 18 December 1989, Bundesgesetzblatt 1989, Part I, 2255.

[23] See Verordnung über Allgemeine Bedingungen für die Gasversorgung von Tarifkunden (AVBGasV – Regulation On The General Terms And Conditions Of Gas Supply To Tariff Customers) of 21 June 1979, Bundesgesetzblatt 1979, Part I, 676, as amended on 25 September 1990, Bundesgesetzblatt 1990, Part I, 2106; Bundestarifordnung Gas (BTOGas – Federal Tariff Order On Gas) of 26 November 1959, Bundesgesetzblatt 1959, Part I, 46, in the version of 21 June 1979, Bundesgesetzblatt 1979, Part I, 676.

[24] For a brief survey see A.-R. Börner, "Germany" in: C. Zach (ed.), *Energy and Resources Law*, International Financial Law Review, Special Supplement (London, October 1994), 25; for more detailed figures see H.-W. Schiffer, "Deutscher Energiemarkt '99", *Energiewirtschaftliche Tagesfragen* (2000), 114 at 122.

[25] A.-R. Börner, "The German Gas Industry in a Changing Environment" in M. Crisdell (ed.), *International Oil & Gas Finance Review* 2000 (London, 1999), 77; For more detailed figures see H.-W. Schiffer, "Deutscher Energiemarkt '99", *Energiewirtschaftliche Tagesfragen* (2000), 114 at 122.

B. The "Transitional" Period

In Germany, the discussion over the future of the system of territories of exclusive supply re-started in 1994.[26] For many years, the efficiency of this system had already been discussed time and again.[27] A lot of the criticism was due to the interdependent challenges of globalization and the economic downturn in Continental Europe, both of which led to a call for lower energy prices.[28]

The discussion intensified due to proposals for a Single European energy Market[29] and due to discussions over the drafts of Directive 96/92/EC on common rules for the internal electricity market[30] and Directive 98/30/EC on common rules for the internal market in natural gas.[31]

In Germany as well as in the EC, the idea of consumer protection guaranteed by market mechanisms gained ground. It became the prevalent opinion that a competitive organization of the market would achieve superior results in the field of network-bound industries.

This has led to a two-pronged approach:

First, the Federal Cartel Office began to apply Articles 81 and 82 (ex-Articles 85 and 86) of the EC Treaty in order to liberalize the markets.[32] With regard to the above-mentioned concession agreements, it was argued that they guaranteed the supply of services of general economic interest according to Article 86(2) (ex-Article 90(2)) of the Treaty.[33] To a certain extent, this argument was correct since these contracts were part of a whole legal system and the basic rules did not need to be repeated by them.[34] In order to justify these contracts,

---

[26] For a survey of the transition from the old law to the new law, see A.-R. Börner, "Recent Developments in Germany Energy Law and Policy", *Oil & Gas Law Taxation Review* (1997), 117-127, 153-159.

[27] W. Danner in W. Obernolte and W. Danner (ed.), *Energiewirtschaftsgesetz,* (Munich, January 1999), Einführung (Introduction).

[28] M. Kley, "Aktuelle Perspektiven der industriellen Energiewirtschaft 1991", *VIK-Mitteilungen* (1991), 147; H.-J. Budde, "Die leitungsgebundene Energieversorgung der Industrie am Standort Deutschland im Spannungsfeld politischer Zielkonflikte", *VIK-Mitteilungen* (1993), 54.

[29] European Commission, *White Book: The Accomplishment Of The Internal Market In Electricity And Gas,* COM (1991) 548 final of 21 February 1992.

[30] Directive 96/92/EC of the European Parliament and of the Council concerning common rules for the internal market in electricity of 19 December 1996, OJ 1997 L 27/20.

[31] Directive 98/30/EC of the European Parliament and the Council concerning common rules for the internal market in natural gas of 22 June 1998, OJ 1998 L 204/1.

[32] For an overview see W. Löwer, "Das Bundeskartellamt als Rechtsreformer im Energierecht" in J. Ipsen, H.-W. Rengeling, J. Mössner and A. Weber (ed.), *Verfassungsrecht im Wandel,* Festschrift zum 180jährigen Bestehen des Carl Heymanns Verlag KG (Cologne, 1995), 425.

[33] For a recent and complete survey see H., Decker, "Art. 86 (90) EGV Note 24 et seq.", in W. Ludwif and H. Odenthal (ed.), *Recht der Elektrizitäts-, Gas- und Wasserversorgung* (Neuwied, December 1999).

[34] See A.-R. Börner, "Der Energiemarkt und die geschlossenen Versorgungsgebiete der Strom- und Gaswirtschaft im Übergang zum Wettbewerb", *Zeitschrift für öffentliche und gemeinwirtschaftliche Unternehmen, Beiheft 20* (Baden-Baden, 1996), 23; B. Scholtka, *Das Konzessionsabgabenrecht in der Elektrizitäts- und Gaswirtschaft,* Veröffentlichungen des Instituts für Energierecht an der Universität zu Köln (Baden-Baden, 1999), 30.

one could also advance the applicability of other antitrust exceptions. Although this matter has been brought before it, the European Court of Justice has never rendered a judgment in these cases because they were withdrawn before judgment could be delivered. In fact, the questions had become obsolete due to the liberalization legislation.[35]

At the same time, the German legislator embarked on a complete revision of the Energy Business Act and the antitrust exceptions. In spite of serious objections raised by some members of the Bundestag and the Federal Council, the Parliament passed the Act on the New Regulation of the Law on Energy Industry,[36] which entered into force in April 1998. The Act provides for a nearly unrestricted liberalization of the electricity and gas markets which goes far beyond the EC minimum requirements.

C. The "New" Model

The Act on the New Regulation of the Law on Energy Industry is subdivided into four sections: (i) the Energy Business Act, (ii) the amendments of the Antitrust Act, (iii) the amendments of other laws such as, for instance, the Electricity Intake Act and (iv) transitional provisions. This Act, which seeks to transpose the EC Electricity Directive, contains provisions applicable to the electricity as well as the gas industries although they are affected differently. A draft of a law amending the Act in order to transpose completely the EC Gas Directive is being drawn up at the moment.

The new Energy Business Act seeks to achieve the following objectives:[37] to ensure — in the public interest — a reliable, price efficient and environmentally compatible supply of electricity and gas by direct connection.

The first major novelty of the Act on the New Regulation of the Law on Energy Industry is the abolition of those sections of the Antitrust Act which granted antitrust exemptions to the electricity and gas industries.[38] As a consequence, contractual provisions based on these exemptions, which means all provisions aimed at the establishment or maintenance of closed areas of supply are void. During the transitional period, it is a difficult legal task to find out whether the nullity or contestability of these clauses affects other contractual obligations or not. As regards the already existing concession contracts, their continuing validity is explicitly provided for in spite of the nullity of the exclusivity clauses concerning the rights of way.[39] This provision aims to preserve the concession fees which — for

---

[35] For further information see A.-R. Börner, "XII. Hauptgutachten", *Zeitschrift für öffentliche und gemein-wirtschaftliche Unternehmen* (1999) 231 at 253 note 96; as regards the new legal situation see F. Hölzer, *Der Energiesektor zwischen Marktwirtschaft und öffentlicher Aufgabe*, Verwaltungswissenschaftliche Abhandlungen No. 16 (Cologne, 2000), 313.

[36] Gesetz zur Neuregelung des Energiewirtschaftsrechts of 24 April 1998, Bundesgesetzblatt 1998, Part I, 730.

[37] See Article 1 of the new Energy Business Act.

[38] Article 2 of the Act On The New Regulation Of The Law On Energy Industry.

[39] Article 4, para. 1, of the Act On The New Regulation Of The Law On Energy Industry.

obvious reasons — are essential for the municipalities. As regards other contracts, such as for instance supply contracts, their validity has to be determined case by case according to the general antitrust rules and the general rules of contract law.[40]

The second major novelty of the Act lies in the grant of third party access rights to the electricity grid. The Act grants rights of access to all competitors as well as to all customers regardless of the amount of energy they consume. According to Article 6 of the Act on the New Regulation of the Law on Energy Industry, negotiated third party access (NTPA) is the general rule. There is an exception allowing for a single buyer model which is limited in time and subject to the following conditions.[41] The provision of such access must lead to the same economic effects being achieved as under the NTPA, as well as market opening and access to the electricity markets which would be directly comparable to what would be achieved under the NTPA. The single buyer system has been selected by a number of local distributors because the integrity of the network is safeguarded slightly more than under the NTPA. It is prohibited, for instance, to form new sub-local distributors in a single buyer area.[42] The rules on third party access go hand in hand with the unbundling and operating provisions which transpose the EC Directive.

It should be noted that third party access is limited in the following circumstances: (i) when foreign electricity producers want to enter the German market and there is a lack of reciprocity,[43] (ii) in case of competition with East German lignite power[44] and (iii) in case of harmful competition between combined heat and power production plants.[45]

In spite of the liberalization, the new Energy Business Act continues to oblige local distributors to connect with and to supply all customers in their grid area at general tariffs and controlled prices.[46] As regards areas which are furnished with electricity by many suppliers, it may become questionable whether this is the duty of the network operator, who concentrates on energy transport, or of the most important local supplier.

The Energy Business Act also leaves antitrust remedies untouched.[47] The latter have been strengthened by an amendment to the Antitrust Act.[48] In German competition law,

---

[40] For further information see A.-R. Börner, "XII. Hauptgutachten", *Zeitschrift für öffentliche und gemeinwirtschaftliche Unternehmen* (1999), 231 at 241 note 58.

[41] Articles 7 and 8 of the new Energy Business Act.

[42] A.-R. Börner, "Das Alleinabnehmersystem" in M. Bartsch, A. Röhling and P. Salje (ed.), *Handbuch des Energierechts* (Cologne, to be published soon).

[43] Article 4, para. 2, of the Act On The New Regulation Of The Law On Energy Industry.

[44] Article 4, para. 3, of the Act On The New Regulation Of The Law On Energy Industry.

[45] Article 6, para. 3 of the new Energy Business Act.

[46] Article 10 of the new Energy Business Act.

[47] See e.g. Article 6, para. 1, sentence 4, of the new Energy Business Act.

[48] 6th Act amending the Act Against Restrictions Of Competition (Sechstes Gesetz zur Änderung des Gesetzes gegen Wettbewerbsbeschränkungen) of 26 August 1998, Bundesgesetzblatt 1998, part I, 2521; for the complete new version of the Antitrust Act see Bundesgesetzblatt 1998, Part I, 2546.

there is now a provision that explicitly declares that a denial of access to essential facilities constitutes an abuse of a dominant position under certain conditions.[49] However, antitrust procedures and claims are not necessarily compatible with the provisions of the Energy Business Act.[50]

IV. MAKING THE NEW MODEL WORK

In theory, only a few provisions are necessary in order to open up the market and create competition. In practice, opening the market to competition is not so simple and may require additional regulatory intervention.

A. Electricity

There are a number of models for power wheeling such as point-to-point transmissions, one-point-tariffs, copper-plate-tariffs, market tariffs and others that have been devised in the US.[51] The industry must agree on specific "codes" in order to ensure the smooth transmission of electricity. This is particularly true as regards Germany with its high densities of transmission, its regional and local networks, its short average distances between power plants and consumers, as well as its enormous number of market participants, including producers, importers, traders, transmitters, distributors and customers.

A number of codes have been established in the form of association agreements. The

---

[49] Article 19, para. 4, point 4, of the Act against Restrictions of Competition: "An abuse (scil.) of a dominant market position) exists in particular, if a dominant undertaking as a supplier or purchaser of certain kinds of goods or commercial services,

4. refuses to allow another undertaking access to its own networks or other infrastructure facilities, against adequate remuneration, provided that without such concurrent use the other undertaking is unable for legal or factual reasons to operate as a competitor of the dominant undertaking on the upstream or downstream market; this shall not apply if the dominant undertaking demonstrates that for operational or other reasons such concurrent use is impossible or cannot reasonably be expected."

[50] See for the prevailing opinion U. Büdenbender, "Durchleitung elektrischer Energie nach der Energierechts-reform", *Recht der Energiewirtschaft* (1999), 1 at 8 forth following; J. F. Baur (ed.), *Energiewirtschaft – Der neue energie- und kartellrechtliche Rahmen*, Veröffentlichungen des Instituts für Energierecht an der Universität zu Köln, vol. 91 (Baden-Baden, 1999), at 73 and 81; W. Möschel, "Energierechtsreform und wettbewerbliche Prognoseentscheidungen", *VIK-Mitteilungen* (1998), 133 at 134 and 136; W. Möschel, "Strompreis und kartellrechtliche Kontrolle" in J. F. Baur (ed.), *Energiewirtschaft – Der neue energie- und kartellrechtliche Rahmen*, Veröffentlichungen des Instituts für Energierecht der Universität zu Köln, vol. 91 (Baden-Baden, 1999), 27 at 29; A.-R. Börner, "Zum Verhältnis von § 6 EnWG-neu und Kartellrecht", *Versorgungswirtschaft* (1999), 77; A.-R. Börner, "XII. Hauptgutachten", *Zeitschrift für öffentliche und gemeinwirtschaftliche Unternehmen* (1999), 231 at 237; W. Harms, "Zur Anwendung der Schutzklauseln für Öko-, KWK- und Braunkohlestrom im Neuregelungsgesetz vom 24.4.1998", *Recht der Energiewirtschaft* (1999), 165 at 166.

[51] See A.-R. Börner, *Stromdurchleitung: Anregung aus US-Regulierung*, Kölner Miszellen zum Energierecht (KME), vol. 6 (Baden-Baden, 1998), at 66.

first generation of codes was based on the model of point-to-point transmission which amounts to a fictitious contract path to the customer.[52] This had to be negotiated by the supplier with the different network operators. The experience with this model has shown that it has the disadvantage of adding technical, economic and legal problems such as, for instance, diverging physical load flows, calculation models which tended to overcharge wheelers, pancaking, a lack of price transparency and high transaction costs due to the multitude of individual contractual arrangements.

In response to continuous pressure from the German Ministry of Economics and its threat to enact an access regulation and to establish a new authority if they did not reach a satisfactory agreement, the parties to the first generation of codes agreed on a revision of the latter in December 1999.[53] This revision has led to a fundamental change of the energy access system. The new system is based on the idea that the final consumer buys access to a "copper-plate". The new system works as follows.

The local distributor concludes an access agreement with the consumer and calculates the access fee. He should be reimbursed for all of his costs. All higher voltage grids calculate their full costs and pass them on to the local networks according to their respective consumption, reserve power included, and average load curve. The local distributors charge their customers the total amount of costs according to their respective consumption and load curve, which is the actual load curve in case of large consumers and an average load curve in case of small consumers. The aggregate sum of the distribution costs is increased by the hypothetical cost for wheeling of locally produced power and accordingly the surplus charge levied from consumers is reimbursed to the local power producers due to their function of minimizing system load.

The old antitrust rule of comparing monopoly prices[54] rather than fictitious prices[55] is being revived; the charges levied in one grid zone may not exceed those levied in another comparable zone.

---

[52] "Verbändevereinbarung über Kriterien zur Bestimmung von Durchleitungsentgelten vom 22. Mai 1998", *VIK-Mitteilungen* (1998), 57 = *Recht der Energiewirtschaft* (1998), p. XXI = W. Obernolte and W. Danner (ed.), *Energiewirtschaftsrecht* (Munich, January 1999), Chapter I. C. 30; Deutsche Verbundgesellschaft (ed.), *Der Grid Code – Netz- und Systemregeln der deutschen Übertragungsnetzbetreiber* (Heidelberg, September 1998); Deutsche Verbundgesellschaft (ed.), *Der Grid Code – Kooperationsregeln für die deutschen Übertragungsnetzbetreiber* (Heidelberg, September 1998); VDEW (ed.), *Netzregeln für den Zugang zu Verteilungsnetzen – "Distribution Code"*, VDEW-Materialien M-11/99 (Frankfort on the Main, June 1999); VDEW (ed.), *VDEW-Richtlinie "Abrechnungszählung und Datenbereitstellung" – "Metering Code"*, VDEW-Materialien M-12/99 (Frankfort on the Main, June 1999).

[53] Verbändevereinbarung II of 13 December 1999 (VV II, in short); for its content see W. Ohlms, "Umsetzung als Kraftakt", *Zeitschrift für Kommunale Wirtschaft* (1999), 6; W. Ohlms, "Die Verbändevereinbarung II Strom ist unterschrieben – was nun?", *VKU-Nachrichtendienst* No. 613 (January 2000), Annex; for some logical and antitrust problems see A.-R. Börner, "Erste Überlegungen zu den privaten Normierungen der Stromdurchleitung: Stringenz und Kartellrecht", *Recht der Energiewirtschaft* (2000), 55 and 94.

[54] See Article 103, para. 5, point 2, of the old Antitrust Act.

[55] See Article 19, para. 4, point 2, of the new Antitrust Act.

The eight German high-voltage network operators who take care of the ancillary services, especially the frequency regulation, have neither insisted on considering the eight high-voltage grids as to be isolated nor on charging a toll for each transmission from or to another high-voltage grid. Instead of this and in order to lower the charges for high-voltage wheeling and to simplify long distance transmissions, it has been agreed that the former eight zones should be merged into a northern and a southern zone and that permission should be granted for set-offs of incoming and outgoing transmission.[56]

As a result of the new association agreement, competition for small consumers has now become possible. Many technical and economic obstacles have been removed by the agreed rules, the standardization of procedures and agreed transmission charges. Instead of metering, for instance, one of the following two methods to classify a given small consumer can be chosen by the local distributor: an artificial load profile inferred from the observation of the average consumption or an analytical load profile calculated by deducting the metered and the calculated consumption from the actual load profile and by attributing the remainder to customer groups (e. g. private households, small producers, service companies etc.) and the average customer.

However, the rules according to which the charges are to be calculated and the channels of information and cash flows under the new agreement are quite complex and elaborate. The system has to operate for a certain time before it can be evaluated in a reasonable way.

It will certainly take some time to implement the new Association Agreement. Companies will have to adjust their model contracts, software, metering etc, but this is being done now and the final system can be expected to operate soon.

In the author's opinion, the new system is particularly appropriate to the German situation. Although it goes beyond the minimum obligations as regards third party access provided for by the Energy Business Act and the Antitrust Act, it enables industry to draw up simple and clear rules for third party access which is a precondition for successful and significant trade and price mechanisms for electricity trade, especially in view of the power exchanges which are being set up. The new association agreement on electricity transmission will prove to be the most effective for a lively and significant electricity market in continental Central Europe.

This opinion seems to be shared by the German legislator. It has just enacted a law

---

[56] As can be inferred from the Commission's letter to the German associations of 7 January 2000, DG Competition has obviously not understood the historical perspective in which the new two-zones model has to be seen: The alternative to the agreement establishing two zones would be an agreement providing for the continuation of the former eight zones and not an agreement providing for the merger into a single zone without any delimitation as regards foreign grids. As of 1 July 2000, the grid companies have agreed to discontinue the levying of the zonal transmission charges.

amending the Power Intake Act.[57] The new Act obliges the grid operators to buy electricity originating from renewable energy sources for 0.17 Deutsche Mark per kWh and photovoltaic power for 0.99 Deutsche Mark per kWh.[58] The German Parliament has based its decision on the assumption that under the new association agreement, the grid operators will pass on their total costs to their clients.

In a new law, financial aid for hard coal cogeneration will be set at 0.09 Deutsche Mark per kWh and decrease over five years by 0.005 Deutsche Mark each year.[59] For today, it will enable cogeneration plants to obtain an income from the – unavoidable – power generation and thus to survive for the sake of providing hot water or vapour for district heating. This subsidy shall also ultimately be paid by the consumer through a cost rollover via the grids.

Both systems bear a resemblance to the old "Kohlepfennig", which was a levy on electricity introduced in order to support the German hard coal pits. The German Federal Constitutional Court declared the law implementing the "Kohlepfennig" as to be unconstitutional on the grounds that it introduced an illicit parafiscal tax.[60]

B. Gas

An association agreement for gas transmission is also being developed. As already mentioned, third party access to gas networks involves far more complicated issues than power wheeling due to less flexible production volumes, insufficient domestic production having as its result a dependence on imports, the divergent quality of gas in the deposits, the changing technical rules for conditioning, the necessity of physical transport, the volatility of load curves reflecting gas consumption over the seasons and during a given day (varying 4 to 5 times more than electricity), the storage effect of pipelines, the costly underground and tank storage, and finally the cost of delivery flexibility in sales contracts etc.[61] Accordingly, the negotiations over the gas association agreement have made little progress. However, the main aspects of the agreement have just been published.[62] The fees

---

[57] Gesetz über die Einspeisung von Strom aus erneuerbaren Energien in das öffentliche Netz (StromEG, in short), Bundesgesetzblatt 1990, part I, 2633, finally amended in 1998 by Article 3 of the Act On The New Regulation Of The Law On Energy Industry, Bundesgesetzblatt 1998, part I, 730; In an application for judicial review of the constitutionality of laws filed at the Federal Constitutional Court, the constitutionality of the Power Intake Act is being disputed; The Act has also been challenged for violating EC Competition Law (including the State Aid rules), for further references see the article of A. Heinen in this book.

[58] Erneuerbare-Energien-Gesetz (Renewable-Energies-Act), Bundesgesetzblatt 2000, part I, 305.

[59] Kraft-Wärme-Kopplungs-Gesetz (Cogeneration-Act), Bundesgesetzblatt 2000, part I, 703.

[60] Entscheidungen des Bundesverfassungsgerichts vol. 91 (1994), 186.

[61] See European Commission, *Report to the Council and the European Parliament on the harmonization requirements for Directive 98/30/EC*, COM (1999) 612 final.

[62] See *Frankfurter Allgemeine Zeitung* of 18 March 2000.

for transport by the central network will be calculated on a point-to-point basis. They will vary according to the respective pressure group and pipeline diameter. There will be flat fees for three transport zones at the regional distribution level and flat fees for transport by each local network. While the fee will include the costs of system services and limited load flexibility, services supplied by storage facilities will be charged separately. A preliminary version of the association agreement has been concluded in summer 2000. It permits retail competition for industrial consumers.

*Gian Carlo Scarsi**

COUNTRY REPORT: ITALY

I. INTRODUCTION

Italy has the world's fifth largest economy. It is one of the original members of the European Union (EU), and one of the "Group of Seven" (G-7) industrialized countries. EU membership has brought about important changes in Italy's energy sector, requiring liberalization of Italy's dominant energy monopolies. Hence, Italy's energy sector has undergone considerable restructuring in recent years. ENI, the state-held oil and gas conglomerate, along with its main subsidiaries, Agip (hydrocarbons exploration and production) and SNAM (gas supplies and distribution), and the state-owned electricity company, ENEL, had to be privatized. Both ENEL and ENI became joint stock companies in 1992. The Italian government sold off shares of ENI between 1995 and 1998, and now holds 35% of the company. The semi-monopolistic position of the national gas utility was attractive to investors and the sale raised ITL 6,300 billion for the Italian Treasury. Privatization of ENEL has been held up due to internal opposition from a small left-wing party (*Rifondazione Comunista*) which is part of the government coalition. According to EC Directives, plans for liberalization must proceed quickly in coming years, even though a formal deadline has not been specified.

State-held ENEL owns 85% of Italy's generating capacity, and is the world's fifth largest power generator. It owns 100% of transmission capacity and 93% of the distribution network in Italy. ENEL is also the country's only cross-border trader (Italy imports about 15% of its electricity, mostly from France, Switzerland, Germany, Austria, and Slovenia), although the governmental decree incorporating EC Directive 92/96/EC on the liberalization of electricity markets (the "Electricity Directive") within the Union has recently lifted the ban preventing operators other than ENEL from entering into direct trade in electricity with foreign countries. ENEL has had a legal monopoly in Italy's electricity sector since the industry was nationalized in 1962. The Italian Ministerial Decree transposing the Electricity Directive bans any generator from supplying/importing more than 50% of national demand from 1 January 2003.[1]

The deadline for implementing the Directive imposed on Member States was 19 February 1999, which Italy met just on time by means of the so-called "Bersani Decree" on electricity (see Section 3). The Bersani Decree – which entered fully into force by early spring 1999

---

* I hold responsibility for the views expressed in this article. Such views are not necessarily those of London Economics Limited. I would like to thank Anna Francescangeli for her valuable research assistance, but any mistakes remain my own.

[1] "Bersani Decree" (1999), Art. 8.

Damien Geradin (ed.), The Liberalization of Electricity and Natural Gas in the European Union, 169–195
©2001 Kluwer Law International. Printed in the Netherlands.

– finally ended ENEL's legal monopoly. Before the end of 1999, 30% of Italy's electricity market was opened to competition, and a total of 40% will be opened by 2002. In September 1999, ENEL formed three new power generation companies out of its current holdings, in what is likely to be the world's largest initial public offering in 2000. The three generation companies account for about 25% of ENEL's current generation capacity (around 15,000 MW).

In addition to opening up the Italian electric power generation market, the Bersani Decree also ended ENEL's monopoly on imports and sales. Finally, it allowed Independent Power Producers (IPPs), which previously sold only to ENEL at publicly regulated bulk prices, to sell directly to industrial consumers. ENEL's most recent policies in response to increasing market liberalization and regulation are multi-faceted. As ENEL reduces its Italian holdings, it is becoming increasingly involved in joint ventures abroad. In August 1999, ENEL signed an agreement with the Greek firm Prometheus Gaz to establish ENELCO, which will develop, finance, and implement energy projects in Greece and other South-Eastern European countries. This joint venture may jeopardize previous plans for the construction of a pipeline under the Adriatic Sea to link Greece and Italy.

Italy is heavily reliant on oil for its electricity generation. Largely for environmental reasons – and also under the pressure of Kyoto-related commitments and subsequent increases in fossil-fuel taxation – natural gas for electricity generation (CCGT) is now subject to heavily increasing demand. Coal is far more polluting than either gas or oil, and EU and Kyoto Protocol agreements, as well as strongly opposed public opinion, have prevented Italy from opening any new coal-fired plants.

Italy has four nuclear power plants, all owned by ENEL. None of them is currently in operation. In 1987, in the emotional wake of the Chernobyl accident, a public referendum decided against the use of nuclear power. The plants have remained idle since that time, and no nuclear generation is expected in the foreseeable future. Decommissioning costs related to nuclear power will be treated as stranded costs by ENEL, with an ex-post recoupment approach probably leading the European Commission to consider (and sanction) the recovery mechanism – if applied in its current form – as plain State aid.

With limited domestic energy sources, Italy is highly dependent on energy imports. As of 1998, Italy was estimated to be less than 20% self-sufficient in terms of energy. Historically, the country has relied heavily on imported oil, much of it from North Africa (Libya). In recent years, oil consumption has declined (although Italy remains one of the largest oil consumers in Western Europe) in favour of natural gas. Natural gas is a much cleaner fossil fuel that helps Italy to meet domestic, European, and broader international requirements for a cleaner environment. As with oil, North Africa is a large exporter of natural gas to Italy. Algeria (Sonatrach) is the largest single supplier, and a new agreement with Libya makes the region an even more important supply source. The second-largest high-risk exporter to Italy is Russia's Gazprom. There have been concerns that this reliance on North African and Russian sources has potentially negative implications for Italian energy security.

The next Sections will in turn analyze the electricity and natural gas markets.

II. THE ELECTRICITY MARKET

The Italian energy market is characterized by a lack of indigenous resources, which makes Italy heavily dependent on imports. Oil is imported together with gas, whereas electricity is mainly self-produced from fuel imports. Nonetheless, a fraction of the country's electricity requirements is also imported, with France, Switzerland, Germany, Austria and Slovenia being the main sources of supply. Ironically enough, imported electricity generally comes from massive foreign nuclear plants, which are sometimes located not far from the Italian border (Swiss sub-Alpine regions, and South-Eastern France), thus making Italy's choice to give up nuclear power (1987) a curious affair.

Italy's energy policy has been centralized since 1962, when the government decided to take over the electricity industry and create a fully integrated monopolist, named ENEL (or *Ente Nazionale per l'Energia Elettrica,* i.e. National Electricity Board). Private generators were then *de jure* transferred to public ownership at symbolic prices, whereas the transmission/distribution network, which had enjoyed a mixed ownership structure with the State already being involved in high-voltage transmission, was almost completely transferred to the newly created ENEL. Finally, town-based distribution and retail supply went public, too, with some exclusive franchises being granted to local authorities in some (especially Northern) mid-sized towns and large conurbations. Municipal distribution was also devised for several mountain villages located in South Tyrol.

ENEL was kept separated from ENI *(Ente Nazionale Idrocarburi,* or National Fuels Board), which mainly managed the processing of oil and gas. Some links were – however – established, since the two companies enjoyed some scale economies relating to the joint production of refined oil, gas and heat for power co-generation. The previously mixed structure of electricity generation and supply was reformed in such a way so as to leave industrial customers with their own generation and co-generation plants (FIAT in Turin, Breda/Ansaldo in Genoa, Italsider/ILVA in Naples and Taranto, and so on). Nonetheless, auto-generated electricity, as a by-product of industrial activities, was legally confined to self-consumption, thus preventing large industrial firms from entering the electricity market, which was then structured as a legal monopoly. *De jure* importing rights were also granted, so as to make ENEL the only Italian firm being entitled to trade electricity on an international basis. Both imports and exports were then conveyed through the national publicly owned incumbent.

On the other hand, retail supply was regulated according to a three-party licensing scheme among the government, ENEL and some municipal authorities, ending up in a mixed structure where smaller towns, rural areas and almost all territories in the South were served by ENEL itself as a final supplier, whereas separate local concerns were licensed as retailers – and often distributors – to operate within more developed, especially Northern urban contexts.

Pricing policies for public utility services have traditionally been highly centralized in Italy. With special reference to electricity, the Interministerial Committee for Prices *(Comitato Interministeriale Prezzi,* or CIP) directed prices and tariff structures according to a command-and-control criterion since energy nationalization took place. CIP was abolished on 1 January 1994, when a presidential decree transferred responsibility for the regulation of electricity tariffs to the Ministry of Industry and CIPE *(Comitato Inter-ministeriale per la Programmazione Economica),* which is the main economic planning body in Italy. This was bound to be a provisional arrangement, since the government also decided in 1996 to establish certain independent authorities to regulate the public utilities.

The first proposed regulatory option was to create a single regulatory body for all utilities. However, staggered divestiture plans for different utilities, as well as technical reasons, suggested that separate regulators should be set up for each sector, in a similar structure to that in the United Kingdom. The Milanese electricity regulatory body *(Autorità per l'Energia ed il Gas)* was finally set up in September 1996, and is currently organized as a non-governmental department, being responsible towards the Parliament. It has an independent chairman and two deputies, who are in charge for seven years, and its full staff is around eighty people.

The salient features of the Italian electricity supply industry as it stands today (early 2000) may be summarized as follows:
–   mixed thermal-hydro generation base;
–   high concentration with significant interconnection and imports;
–   some transmission constraints; and
–   forthcoming liberalization of the wholesale electricity market (2001).

Gross capacity and output in 1998 (ENEL data) are shown in Table 1 below.

Table 1. Capacity and output figures, Italy, 1998 (source: ENEL)

	Gross			**Net**		
	ENEL	*Others*	*Total*	*ENEL*	*Others*	*Total*
Capacity (MW)	58,906	16,050	74,956	56,894	15,619	72,513
Output (MWh)	189,684	70,102	259,786	179,484	67,459	246,943

As Table 2 shows, concentration is a prominent issue, together with import-dependence. In a nutshell, ENEL dominates the market but imports – no longer subject to ENEL's monopoly since 1999 – are significant.

Table 2. ENEL and other operators, Italy, 1998 (source: ENEL)

1998	ENEL	Munici-palities	Auto-producers	Others	Total
Gross output (MWh)	189,684	9,754	57,785	2,563	259,786
Net output (MWh)	179,484	9,332	55,627	2,500	246,943
% gross output	73.0	3.8	22.2	1	100
% net output	72.7	3.8	22.5	1	100

Capacity ownership remains concentrated – even accounting for planned power station divestment as devised by the Bersani Decree (see Table 3 and Section 3).

Table 3. ENEL's generating capacity (MW) before and after divestment (source: Power in Europe, 27 September 1999)

	Thermal	Hydro	Other	Sum
ENEL – before divestment	41,008	16,639	576	58,223
A	6,242	766	0	7,008
B	4,424	1,014	0	5,438
C	2,548	63	0	2,611
	13,214	1,843	0	15,057
ENEL – after divestment	27,794	14,796	576	43,166

Transmission constraints are an issue in Italy, even though their relevance is probably limited once we exclude a bottleneck just South of the Apennines in the Florence area. Figure 1 below is a map of Italy's 380kV transmission grid in 1998 – please notice that the rectangle on the top right corner of the map zooms in on the North-Eastern area bounded by Milan and Brescia (Lombardy), where a separate "mini-grid" operated by a number of municipalities is also present.

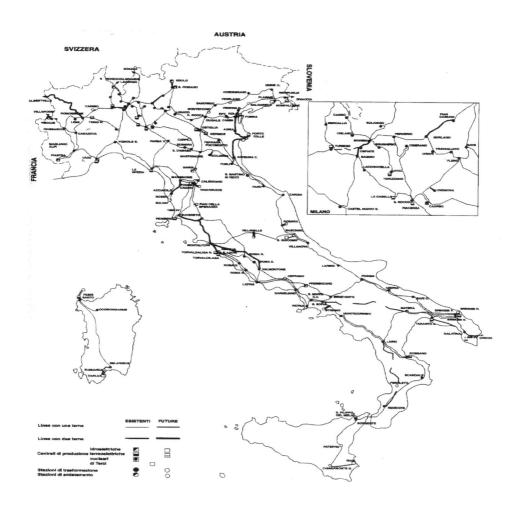

Figure 1. Map of ENEL's transmission grid, 1998 (source: ENEL)

Finally, on the liberalization of the wholesale electricity market, we refer the reader to Section 3 on institutional changes and the Bersani Decree in particular.

The Italian generating capacity in 1998 (ENEL data) was based on:

– imports from Switzerland, France, Germany (via Switzerland), Austria, and Slovenia (16.9% of total supplies);
– own generation, totalling 72.5 GW at end-1998, subdivided into oil-fired and orimulsion[2] generation (47.4%), hydro power (19.6%), gas turbines (21.2%), coal generation (9%), plus some geothermal generation (2.8%).

Provisional 1999 data from the newly-established *Gestore della Rete di Trasmissione Nazionale* (GRTN) show that total electricity demand in Italy (1999) has risen to 285.8 TWh from 279 TWh in the previous year (+2.3%).[3] ENEL's total losses in the generating system are mainly due to the low efficiency of older plants, which are now being replaced by new CCGT generators (11.7 GW of new gas plant capacity was planned by ENEL over the period 1996-2000). Gas/oil substitution will cause a massive switch from oil to natural gas (thanks to some new flexible multi-fired plants) in such a way that oil-based generation should fall to 36.5% of the total by end-2001. Hydro-power should be retained, albeit with some restructuring, and coal-fired generation will be gradually reduced, although not phased out completely in view of heavy labour-market pressures.

However, electricity imports are bound to go up in the foreseeable future because of the government's difficulties in reaching agreement with local authorities on the location of new multi-fired – and potentially polluting – stations. Nevertheless, some nuclear research is under way in order to convert old nuclear stations to a brand-new, cleaner technology which could make the nuclear option politically more appealing in the medium term.

III. ELECTRICITY LIBERALIZATION

Except for auto-generation as a by-product of some big industrial firms, power generation has continuously been under ENEL's monopolistic control from 1962 to 1991. The first concrete moves aimed at tackling the liberalization problem in electricity generation coincided with Laws No. 9 and 10 of 1991. Law no. 9/1991 partially deregulated independent generation, and – as a result of this – some 5,300 MW of capacity was commissioned to independent producers over the period 1993-1998. Independent capacity (municipal utilities, industrial co-generators and other producers such as Edison and FIAT) responded with a 240 MW rise.

---

[2] Orimulsion is a water-based heavy petroleum emulsion developed in Venezuela. The bitumen is increasingly used to generate electricity. In 1999, Italy bought two million tons of orimulsion, followed by Canada with 1.8 million tons. Japan and Denmark are also big buyers.

[3] Macroeconomic recovery in Italy has pushed up demand in 1999 – as opposed to 1998 – especially in the North-Eastern districts and the islands, according to GRTN's provisional figures. Always notice that the difference between demand and internal production is covered by imports.

As a result of generating capacity being partially shifted to independent operators, ENEL is now expecting that its share in total generation will be reduced from more than 80% in 1993 to less than 50% by 2002.

Before Italian legislation provided for the compulsory restructuring of some of ENEL's activities, the incumbent had already put in place a number of self-imposed restructuring measures, including the accounting and legal separation of generation, transmission, distribution, and retail supply. Moreover, non-core activities such as mobile communications and water services have been incorporated as separate joint stock companies.

The so-called "Bersani Decree" transposed Directive 92/96 in early 1999. Its main restructuring measures are listed below:

– Establishment of an Independent System Operator – physically separated yet majority-owned by ENEL – to regulate access to the incumbent's transmission and distribution network (the inconsistency is clear, as pointed out by several academic sources in Italy, and by the industry regulator);

– Forced divestment of capacity by ENEL – 15 GW of plant by 2003 into three separate companies (the list of plants has been published, and the companies were legally set up in the second half of 1999);[4]

– Introduction of a Power Pool by 2001, with a parallel bilateral contract market (the regulatory by-laws aimed at regulating its functioning have not been published yet, though);

– Establishment of a Single Buyer with the duty of procuring energy for 'franchise' (i.e. domestic) customers;

– Obligation for ENEL to purchase or produce at least 2% of output in the form of "new" renewable generation (so-called "CIP 6" obligations);

– Rationalization of distribution – for large cities (exceeding 300,000 customers), ENEL has been obliged to offer its assets for sale to municipalities by the end of March 2000;

– Definition of a phased timetable for retail market eligibility (eligible vs. "franchise", or "captive", customers) spanning from 1999 to 2004;[5] and

– Definition of Third Party Access (TPA) transmission tariffs: the 'postage stamp' principle has been adopted as a rule, thus making third-party access pricing (almost) independent of distance. A distance-related component has – however – been introduced on top of the flat postage-stamp fee.

---

[4] The three generating companies have a similar plant mix, and are evenly headquartered across the Italian territory – one in the North, one in the Centre, and one in the South. The location of their headquarters, however, does not reflect any particular geographical plant bias: plants belonging to each of the three companies are evenly spread throughout the country.

[5] The Bersani Decree states that any customer having consumed at least 20 GWh in the previous year shall be considered as "eligible" from 1/1/2000. The threshold will come down to 9 GWh from 1/1/2002. From the same day, any customer having consumed at least 1 GWh in the previous year will also be considered as "eligible", provided that such a customer is part of an organization having consumed at least 40 GWh overall on the national territory.

ENEL's plant divestment as devised by the Bersani Decree entails the sale of around 15 GW of generating power. Notwithstanding the 2003 deadline, ENEL declared that it is ready to sell by the end of 2000 – or, ideally, as soon as possible – the three companies being already put in place in 1999. Criticism has arisen on the fact that ENEL is simply getting rid of old and inefficient thermal plant. The capacity mix being identified by ENEL to abide by the Bersani Decree's provisions is a mixed hydro-thermal one with some emphasis being put on big, middle-aged heavy-fuel stations. Notice that the plant mix has still to be granted final approval by the energy regulator.

The geographical spread of ENEL's 15 GW plant divestment programme is varied, encompassing areas from all of Italy's regions (including Sicily and Sardinia). Moreover, ENEL has already implemented accounting and vertical separation, as well as some multi-utility diversification leading to the expression of some public concerns. ENEL's privatization is stalled at the moment, in view of the results of the regional elections held in April 2000 (which triggered a change of government following the right-wing majority in Italy's leading regions). Should the regional results lead to a general election, there exists a chance of right-wing victory, probably leading to a change of policy towards ENEL's privatization. However, it is not clear whether a right-wing coalition will be successful in forcing ENEL's 100% privatization in the short term.

IV. ENVIRONMENTAL ISSUES

Even though electricity is not as polluting *per se* as other kinds of energy, the choice among different generating technologies is crucial in determining the industry's contribution to global CO_2 emissions, which Italy has accepted to reduce by 6.5% as compared to 1990 levels by 2010 (according to the Kyoto Protocol). For instance, oil and coal-based generation poses problems in terms of air pollution, whereas even hydro power, which is the least polluting of all technologies, may result in earthquake – as well as landslide – risks being increased, let alone visual amenity problems.

In this respect, Law no. 61/1994 established a new national environmental protection agency, called ANPA *(Agenzia Nazionale per la Protezione Ambientale),* which has been charged with promoting and conducting environmental research, providing technical support to regulators in formulating standards, and co-operating with the European Environment Agency (EEA).

As a general consideration, the Italian government should increase efforts to resolve conflicts of national, regional and local jurisdiction in order to operate new environmentally friendly stations (CCGTs, renewables, and some new hydro power) to provide for greater flexibility in the choice of fuel inputs, within the constraints of national, European, and global CO_2 emissions targets.

The set-up of ANPA (the national environmental protection agency) has to be considered as a positive event, subject to the caveat that some form of co-ordination is now needed between ANPA and the other regulatory bodies at various levels, in order to implement a common environmental policy which could be defended against external pressure groups. Some co-ordination would also be necessary between ANPA and ENEA, the Italian board for technological research in the energy sector.

In addition, the use of renewable fuels should be encouraged. ENEL has recently phased in three experimental wind farms based in Central Italy's Apennines and in Sardinia, so as to increase Italy's alternative generation capacity, which stood at a modest 45 MW of wind power capacity in the mid nineties.

The last environmental prescription for the Italian government is to try curbing energy demand growth, with special reference to the road transport sector (motorways) – whose congestion has reached unacceptable levels – especially by stimulating freight demand on railways.[6]

V. MUNICIPAL UTILITIES

Local utility services in Italy have traditionally been operated by municipally-owned concerns. Such firms, known as *Aziende Municipalizzate*, have been structured in such a way that almost all public utility services at city levels were transferred from national utility monopolists to City Councils, which were granted concessions from the government to run those services by using their own plants and personnel.

Both price and quality levels, however, are set by Ministerial Decrees according to 'geographic uniformity' criteria, and generally set price/quality mixes at the same levels as those being imposed upon national utilities. This clearly stimulates local utilities to cream-skim at ENEL's territorial borders whenever possible. They are also allowed to retain the profits stemming from urban services being priced at the nation-wide average. The rationalization process which municipal utilities underwent during the past few years downsized municipal electricity distribution to a considerable extent – from 12% in the Sixties to 7% in 1994.

Local distributors are now serving around 2.5 million customers and distributing almost 17,000 MWh energy – around 7% of Italy's total electricity output in 1998. However, they generate only 9,300 MWh (less than 4% of Italy's overall figure), the remainder being

---

[6] Note that Italy has signed up to the Kyoto Protocol. The Convention on Climate Change was initiated at the UN Headquarters, New York City, in May 1992; it was open for signature at Rio de Janeiro from 4 to 14 June 1992, and thereafter at the UN Headquarters themselves until 19 June 1993. By that date, the Convention had received 166 signatures. It entered into force on 21 March 1994. Ratification of the Convention went on until the Kyoto Conference on Climate Change (December 1997) and is still taking place. Italy ratified the Convention on 15 April 1994, after signing it on 5 June 1992. Following ratification, the agreement entered into force on 14 July 1994 in Italy. Italy confirmed its emissions commitments (CO_2) for the year 2000 at the Kyoto Conference on Climate Change, and also promised to reduce its carbon dioxide emissions by 6.5% (as compared to 1990 levels) by 2010. This is not a tremendous commitment, since e.g. Germany committed to a 21% reduction from 1990 levels by the year 2010.

covered by ENEL's medium-voltage power. Electricity liberalization in Italy has stimulated some of these municipal concerns to set themselves up as joint stock companies, thus paving the way for stock market flotation of the largest municipalities (Milan, Rome, Turin) – which took place in 1999.

Industry concentration for local distributors in Italy is very high: there are a few municipal firms serving highly populated areas, plus a substantial fringe of smaller, provincial units which hold concessions in the countryside and the mountains (mainly in the North-Eastern districts).[7] In fact, only four municipal distributors own distribution plants and networks which exceed 100 MW capacity, with more than 100,000 customers and 100 employees: these are Milan (AEM Milan), Turin (AEM Turin), Rome (ACEA), and Brescia (ASM).

Nonetheless, it is worth noticing that only Rome and the Northern industrial district of Brescia enjoy complete territorial coverage over their municipal jurisdictions, whereas Milan and Turin currently feature a 'double' distribution system, with their municipal operators and ENEL co-existing to some extent within municipal territories. As previously noted, the Bersani Decree has now determined the amalgamation of electricity distribution for those urban areas featuring at least 300,000 customers, thus letting Rome, Milan, and Turin have a 'global' electricity distributor – not necessarily ENEL-owned.

Furthermore, a parliamentary bill (Law no. 142/1990) introduced the concept of 'metropolitan area', and granted such status to nine Italian towns (Turin, Milan, Venice, Genoa, Bologna, Florence, Rome, Bari, and Naples), which now have the right and duty – among other things – to distribute and supply both water and energy services to all kinds of customers throughout their cities and outskirts. Unfortunately, due to the fact that some of these towns had never run a proper local utility company before, electricity – as well as gas – distribution is currently being delegated to ENEL and SNAM (ENI's pipeline subsidiary). Finally, metropolitan councils should – in theory – run local railways, and operate sewage and sewerage services.

There are about forty local electric utilities. Except for a couple of distributors in the Centre and just one in the South-East, all remaining municipal firms are concentrated in Northern towns. They are regarded as being efficiently run overall, even though it is not always easy to separate their electricity business from other public utility services. Internal cross-subsidization has traditionally been widespread, in particular in those firms also operating local bus and underground services.

ENEL has often suggested that local distributors are too small in terms of efficient production scale, which would lead to either closing them down, or merging them into ENEL's distribution arm. However, the most advanced local utilities enjoy substantial scale and scope economies by operating electricity, water, sewage and sewerage, gas, district heating from co-generation, public lighting, public transport, and the processing of urban waste. They may be regarded as full multi-utility companies, albeit their scale of

---

[7] See Kwoka (1996) on the limited amount of competition in electricity distribution which exists in the US. With respect to the US case, the author finds that competition in distribution does reduce costs.

operations is strongly constrained by the presence of nation-wide suppliers managing public utility services throughout the country.

Even though national monopolists such as ENI and ENEL would like local distributors to be either absorbed or shut down, the debate is open with reference to the optimal scale of production at which such concerns should be allowed to operate. Some provincial expansion is being observed at the moment for Northern local utilities. This is broadly consistent with the outcomes of a number of efficiency studies.[8]

Local utilities usually co-generate electricity and heat, which is carried through (under-ground) heating pipelines and conveyed to the customer's premises.[9] Their distribution networks and substations are connected to ENEL's national grid, as well as to the micro-systems of neighbouring municipal concerns. Similarly, natural gas, which was introduced in Italy during the 1950s to replace coal-based gas, is distributed to both households and industrial customers by means of micro-grids being connected to SNAM's high-pressure pipelines.

Electricity voltage is scaled down thanks to municipally-owned substations and capacitors, whereas SNAM's raw natural gas is de-pressurized at the local Council's expense. On the other hand, industrial customers are directly provided with medium or high-pressure gas. Water pumping businesses are sometimes owned by municipalities for both water storage and hydro-electricity.[10] However, CCGTs (Combined Cycle Gas Turbines) are rapidly becoming the favourite technology in terms of both cost efficiency and environmental friendliness.

Local utilities have long complained about administrative prices for wholesale electricity or 'Tariffe Uniche Nazionali' (TUN) – which were equivalent to bulk supply tariffs. Apart from buying ENEL's high-voltage electricity and producing some by themselves, local distributors are also interconnected to neighbouring networks owned by bordering municipal utilities.[11]

Even though 'consumer charters' are present to establish and enforce customer rights

---

[8] See *Scarsi* (1998) and *Scarpa* (1999).

[9] The first Italian operator to introduce networked heating in Italy was the Northern industrial centre of Brescia, which started to 'distribute' heat to households in 1972, and implemented electricity and heat co-generation from waste in 1978.

[10] This is particularly true of North-Eastern utilities situated in the East of Lombardy and in the Northern provinces of the Venetian area (Veneto's highlands and Trentino-Südtirol).

[11] Municipal distributors are connected to both ENEL and other municipal networks. This stems from the past, municipal structure of electricity distribution in the North of Italy prior to nationalization (1962). For instance, the Northern and North-Eastern municipal utilities based in Milan, Brescia, Verona, Rovereto, and Vicenza (located in Lombardy, Veneto, and Trentino) jointly own a co-ordinating centre managing electricity transfers and swaps on both their distribution and transmission networks. Of course, ENEL also takes part in this process, but the municipal links are older and generally prioritized by MUNIs, which turn to ENEL's supply as a last resort option only (for peaks in demand). Gas pipelines are run by municipalities according to similar criteria. Gas, as well as electricity, might be distributed on a regional basis by some municipalities in the near future. Milan's privatized AEM has also embarked upon ambitious Internet and multi-media ventures.

with respect to low-voltage (domestic) electricity supply, it is worth noting that local distributors are still 100% retail supply monopolists. Phased liberalization of retail supply, however, is now under way in Italy following the Bersani Decree's provisions.

The main differences between ENEL's distributing arm and local utilities – apart from size – are the following:

- municipal authorities sometimes co-generate electricity and heat, which is distributed to final customers along with electricity itself, with possible scope economies and (in some cases) no accounting separation;
- several public utility services are provided by local concerns. This – once again – gives rise to scope effects, together with non-trivial common cost allocation problems;
- even though municipal concerns serve industrial demand as well, their customer structure is generally biased in favour of domestic users (with the noticeable exception of some medium-sized industrial districts in Northern Italy); and
- ENEL's capital structure is significantly 'heavier' than that of municipal firms, even after adjusting for size, as the national monopolist is legally required to operate below its real plant capacity because of obvious security reasons. In other words, ENEL is compelled to maintain excess capacity to some extent, whereas local distributors are not.[12]

During 1998, Italy's municipal distributors (MUNIs) applied for the status of 'exclusive dealers' of electricity (distribution, supply, and sometimes generation) within those urban areas which currently feature a mixed distribution structure (MUNIs plus ENEL). Such a move on the municipal side was obviously aimed at gaining complete dominance over those urban and metropolitan areas which are today shared with ENEL's local branches. ENEL rejected municipal claims by counter-proposing a different scenario in which urban and metropolitan areas would be served by an exclusive franchisee stemming from a consortium between ENEL itself and the local MUNI. Alternatively, ENEL was willing to take over municipal assets and serve urban areas as an exclusive dealer. The Bersani Decree seems to be consistent with ENEL's view, but gives municipalities the right of choice by forcing ENEL to offer its urban distributing assets for sale first (under regulatory scrutiny). Thus, ENEL is left as a residual buyer should the local utility decline the offer.

VI. FURTHER ISSUES IN THE ELECTRICITY SECTOR

Even following the Bersani Decree's enforcement, some regulatory issues remain undecided. We list them in turn:

---

[12] In other words, ENEL may be regarded as the last-resort distributor with respect to all municipally-served customers.

– Stranded costs:[13] Italy has asked for a maximum of ITL 15,000bn (£ 5bn) of stranded costs. The recovery mechanism has been set out in January 2000. In practice, it appears that stranded costs will be recovered on an 'ex post' basis, i.e. after they have been listed by the incumbent and reimbursed by the government. This entails that the European Commission is likely to consider these mechanisms as straight-forward state aids;

– Financial incentives for renewable generation (so-called "CIP 6") have not been clarified yet;

– Some 5 GW of new "CIP 6" generation is expected on the system by 2003, but the regulator's recent interventions on this issue may affect the set-up of some of the new ecological plants; and

– Retail tariff controls seem to remain an open issue, even though the energy regulator set out RPI-X price caps for retail supply in July 1999 (with the price cap being initially fixed at RPI-4%).

However, the main issue is that, even after divestment, ENEL will be likely to dominate the Electricity Pool. The incumbent's market share will be unlikely to fall below 50% unless the policy-maker imposes further plant divestment. ENEL's likely dominance of the Pool stems from the fact that the incumbent will still be able to act as a "residual monopolist" on the top of the demand curve, as Figure 2 below shows.

Looking at the modelling of wholesale electricity markets, and considering Italy's peculiar features in the energy sector, the main price drivers are likely to be both static and dynamic. The static price drivers for the future are likely to be:

– fuel prices, especially gas and oil (the latter accounts for 60% of domestic thermal production, but ENEL now intends to re-power a substantial number of its plants);

– the "exogenous" (non-controllable) behaviour of pondage hydroelectric energy, mainly depending on weather;[14]

– demand behaviour; and

– short-run evolution of renewable and interconnection capacity.

Among the dynamic price drivers, we shall be likely to see long-run effects stemming from the adjustment of fixed factors such as further plant divestment, phasing-out, re-powering, and re-building. Since more than 50% of output will be likely to be controlled by ENEL even after divestment, strategic behaviour is likely to take place in the forthcoming Pool market. Frequently repeated interaction in the day-ahead Pool may give rise to the potential for "tacit collusion" between the incumbent and a fringe of smaller players – as already observed in the Electricity Pool of England and Wales. On the other hand, the

---

[13] Stranded costs relate to those inputs which, following entry in a previously foreclosed market, become economically infeasible for the incumbent player (in this case, the formerly legal monopolist ENEL).

[14] Note that, in Italy, hydro-electric generation accounts for about 20% of domestic output.

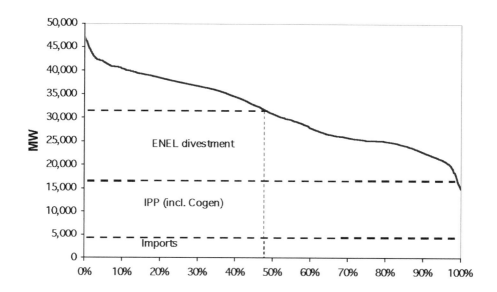

Figure 2. ENEL's residual monopoly power following 15 GW divestment: load curve with 12 GW IPP capacity and 4.5 GW imported electricity (source: author's and London Economics' calculations based on ENEL data)

'static' exercise of market power may result in the following:
- non-cost reflective bidding in the form of price-cost "mark-ups" (i.e., surcharges above marginal cost);
- non-innocent "withdrawal", or hold-up, of thermal capacity (suspect early plant retirement?); and
- strategic dispatch of hydroelectric energy in order to "peak-shave" demand – a phenomenon being widely observed in Spain in recent years.[15]

On the other hand, the so-called 'dynamic' exercise of market power can take the form of entry deterrence measures such as:
- short-term drops in prices which increase price uncertainty;

---

[15] "Peak-shaving" takes place when the incumbent takes control of demand peaks by strategically despatching plants characterized by low marginal cost (such as hydro and nuclear) at a moment when demand for all competitors is already saturated.

- capacity pre-commitment over time (a credible threat of fighting) obtained via the long-term deployment of extra plants even when apparently superfluous; and
- systematic retail foreclosure via downstream price wars, unfair advertizing, territorial pre-emption, and the like.

In addition, market rules for the Electricity Pool should be specified by the regulatory agency. The economic regulator is also expected to restructure the downstream market for electricity supply to final customers (both industrial and residential), in order to scrutinize ENEL's negotiations with retailers and open up the retail supply subset of production to competition. Finally, the regulatory authority is expected to set standards for investment in transmission and distribution, as well as quality and environmental[16] parameters.

Economic regulation affects electricity prices by changing the players' incentives and constraining their bidding behaviour. In the generation market, the regulator may seek to limit the exercise of market power by ENEL in the wholesale market via a number of measures, namely:

- the imposition of contracts between ENEL and the Single Buyer (the latter not ENEL-owned, preferably?);
- the imposition of a stranded cost recovery mechanism (not *ex post*);
- the credible threat of further ENEL divestment; and
- the auctioning off of ENEL-related Power Purchase Agreements to third parties (Independent Power Producers).

In addition to regulatory scrutiny, new entrants should be encouraged by the fact that apparently ample room for manoeuvre still exists for cost-effective entry. Indeed, ENEL claims its average wholesale costs are at around 90 ITL/kWh, whereas the short-run marginal cost (SRMC) of an oil plant is commonly estimated at 50-55 ITL/kWh. The long-run marginal cost (LRMC) of a combined-cycle gas turbine (CCGT) plant should not exceed 60-70 ITL/kWh. Will it be possible for the whole Italian generation system to converge towards cost efficiency? Convergence to cost (and, given free entry, price) efficiency will be affected by a number of technical and economic factors:

- plant retirement (ENEL has announced plans to place 6 GW on reserve capacity);
- plant conversion and new entry; and
- market re-organization via financial arrangements such as the so-called "Contracts for Differences" (CfDs), which are akin to financial options on bulk electricity.

---

[16] The importance of environmental regulation should not be understated: for example, in his analysis of productivity growth in the American electricity generation industry, Gordon (1992) found that productivity growth was actually negative between 1968 and 1987, this being partially due to higher environmental costs imposed by energy regulators (electricity regulation in the USA is co-ordinated by the Federal Energy Regulatory Commission or FERC).

VII. RPI-X REGULATION OF DOWNSTREAM ACTIVITIES

The regulatory price formula which was first devised in 1994 is aimed at calculating annual tariff adjustments. Its first version actually dates back to 1991, when the electricity supply industry's tariff structure was still under CIP's control. According to such a rule, price changes on a yearly basis could not exceed the Retail Price Index (RPI) minus a productivity parameter, which should reflect expected technological improvements in the industry. In fact, the X factor has actually been set for the first time in July 1999, when the energy regulator imposed RPI-4 for the first 5-year regulatory period (retail supply).

The authority is setting price caps according to a RPI-X+Y scheme (Y being the cost pass-through element onto final customers for those input prices which will be deemed exogenous to the electricity industry). X at 4% covers franchise, or 'captive', customers (eligible customers face unregulated retail supply), whereas Y has still to be announced.

The future regulatory scheme will also include some indicators for service quality (which have not been specified so far), as well as fluctuations in exogenous costs (such as fuel input costs, to be passed on to consumers). Notably, some input costs are not properly exogenous under the current circumstances, since the Italian government is entitled to alter them by means of several economic policy measures. Once the whole energy industry is privatized, exogeneity of fuel prices will probably be more plausible, especially now that ENEL's monopoly rights on foreign trade have been removed.

Tariff issues, as well as quality regulation, are now among the regulatory body's responsibilities, together with the resolution of pricing disputes. Some co-ordination is also being sought between the industry regulator and the Italian Antitrust Authority (AGCM, or *Autorità Garante della Concorrenza e del Mercato).* Since energy taxes still remain quite high in the country (fossil fuels being the most heavily taxed), Italy decided to say 'no' to a proposed EU energy/carbon tax in 1996. In this respect, it is worth noticing that heavy energy taxation in Italy is not due to any environmental or 'Pigouvian' concerns. On the contrary, it is just aimed at raising revenue by overtaxing inelastically demanded commodities such as oil and, albeit to a lesser extent, gas: in other words, it is a 'Ramsey' tax. General taxation pressures are, therefore, undermining Italy's energy intensity,[17] which already ranks quite low as compared to the average of the industrial set of OECD countries which are periodically surveyed by the International Energy Agency.

The Italian government has clearly stated that geographic uniformity of electricity prices will be kept as part of universal service commitments. Therefore, cross-subsidization among customers is likely to persist, unless a compensation fund is set up to smooth out differences in local supply costs. Quantity discounts to large customers are likely to be reduced, as a price discrimination ban is under way.[18] However, individual negotiation with large

---

[17] 'Energy intensity' is defined by the IEA (International Energy Agency) as the ratio between Total Primary Energy Supply (TPES) and Gross Domestic Product (GDP).

[18] Nonetheless, quantity discounts might well be justified by corresponding differences in underlying costs.

industrial customers will be maintained in view of the European Directive, provided that all negotiated terms are published by the utility. This should discourage undue preference, even though the real applicability of such a measure is highly jeopardized by asymmetric information problems. In any case, even when publication requirements are met with no cheating, no legal 'most favoured nation clause' will constrain the utility's pricing policies.

According to the government's plans, a transition period of no less than five years will be required for the gradual phasing out of cross-subsidies. The so-called 'social tariff' has also been abolished, thus pushing up Italian electricity prices to final customers considerably over the last three years. Fixed rentals, which once had been set to purely symbolic levels, have experienced the most dramatic rise. The phasing out of cross-subsidies has also increased prices at peak hours, as network congestion requirements induced the Italian authorities to adopt more severe time-of-day tariff schedules.

VIII. THE NATURAL GAS MARKET

Italy's reliance on natural gas imports has risen substantially since massive imports began in the early 1970s, when the then state-held *Ente Nazionale Idrocarburi* (ENI) started to purchase gas from the Netherlands and Russia. Italy is currently the third-largest gas market in Europe, behind Germany and the United Kingdom. Natural gas use has increased sharply in recent years, especially for power generation (CCGT). Gas now represents about 30% of total energy consumed in Italy, and this share is expected to grow in the coming years. According to ENEL officials, 60% of electricity in Italy will be generated by natural gas and only 10% by oil by 2010; currently, oil accounts for about 47% of generation and gas for only 21%.

ENI, a massive oil and gas conglomerate, used to hold *de facto* monopoly control over the Italian gas market through its pipeline subsidiary, SNAM. In a similar fashion to the electricity sector, a European Directive requires deregulation in the Italian gas industry. Italy implemented the Directive by means of a recent ministerial decree – which shadows the one already approved for electricity in 1999. The gas decree came into effect in February 2000.

ENI has been a publicly traded, joint stock company since 1992. Shares were sold off in four separate offerings between 1995 and 1998, and the state now holds 35% of the company. Prior to the gas liberalization decree, SNAM has retained its *de facto* – not legal – monopoly in the pipeline business, controlling almost 90% of the market. According to the EC Directive, though, 30% of the sector must be deregulated by June 2000, 38% by 2003, and 43% by 2008.

Edison (Electricity and Gas), the power-related arm of the formerly public Montedison Group, is the leading independent power producer in Italy, and its role in – and share of – the gas industry are expected to increase as deregulation continues. Edison Gas signed a deal to have Algerian gas delivered to Italy through the TransMed pipeline beginning in

2003. When negotiating third-party access with SNAM, the operator of the nation-wide pipeline, for use of the TransMed interconnector, Edison – as well as the incumbent – will be subject to regulatory scrutiny in order to complete the deal. Edison Gas is also pushing for a marine pipeline to link Algeria with the Mediterranean islands of Sardinia and Corsica.

As previously underlined, diversification of supply is an important issue, as Italy relies heavily on two high-risk suppliers (Algeria and Russia). In 1997, Italian gas sources were estimated to be 30% domestic, 30% Algerian, 26% Russian and 10% Dutch (the remaining 4% was in the form of liquefied natural gas, and was imported from Algeria). The major alternative suppliers that Italy is considering are Libya and Norway. The biggest project under consideration is the proposed construction of a pipeline to link Libya and Sicily. This "West Libya Gas Project" was finalized in July 1999 as a joint venture between Libya's state-held National Oil Company and ENI. A 600-kilometre (372-mile) pipeline will run under the Mediterranean and connect with the TransMed, delivering a total of 8 billion cubic metres per year, starting in 2003/2004. SNAM has also signed a 25-year contract to receive 6 billion cubic metres per year of Norwegian natural gas through existing pipelines, beginning in 2000.

Prior to the outbreak of further hostilities in Yugoslavia in the spring of 1999, a conference was held in Italy to discuss the possible construction of pipelines to connect the Caspian region, Libya and Russia. The connection of the pipelines would have made Italy a transit centre for the producing regions. No further action has been taken on these plans. Problems in Yugoslavia also halted a deal between SNAM and Romania's SNGN Romgaz. According to their agreement in the summer of 1998, gas would be piped from Romania to Italy via an extension of the Adria line that links Croatia to the European network. Even after the relative political improvements in Southern Yugoslavia, it is uncertain whether the project will continue.

ENI is also involved in projects outside Italy. In the late winter of 1999, the Russian natural gas monopoly Gazprom and ENI signed an agreement to co-operate on the 'Blue Stream' project. The project will involve laying a 400-kilometre (250-mile) pipeline on the floor of the Black Sea to connect Russia and Turkey. Each company will hold a 50% share in the project, and the gas will be sold jointly by the two companies in Turkey. SNAM is also planning to be involved in a joint venture with South Korea's Hyundai Engineering and Construction in a gas project in Qatar.

Liquefied Natural Gas (LNG) accounts for less than 5% of total Italian gas consumption. Italy receives Algerian LNG at its La Spezia terminal, under a 25-year contract that runs until 2015. ENEL also signed a contract in 1992 under which Nigerian LNG will be delivered to ENEL for 22 years, beginning in 1999. In 1996, ENEL attempted to terminate the contract because environmental restrictions had blocked its planned construction of re-gasification terminals in North-Eastern Italy (Monfalcone, Gulf of Trieste). The attempt was unsuccessful. The Nigerian gas will then be delivered to a Gaz de France (GdF) terminal at Montoir de Bretagne (Saint-Nazaire), and an equal volume of Algerian and Russian pipeline gas will be re-routed to Italy in a "roundabout" system. GdF is responsible for delivering equivalent pipeline gas to ENEL via SNAM's network (connecting at the Franco-Italian border).

Currently, the whole of ENI is regulated by the Italian Authority for Electricity and Gas (AEG). Since ENI is a vertically integrated company, regulation pervades the whole industry, i.e. production, storage, transport and primary distribution. Secondary distribution is theoretically liberalized with respect to "eligible" customers (Directive 98/30/EC, incorporated into Italian legislation in February 2000), even though the AEG has determined that price-cap regulation will apply to it in the future, similarly to what has been devised for electricity distribution. SNAM, ENI's subsidiary dealing with high-pressure transport, is regulated by the AEG and – by virtue of its 9/10 market power in transport capacity – is frequently scrutinized by the Italian Antitrust Authority.[19]

Around 65% of Italy's gas comes from Algeria, Russia and the Netherlands. It is forecast that imports will go up in the future to satisfy growing demand, in the absence of any substantial rise in indigenous production. Take-or-pay contracts have also been negotiated with Norway and Libya. From 2001, SNAM will be able to import 66.5bn cubic metres (cm) gas a year, of which 10bn from the Netherlands, 22 from Algeria, 28.5 from Russia, and 6 from Norway. There are also additional 7.5bn cm being imported by ENEL, 4bn of which is supplied by Algeria via SNAM's Mediterranean pipeline, and 3.5bn by Nigeria. The Nigerian imports come from the LNG take-or-pay contract which ENEL failed to renegotiate in 1996.

Finally, from 2003 Edison Gas, ENI's only significant competitor supplying 7% of the Italian gas market, will import 4bn cm of gas per year thanks to a joint venture with Sonatrach (Algeria) and BP Amoco. Forecast imports will also come from the North Sea (1.5bn cm per year, Edison Gas), and from a joint venture between Edison Gas and Mobil (4-5bn cm per year). This joint venture is leading to the building of a re-gasification plant in the Adriatic Sea off the Ravenna coast.

Bypass of pipeline gas for export is not a substantial business in Italy, since the domestic market absorbs all imports, and is forecasted to be saturated by 2003-2005, in spite of the massive import plans of ENI and Edison Gas for the years to come.

Third-party access to SNAM's pipelines is guaranteed by Italian law. However, there are no clear access pricing rules yet, even though this is currently being studied by the regulator's tariffs unit. For the time being, all disputes between SNAM and third-party operators (mainly Edison Gas) have been resolved by either the AEG or the Antitrust Authority – as a last resort adjudicator – on a case-by-case basis. Notably, in February 1999 the Antitrust Authority fined SNAM around ITL 3bn (£1m) due to the abuse of its

---

[19] SNAM's pipelines cover 97% of Italy's gas transport capacity, and satisfy 95% of annual demand. 93% of demand is satisfied by ENI-SNAM gas, and the remaining 7% by Edison Gas and by a fringe of very small, local operators. Edison Gas has recently acquired *Societa' Gasdotti Meridionali* (SGM) from Elf Italie, thus expanding its pipeline capacity in the South-East of Italy. Otherwise, its main strong points are on the Adriatic Coast (NE and C Italy).

dominant position vis-à-vis Edison Gas.[20] Edison Gas wished to use some of SNAM's pipelines in order to transfer its gas between its networks in the Centre and North-East of Italy, and from its re-gasification plant at La Spezia's harbour (NW Italy) to the Po Valley (N Italy). Following SNAM's refusal on grounds of "technical difficulties", Edison brought the matter to the antitrust adjudicator, and easily got SNAM fined. Since then, Edison Gas has had no major difficulties in gaining access to SNAM's high-pressure pipelines on (arguably) reasonable terms.

IX. TARIFF-SETTING AND GENERAL REGULATORY ISSUES

Created in 1996, the Authority for Electricity and Gas (AEG) was initially endowed with tariff-setting and regulating powers with respect to the electricity industry only. Subsequently, it has been given full powers with reference to gas too (especially since 1999). It is now responsible for future price-cap regulation of both gas distribution and third-party access to SNAM's pipelines (see Table 4). It has also some responsibilities in the field of quality and safety regulation. SNAM is entrusted with the supply of pipelines and made responsible for safety, under the regulator's supervision. The Authority has a (short) tradition of interventionism, even though the AEG's determinations have always been accepted by the gas industry with relative acquiescence (in contrast with the electricity monopolist ENEL, which consistently appeals against the regulator's determinations).

Table 4. Transport of Natural Gas by Third-Parties on SNAM's Pipelines, (billion cubic metres, 1995-2000). Source: AEG Annual Report (1999)

	1995	1996	1997	1998	2000 (forecast)
ENEL	0	0.5	2.4	4	7.5
Edison Gas	1	1.5	1.5	1.5	2
Imports (Edison)	0	0	0	0.2	1
Transit Gas (Geoplin)	0.4	0.4	0.4	0.4	0.4
Total	1.4	2.4	4.3	6.1	10.9

---

[20] It must be noted that SNAM's domestic monopoly is not enforced *ex lege*: it has just strengthened over time for historical reasons (aggregation of pipelines, Italy's former "champions nationaux" policy with ENI and ENEL, and the like).

AEG (based in Milan) is responsible for customer complaints and the resolution of disputes in the first place, with the Antitrust Authority (based in Rome) acting as the adjudicator of last-resort. The Antitrust Authority also deals with commercial issues and unfair business practices (e.g. in advertizing), which are generally not examined at a regulatory level. Customer complaints relating to regulated tariffs, however, are a primary responsibility of the AEG. Following Italy's incorporation of the EC Directive on gas liberalization, the distinction between "eligible" and "captive" customers has come into effect. Disputes relating to "captive" or "franchise" customers will be resolved by the AEG. All other disputes involving eligible customers will be dealt with by the AEG and by the Regional Administrative Tribunals. The Antitrust Authority will again act as a last-resort body.

Italian gas prices have long been regulated by the Interministerial Committee for Economic Planning (CIPE), which had conferred upon it in 1974 the right to fix the price of gas for industrial, domestic and technology use. CIPE issued precise instructions on the method of calculating the different rate levels for each type of customer (a complex method of price calculation was used). The prices calculated by CIPE were intended to allow distribution companies to recover all their costs, and to make a return on the capital employed. Standard historic-cost formulae were used and prices were reviewed annually.

A different tariff regulation system took effect in 1993. It was halfway between a cost-plus and a price-cap mechanism, gradually moving towards a pure price-cap system. Following the gas liberalization decree (in 2000), gas prices will be periodically regulated by the AEG on a price cap (RPI-X) basis. As previously mentioned, there are no clear "interconnection pricing" rules with respect to third-party access to SNAM's pipelines: this area is currently one of the hot topics being studied by the regulatory authority. Prices for supplying large industries and hospitals are governed by statutory agreements between SNAM and buyer associations (Confindustria, Confapi, Federelettrica). Third-party suppliers are still referred to the "vettoriamento" agreement signed in 1994 between SNAM, Unione Petrolifera and Assomineraria. According to this agreement, marginal access prices are distance and pipeline diameter-based, with a standing charge component being added to the marginal price. Third-party access prices, according to the "vettoriamento" agreement, are indexed as follows: ¼ to labour cost inflation and ¾ to the Producer Price Index (PPI).

Prior to the new legislation conferring ample powers for price regulation upon the regulatory authority, Italy's domestic consumers used to buy gas under a system of centrally planned prices. The basis for this regime was a decree issued by CIP (Interministerial Committee for Prices) on 26 June 1974. Later on, CIP's competence was transferred to the Ministry of Industry (April 1994), and then to the Energy Authority (April 1997). Since then, new criteria for determining retail tariffs have been issued almost every year. At the moment, the Energy Authority is working towards the establishment of a "pure" and definitive price-cap system. To the best of our knowledge, SNAM's tariff approaches for meeting the EC Gas Directive have not been put in the public domain yet.

The price regulation of gas distribution dates back to a 1993 CIPE ruling. The CIPE tariff regulation stated that a "standard cost" must be calculated for each territorial area in which a distributor or supplier operates. This standard cost is the sum of the following elements:

– the cost of raw materials, made up of the costs incurred by the distributor/supplier for gas purchases and system losses;

– the distribution cost, made up of the technical and economic operating costs of the distribution/supply service. This distribution cost is in turn made up of two elements:

(*a*) operating costs – these include non-raw material expenses incurred in providing the service. The total amount for each area is evaluated each year on the basis of the rate of inflation discounted by a factor "X" (representing expected productivity gains);

(*b*) investment costs – these relate only to those investments carried out in the last three years.

The "standard cost" calculated in this way is used as a constraint on the average revenue of distribution/supply companies. Final tariffs are calculated for categories of consumer, subject to the standard cost constraint. Yardstick competition in gas distribution might also be considered by the energy regulator. This requires a sufficient number of comparable regional monopolies, though:[21] clearly, only five or six supra-regional gas distribution companies would not suffice.

X. CONCLUSIONS

The Italian energy market presents peculiar features that put Italy in a special position within the European context. First of all, the country's dependence upon imports (determined by the lack of indigenous resources) has shaped both the gas and electricity markets in such a way as to jeopardize domestic competition. This has mainly been driven by a policy choice aimed at controlling internal production and import rights through the nationalized incumbents such as ENI and ENEL.

However, the EC Directives on electricity and gas have pushed the Italian government to set up a restructuring plan for both industries. The plan has been delayed during the second half of the Nineties mainly because of political instability. However, in 1999 and 2000 Italy finally incorporated the two EC Directives on energy into its national legislation, thus starting the restructuring – and partial privatization – process of its two energy incumbents. We summarize below the future prospects for electricity and natural gas in turn.

---

[21] The MMC (1995) Report on the take-over of Northumbrian Water by Société Lyonnaise des Eaux discusses the issue of the value of the loss of a comparator firm following mergers and take-overs. It must be said that the accuracy of regulatory price controls may be reduced by the loss of comparators, which also introduces a clear trade-off between the effectiveness of yardstick controls and the possible exploitation of scale/scope economies.

The Italian electricity industry is finally moving, after almost forty years of nationaliza-tion, towards liberalization. The electricity generation market will be structured from 2001 as a wholesale "Pool" in which generators will be free to bid on a day-ahead basis. As the UK experience with the electricity Pool of England and Wales shows, though, the proper functioning of the bulk electricity market will crucially depend upon market structure. A limited number of players in the generation market are likely to lead to tacit collusion and price co-ordination, irrespective of the fact that the day-ahead bidding system may function well from a technical standpoint.[22] Even after the planned 15GW plant divestment, ENEL will still dominate the Pool market, with probably more than 50% of residual capacity. This might push the energy regulator to require further ENEL divestment in the near future.

Electricity transmission is – together with distribution – the only production subset still characterized by naturally monopolistic conditions. However, whereas distribution is commonly regarded as a natural monopoly at local levels only – thus leading to the possibility of "yardstick regulation" mimicking actual market competition via direct efficiency comparisons – transmission is naturally monopolistic on a national scale. For medium-sized countries, benchmarking transmission companies against best practice is virtually impossible unless an international sample is constructed.

As with other countries of similar size, Italy could not economically duplicate its high-voltage transmission grid, which has traditionally been under ENEL's direct control. However, the Bersani Decree has now created a separate national grid operator (*Gestore della Rete di Trasmissione Nazionale*, or GRTN), incorporated as a joint stock company in Rome in 1999, which is taking charge of ENEL's high-voltage responsibilities. Nonetheless, contrary to the regulator's views, the Italian government decided to retain GRTN under ENEL's corporate control. ENEL's ownership of the transmission operator might lead to strategic behaviour of the grid operator with respect to the interconnection terms of independent power producers (IPPs) – or any other non-ENEL owned plant – with the national high-voltage network.[23]

Electricity distribution in Italy has long been an exclusive business of ENEL's local departments and of municipal utilities. In a limited number of cases, ENEL and the local operators have co-existed at the municipal borders of those towns being served by a local distributor. However, ENEL and municipal distributors have never been benchmarked against each other formally, mainly because of dimensional and territorial disparity. The Bersani Decree obliged ENEL to offer its urban distributing assets for sale to interested

---

[22] Green and Newbery (1991) are the authors of a famous study on the influence of market power upon the level of bulk prices observed during the very first period of operation of the English and Welsh electricity spot market (also known as "The Pool").

[23] Using the British experience as a basis, Vickers and Yarrow (1991) give a convincing explanation of the grid operator's possibly perverse access-granting incentives.

municipalities in towns with at least 300,000 customers.[24] This, coupled with the recent privatization and multi-utility expansion of some big municipalities, is likely to pave the way for really "alternative" electricity distribution structures – to which yardstick regulation via efficiency comparisons or "benchmarking" might in principle be applied.

Retail electricity supply is now a partially regulated business. No competition is in sight at the moment in Italy with regard to the franchise (domestic) market, for which the regulator has already put in place a price cap of RPI-4. However, in a limited number of circumstances, even residential customers will be able to buy comprehensive multi-utility packages from the newly privatized municipal operators of Rome, Milan, and Turin. Eligible customers (industrial and large commercial ones), on the other hand, face a liberalization plan spreading over 5 years, according to which all of them will be gradually set free to choose their electricity supplier (in accordance with the requirements of the EC Directive).

The Italian natural gas market has been dominated by *Ente Nazionale Idrocarburi* (ENI) for more than sixty years. Italy's ENI was nationalized under the Fascist administration in the 1930s, and is currently Italy's largest industrial company. ENI's privatization has only been very recent, with the first 14.7% of shares being sold to the public in 1995 for US $4.1 bn. ENI also has an oil refining capacity of 933,000 barrels per day, making it Europe's third-largest refiner. Following market liberalization at home, ENI has recently concentrated upon diversifying away from Italy. The EC Directive on gas liberalization was incorporated into Italian legislation in February 2000. It will force ENI to relinquish its *de facto* extraction monopoly, while SNAM – ENI's pipeline subsidiary- has been already compelled to negotiate fair third-party access terms with ENI's competitors (mainly Edison Gas). TPA conditions are now regulated by the Italian Energy Authority (AEG).

Gas distribution and supply are run by Italgas – again, part of the ENI group – and by a multitude of small companies, either municipally or privately run, for which rationalization is now being sought. Since the technical distinction between gas transmission (high pressure) and distribution (medium-to-low pressure) is blurred, SNAM/Italgas are likely to retain control of the naturally monopolistic production subset in the future, unless the Italian government decides in favour of ENI's break-up. Again, at the retail gas supply level yardstick competition on a territorial basis would be a feasible option, whereas direct scrutiny of SNAM's pipeline network seems, on the other hand, to be the only feasible option for the AEG. Finally, the EC Directive has introduced for gas, too, a distinction between "eligible" and "captive" (or franchise) customers – as already observed for electricity. This will lead to gradual liberalization of retail supply – albeit at an arguably slower pace than for electricity.

To conclude, the speed of liberalization in Italy's energy markets depends to a large

---

[24] Both Scarsi (1998) and Scarpa (1999) found that the minimum efficient scale in distribution for Italy's urban contexts ranges from 300,000 to 360,000 customers. This suggests that the largest municipalities may already be operating at efficient scale. The Bersani Decree should perhaps have set a lower customer threshold for the hand-over of ENEL's distributing assets to municipal operators.

extent on the political will to take the process forward, in line with the EU's principles. Privatization should not be the most relevant issue; the problem of market structure should be the first to be sorted out. Nevertheless, given Italy's peculiar features in terms of the politicization of ENI and ENEL, one is led to believe that privatization and restructuring must be tackled together (this did not turn out to be the case, for instance, in the U.K.). Undoubtedly, restructuring remains the main question.

The two liberalization decrees of 1999 (electricity) and 2000 (gas) are somewhat unsatisfactory in terms of the push for a free market in the non-naturally monopolistic production subsets of the two industries. This is evidence of the fact that ENEL and ENI's powerful lobbying activities have been so far successful in preventing the Italian government from rapidly catching up with the European Union's prescriptions. Greater political stability and impartiality would have probably allowed Italy to easily exceed the requirements of the two European Directives (especially in natural gas, where no legal, but only *de facto*, monopolies are present). However, the reality is different: the government only just met the two statutory EC deadlines by issuing a couple of last-minute, rather disappointing ministerial decrees.

References

Autorita' per l'Energia Elettrica ed il Gas (AEG) (1999). Relazione Annuale (Annual Report). Rome, Italy: Istituto Poligrafico e Zecca dello Stato.

ENEL (1999). Statistical data on electricity in Italy 1998. Rome, Italy: ENEL.

ENI/SNAM Websites (2000): www.eni.it, www.snam.it.

Gordon, R.J. (1992). "Forward into the Past: Productivity Retrogression in the Electric Generating Industry". *NBER Working Paper Series*, Working Paper No. 3988.

Green, R.J., and D.M. Newbery (1991). "Competition in the British Electricity Spot Market". *Journal of Political Economy* (100): 929-953.

GRTN (*Gestore della Rete di Trasmissione Nazionale*) Website (2000): www.grtn.it.

Kwoka, J. (1996). *Power Structure*. Boston (MA): Kluwer Academic Publishers.

Monopolies and Mergers Commission (MMC) (1995). *Report on the take-over of Northumbrian Water by Société Lyonnaise des Eaux*. London (UK): HMSO.

Scarpa (1999). *I costi di distribuzione dell'energia elettrica in Italia: un'analisi quantitativa*. Department of Economics, University of Bologna: mimeo.

Scarsi (1998). Electricity Distribution in Italy: Microeconomic Efficiency Analysis of Local Distributing Units with Methodological Cross-Checking. D.Phil. Thesis, University of Oxford.

Vickers, J.S., and Yarrow, G.K. (1991). "The British Electricity Experiment". *Economic Policy* (12): 187-232.

miliardi di metri cubi	1998	2010	Δ
Austria	8,1	9,0	0,9
Belgio	15,0	20,4	5,4
Danimarca	4,6	6,2	1,6
Finlandia	3,5	6,1	2,6
Francia	40,4	50,8	10,4
Germania	87,0	103,0	16,0
Grecia	0,4	6,7	6,3
Irlanda	3,4	6,7	3,3
Italia	62,4	88,7	26,3
Lussemburgo	0,5	0,7	0,2
Paesi Bassi	42,4	49,8	7,4
Portogallo	0,8	5,8	5,0
Spagna	14,3	30,3	16,0
Svezia	0,9	4,8	3,9
U.K.	90,9	113,5	22,6
Totale	374,6	502,5	127,9

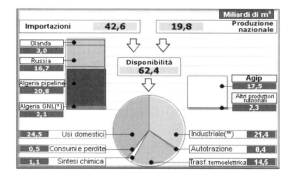

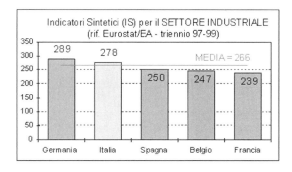

Figure 3. Figures from www.snam.it

Dr. Martha M Roggenkamp[1]

COUNTRY REPORT: THE NETHERLANDS

I. GENERAL INTRODUCTION

The most important primary energy resource in the Netherlands is natural gas which is produced offshore as well as onshore. The production of other hydrocarbons is limited. Although there are some exploitable oil fields, they are small in size and in number. The coal-mines in the province of Limburg were gradually closed as a result of the discovery of the Groningen gas field in 1959.[2] Ever since, natural gas is the most important domestic energy resource. Some 97% of all households apply gas for cooking and heating purposes. Following the large-scale penetration of natural gas in the energy supply market the share of electricity is also relatively small. As far as electricity generation is concerned, natural gas is used more extensively in the Netherlands than in any other EC Member State (49%).[3]

As the Groningen gas field proved to be one of the largest gas fields ever discovered, it was decided at an early stage to sell large quantities abroad instead of limiting the sales to the domestic market. Consequently, the Netherlands has been a net exporter of natural gas since the 1960s. This Dutch gas policy has, therefore, not only changed the entire domestic energy market but also had an enormous impact on the European situation. The development of the Groningen field is basically the birthplace of the (current) European gas market.

Surprisingly, the above mentioned shift in the Dutch energy resource base has not led to important changes with regard to the regulatory framework. In contrast to other countries in Europe, energy regulation has been rudimentary. Until the end of the 1980's few statutory laws applied to the energy sector. Whereas the electricity sector was regulated by an incomplete Electricity Act of 1935[4] which finally was replaced by a new Electricity Act in 1989, the gas supply sector has operated on the basis of private law agreements without statutory legislation. Moreover, the legal basis for the exploration and production of

---

[1] This paper has, *inter alia*, been based on research conducted within the framework of the XIX FIDE Conference in Helsinki, 1-3 June 2000. See also J.E. Janssen, L. Hancher, M.M. Roggenkamp, "Community Law and Competition Rules affecting 'Networks' and its Consequences for the Member States: The Netherlands", *SEW – Tijdschrift voor Europees en Economisch Recht*, 48e jaargang, no. 4, April 2000, pp. 154 – 169.

[2] The last two coalmines were closed in 1974.

[3] In addition, use is made of (imported) coal (45%) and nuclear energy (6%). In 1998 the total inland electricity production was 87.570 GWh (60.329 GWh through SEP). Production capacity is some 20.000 MW (14.000 MW through SEP). Some 11.939 GWh is imported.

[4] Only view provisions of the Act entered into force.

Damien Geradin (ed.), The Liberalization of Electricity and Natural Gas in the European Union, 197–223
©2001 Kluwer Law International. Printed in the Netherlands.

hydrocarbons onshore (including the Groningen gas field) was the "temporary" French Mining Act of 1810 and the Mining Act 1903.[5]

Hence, the EC liberalization process is of special importance for the Dutch energy sector as, to an important extent, it has triggered the legislative and regulatory developments. Since the Minister of Economic Affairs Mr. Weijers published the Third Energy Policy Note in 1995, new energy legislation has been proposed (and partially entered into force) for each of the above energy sectors. In addition to the new Electricity Act 1998 (hereafter E-Act 1998), a Gas Bill was sent to Parliament in 1999 as well as a Mining Bill integrating and modernizing the onshore and offshore hydrocarbons regimes. This chapter, however, will concentrate on developments in the electricity and the gas sector.

II. THE ELECTRICITY SECTOR AND THE IMPLEMENTATION OF DIRECTIVE 96/92

A. Introduction

The E-Act 1998 which entered into force in 1999, implements the EC Electricity Directive.[6] It governs the generation, transport and supply of electricity and aims to foster competition at all stages of the electricity chain. In this respect the E-Act 1998 differs significantly from its predecessor, the Electricity Act 1989. This Act was mainly based on a system of central planning via the National Electricity Plan and licensing of generation facilities.[7] Although the 1989 Electricity Act tried to introduce some competition between distribution companies, these attempts were not very successful. On the other hand, some competition has been realized on the generation side. The reason is that the Electricity Act 1989 specifically differentiated between electricity generated on the basis of fossil fuels and renewables and thus enabled distribution companies, and others, to establish CHP installations without a licence. As these non-licensed generators were not required to take

---

[5] Offshore exploration and production is based on a more modern petroleum law, i.e. the Continental Shelf Mining Act of 1965 and its implementing royal Decrees.

[6] The framework provisions (Stb. 1998, 428) entered into force on 1 August 1998 (Stb. 1998, 429); certain provisions primarily dealing with imports and exports entered into force on 1 January 1999 (Stb. 1998, 681); an amendment to the Act (Stb. 1999, 260) dealing *inter alia* with tariffs for TPA and supply entered into force on 1 July 1999 (Stb. 1999, 261). Articles 96-102, dealing with "stranded costs", have not entered into force. An amendment to the E-Act 1998 dealing with stranded costs will be submitted to Parliament shortly. For a translation in English of the E-Act 1998 and various policy documents with respect to electricity and gas, see the web site of the MEA: www.minez.nl/energie.

[7] For a description of the old regulatory regime, see Annelies E.H. Huygen, *Electricity Regulation in the Netherlands*, DSWO Press, 1995 and E.D. Cross, *Electric Utility Regulation in the European Union – A Country by Country Guide*, Chapter 9, Wiley 1996.

into account the estimates of the National Electricity Plan, numerous decentralized generators (mostly co-generation or CHP) were established. This has, however, resulted in a surplus capacity during the 1990s. In order to handle the creation of surplus capacity the distribution and production companies entered into an agreement (the "protocol agreement") in 1996 as a result of which the distribution companies committed themselves to continue their electricity off-take from the central production power pool (i.e. "N.V. Samenwerkende elektriciteits-productiebedrijven" or SEP) against an aggregate remuneration, and a commitment by SEP and the four production companies not to compete with the distribution companies in the electricity market. This agreement runs until 1 January 2001. The fact that the agreement continues to run after the E-Act 1998 entered into force has complicated the electricity liberalization process, as will be discussed below.

B. Market Opening

1. Schedule of Market Opening

By contrast to the EC Electricity Directive which only requires Member States to partially open their electricity market, the Dutch legislator has opted for a complete market opening in three separate stages. In order to achieve such phased liberalization, a distinction is made between three categories of consumers. Distribution companies have not been designated as "eligible customers" within the meaning of the Electricity Directive. The E-Act 1998 specifically appoints as eligible customers:
–   large industrial users (defined as having a connection to a network with a maximum capacity of more than 2 MW);
–   medium-sized industrial users (defined as having a connection with a total maximum transmission value of more than 3 x 80 Ampere and an available capacity of no more than 2 MW); and
–   small business users and households (defined as having a connection with a total maximum transmission value of no more than 3 x 80 Ampere).

Large industrial users have been free in their choice of supplier since the entry into force of the E-Act 1998.[8] Until recently, it was envisaged that the medium-sized industrial users and the small business consumers and households would remain captive consumers until 31 December 2001 and December 2006 respectively.[9] However, following the Parliamentary debates on the implementation of the Gas Directive, amendments to the E-Act 1998 have

---

[8]   In reality the Act entered into force when the TPA provisions became effective in July 1999.

[9]   Article 1(1)(d) of the E-Act 1998.

been made as a result of which small business users and households will be eligible as early as 1 January 2004.[10] Besides, Parliament proposed to open up the market for (small-scale) sustainable energy by allowing e.g. hydropower and solar-projects to supply captive customers directly.[11]

2. Supply of Electricity

2.1. LICENCE TO SUPPLY NON-ELIGIBLE OR PROTECTED CUSTOMERS

Until customers become eligible, the law regards them as "protected customers". These customers can only be supplied by the (legal) person which has been given an exclusive supply licence (the licensed supplier or "vergunninghouder") for a certain area against regulated tariffs and conditions. In turn, the licensed supplier has an obligation to supply electricity to every protected customer in its designated supply area.[12] Licensed suppliers are required to keep separate accounts of the electricity they supply to captive and eligible customers.[13] Besides, each licensed supplier which gains access to data which it knows or may reasonably assume to be of confidential character is obliged to maintain the confidentiality of such data.[14] To start with, supply licenses have been granted to all existing distribution companies.[15]

The (maximum) tariffs for the supply of protected customers will each year be set by the Minister for each license holder. The CPI-X regulation methodology described in more detail below with respect to the network rates applies equally to supply tariffs to protected customers. Commodity prices for the supply of electricity to free customers are of course not regulated.

---

[10] TK 1999-2000, 26 463, no. 10.

[11] Article 53 under (d) of the E-Act 1998. This provision has not yet entered into force.

[12] See the E-Act 1998, Articles 36 ff. For the requirements of a supply license, see Staatscourant 1998, no. 141, p. 6.

[13] Article 44 of the E-Act 1998. According to Article 65a of the E-Act all suppliers and producers are required to keep separate accounts for the production of electricity and the supply of electricity to free customers.

[14] Article 79 of the E-Act 1998.

[15] Article 74 (1) of the E-Act 1998.

2.2. LICENCE TO SUPPLY HOUSEHOLDS

As of 2004 an additional licence will apply for the supply of electricity to small consumers, i.e. households.[16] Within the framework of the Parliamentary debate on the new Gas Bill this additional supply licence has been introduced in order to give these small consumers some further protection so that they can be assured of permanent and reliable electricity supply against reasonable conditions and tariffs. Every electricity supplier (i.e. distribution companies, traders and foreign suppliers) intending to supply households after 2004 is required to apply for such a licence. Consequently, the number of licensees will increase compared to those supplying "protected customers" before 2004. Moreover, these "new" licensees are not restricted to operate within specific supply areas but entitled to supply consumers everywhere in the Netherlands. Although the Minister can award a licence upon certain conditions, the tariffs and conditions for electricity supply will be subject to the rules of competition. Besides, the licensees are not subject to a firm supply obligation but to a more broadly phrased obligation which states that they should take care of the supply of electricity to small consumers on the basis of reasonable tariffs and conditions.

3. Generation

The Directive aims at full competition in the generation sector. Article 4 of the Directive gives Member States the choice between an authorization and/or a tendering procedure for the construction of new generating capacity. Neither system has, however, been applied in the Netherlands. Contrary to the former Electricity Act, the E-Act 1998 does not impose any restrictions on the production of electricity. In line therewith, the inventory for new means of production is no longer drawn up centrally via a licensing regime.[17] Governmental planning is limited to (i) a Physical Planning Document facilitating the construction of high voltage lines and generation facilities ("Structure Scheme for Electricity Supply" or *structuurschema electriciteitsvoorziening*)[18] and (ii) the Energy Report ("Energierapport"), which is a policy document that is intended to give guidance on the decisions to be taken by the Dutch Government in the following next four years "to the extent the importance of reliable, renewable, efficient and environmentally hygienic electricity supplies must or may be taken into account".[19]

The implementation of the rules on generation of the EC Electricity Directive did not

---

[16] Article 95a – 91i of the E-Act 1998 as proposed by the Gas Bill.

[17] Licensing was to a large extent based on the content of the Electricity Plans ("Elektriciteitsplannen").

[18] The first *Structuurschema Elektriciteitsvoorziening* was issued in 1981. A proposal for a second Structure Scheme was presented in 1992. Further amendments to this Schema have been initiated as of 1993 (Tweede Kamer 1993-1994, 23 424).

[19] E-Act 1998, Article 2(1). In November 1999, the first Energy Report was published.

give rise to special discussions in the Netherlands. The primary problem for the Dutch production sector, which is suffering from over-capacity, is formed by "stranded costs". In order to solve the issue of "stranded costs", the Minister of Economic Affairs may impose a binding arrangement on the four production companies and their joint subsidiary SEP.[20] If they will assume the liability for and the payment of the stranded costs, they may in return receive *inter alia* a partial compensation of these stranded costs by means of a surcharge on the transportation rates.[21] However, since the parties cannot agree on the division of the stranded costs and the extent of compensation, the legislature is currently preparing a Bill dealing with the issue of stranded costs.[22] It is most likely that this Bill will be based on the advice presented in November 1999 by a special Committee "of Three Wise Men", commonly referred to after the name of its chairman as the Herkströter report.

4. Transmission and Distribution

4.1. APPOINTMENT OF A NETWORK OPERATOR

The E-Act 1998 is based on a system of legal unbundling and subsequently prescribes a (legal) separation between i) supply and ii) transmission and distribution.[23] Therefore, owners of the electricity networks are required to establish separate legal entities for the transport of electricity (i.e. the "network operators").[24] This provision applies to SEP as far as it concerns the national high-voltage network as well as the distribution companies with regard to the regional distribution networks.

---

[20] In practice, SEP has operated as the economic and technical dispatcher. Whereas economic dispatch has now been transferred to the transmission system operator (TenneT), technical dispatch will be performed by the production companies individually when the current co-operation arrangement between SEP and the four large-scale production companies (embodied in the Co-Operation Agreement or "OVS") ends. The E-Act 1998 gives the OVS a statutory basis until 1 January 2001. Thereafter, it is expected that the OVS or at least the key elements thereof (i.e. pooling of costs, joint technical dispatch) will cease to apply as they are generally deemed to violate Article 6 of the Dutch Competition Act (and 81 EC).

[21] See Articles 96-102 of the E-Act 1998.

[22] At the time of writing, the Bill is under review by the Council of State.

[23] The term "transmission" means "the transport of electricity on the high-voltage interconnected systems with a view to its delivery to final customers or to distributors", whereas "distribution" means "the transport of electricity on medium-voltage and low-voltage distribution systems with a view to its delivery to customers" (Electricity Directive, Article 2 under 5 and 6). Hereafter the term "transport" refers to transmission and distribution.

[24] See E-Act 1998, Articles 10(2) (for national high-voltage network), 10(3) (for the other networks) and 15 (for the exceptions to the general obligation to appoint a network manager). Such an appointment usually runs for a period of 10 years.

The appointment of the network operators requires the approval of the Minister.[25] There is one network operator for the national high-voltage (380 kV and 220 kV) grid: TenneT. Separate network operators have been appointed for each of the regional grids. The respective owners of the networks are allowed to remain shareholders of the network company[26] and may also retain ownership of the grid. The E-Act 1998 and the implementing rules contain various provisions that guarantee the independence of the network operators from its shareholders, so as to ensure truly non-discriminatory TPA (see below).

The Minister has approved the appointment of most network operators. In some cases, however, there are doubts about the independence of the network company. The Minister has, for example, not approved the appointment of TenneT as a separate network operator. Recently, the Minister has, at the urgent request of Parliament, announced[27] that the Government intends to acquire for the period of two to three years the smallest majority (50% + 1) of the shares of TenneT against "market value" for a transitional period.[28] During this period the supervision of the "*Dienst toezicht en uitvoering Energie*" (hereafter DTe) could then be firmly established and certain structural amendments to the E-Act 1998 to strengthen the independence of TenneT could be introduced.

4.2. DUTIES OF THE NETWORK OPERATOR

The E-Act 1998 defines the duties of a network operator. The legal duties are:[29]
- to operate and maintain the networks managed by it
- to guarantee in the most effective manner the safety and reliability of the networks and of the transport of electricity over its networks
- to construct, repair, renew or extend the networks
- to maintain sufficient spare capacity for the transport of electricity
- to provide in a non-discriminatory manner third parties with a connection to the network, and to make a meter available to them upon request in a non-discriminatory manner
- to carry out the transport of electricity on behalf of third parties in a non-discriminatory manner and against regulated (maximum) tariffs

---

[25] Article 12(2) of the E-Act 1998.

[26] I.e. the distribution companies are the shareholders of the respective regional network managers and SEP is (currently) the sole shareholder of TenneT.

[27] TK 1999-2000, 25087, no. 32.

[28] Within Parliament there is a tendency, however, to push for 100% government ownership of TenneT. The discussion concerns not only the independence of the network but should also be judged in the light of the "stranded costs" discussion. It seems, however, unlikely that SEP (and its shareholders) would agree to a sale of a majority of its shares in TenneT for approximately half the market value for the total network (i.e. ignoring any control premium).

[29] Article 16(1) of the E-Act 1998.

–   to promote the usage safety of appliances and installations that consume electricity.

In addition to the above duties, TenneT has the overall responsibility for the safe and reliable transmission of electricity and to transport on behalf of third parties electricity exported from or imported to the Netherlands over the national high-voltage network.[30] This poses additional problems with regard to the division of scarce capacity on the interconnectors by TenneT (see below).

It also follows from the above that the E-Act 1998 does not provide for "grid-to-grid" competition. Since the original transmission and distribution companies appoint their own network operator and the construction of new transmission grids is limited to the network operators, the establishment of new and additional grids is effectively blocked. An exception can only be made in case of the establishment of direct lines and networks in new locations for large-scale building (suburbia).

4.3. INDEPENDENCE OF THE NETWORK OPERATOR

The organizational unbundling prescribed by the E-Act 1998 is accompanied by a large number of provisions that (i) ensure the organizational and financial independence of the network manager, (ii) prevent cross-subsidization and the dissemination of strategic and confidential information, and (iii) enable the implementation of a system of price regulation on the basis of output steering.

Hence, producers and suppliers are prohibited from interfering with the exercise of the duties of a network operator.[31] Moreover, each network operator must have a supervisory board with extensive powers of which the majority, as well the majority of the management board, may not have any direct or indirect link with a producer, supplier or shareholder.[32] Network operators may not engage in any activities other than those prescribed by law (see above). Other than its statutory duties the range of permissible activities is very limited.[33] The requirement in the E-Act 1998 regarding a network operator's independence has been further developed in some "Policy Rules on the Designation of Network Operators".[34]

In addition, network managers may not provide any company within the group with preferential treatment or grant to it any other advantages beyond what is customary in normal business practice. Supplying a group company with details on customers, not being captive customers (which by law are bound for a transitional term to the relevant supply

---

[30]   Article 16(2) of the E-Act 1998.

[31]   Article 16(4) of the E-Act 1998.

[32]   With respect to TenneT only, the appointment of the supervisory directors of TenneT must moreover be approved by the Minister (Article 11).

[33]   Article 17 of the E-Act 1998.

[34]   *Beleidsregels aanwijzing netbeheerders,* Stcrt. 1999, no. 1, p. 6.

company in the network operator's region), is for example defined as a forbidden form of preferential treatment.[35] Finally, each network operator is obliged by law to use the information made available to him on captive customers only for the performance of its statutory tasks[36] and each network operator is required to respect what should reasonably be understood as constituting confidential information.[37]

5. Access to the System

5.1. GENERAL

The Electricity Directive gives the Member States the choice between three different forms of access to the system: negotiated TPA (nTPA), regulated TPA (rTPA) or the single buyer system. The Netherlands has, without much debate, opted for rTPA, whereby the director of the DTe sets the (maximum) tariffs and conditions.

5.2. PROVISIONS ON ACCESS AND CONNECTION

Each network operator is required to make an offer to an applicant that so requests for the transport of electricity via its network.[38] Similarly, each network operator is upon request required to provide connection to its network.[39] The tariffs and conditions for transportation and connection have to comply with the provisions in the E-Act 1998 (see below). Moreover, the network operator has to refrain from any discrimination between applications requiring access and/or connection to the grid. The network operator may thus not give an applicant priority for capacity on its network unless it concerns the mutual assistance within the UCTE agreement, the construction of the NorNed cable or other new cables. In addition, capacity can be reserved by the Minister in order to promote more effective competition in the electricity market.[40] Access to the grid can only be restricted to the extent that the network operator "reasonably" has no capacity available.[41] This restriction is refined by the prohibition on "speculative reservation" of capacity contained in Article 25 of the E-Act 1998.

---

[35] Article 18 of the E-Act 1998.
[36] Article 19 of the E-Act 1998.
[37] Article 79 of the E-Act 1998.
[38] Article 24 of the E-Act 1998.
[39] Article 23 of the E-Act 1998.
[40] Article 25 and Article 26 of the E-Act 1998.
[41] Article 24(2) of the E-Act 1998.

Subsequently, each network operator has a duty to maintain sufficient spare capacity on its networks. Therefore, every two years he must provide the director DTe with estimates of the total capacity requirements for its networks for a period of seven years. The director DTe will notify the Minister if he is of the opinion that such network operator may have insufficient capacity. The Minister is entitled to order the network operator to take the necessary measures so that (future) transport can be carried about.[42]

5.3. TARIFFS AND CONDITIONS

The E-Act 1998 distinguishes between connection rates,[43] transport rates[44] and the rates for the system services provided by TenneT.[45] Each year the director DTe will set (maximum) rates for each individual network manager.[46] The (starting) rates for the year 2000 have been set following a lengthy consultation procedure.[47] The Netherlands has introduced an uniform producers' transport rate or distance unrelated "point tariff" for electricity fed into the grid through high-voltage networks. The concept of a producers' transport rate was primarily motivated to reward environmentally friendly generation that feeds into lower level networks. This producers' transport rate will also be levied from foreign suppliers as an import duty. As from the year 2001, the individual network rates will be adjusted by the director DTe on the basis of a CPI-X methodology, whereby "CPI" refers to consumer price index and "X" to an efficiency discount that will be set by the director Dte.[48]

Further rules regarding these tariffs and conditions as briefly described in Article 31(1) of the E-Act 1998 are included in the so-called Technical Codes which are established by the DTe. Whereas the first part of these codes entered into force in October 1999, the remaining part has entered into force following a notification procedure with the EC Commission. These technical conditions are actually embodied in three separate codes, i.e. the NetCode, SystemCode and MeasuringCode. The NetCode also contains rules for

---

[42] Articles 21-22 of the E-Act 1998.

[43] Article 28 of the E-Act 1998.

[44] Article 29 of the E-Act 1998.

[45] Article 30 of the E-Act 1998.

[46] Article 36 of the E-Act 1998.

[47] See Article 25 ff. of the E-Act 1998.

[48] See Article 41 of the E-Act 1998. Reference is made to the recent documents "Guidance for price-cap regulation in the Dutch electricity sector for the period 2000-2003" and "Determination of the Regulatory Asset Base of Network Companies" published on the DTe's website. On 1 March 2000 the Dte announced that in the second regulatory period (from 2004 onwards) companies will no longer be assessed against a group of "best practice" companies defined by DTe (the method for the years 2001-2003) but against the average performance of the sector as a whole ("yardstick regulation").

the determination and allocation of transport capacity on the cross-border connections or "interconnectors" (see below).[49]

6. International Trade in Electricity

6.1. CROSS-BORDER TRADE

International trade in electricity is hampered by the lack of sufficient cross-border connections and transport capacity. Pursuant to Article 31 of the E-Act 1998 the director of the DTe has provided special rules in the Netcode for the allocation of capacity on the interconnectors for the year 2000.[50] The Netcode identifies three categories of importers, i.e. SEP on the basis of long-term take-or-pay contracts, annual supply contracts which have been concluded more recently and imports within the framework of the Amsterdam Power Exchange (APX).[51] In order to avoid "gaming" (i.e. reservation of capacity) the DTe requires the existence of a firm supply contract. With respect to the allocation of capacity for annual contracts for the year 2000, TenneT interpreted these rules and the E-Act 1998 to the effect that both an underlying supply contract as well as an ongoing sales contract with end-users (or Dutch distribution companies) are required for the allocation of capacity. It has been argued that this allocation method discriminates against new entrants, in particular (wholesale) traders. From the year 2001 onwards it is most likely that another system will apply as a result of which available interconnector capacity will be allocated by means of, e.g., an auction.

6.2. IMPORT/EXPORT: THE RULES ON RECIPROCITY

Article 19(5) of the Directive provides a mechanism for redressing any imbalances that may occur as a result of unequal liberalization. Under the procedure established by this provision it is for the Commission to adopt measures at the request of the Member State

---

[49] Chapter 5.6 Netcode.

[50] These rules have again been set by the DTe following a lengthy consultation procedure (*inter alia* on the basis of the Information and consultation document "Transport Capacity on International Electricity Networks).

[51] The E-Act 1998 does not provide specific rules with regard to the organization and regulation of the APX, neither does any of the financial laws. This means, for example, that neither the Dte nor the Ste supervising the financial institutions in the Netherlands is charged with the supervision of the APX. More information about the APX is to be found on http://www.APX.nl.

where the eligible customer who is refused a contract or access is located.[52]

The reciprocity provisions contained in the E-Act 1998[53] and the implementing ministerial regulation[54] derive from an opposite angle, whereby TenneT is prohibited from making a transport offer if the electricity originates from a country that has not yet sufficiently opened its market. When a customer (or a supplier on behalf of a customer) wants to import, the ministerial regulation distinguishes between: countries from which imports are always allowed (e.g., Germany); countries from which imports are allowed provided the customer consumes more than 20 GWh per annum (e.g., Italy); and countries from which imports are not allowed unless the customer consumes more than 100 GWh per annum (being the minimum market opening prescribed by the Directive), such as France and Belgium. It should be noted, however, that to an increasing extent "foreign" electricity is traded on the Amsterdam Power Exchange or APX and that is not possible to trace the electricity traded on the exchange back to the country of origin.

7. Dispute Settlement Mechanism

The legislator has opted for a specific regulator for the energy sector: DTe.[55] The DTe is a chamber within the Dutch competition authority Nma and is responsible for activities relating to the administration of the E-Act 1998 and to the supervision of compliance therewith.[56] In addition, the director of the DTe has certain specific duties such as the setting of rate structures referred to above and conditions for the transport of electricity and advising the Minister on the exercise of his responsibilities under the E-Act 1998.

TPA disputes are, however, settled pursuant to the general competition rules by the Nma.[57] The director-general of the Nma may issue "general and specific instructions" to the director DTe where, in the opinion of the director-general of the Nma, an interpretation of the terms used in the application of the DCA can or should be provided.[58] Information

---

[52] For a justification thereof, reference is made to the notice of the Commission's Legal Service published on: http://europe.eu.int/en/comm/dg17/elec/memor.htm.

[53] Article 29 ff of the E-Act 1998.

[54] Regulation containing further rules on the import and export of electricity (Stcrt. 1998, no. 229, as amended by Stctr. 1999, no. 234).

[55] See www.dte.nl. Originally the DTe was only responsible for the supervision of compliance with the E-Act 1998. As a result of the implementation of the Gas Directive, the tasks of the DTe have been extended to ensure compliance with the Gas Act.

[56] Article 5 of the E-Act 1998.

[57] Article 34 of the E-Act 1998.

[58] E-Act 1998, Article 8. In addition, the Minister may – while the Nma is still a service of the Ministry (a Bill making the Nma more independent was announced but has still not been submitted to Parliament) – give instructions to both the director-general of the Nma and the director of the DTe (Article 2 of the DCA and Article 6(1) of the E-Act 1998). Before issuing instructions to the director DTe, the Minister must give the director-general Nma the opportunity to present his views (E-Act 1998, Article 6(2)).

relating to a producer, a trader or a network manager which the (director) DTe obtains in connection with any operations for the purpose of administering the E-Act 1998 may only be used for the application of the E-Act 1998 and not for competition purposes.[59] The resulting situation is somewhat complex; in the performance of certain of his duties the director of the DTe reports to the Minister, but at the same time in the exercise of the powers attributed to him under the E-Act 1998, the director may also receive directions of a general as well as an individual character from the director-general of the Nma.[60] The role of the Nma and those of the DTe are therefore likely to become blurred. Moreover, energy liberalization in the United States and the United Kingdom illustrates that this process to a large extent depends on the existence of a pro-active regulator.

8. Future developments

The liberalization process of the Dutch electricity market has not been easy, mainly because of the unresolved issue of stranded costs and the existence of the protocol agreement that runs to the year 2001. It is expected that the market will be more transparent in 2001 when this agreement comes to an end, a final decision is made about the allocation of interconnector capacity and the Amsterdam Power Exchange has extended its portfolio to include financial products such as futures.

III. THE GAS SECTOR AND THE IMPLEMENTATION OF COUNCIL DIRECTIVE 98/30

A. Introduction

By contrast to other Member States, the Dutch gas supply sector has not been based on extensive statutory regulation. Public regulation is limited to the exploration and production of natural gas on the one hand (upstream activities) and the distribution of gas on the other

---

[59] Article 7(3) of the E-Act 1998. However, pursuant to Article 91 DCA, the director-general of the Nma may give information to the director-general of the DTe if necessary for the performance of his tasks by the director of the DTe that also involve the application of competition rules.

[60] Article 34 of the E-Act 1998. The director-general of the Nma is, however, not competent where the manager of a network located in another Member State refuses to carry out the relevant transport or has established allegedly unfair tariffs or conditions (Article 35 of the E-Act 1998).

hand (downstream activities), i.e. the onshore and offshore Mining Acts[61] and the Energy Distribution Act of 1997 (Wet Energie-Distributie).[62] The storage of natural gas and the construction of upstream pipelines are so-called midstream activities. Currently the regulatory regime for these activities is limited to the provisions on safety and the environment in the onshore and offshore Mining regulations.

As a result of the implementation of Directive 98/30 the gas supply sector will be completely regulated by statutory law. However, before examining the way in which the Gas Directive will be implemented in the Netherlands, an overview will be presented of the organization of the Dutch gas market since the discovery of the Groningen gas field in 1959.

B. Organization of the Dutch Gas Market

1. Organization of the Gas Supply Market: Policy Note of De Pous

Since the discovery of the Groningen gas field, the transmission of gas has been based on a policy note issued by Minister De Pous in 1962.[63] The basic principle of this policy note was that there should be a close co-ordination between the extraction and the marketing/sales of gas. The Dutch State should be involved in both activities. As a consequence, State participation was introduced in the production of gas. Although the concession for the exploitation of the Groningen field was awarded to the Nederlandse Aardolie Maatschappij or NAM (= 50% Shell and 50% Exxon), a separate partnership (Maatschap) was established in which the Dutch State (through Energie Beheer Nederland or EBN) holds 40% shares and NAM 60% shares. All decisions related to off-take and production at the Groningen gas field are taken by this partnership. The close co-ordination between extraction and sales is also warranted by the fact that the same parties hold the shares in the gas supply company: NV Nederlandse Gasunie (25% Shell, 25% Exxon, 40% EBN and 10% Dutch State directly). Although some of Gasunie's shareholders (Shell and Exxon) participate in the upstream activities through the NAM, the latter is not to be considered as a related undertaking.

Even though Minister De Pous wished to establish close co-operation between the production and marketing of gas, the Government did not opt for a system of vertical

---

[61] "Loi concernant les Mines, les Minières et les Carrières" of 21 April 1810; "Mijnwet 1903" of 27 April 1904, Stb. 73; "Wet Opsporing Delfstoffen" of 3 May 1967, Stb. 258. "Mijnwet Continentaal Plat" of 23 September 1965, Stb. 428. These Acts have most recently been amended by the Act of 18 March 1996 implementing EC Directive 94/22/EC, Stb. 199.

[62] Act of 14 December 1996, providing rules for the distribution of electricity, gas and heat (Stb. 642).

[63] Tweede Kamer 1961-1962, no. 6767.

integration between production, transmission and supply. Separate undertakings are responsible for each and individual activity within the gas chain. The upstream market is a liberalized market where several oil companies (such as NAM, Elf Petroland, BP/Amoco, Wintershall and Veba) hold concessions and licences for the exploration and production of gas onshore as well as offshore. Almost all concessions and production licences awarded since 1959 include the provision that gas produced in the Netherlands and destined for the Dutch market should be sold to the Gasunie. As a result of the implementation of the Hydrocarbons Licensing Directive by the amended Mining Act of 1996 this supply obligation has been deleted.[64] Be that as it may, most gas produced in the Netherlands is still contracted to Gasunie which in turn supplies gas to the distribution companies and to some large consumers directly.

At the same time as Gasunie was established, the Minister obtained a number of powers of approval on the basis of a private law agreement with Gasunie, i.e. the right of approval of the Gas Marketing Plan forecasting Dutch medium and long term gas supply and demand, the right and approval of the conditions and tariffs for the delivery of gas in- and outside the Netherlands, the right of approval of gas purchasing contracts between Gasunie and suppliers and the right to approve plans for the laying of pipelines.[65]

2. Organization of the Distribution Sector

Since the 1960s there has been a debate about horizontal or vertical integration of the distribution sector. As a result of the long-lasting discussion concerning the scope and content of the (draft) Energy Distribution Act, most gas and electricity distribution companies started to merge into major energy distribution companies (horizontal integration). Gasunie holds shares in two distribution companies. Hence, there is also a very limited extent of vertical integration in the gas distribution sector.

Since 1997 the distribution of gas is regulated on the basis of the earlier mentioned Energy Distribution Act.[66] This Act does not contain a supply obligation, i.e. no public service obligation for the gas supplier. The main tasks of the distribution companies are reliable energy supply at low cost, the promotion of safety as far as the use and the equipment is concerned and the promotion of an efficient and environmentally sound use of energy.[67] Other activities are basically prohibited as these are not covered by the principle of public

---

[64] The implementation of the Hydrocarbons Licensing Directive is further examined by Martha M. Roggenkamp in "Energy Law in the Netherlands", Chapter 10 in the monograph *Energy Law in Europe*, to be published by Oxford University Press, Autumn 2000.

[65] See further Martha M. Roggenkamp, "Oil & Gas: Netherlands Law and Practice", *Chancery Law* 1991, pp. 169-172.

[66] Energy Distribution Act (Wet Energie Distributie) of 20 December 1996, Stb. 654, most recently amended on 2 July 1998, Stb. 427.

[67] Article 2 of the Energy Distribution Act.

supply (i.e. at low cost) as a result of which competition could be distorted.[68]

The Energy Distribution Act has no direct impact on the gas supply contracts between Gasunie and the energy distribution companies. In the early 1960s Gasunie entered into an exclusive evergreen contract with the energy distribution sector through the association of energy distribution companies "EnergieNed". This contract was designed to give the distribution companies the maximum guarantee with regard to a regular and continuous gas supply, but also to give Gasunie a maximum security with regard to the off-take of gas as the contract was designed to continue to run for 15 years after termination. Although during the past years the contract has been amended regularly, the Nma received several complaints about the exclusive character of this contract. Although the Nma has not yet issued a ruling yet, Gasunie announced in March 2000 that it is prepared to give up its exclusive contracts for the sector of protected end-users as of 1 January 2004.

C. Market Opening: Liberalization versus Regulation

1. The Gas Bill

In March 1999 the Gas Bill implementing Directive 98/30 concerning common rules for the internal market in gas was sent to Parliament.[69] After some intense debates the Second Chamber of Parliament approved the Bill on 5 April 2000. The First Chamber has no right of amendment and the Gas Bill was thus accepted without voting by call on 20 June 2000. The date on which the Gas Act enters into force will be decided by separate Royal Decree.

The Gas Act aims to secure (i) the regular supply of gas as well as (ii) the introduction of competition in the gas sector. Like the energy distribution companies under the Energy Distribution Act (see above), the Gas Act provides that each gas transmission, gas storage or LNG-undertaking shall operate, maintain and develop under economic conditions secure, reliable and efficient transmission, storage or LNG facilities, with due regard to the environment. Moreover, all natural gas supply companies are under an obligation to promote an environmentally prudent use of natural gas both by themselves and by their customers.[70]

Pursuant to the aim to promote competition in the gas sector, the Act requires gas undertakings to provide other gas undertakings with sufficient information to ensure that

---

[68] Article 12 clearly defines these activities as including the supply of goods and services necessary for energy supply (at low cost), safety inspections, collection of payments, the construction of supply infrastructure and, finally, the construction and exploitation of public lighting systems and traffic regulation systems in so far as these latter activities are connected with electricity supply.

[69] Tweede Kamer 1998-1999, 26 463, nos. 1-3.

[70] Article 29 of the Gas Act.

the transport and storage of natural gas with the use of the transmission grid and/or storage and LNG facilities, may take place in a manner compatible with the secure and efficient operation of the interconnected grid. More particularly, gas undertakings shall refrain from any form of discrimination between network users.

2. Gradual Market Opening

Similar to the electricity sector, the Government aims at a 100% liberalization of the gas market in three different stages. Again a distinction is made between three categories of customers. Those customers who are not (yet) considered to be eligible are regarded as "protected customers". These consumers are protected by the law as the distribution companies supplying these customers have an obligation to supply them and the supply tariff is set by the Minister (see below).

The first category of "eligible" customers consists of those companies using more than 10 million m^3 gas per year.[71] As a result some 44% of the market will be liberalized, instead of the minimum required 20% (and eventually 33%) provided for by the EC Gas Directive. In the absence of statutory provisions, these consumers are in theory already free to choose their suppliers. The market liberalization process is, therefore, not completely dependent on the entry into force of the Gas Act.

The next category of consumers that will be considered eligible are those consumers using less than 10 million m^3 and more than 1 million m^3 gas per year. These medium-sized customers will be eligible as from 1 January 2002. Finally all consumers using less than 1 million m^3 gas per year will be free to choose their suppliers as of 1 January 2004.[72] The Gas Act originally provided that the latter category of gas customers would be eligible as of 1 January 2007. However, as a result of the experiences in the electricity sector it was decided to speed up the liberalization process and cut back the liberalization date to 2004. At the same time, the original Bill applied a different categorization of eligible customers. Instead of customers using more or less than 1 million m^3 gas per year, it referred to consumers using more or less than 170,000 cubic metres gas per year, i.e. households.[73] However, as some customers like horticulturists expect to be worse off as a result of the new gas pricing system following the liberalization process, it was decided to give them a two year's grace period, as most horticulturists consume less than 1 million m^3 gas per year.

---

[71] Tweede Kamer 1998-1999, 26 463, no. 3, p. 10.

[72] Article 1 (1n) of the Gas Act.

[73] It should be noted that the references in the original Gas Bill to the three mentioned categories of consumers were not arbitrary but taken directly from the old tariff structure of Gasunie, i.e. the zoning tariff which currently still applies to all consumers using less than 10 million m^3 gas.

3. Supply Licences

During the transitional period which runs to 2004, the Gas Act requires gas undertakings to apply for a license in order to supply natural gas to "protected customers".[74] This license will only be granted when the undertaking demonstrates that sufficient arrangements are made to fulfil the obligation to supply natural gas to the protected customers in a certain area.[75] The obligation to supply does not apply if it is considered to be unreasonable for the license holder. In case a licence is awarded, the license holder is obliged to supply natural gas to these protected customers for a certain price.[76] The Minister determines the maximum prices thereof.[77] As the Natural Gas Prices Act (Wet Aardgasprijzen)[78] remains valid after the Gas Act has entered into force; the Minister may continue to influence the minimum price of gas. The Natural Gas Prices Act states that the Minister may prohibit supplies of natural gas at a price lower than the price set by him. In addition, the Gas Act requires licence holders to keep annual accounts of their supply of gas to protected customers.[79] Further rules shall be laid down by ministerial regulation relating to the way in which these obligations should be complied with.

The original Gas Bill included a provision imposing on gas companies an obligation that small customers (using less than 170,000 m³ gas per year) should be guaranteed a regular supply of gas after the market had been completely opened.[80] This obligation has been made more concrete as the Gas Act introduces a separate licensing requirement for suppliers (distribution companies as well as others) delivering gas to households after 2004. This licensing requirement was specifically introduced to give small consumers some additional protection. Such a supply licence will be awarded by the Minister of Economic Affairs upon certain conditions. In contrast with the licence applying to eligible customers and which runs until 2004, this new or additional supply licence does not include a specific obligation to supply but a more general obligation to take care of the supply of gas upon reasonable terms and conditions.

The Gas Act like the Electricity Act establishes in fact a transitional period in which two separate markets exist side by side. A liberalized gas market for large and medium sized consumers for which there are no licensing requirements and a non-liberalized market for the supply of gas and electricity to "protected customers". The latter market is a regulated market.

---

[74] Article 11 of the Gas Act.

[75] Article 12 of the Gas Act.

[76] Article 15 of the Gas Act.

[77] Article 16 of the Gas Act.

[78] Stb. 1974, no.765.

[79] Article 23 of the Gas Act.

[80] Article 32 of the Gas Act. The Minister is given specific enforcement powers.

4. The Role of Gasunie

Surprisingly, the first draft of the Gas Bill did not address the position of Gasunie, its tasks and more specifically its relationship with the Government. However, the revised draft of December 1999 included an additional paragraph on the systematic management of gas reservoirs within which Gasunie is given a crucial role.[81] It requires Gasunie (i) to purchase gas from the Groningen field, (ii) to purchase gas at the request of producers from other fields according to reasonable conditions and market-value prices, and (iii) to submit annually a forecast of Dutch supply and demand for the next 20 years. It confirms Gasunie's central role in the Dutch gas market co-ordinating the production and sale of gas and concerns particularly the balancing function of the Groningen field. This paragraph has specifically been included in order to safeguard the Government's small field policy and has to be considered as a public service obligation. The Minister can decide that Gasunie should be exempted temporarily of the above obligation if Gasunie would (possibly) suffer financial or economic difficulties as a result of this task (cf. Article 86 of the EC Treaty).[82] Further estimates of Dutch supply and demand will be included in the Energy Report. The Minister is given the explicit right to give Gasunie instructions as far as they are necessary for carrying out the specific tasks assigned to it. These new provisions are also intended to replace the above mentioned private law agreements between the State and Gasunie.[83]

5. Unbundling

The original Gas Bill deviated from the Electricity Act as it did not require the transmission and distribution companies to establish separate network and supply companies. Following the provisions in Directive 98/30, the Gas Bill only required gas undertakings[84] like Gasunie and the distribution companies to keep separate accounts for transportation and storage of gas.[85]

However, as a result of the Parliamentary debate the legislature had to provide for a limited legal unbundling along the lines of the E-Act 1998. The Gas Act requires the distribution companies to appoint an independent network operator for the regional grid. As a result, the exploitation of the regional grid will be legally separated from the supply activities. The Gas Act contains similar provisions for the appointment of a network operator

---

[81] Chapter 5.3a or Articles 33a – 33d of the Gas Act.

[82] Article 33b of the Gas Act.

[83] Tweede Kamer 1998-1999, 26 463, no. 7, p. 9.

[84] Article 1 (1 under j) of the Gas Act includes in the definition of "gas company" (gasbedrijf) a company which produces gas, without distinguishing the place of origin.

[85] Article 22 of the Gas Act. It seems that this obligation also applies to the petroleum-producing companies operating upstream pipelines.

as the E-Act 1998.[86] As most distribution companies are horizontally integrated, some distribution companies may already have appointed a separate network operator for the gas and the electricity grid. The high pressure grid (i.e. Gasunie's grid) is excluded from the obligation to appoint a separate network operator without any specific reason.

The absence of legal unbundling emphasises the need to protect confidential information acquired in the process of negotiating access and/or supply. Article 26 of the Gas Act, therefore, provides that a gas transmission, storage or LNG undertaking which, in the discharge of its duties, acquires data/information that it knows to be or must reasonably presume to be confidential shall be obliged to keep those data secret.

Moreover, gas transmission undertakings (i.e. Gasunie) shall, in purchasing or selling gas through the gas transmission undertaking itself or through an allied undertaking, not misuse commercially sensitive data relating to others that it has obtained in negotiations or during negotiations about transport. This provision limits the confidentiality clause to information that is obtained in negotiations about transport. No such clause seems to apply if negotiations about the delivery of gas are unsuccessful and separate negotiations start for the transport of third party's gas.

Nevertheless, Gasunie is aware of the need to distinguish between gas supply and gas transport and has as of 1 April 2000 established a separate Transportation and Services Office. In addition, special accountancy procedures have been introduced to guarantee the independent position of the Gas Transportation and Services Office. The Nma supervises these activities. An infringement forms an economic offence under the Financial Offences Law ("Wet Economische Delicten").[87]

6. Access to the System

6.1. INTRODUCTION

From the start of the liberalization process, the legislature has opted for a system of negotiated access.[88] This may be surprising as the earlier mentioned E-Act 1998 is based on a system of regulated access and both laws are based on similar assumptions of market opening and liberalization. The legislator argues, however, that the gas market (by contrast to the electricity sector) always has been an international market within which third parties have acquired access on the basis of free and commercial negotiations. Although this argument is in itself true, it should be noted that such access negotiations only took place

---

[86] Article 2 – Article 9 of the Gas Act.

[87] Article 44 of the Gas Act.

[88] See "Nota Gasstromen" (Policy Paper "Gas Flows") and the explanatory notes to the Gas Bill.

between the incumbent national gas companies like Distrigaz, Ruhrgas, Gaz de France etc. In other words, only the national monopolies were in the position to negotiate access.[89] Major consumers have never had (or taken) the opportunity to negotiate access with Gasunie.

6.2. NEGOTIATED AND REGULATED ACCESS

Following the choices made with regard to unbundling, the current Gas Act provides for two different systems of TPA. In case of the unbundled activities of the regional grid, the legislator now provides for a system of regulated access (rTPA). The provisions on rTPA are based on the same principles as the E-Act 1998. This means that the CPI-X methodology will apply to the gas sector as well. The provisions on negotiated access remain valid as far as it concerns the Gasunie grid (nTPA). Access can be denied if there is insufficient capacity or if an undertaking is experiencing or is threatening to experience serious economic and financial difficulties in connection with one or more existing Take or Pay contracts.[90] In assessing the application the director-general of the Nma shall take into account the provisions of the Gas Directive. Moreover, such assessment has to take place within a given time frame,[91] which is noteworthy since the Gas Act does not provide for specific time limits with regard to the negotiations on access.

The provisions in the Gas Act regarding negotiated access have also been developed gradually. At first the Bill merely stated that a gas business is obliged to negotiate access if a request for access is made.[92] The absence of any time limits and/or guidelines for negotiations could lead to very lengthy negotiations as a result of which an applicant could easily lose its interest or need for access. The extent to which the gas undertakings' indicative tariffs may lead to further negotiations was another matter of discussion. Free

---

[89] See also the requirement under the Council Directive 91/296 on Gas Transit that negotiations regarding transit are limited to those main transmission companies listed in the annex to the Directive.

[90] See Articles 15 and 16 of the Gas Act, which in turn refer to Article 25 of the Gas Directive. The provision in the Gas Act does not deviate in any important way from the Directive. It provides that the director-general of the Nma may, on application, grant a gas transmission undertaking temporary exemption from the obligation to negotiate access if such a request for transport is made and the undertaking is experiencing or may experience difficulties in connection with agreements already entered into which contain an obligation for it to purchase a certain quantity of gas or, failing that, to make a payment to the value of that quantity of gas or a part thereof.

[91] He shall rule on the application as soon as possible, but at the latest within 4 months following receipt of the application. If an exemption is granted, he shall immediately notify this (together with all relevant details) to the Commission. If the Commission decides to amend or withdraw the exemption (as referred to in Article 25(2) of the Directive) the director-general is obliged to put this into effect.

[92] Article 5 (first version) reads:(1) A gas business shall be obliged, where appropriate with an allied business, to negotiate with the party who requests this concerning the performance of the transport of gas via its gas transportation network and via one or more installations of its own or of the allied business, in so far as the use of those installations is necessary for transport. (2) The transport of gas and the services necessarily connected therewith shall be performed on the basis of what has been agreed by virtue of section 1. (3) Application of section 1 and 2 shall take place under conditions which are reasonable, transparent and non-discriminatory".

negotiations about access could result in different tariffs being set for similar customers and this was argued to be contrary to the basic principle of non-discrimination of the Directive and the EC Treaty. Consequently the Gas Bill has been revised drastically as a result of which the nTPA has become more regulated.

A crucial role is given to the Nma, with regard to both the aspects of regulation and supervision. First, the Gas Act provides that indicative gas transportation tariffs can only be set on the basis of guidelines issued by the Nma. These guidelines are supposed to give applicants increased security that the tariffs are reasonable and non-discriminatory. In practice these guidelines will probably be set by the DTe. As a result, there will be a clear division between the regulatory tasks of the DTe and dispute settlement by Nma.

Secondly, the Gas Act provides that the director-general of the Nma can decide on a certain time frame within which the negotiations have to take place. If such negotiations are unsuccessful, the gas undertaking has to inform the director-general of the Nma of the reasons for the failure.[93]

Thirdly, the director-general of the Nma may apply a provisional measure in case the parties (gas undertaking and the undertaking requesting access) cannot agree upon the terms and conditions for access. Such a provisional measure would facilitate access for the applicant party and will apply for a certain period set by the director-general.[94] Although these amendments are improvements, they are still considered to raise some (future) problems. After all, the final terms and conditions which may finally be set by the Court of Appeal for Trade and Industry ("College van Beroep voor het Bedrijfsleven"), a specialist forum of independent judges, could be so strict that the applicant under normal circumstances would never have accepted them.

6.3. ACCESS TO GAS STORAGE FACILITIES

It is striking that the legislature has also included special provisions regarding access to gas storage facilities. The Gas Act states that the rules on nTPA apply to gas storage as long as the storage facility has a dominant position. Moreover, the Act declares explicitly that Gasunie as well as the holders of the Groningen concession (NAM) and the Bergen concession (Amoco) enjoy such a dominant position. Currently, all underground storage facilities are situated in these two concession areas and are leased by Gasunie. Be that as it may, the Gas Act gives NAM and Amoco a special role. It seems that NAM and Amoco can be required to present indicative tariffs on the basis of which they can negotiate TPA with third parties, including Gasunie. Examining the Gas Bill it also seems that gas storage and gas transportation are two completely separate activities. In practice, however, these activities are very closely related. Gasunie's new tariff structure "Commodity Services

---

[93] Article 5 of the Gas Act.

[94] Article 9 of the Gas Act

System" (CSS) is, to a large extent, based on the combined services of transportation and storage.

6.4. TARIFFS

Gasunie published a new tariff structure in 1999. This new structure is called "Commodity Services System" (or CSS). The Minister has approved the CSS. The Minister's power of approval is based on the private law agreements which are part of the "old" regime (see above).

The CSS originally applied to the major consumers (i.e., above 50 million m³). As from the year 2000 it also applies to customers consuming more than 10 million m³ gas. This new tariff structure makes a distinction between the volume sold (= commodity) and the capacity sold (= transportation and services). The commodity is priced the same way as before, i.e. on the basis of an alternative energy source like heavy fuel oil (oil parity) or coal. An independent market price for gas, as in the US and/or UK, has not yet been envisaged. It will *inter alia* depend on the establishment of an Energy Exchange.[95] The capacity tariff is more complicated as there are several capacity charges. The contractual capacity consists of a base load capacity and the additional capacity. The base load capacity is determined on the basis of a yearly consumption of 8000 hours. Basically the base load capacity consists of a regular and even off-take of gas. The transport of base load capacity is free under the CSS. The difference between the contractual and base load capacity is called additional capacity. Additional capacity refers to all capacity that exceeds the base load capacity. The off-take of additional capacity is more unpredictable. By contrast to the base load capacity, a special capacity charge is included in the CSS. Besides, companies have to pay a distance-related transportation charge for the transport of base load and additional capacity. The distance is determined on the basis of five entry points so that the distance will never exceed 200 km. These five entry points are Noordbroek, Balgzand, Maasvlakte, Zelzate and 's Gravenvoere. With the exception of the latter entry point, these places represent the locations where gas is entering the Dutch market.

The CSS applies to contracts with a one-year term and is based on an hourly flexibility. For third parties the hourly flexibility may cause problems as they have to guarantee the input and off-take of gas at a given place and time. If not, third parties have to pay additional service charges. In addition, the CSS is presented as providing fixed tariffs as negotiations could lead to discriminatory behaviour between the same type of users. The industry, however, argues that the CSS seems to be applied as a regulated tariff, which has been established without any democratic control or involvement or negotiations by the other parties involved. It remains to be seen whether the CSS will be amended after the entry into force of the Act and whether the Nma (or DTe) will provide general guidelines to which the Gasunie will have to adhere.

---

[95] The Minister has asked the Amsterdam Power Exchange to investigate the possibilities for such an exchange.

7. Access to Upstream Pipelines

The Gas Directive also provides for access to upstream pipelines. The reason that these pipelines are included in the Gas Directive is of course that free negotiations between producers and consumers have no sense if there is no access to these pipelines as well. It is a basic point of discussion, however, whether production/upstream pipelines should be regulated by the Gas Directive or the (upstream) Hydrocarbons Licensing Directive. Most gas producing countries have on the basis of the Law of the Sea Conventions included basic regulations (i.e. a licensing regime) for the construction and use (including the connection to the grid by third parties) of upstream pipelines in their petroleum laws. This is not the case in the Netherlands. Neither the Gas Act nor the Mining Bill[96] propose to introduce such a licensing regime. Article 8 of the Gas Act only provides that competition law also applies to the transportation of gas through those production networks (i.e. upstream pipelines)[97] over which the Netherlands may exercise sovereign rights by virtue of the Treaty concerning the rights of the sea concluded at Montego Bay on 10 December 1982.[98]

Neither the mining laws nor the Gas Act provide any direct obligation/provisions regarding a connection between production pipelines. A possible exception is the existence of safety rules and technical provisions/standards issued by the NNI (Nederlands Normalisatie Instituut) or other standardization institutes such as ISO or CEN. The connection of production facilities to the grid (i.e., production pipelines) depends on the capacity in the grid (and to a lesser extent gas quality). There are no provisions regulating the connection of production pipelines to the transmission grid.[99]

8. Dispute Settlement

The director-general of the Nma is the competent dispute settlement authority for the gas sector. The DTe is a chamber of the Nma and has recently been charged with the supervision of the compliance with the Gas Act. As with the Electricity Act, it is the DTe who supervises the gas sector (and thus the entire downstream energy sector) and the director-general of the Nma who is required to settle disputes on access and the refusal of access.[100] The director-general is not competent in cases of cross-border transportation if the refusal of access or the refusal to indicate the conditions of transport is due to a company which controls transport- or production facilities which are totally in the sphere of another Member

---

[96] Draft Mining Act ("Mijnbouwwet"), TK 1998, 26219.

[97] The term "gas production network" shall not be understood to mean the pipelines used on the site within an oil or gas extraction project (Article 8 (2) of the Gas Act).

[98] *Tractatenblad* (Treaty Gazette) 1983, 83.

[99] See Article 23 of the Gas Directive which refers to existing upstream pipeline facilities.

[100] Article 9 of the Gas Act.

State. In cases of disputes related to a transport which fall also in the sphere of another Member State, the director-general will consult the competent dispute-settlement authority in the other Member state. It is not clear how this provision will evolve in practice.[101] Any decision by the director-general taken in this respect is subject to review by the Court of Appeal for Trade and Industry.[102]

D. Pipeline Competition and the Construction of (Direct) Lines

Examples in other jurisdictions show that the absence of a separate network operator is an important barrier to the liberalization of the gas market. It is also a psychological barrier for companies to negotiate access. Companies may wish to turn to direct pipeline competition instead of gas-to-gas competition. In the Netherlands companies have the possibility to construct and exploit a competitive pipeline as there is a general freedom to construct pipelines. A typical example of this development is the establishment of the Zebra pipeline between the Belgian border and the Europoort area by Delta Nutsbedrijven. This pipeline runs parallel to a Gasunie pipeline.

In the absence of specific pipeline legislation, no licences are required for the construction and operation of direct lines either. Basically, there is a general freedom to construct (subsoil) pipelines. Unlike the E-Act 1998, the Gas Bill does not include any constraints on this freedom. However, in case a landowner does not wish to co-operate with the construction of a subsoil pipeline, a special permission (gedoogplicht) can be issued on the basis of the Act on Hindrances of Private Law ("Belemmeringenwet privaatrecht") of 1927.[103] In order to receive such permission, the pipeline company will need a concession and a declaration of public interest. As Gasunie and the distribution companies have been awarded such documents in the past, new pipeline companies could have a disadvantage. On the other hand, as the Act on Hindrances of Public Law of 1927 is specifically intended for the construction of public works, it is a matter of discussion whether pipelines/direct lines within a liberalized gas market are to be considered as public works at all.

E. The Consequences of the Liberalization Process

The implementation of Directive 98/30 is of special importance as it abolishes the regional monopolies of the distribution companies. A less rigorous regime applies to the transmission sector. By contrast, the Gas Act seems to give Gasunie a legal basis for its monopoly

---

[101] Article 10 of the Gas Act.

[102] Article 35 of the Gas Act.

[103] Act of 13 May 1927, Stb. 159. See further Martha M. Roggenkamp, "Het Juridisch Kader van Pijpleidingen in de Olie- en Gasindustrie", *Energie en Recht*, deel 1, Intersentia, 1999.

position. Be that as it may, the above changes in the regulatory framework will certainly have some consequences for the companies' ownership structure. Currently the distribution companies are mostly owned by public bodies such as municipalities and provinces. Gasunie is 50% owned by the State and 50% by Shell and Exxon. There are clear signs that the shareholders' position in these companies may change in the (near) future. Despite objections from the Minister of Economic Affairs, the gas distribution company of Haarlemmermeer has already decided that it will privatize.

It is most unlikely that the privatization process which is currently taking place within the electricity supply and energy distribution sector will fail to touch the gas transmission sector as well (i.e. Gasunie.). The Minister has already announced that further privatization of Gasunie may be discussed after the Gas Act has entered into force. It is also unclear to what extent the oil companies Shell and Exxon will apply a similar (and parallel) policy with regard to their shares in Gasunie. Although members of parliament have raised the issue of (State-) ownership in Gasunie, it is too early to tell which way the shareholders' position in Gasunie will develop. Be that as it may, liberalization of the gas sector will lead to privatization one way or another.

The above has also shown that liberalization leads to further regulation of the gas sector. Although the Gas Act is an important document since it provides the gas sector with a statutory law, it remains to be seen to what extent the gas market actually will be liberalized. In practice it will be difficult to introduce competition in the gas sector. Firstly, the supply of gas is restricted. Dutch gas is for the most part contracted to Gasunie. This policy seems to be continued in the future on the basis of the small fields policy and Gasunie's co-ordinating role. As there are no signs that the Dutch Government wishes to interfere in existing gas contracts,[104] the possibilities for liberalizing the Dutch gas market are in fact very scarce. The supply from other gas sources is also considered to be limited. UK's gas bubble will soon come to an end, as a result of which the UK will become an importing instead of an exporting country. Hence, "free" gas supply is limited to Norwegian, Russian and Algerian gas, i.e. long distance gas from countries dominated by gas supply monopolies. Secondly, examples from the Canadian, US and UK gas markets illustrate that the introduction of competition relies on a pro-active regulator and regulated access to the gas transmission networks. Although the Dutch legislator has finally opted for regulated access to the distribution grid and for the appointment of the DTe as the supervisory authority, it seems that this is just a first but necessary step towards liberalization. Regulated access to the transmission grid is a *sine qua non* for liberalization. Maybe the current system of negotiated access to transmission lines is just a transitional regime. Moreover, the proposed regime also includes some important regulatory elements. Whether the DTe has sufficient instruments to steer the liberalization process is another issue indeed. After all, the DTe is charged with the supervision of compliance with the Gas Act and not with the explicit task to promote competition.

---

[104] As the UK Government did by introducing the 90/10 rule, i.e. 10% of the gas contracted to the former State gas company British Gas should be brought on the open market.

IV. CONCLUDING REMARKS

The above examination of the developments in the Dutch gas and electricity sector illustrate the impact the EC Directives have (had) on the legal framework applying to the energy sector. Although the E-Act 1998 and the Gas Act to a large extent are based on similar assumptions (i.e. a 100% market opening), some difference can be noted as well. Most importantly, these differences concern the choices made with regard to unbundling and access to the grid. While the E-Act 1998 from the start has opted for a liberalized regime, the Gas Act is slowly moving towards a regime of legal unbundling and regulated access. Whether this will result in a further integration of both laws into one integrated energy law remains to be seen. Despite the Minister's announcement in the third Energy Policy Note of 1995, the feasibility of such an integrated law is small. It is more likely that the legislator will be forced by the market to regularly amend both the E-Act 1998 and the Gas Act as the liberalization process is on its way. Moreover, an important difference appears between both sectors and that concerns the supply side. In contrast with the electricity sector, major Dutch interests are involved in the production of gas. Although the Gas Act aims at safeguarding these interests, it is doubtful whether this can be done in the long term within a process of continuing liberalization.

LIST OF CONTRIBUTORS

Dr. Michael Albers, Head of Unit, Direction E-3, Competition Directorate, European Commission

Dr. Achim-Rüdiger Börner, Börner Rechtsanwalt, Köln

Nicolas Charbit, Avocat à la Cour d'Appel, Paris

Dr. Wolgang Fritz, Director, Consentec Consulting, Aachen

Damien Geradin, Associate Professor of Law, University of Liège; Professor, College of Europe, Bruges

Francis McGowan, Lecturer, European Institute, Sussex University

Anne Heinen, Research Assistant, University of Liège

Martha Roggenkamp, Member of the Energy Group, Trénité Van Doorne, Rotterdam; Fellow, International Institute of Energy Law, University of Leiden

Gian Carlo Scarsi, Senior Economic Consultant, London Economics.

Dr. Sabine Schulte-Beckhausen, Expert, Verband kommunaler Unternehmen e.V. (Association of Municipal Utilities)

Piet Jan Slot, Professor of Law and Director, International Institute of Energy Law, University of Leiden

Dirk Vandermeersch, Partner, Cleary, Gottlieb, Steen and Hamilton, Brussels; Visiting Professor of Energy Law, Ghent University

Annex 1

DIRECTIVE 96/92/EC OF THE EUROPEAN PARLIAMENT AND OF THE COUNCIL OF 19 DECEMBER 1996
concerning common rules for the internal market in electricity

THE EUROPEAN PARLIAMENT AND THE COUNCIL OF THE EUROPEAN UNION,

Having regard to the Treaty establishing the European Community, and in particular Article 57 (2), Article 66 and Article 100a thereof,

Having regard to the proposal from the Commission (1),

Having regard to the opinion of the Economic and Social Committee (2),

Acting in accordance with the procedure laid down in Article 189b of the Treaty (3),

(1) Whereas it is important to adopt measures to ensure the smooth running of the internal market; whereas the internal market is to comprise an area without internal frontiers in which the free movement of goods, persons, services and capital is ensured;

(2) Whereas the completion of a competitive electricity market is an important step towards completion of the internal energy market;

(3) Whereas the provisions of this Directive should not affect the full application of the Treaty, in particular the provisions concerning the internal market and competition;

(4) Whereas establishment of the internal market in electricity is particularly important in order to increase efficiency in the production, transmission and distribution of this product, while reinforcing security of supply and the competitiveness of the European economy and respecting environmental protection;

(5) Whereas the internal market in electricity needs to be established gradually, in order to enable the industry to adjust in a flexible and ordered manner to its new environment and to take account of the different ways in which electricity systems are organized at present;

(6) Whereas the establishment of the internal market in the electricity sector must favour the interconnection and interoperability of systems;

Damien Geradin (ed.), The Liberalization of Electricity and Natural Gas in the European Union, 227–286
©2001 Kluwer Law International. Printed in the Netherlands.

(7) Whereas Council Directive 90/547/EEC of 29 October 1990 on the transit of electricity through transmission grids (4) and Council Directive 90/377/EEC of 29 June 1990 concerning a Community procedure to improve the transparency of gas and electricity prices charged to industrial end-users (5), provide for a first phase for the completion of the internal market in electricity;

(8) Whereas it is now necessary to take further measures with a view to establishing the internal market in electricity;

(9) Whereas, in the internal market, electricity undertakings must be able to operate, without prejudice to compliance with public service obligations, with a view to achieving a competitive market in electricity;

(10) Whereas Member States, because of the structural differences in the Member States, currently have different systems for regulating the electricity sector;

(11) Whereas, in accordance with the principle of subsidiarity, general principles providing for a framework must be established at Community level, but their detailed implementation should be left to Member States, thus allowing each Member State to choose the regime which corresponds best to its particular situation;

(12) Whereas, whatever the nature of the prevailing market organization, access to the system must be open in accordance with this Directive and must lead to equivalent economic results in the States and hence to a directly comparable level of opening-up of markets and to a directly comparable degree of access to electricity markets;

(13) Whereas for some Member States the imposition of public service obligations may be necessary to ensure security of supply and consumer and environmental protection, which, in their view, free competition, left to itself, cannot necessarily guarantee;

(14) Whereas long-term planning may be one means of carrying out those public service obligations;

(15) Whereas the Treaty lays down specific rules with regard to restrictions on the free movement of goods and on competition;

(16) Whereas Article 90 (1) of the Treaty, in particular, obliges the Member States to respect these rules with regard to public undertakings and undertakings which have been granted special or exclusive rights;

(17) Whereas Article 90 (2) of the Treaty subjects undertakings entrusted with the operation of services of general economic interest to these rules, under specific conditions;

(18) Whereas the implementation of this Directive will have an impact on the activities of such undertakings;

(19) Whereas the Member States, when imposing public service obligations on the

undertakings of the electricity sector, must therefore respect the relevant rules of the Treaty as interpreted by the Court of Justice;

(20) Whereas, in establishing the internal market in electricity, full account should be taken of the Community objective of economic and social cohesion, particularly in sectors such as the infrastructures, national or intra-Community, which are used for the transmission of electricity;

(21) Whereas Decision No 1254/96/EC of the European Parliament and of the Council of 5 June 1996 laying down a series of guidelines for trans-European energy networks (6) has contributed to the development of integrated infrastructures for the transmission of electricity;

(22) Whereas it is therefore necessary to establish common rules for the production of electricity and the operation of electricity transmission and distribution systems;

(23) Whereas there are two systems which may be applied for opening up the production market, an authorization procedure or a tendering procedure, and these must operate in accordance with objective, transparent and non-discriminatory criteria;

(24) Whereas the position of autoproducers and independent producers needs to be taken into consideration within this framework;

(25) Whereas each transmission system must be subject to central management and control in order to ensure the security, reliability and efficiency of the system in the interests of producers and their customers; whereas a transmission system operator should therefore be designated and entrusted with the operation, maintenance, and, if necessary, development of the system; whereas the transmission system operator must behave in an objective, transparent and non-discriminatory manner;

(26) Whereas the technical rules for the operation of transmission systems and direct lines must be transparent and must ensure interoperability;

(27) Whereas objective and non-discriminatory criteria must be established for the dispatching of power stations;

(28) Whereas, for reasons of environmental protection, priority may be given to the production of electricity from renewable sources;

(29) Whereas, at the distribution level, customers located in a given area may be granted supply rights and a manager must be designated to manage, maintain and, if necessary, develop each distribution system;

(30) Whereas, in order to ensure transparency and non-discrimination, the transmission function of vertically integrated undertakings should be operated independently from the other activities;

(31) Whereas a single buyer must operate separately from the generation and distribution activities of vertically integrated undertakings; whereas the flow of information between the single buyer activities and these generation and distribution activities needs to be restricted;

(32) Whereas the accounts of all integrated electricity undertakings should provide for maximum transparency, in particular to identify possible abuses of a dominant position, consisting for example in abnormally high or low tariffs or in discriminatory practices relating to equivalent transactions; whereas, to this end, the accounts must be separate for each activity;

(33) Whereas it is also necessary to provide for access by the competent authorities to the internal accounts of undertakings with due regard for confidentiality;

(34) Whereas, owing to the diversity of structures and the special characteristics of systems in Member States, there should be different options for system access operating in accordance with objective, transparent and non-discriminatory criteria;

(35) Whereas provision should be made for authorizing the construction and use of direct lines;

(36) Whereas provision must be made for safeguards and dispute settlement procedures;

(37) Whereas any abuse of a dominant position or any predatory behaviour should be avoided;

(38) Whereas, as some Member States are liable to experience special difficulties in adjusting their systems, provision should be made for recourse to transitional regimes or derogations, especially for the operation of small isolated systems;

(39) Whereas this Directive constitutes a further phase of liberalization; whereas, once it has been put into effect, some obstacles to trade in electricity between Member States will nevertheless remain in place; whereas, therefore, proposals for improving the operation of the internal market in electricity may be made in the light of experience; whereas the Commission should therefore report to the Council and the European Parliament on the application of this Directive,

HAVE ADOPTED THIS DIRECTIVE:

CHAPTER I

Scope and definitions

Article 1

This Directive establishes common rules for the generation, transmission and distribution of electricity. It lays down the rules relating to the organization and functioning of the electricity sector, access to the market, the criteria and procedures applicable to calls for tender and the granting of authorizations and the operation of systems.

Article 2

For the purposes of this Directive:

1. 'generation' shall mean the production of electricity;

2. 'producer' shall mean a natural or legal person generating electricity;

3. 'autoproducer' shall mean a natural or legal person generating electricity essentially for his own use;

4. 'independent producer' shall mean:
   (a) a producer who does not carry out electricity transmission or distribution functions in the territory covered by the system where he is established;
   (b) in Member States in which vertically integrated undertakings do not exist and where a tendering procedure is used, a producer corresponding to the definition of point (a), who may not be exclusively subject to the economic precedence of the interconnected system;

5. 'transmission' shall mean the transport of electricity on the high-voltage interconnected system with a view to its delivery to final customers or to distributors;

6. 'distribution' shall mean the transport of electricity on medium-voltage and low-voltage distribution systems with a view to its delivery to customers;

7. 'customers' shall mean wholesale or final customers of electricity and distribution companies;

8. 'wholesale customers' shall mean any natural or legal persons, if the Member States recognize their existence, who purchase or sell electricity and who do not carry out transmission, generation or distribution functions inside or outside the system where they are established;

9. 'final customer' shall mean a customer buying electricity for his own use;

10. 'interconnectors' shall mean equipment used to link electricity systems;

11. 'interconnected system' shall mean a number of transmission and distribution systems linked together by means of one or more interconnectors;

12. 'direct line' shall mean an electricity line complementary to the interconnected system;

13. 'economic precedence' shall mean the ranking of sources of electricity supply in accordance with economic criteria;

14. 'ancillary services' shall mean all services necessary for the operation of a transmission or distribution system;

15. 'system user' shall mean any natural or legal person supplying to, or being supplied by, a transmission or distribution system;

16. 'supply' shall mean the delivery and/or sale of electricity to customers;

17. 'integrated electricity undertaking' shall mean a vertically or horizontally integrated undertaking;

18. 'vertically integrated undertaking' shall mean an undertaking performing two or more of the functions of generation, transmission and distribution of electricity;

19. 'horizontally integrated undertaking' shall mean an undertaking performing at least one of the functions of generation for sale, or transmission or distribution of electricity, and another non-electricity activity;

20. 'tendering procedure' shall mean the procedure through which planned additional requirements and replacement capacity are covered by supplies from new or existing generating capacity;

21. 'long-term planning' shall mean the planning of the need for investment in generation and transmission capacity on a long-term basis, with a view to meeting the demand for electricity of the system and securing supplies to customers;

22. 'single buyer' shall mean any legal person who, within the system where he is established, is responsible for the unified management of the transmission system and/or for centralized electricity purchasing and selling;

23. 'small isolated system' shall mean any system with consumption of less than 2500 GWh in the year 1996, where less than 5 % of annual consumption is obtained through interconnection with other systems.

CHAPTER II

General rules for the organization of the sector

Article 3

1. Member States shall ensure, on the basis of their institutional organization and with due regard for the principle of subsidiarity, that, without prejudice to paragraph 2, electricity undertakings are operated in accordance with the principles of this Directive, with a view to achieving a competitive market in electricity, and shall not discriminate between these undertakings as regards either rights or obligations. The two approaches to system access referred to in Articles 17 and 18 must lead to equivalent economic results and hence to a directly comparable level of opening-up of markets and to a directly comparable degree of access to electricity markets.

2. Having full regard to the relevant provisions of the Treaty, in particular Article 90, Member States may impose on undertakings operating in the electricity sector, in the general economic interest, public service obligations which may relate to security, including security of supply, regularity, quality and price of supplies and to environmental protection. Such obligations must be clearly defined, transparent, non-discriminatory and verifiable; they, and any revision thereof, shall be published and notified to the Commission by Member States without delay. As a means of carrying out the abovementioned public service obligations, Member States which so wish may introduce the implementation of long-term planning.

3. Member States may decide not to apply the provisions of Articles 5, 6, 17, 18 and 21 insofar as the application of these provisions would obstruct the performance, in law or in fact, of the obligations imposed on electricity undertakings in the general economic interest and insofar as the development of trade would not be affected to such an extent as would be contrary to the interests of the Community. The interests of the Community include, inter alia, competition with regard to eligible customers in accordance with this Directive and Article 90 of the Treaty.

CHAPTER III

Generation

Article 4

For the construction of new generating capacity, Member States may choose between an authorization procedure and/or a tendering procedure. Authorization and tendering must be conducted in accordance with objective, transparent and non-discriminatory criteria.

Article 5

1. Where they opt for the authorization procedure, Member States shall lay down the criteria for the grant of authorizations for the construction of generating capacity in their territory. These criteria may relate to:

    (a) the safety and security of the electricity system, installations and associated equipment;

    (b) protection of the environment;

    (c) land use and siting;

    (d) use of public ground;

    (e) energy efficiency;

    (f) the nature of the primary sources;

    (g) characteristics particular to the applicant, such as technical, economic and financial capabilities;

    (h) the provisions of Article 3.

2. The detailed criteria and procedures shall be made public.

3. Applicants shall be informed of the reasons, which must be objective and non-discriminatory, for any refusal to grant an authorization; the reasons must be well founded and duly substantiated; they shall be forwarded to the Commission for information. Appeal procedures must be made available to the applicant.

Article 6

1. Where they opt for the tendering procedure, Member States or any competent body designated by the Member State concerned shall draw up an inventory of new means of production, including replacement capacity, on the basis of the regular estimate referred to in paragraph 2. The inventory shall take account of the need for interconnection of systems. The requisite capacity shall be allocated by means of a tendering procedure in accordance with the procedure laid down in this Article.

2. The transmission system operator or any other competent authority designated by the Member State concerned shall draw up and publish under State supervision, at least every two years, a regular estimate of the generating and transmission capacity which is likely to be connected to the system, of the need for interconnectors with other systems, of potential transmission capacity and of the demand for electricity. The estimate shall cover a period defined by each Member State.

3. Details of the tendering procedure for means of production shall be published in the Official Journal of the European Communities at least six months prior to the closing date for tenders.

The tender specifications shall be made available to any interested undertaking established in the territory of a Member State so that it has sufficient time in which to submit a tender.

The tender specifications shall contain a detailed description of the contract specifications and of the procedure to be followed by all tenderers and an exhaustive list of criteria governing the selection of tenderers and the award of the contract. These specifications may also relate to the fields referred to in Articles 5 (1).

4. In invitations to tender for the requisite generating capacity, consideration must also be given to electricity supply offers with long-term guarantees from existing generating units, provided that additional requirements can be met in this way.

5. Member States shall designate an authority or a public body or a private body independent of electricity generation, transmission and distribution activities to be responsible for the organization, monitoring and control of the tendering procedure. This authority or body shall take all necessary steps to ensure confidentiality of the information contained in the tenders.

6. However, it must be possible for autoproducers and independent producers to obtain authorization, on the basis of objective, transparent and non-discriminatory criteria as laid down in Articles 4 and 5, in Member States which have opted for the tendering procedure.

CHAPTER IV

Transmission system operation

Article 7

1. Member States shall designate or shall require undertakings which own transmission systems to designate, for a period of time to be determined by Member States having regard to considerations of efficiency and economic balance, a system operator to be

responsible for operating, ensuring the maintenance of, and, if necessary, developing the transmission system in a given area and its interconnectors with other systems, in order to guarantee security of supply.

2. Member States shall ensure that technical rules establishing the minimum technical design and operational requirements for the connection to the system of generating installations, distribution systems, directly connected consumers' equipment, interconnector circuits and direct lines are developed and published. These requirements shall ensure the interoperability of systems and shall be objective and non-discriminatory. They shall be notified to the Commission in accordance with Article 8 of Council Directive 83/189/EEC of 28 March 1983 laying down a procedure for the provision of information in the field of technical standards and regulations (7).

3. The system operator shall be responsible for managing energy flows on the system, taking into account exchanges with other interconnected systems. To that end, the system operator shall be responsible for ensuring a secure, reliable and efficient electricity system and, in that context, for ensuring the availability of all necessary ancillary services.

4. The system operator shall provide to the operator of any other system with which its system is interconnected sufficient information to ensure the secure and efficient operation, coordinated development and interoperability of the interconnected system.

5. The system operator shall not discriminate between system users or classes of system users, particularly in favour of its subsidiaries or shareholders.

6. Unless the transmission system is already independent from generation and distribution activities, the system operator shall be independent at least in management terms from other activities not relating to the transmission system.

Article 8

1. The transmission system operator shall be responsible for dispatching the generating installations in its area and for determining the use of interconnectors with other systems.

2. Without prejudice to the supply of electricity on the basis of contractual obligations, including those which derive from the tendering specifications, the dispatching of generating installations and the use of interconnectors shall be determined on the basis of criteria which may be approved by the Member State and which must be objective, published and applied in a non-discriminatory manner which ensures the proper functioning of the internal market in electricity. They shall take into account the economic precedence of electricity from available generating installations of interconnector transfers and the technical constraints on the system.

3. A Member State may require the system operator, when dispatching generating installations, to give priority to generating installations using renewable energy sources or

waste or producing combined heat and power.

4. A Member State may, for reasons of security of supply, direct that priority be given to the dispatch of generating installations using indigenous primary energy fuel sources, to an extent not exceeding in any calendar year 15 % of the overall primary energy necessary to produce the electricity consumed in the Member State concerned.

Article 9

The transmission system operator must preserve the confidentiality of commercially sensitive information obtained in the course of carrying out its business.

CHAPTER V

Distribution system operation

Article 10

1. Member States may impose on distribution companies an obligation to supply customers located in a given area. The tariff for such supplies may be regulated, for instance to ensure equal treatment of the customers concerned.

2. Member States shall designate or shall require undertakings which own or are responsible for distribution systems to designate a system operator to be responsible for operating, ensuring the maintenance of and, if necessary, developing the distribution system in a given area and its interconnectors with other systems.

3. Member States shall ensure that the system operator acts in accordance with Articles 11 and 12.

Article 11

1. The distribution system operator shall maintain a secure, reliable and efficient electricity distribution system in its area, with due regard for the environment.

2. In any event, it must not discriminate between system users or classes of system users, particularly in favour of its subsidiaries or shareholders.

3. A Member state may require the distribution system operator, when dispatching generating installations, to give priority to generating installations using renewable energy sources or waste or producing combined heat and power.

Article 12

The distribution system operator must preserve the confidentiality of commercially sensitive information obtained in the course of carrying out its business.

CHAPTER IV

Unbundling and transparency of accounts

Article 13

Member States or any competent authority they designate as well as the dispute settlement authorities referred to in Article 20 (3) shall have right of access to the accounts of generation, transmission or distribution undertakings which they need to consult in carrying out their checks.

Article 14

1. Member States shall take the necessary steps to ensure that the accounts of electricity undertakings are kept in accordance with paragraphs 2 to 5.

2. Electricity undertakings, whatever their system of ownership or legal form, shall draw up, submit to audit and publish their annual accounts in accordance with the rules of national law concerning the annual accounts of limited liability companies adopted pursuant to the fourth Council Directive 78/660/EEC of 25 July 1978 based on Article 54 (3) (g) of the Treaty on the annual accounts of certain types of companies (8). Undertakings which are not legally obliged to publish their annual accounts shall keep a copy of these at the disposal of the public in their head office.

3. Integrated electricity undertakings shall, in their internal accounting, keep separate accounts for their generation, transmission and distribution activities, and, where appropriate, consolidated accounts for other, non-electricity activities, as they would be required to do if the activities in question were carried out by separate undertakings, with a view to avoiding discrimination, cross-subsidization and distortion of competition. They shall include a balance sheet and a profit and loss account for each activity in notes to their accounts.

4. Undertakings shall specify in notes to the annual accounts the rules for the allocation of assets and liabilities and expenditure and income which they follow in drawing up the separate accounts referred to in paragraph 3. These rules may be amended only in exceptional cases. Such amendments must be mentioned in the notes and must be duly

substantiated.

5. The annual accounts shall indicate in notes any transaction of a certain size conducted with affiliated undertakings, within the meaning of Article 41 of the seventh Council Directive 83/349/EEC of 13 June 1983 based on Article 54 (3) (g) of the Treaty on consolidated accounts (9), or with associated undertakings, within the meaning of Article 33 (1) thereof, or, with undertakings which belong to the same shareholders.

Article 15

1. Member States which designate as a single buyer a vertically integrated electricity undertaking or part of a vertically integrated electricity undertaking shall lay down provisions requiring the single buyer to operate separately from the generation and distribution activities of the integrated undertaking.

2. Member States shall ensure that there is no flow of information between the single buyer activities of vertically integrated electricity undertakings and their generation and distribution activities, except for the information necessary to conduct the single buyer responsibilities.

CHAPTER VII

Organization of access to the system

Article 16

For the organization of access to the system, Member States may choose between the procedures referred to in Article 17 and/or in Article 18. Both sets of procedure shall operate in accordance with objective, transparent and non-discriminatory criteria.

Article 17

1. In the case of negotiated access to the system, Member States shall take the necessary measures for electricity producers and, where Member States authorize their existence, supply undertakings and eligible customers either inside or outside the territory covered by the system to be able to negotiate access to the system so as to conclude supply contracts with each other on the basis of voluntary commercial agreements.

2. Where an eligible customer is connected to the distribution system, access to the system must be the subject of negotiation with the relevant distribution system operator and, if necessary, with the transmission system operator concerned.

3. To promote transparency and facilitate negotiations for access to the system, system operators must publish, in the first year following implementation of this Directive, an indicative range of prices for use of the transmission and distribution systems. As far as possible, the indicative prices published for subsequent years should be based on the average price agreed in negotiations in the previous 12-month period.

4. Member States may also opt for a regulated system of access procedure, giving eligible customers a right of access, on the basis of published tariffs for the use of transmission and distribution systems, that is at least equivalent, in terms of access to the system, to the other procedures for access referred to in this Chapter.

5. The operator of the transmission or distribution system concerned may refuse access where he lacks the necessary capacity. Duly substantiated reasons must be given for such refusal, in particular having regard to Article 3.

Article 18

1. In the case of the single buyer procedure, Member States shall designate a legal person to be the single buyer within the territory covered by the system operator. Member States shall take the necessary measures for:

(i) the publication of a non-discriminatory tariff for the use of the transmission and distribution system;

(ii) eligible customers to be free to conclude supply contracts to cover their own needs with producers and, where Member States authorize their existence, with supply undertakings outside the territory covered by the system;

(iii) eligible customers to be free to conclude supply contracts to cover their own needs with producers inside the territory covered by the system;

(iv) independent producers to negotiate access to the system with the transmission and distribution systems operators so as to conclude supply contracts with eligible customers outside the system, on the basis of a voluntary commercial agreement.

2. The single buyer may be obliged to purchase the electricity contracted by an eligible customer from a producer inside or outside the territory covered by the system at a price which is equal to the sale price offered by the single buyer to eligible customers minus the price of the published tariff referred to in paragraph 1 (i).

3. If the purchase obligation under paragraph 2 is not imposed on the single buyer, Member States shall take the necessary measures to ensure that the supply contracts referred to in paragraph 1 (ii) and (iii) are implemented either via access to the system on the basis of the published tariff referred to in paragraph 1 (i) or via negotiated access to the system according to the conditions of Article 17. In the latter case, there would be no obligation for the single buyer to publish a non-discriminatory tariff for the use of the transmission and distribution system.

4. The single buyer may refuse access to the system and may refuse to purchase electricity from eligible customers where he lacks the necessary transmission or distribution capacity. Duly substantiated reasons must be given for such refusal, in particular having regard to Article 3.

Article 19

1. Member States shall take the necessary measures to ensure an opening of their electricity markets, so that contracts under the conditions stated in Articles 17 and 18 can be concluded at least up to a significant level, to be notified to the Commission on an annual basis.

The share of the national market shall be calculated on the basis of the Community share of electricity consumed by final consumers consuming more than 40 GWh per year (on a consumption site basis and including autoproduction).

The average Community share shall be calculated by the Commission on the basis of information regularly provided to it by Member States. The Commission shall publish this average Community share defining the degree of market opening in the Official Journal of the European Communities before November each year, with all appropriate information clarifying the calculation.

2. The share of the national market referred to in paragraph 1 will be increased progressively over a period of six years. This increase will be calculated by reducing the Community consumption threshold of 40 GWh, referred to in paragraph 1 from 40 GWh to a level of 20 GWh annual electricity consumption three years after the entry into force of this Directive and to a level of 9 GWh annual electricity consumption six years after the entry into force of this Directive.

3. Member States shall specify those customers inside their territory representing the shares as specified in paragraphs 1 and 2 which have the legal capacity to contract electricity in accordance with Articles 17 and 18, given that all final consumers consuming more than 100 GWh per year (on a consumption site basis and including autoproduction) must be included in the above category.

Distribution companies, if not already specified as eligible customers under this paragraph, shall have the legal capacity to contract under the conditions of Articles 17 and 18 for the volume of electricity being consumed by their customers designated as eligible within their distribution system, in order to supply those customers.

4. Member States shall publish by 31 January each year the criteria for the definition of eligible customers which are able to conclude contracts under the conditions stated in Articles 17 and 18. This information, together with all other appropriate information to justify the fulfilment of market opening under paragraph 1, shall be sent to the Commission to be published in the Official Journal of the European Communities. The Commission may request a Member State to modify its specifications, as mentioned in paragraph 3, if they create obstacles to the correct application of this Directive as regards the smooth

functioning of the internal market in electricity. If the Member State concerned does not comply with this request within a period of three months, a final decision shall be taken in accordance with Procedure I of Article 2 of Council Decision 87/373/EEC of 13 July 1987 laying down the procedures for the exercise of implementing powers conferred on the Commission (10).

5. To avoid imbalance in the opening of electricity markets during the period referred to in Article 26:

(a) contracts for the supply of electricity under the provisions of Articles 17 and 18 with an eligible customer in the system of another Member State shall not be prohibited if the customer is considered as eligible in both systems involved;

(b) in cases where transactions as described in subparagraph (a) are refused because of the customer being eligible only in one of the two systems, the Commission may oblige, taking into account the situation in the market and the common interest, the refusing party to execute the requested electricity supply at the request of the Member State where the eligible customer is located.

In parallel with the procedure and the timetable provided for in Article 26, and not later than after half of the period provided for in that Article, the Commission shall review the application of subparagraph (b) of the first subparagraph on the basis of market developments taking into account the common interest. In the light of experience gained, the Commission shall evaluate this situation and report on possible imbalance in the opening of electricity markets with regard to this paragraph.

Article 20

1. Member States shall take the necessary measures to enable:

(i) independent producers and autoproducers to negotiate access to the system so as to supply their own premises and subsidiaries in the same Member State or in another Member State by means of the interconnected system;

(ii) producers located outside the territory covered by the system to conclude a supply contract following a call for tender for new generating capacity, and to have access to the system to perform the contract.

2. Member States shall ensure that the parties negotiate in good faith and that none of them abuses its negotiating position by preventing the successful outcome of negotiations.

3. Member States shall designate a competent authority, which must be independent of the parties, to settle disputes relating to the contracts and negotiations in question. In particular, this authority must settle disputes concerning contracts, negotiations and refusal of access or refusal to purchase.

4. In the event of cross-border disputes, the dispute settlement authority shall be the dispute settlement authority covering the system of the single buyer or the system operator which

refuses use of, or access to, the system.

5. Recourse to this authority shall be without prejudice to the exercise of rights of appeal under Community law.

Article 21

1. Member States shall take measures under the procedures and rights referred to in Articles 17 and 18 to enable:

– all electricity producers and electricity supply undertakings, where Member States authorize their existence, established within their territory to supply their own premises, subsidiaries and eligible customers through a direct line;
– any eligible customer within their territory to be supplied through a direct line by a producer and supply undertakings, where such suppliers are authorized by Member States.

2. Member States shall lay down the criteria for the grant of authorizations for the construction of direct lines in their territory. These criteria must be objective and non-discriminatory.

3. The possibility of supplying electricity through a direct line as referred to in paragraph 1 shall not affect the possibility of contracting electricity in accordance with Articles 17 and 18.

4. Member States may make authorization to construct a direct line subject either to the refusal of system access on the basis, as appropriate, of Article 17 (5) or Article 18 (4) or to the opening of a dispute settlement procedure under Article 20.

5. Member States may refuse to authorize a direct line if the granting of such an authorization would obstruct the provisions of Article 3. Duly substantiated reasons must be given for such refusal.

Article 22

Member States shall create appropriate and efficient mechanisms for regulation, control and transparency so as to avoid any abuse of dominant position, in particular to the detriment of consumers, and any predatory behaviour. These mechanisms shall take account of the provisions of the Treaty, and in particular Article 86 thereof.

CHAPTER VIII

Final provisions

Article 23

In the event of a sudden crisis in the energy market and where the physical safety or security of persons, apparatus or installations or system integrity is threatened, a Member State may temporarily take the necessary safeguard measures.

Such measures must cause the least possible disturbance in the functioning of the internal market and must not be wider in scope than is strictly necessary to remedy the sudden difficulties which have arisen.

The Member State concerned shall without delay notify these measures to the other Member States, and to the Commission, which may decide that the Member State concerned must amend or abolish such measures, insofar as they distort competition and adversely affect trade in a manner which is at variance with the common interest.

Article 24

1. Those Member States in which commitments or guarantees of operation given before the entry into force of this Directive may not be honoured on account of the provisions of this Directive may apply for a transitional regime which may be granted to them by the Commission, taking into account, amongst other things, the size of the system concerned, the level of interconnection of the system and the structure of its electricity industry. The Commission shall inform the Member States of those applications before it takes a decision, taking into account respect for confidentiality. This decision shall be published in the Official Journal of the European Communities.

2. The transitional regime shall be of limited duration and shall be linked to expiry of the commitments or guarantees referred to in paragraph 1. The transitional regime may cover derogations from Chapter IV, VI and VII of this Directive. Applications for a transitional regime must be notified to the Commission no later than one year after the entry into force of this Directive.

3. Member States which can demonstrate, after the Directive has been brought into force, that there are substantial problems for the operation of their small isolated systems, may apply for derogations from the relevant provisions of Chapter IV, V, VI, VII, which may be granted to them by the Commission. The latter shall inform the Member States of those applications prior to taking a decision, taking into account respect for confidentiality. This decision shall be published in the Official Journal of the European Communities. This paragraph shall also be applicable to Luxembourg.

Article 25

1. The Commission shall submit a report to the Council and the European Parliament, before the end of the first year following entry into force of this Directive, on harmonization requirements which are not linked to the provisions of this Directive. If necessary, the Commission shall attach to the report any harmonization proposals necessary for the effective operation of the internal market in electricity.

2. The Council and the European Parliament shall give their views on such proposals within two years of their submission.

Article 26

The Commission shall review the application of this Directive and submit a report on the experience gained on the functioning of the internal market in electricity and the implementation of the general rules mentioned in Article 3 in order to allow the European Parliament and the Council, in the light of experience gained, to consider, in due time, the possibility of a further opening of the market which would be effective nine years after the entry into force of the Directive taking into account the coexistence of systems referred to in Articles 17 and 18.

Article 27

1. Member States shall bring into force the laws, regulations and administrative provisions necessary to comply with this Directive not later than 19 February 1999. They shall forthwith inform the Commission thereof.

2. Belgium, Greece and Ireland may, due to the specific technical characteristics of their electricity systems, have an additional period of respectively 1 year, 2 years and 1 year to apply the obligations ensuing from this Directive. These Member States, when making use of this option, shall inform the Commission thereof.

3. When Member States adopt these provisions, they shall contain a reference to this Directive or shall be accompanied by such reference on the occasion of their official publication. The methods of making such reference shall be laid down by Member States.

Article 28

This Directive shall enter into force on the 20th day following that of its publication in the Official Journal of the European Communities.

Article 29

This Directive is addressed to the Member States.

Done at Brussels, 19 December 1996.

For the European Parliament
The President
K. HÄNSCH

For the Council
The President
S. BARRETT

(1) OJ No C 65, 14. 3. 1992, p. 4 and OJ No C 123, 4. 5. 1994, p. 1.

(2) OJ No C 73, 15. 3. 1993, p. 31.

(3) Opinion of the European Parliament of 17 November 1993 (OJ No C 329, 6. 12. 1993, p. 150). Council common position of 25 July 1996 (OJ No C 315, 24. 10. 1996, p. 18) and Decision of the European Parliament of 11 December 1996 (not yet published in the Official Journal). Council Decision of 19 December 1996.

(4) OJ No L 313, 13. 11. 1990, p. 30. Directive as last amended by Commission Decision 95/162/EC (OJ No L 107, 12. 5. 1995, p. 53).

(5) OJ No L 185, 17. 7. 1990, p. 16. Directive as last amended by Commission Directive 93/87/EEC (OJ No L 277, 10. 11. 1993, p. 32).

(6) OJ No L 161, 29. 6. 1996, p. 147.

(7) OJ No L 109, 26. 4. 1983, p. 8. Directive as last amended by the 1994 Act of Accession.

(8) OJ No L 222, 14. 8. 1978, p. 11. Directive as last amended by the 1994 Act of Accession.

(9) OJ No L 193, 18. 7. 1983, p. 1. Directive as last amended by the 1994 Act of Accession.

(10) OJ No L 197, 18. 7. 1987, p. 33.

Annex 2

DIRECTIVE 98/30/EC OF THE EUROPEAN PARLIAMENT AND OF THE COUNCIL OF 22 JUNE 1998
concerning common rules for the internal market in natural gas

THE EUROPEAN PARLIAMENT AND THE COUNCIL OF THE EUROPEAN UNION,

Having regard to the Treaty establishing the European Community, and in particular Articles 57(2), 66 and 100a thereof,

Having regard to the proposal from the Commission (1),

Having regard to the opinion of the Economic and Social Committee (2),

Acting in accordance with the procedure laid down in Article 189b of the Treaty (3),

(1) Whereas, according to Article 7a of the Treaty, the internal market shall comprise an area without internal frontiers in which the free movement of goods, persons, services and capital is ensured; whereas it is important to adopt measures to continue the completion of the internal market;

(2) Whereas, under Article 7c of the Treaty, differences in development of certain economies have to be taken into account, but derogations must be of a temporary nature and cause the least possible disturbance to the functioning of the common market;

(3) Whereas the establishment of a competitive natural gas market is an important element of the completion of the internal energy market;

(4) Whereas Council Directive 91/296/EEC of 31 May 1991 on the transit of natural gas through grids (4) and Council Directive 90/377/EEC of 29 June 1990 concerning a Community procedure to improve the transparency of gas and electricity prices charged to industrial end-users (5) constitute a first phase of the completion of the internal market in natural gas;

(5) Whereas it is now necessary to take further measures with a view to establishing the internal market in natural gas;

(6) Whereas the provisions of this Directive should not affect the full application of the Treaty, in particular the provisions concerning the free movement of goods in the internal market and the rules on competition, and do not affect the powers of the Commission under the Treaty;

(7) Whereas the internal market in natural gas needs to be established gradually, in order to enable the industry to adjust in a flexible and ordered manner to its new environment and in order to take account of the different market structures in the Member States;

(8) Whereas the establishment of the internal market in the natural gas sector should favour the interconnection and interoperability of systems, for example through compatible qualities of gas;

(9) Whereas a certain number of common rules should be established for the organisation and operation of the natural gas sector; whereas, in accordance with the principle of subsidiarity, these rules are no more than general principles providing for a framework, the detailed implementation of which should be left to Member States, thus allowing each Member State to maintain or choose the regime which corresponds best to a particular situation, in particular with regard to authorisations and the supervision of supply contracts;

(10) Whereas the external supply of natural gas is of particular importance for the purchase of natural gas in Member States highly dependent on gas imports;

(11) Whereas, as a general rule, undertakings in the natural gas sector should be able to operate without being discriminated against;

(12) Whereas for some Member States the imposition of public service obligations may be necessary to ensure security of supply and consumer and environmental protection, which, in their view, free competition, left to itself, cannot necessarily guarantee;

(13) Whereas long-term planning may be one means of carrying out those public service obligations, taking into account the possibility of third parties seeking access to the system; whereas Member States may monitor take-or-pay contracts undertaken in order to keep up to date with the situation on supply;

(14) Whereas Article 90(1) of the Treaty obliges the Member States to respect the rules on competition with regard to public undertakings and undertakings which have been granted special or exclusive rights;

(15) Whereas Article 90(2) of the Treaty subjects undertakings entrusted with the operation of services of general economic interest to these rules under specific conditions; whereas the implementation of this Directive will have an impact on the activities of such undertakings; whereas, as referred to in Article 3(3), Member States need not apply Article

4, in particular, to their distribution infrastructure in order not to obstruct in law or in fact the fulfilment of obligations of general economic interest imposed on gas undertakings;

(16) Whereas, when imposing public service obligations on undertakings of the natural gas sector, Member States must therefore respect the relevant rules of the Treaty as interpreted by the Court of Justice of the European Communities;

(17) Whereas basic criteria and procedures should be laid down concerning the authorisations which Member States may grant for the construction or operation of relevant facilities under their national system; whereas these provisions should not affect the relevant rules of national legislation subjecting the construction or operation of relevant facilities to an authorisation requirement; whereas, however, such requirement should not have the effect of restricting competition among the undertakings of the sector;

(18) Whereas Decision No 1254/96/EC of the European Parliament and of the Council of 5 June 1996 laying down a series of guidelines for trans-European energy networks (6), contributes to the development of integrated infrastructures for the natural gas sector;

(19) Whereas the technical rules for the operation of systems and direct lines must be transparent and must ensure interoperability of systems;

(20) Whereas basic rules must be laid down with regard to transmission, storage and liquefied natural gas undertakings, as well as to distribution and supply undertakings;

(21) Whereas it is necessary to provide for access by the competent authorities to the internal accounts of undertakings, with due regard for confidentiality;

(22) Whereas the accounts of all integrated natural gas undertakings should provide for a high degree of transparency; whereas the accounts should be separate for different activities when this is necessary in order to avoid discrimination, cross-subsidisation and other distortions of competition, taking into account in relevant cases that transmission for accounting purposes includes re-gasification; whereas separate accounts should not be required for legal entities, such as stock or futures exchanges, which do not, other than in this trading capacity, perform any of the functions of a natural gas undertaking; whereas integrated accounts for hydrocarbon production and related activities may be produced as part of the requirement for accounts for non-gas activities required by this Directive; whereas the relevant information in Article 23(3) should include, where required, accounting information about upstream pipelines;

(23) Whereas access to the system should be open in accordance with this Directive and should lead to a sufficient and, where appropriate, a comparable level of opening-up of markets in different Member States; whereas, at the same time, the opening-up of markets should not create unnecessary disequilibrium in the competitive situation of undertakings in the different Member States;

(24) Whereas, owing to the diversity of structures and the special characteristics of systems

in Member States, there should be different procedures for system access operating in accordance with objective, transparent and non-discriminatory criteria;

(25) Whereas, in order to achieve a competitive market in natural gas, provision should be made for access to upstream pipeline networks; whereas separate treatment is required as respects such access to upstream pipeline networks, having regard, in particular, to the special economic, technical and operational characteristics relating to such networks; whereas the provisions of this Directive do not in any event affect national taxation rules;

(26) Whereas provision should be made regarding authorisation, construction and use of direct lines;

(27) Whereas provision should be made for safeguards and dispute settlement procedures;

(28) Whereas any abuse of a dominant position or any predatory behaviour should be avoided;

(29) Whereas, as some Member States are liable to experience special difficulties in adjusting their systems, provision should be made for temporary derogations;

(30) Whereas long-term take-or-pay contracts are a market reality for securing Member States' gas supply; whereas, in particular, provision should be made for derogations from certain provisions of this Directive in the case of a natural gas undertaking which is or would be in serious economic difficulties because of its take-or-pay obligations; whereas these derogations should not undermine the purpose of this Directive to liberalise the internal market in natural gas; whereas any take-or-pay contracts entered into or renewed after the entry into force of this Directive should be concluded prudently in order not to hamper a significant opening of the market; whereas, therefore, such derogations should be limited in time and scope and granted in a transparent manner, under the supervision of the Commission;

(31) Whereas specific provisions are needed for markets and investments in other areas which have not yet reached a developed stage; whereas derogations for such markets and areas should be limited in time and scope; whereas, for the sake of transparency and uniformity, the Commission should have a significant role in the granting of these derogations;

(32) Whereas this Directive constitutes a further phase of liberalisation; whereas, once it has been put into effect, some obstacles to trade in natural gas between Member States will nevertheless remain in place; whereas proposals for improving the operation of the internal market in natural gas should be made in the light of experience; whereas the Commission should therefore report to the European Parliament and the Council on the application of this Directive,

HAVE ADOPTED THIS DIRECTIVE:

CHAPTER I

Scope and Definitions

Article 1

This Directive establishes common rules for the transmission, distribution, supply and storage of natural gas. It lays down the rules relating to the organisation and functioning of the natural gas sector, including liquefied natural gas (LNG), access to the market, the operation of systems, and the criteria and procedures applicable to the granting of authorisations for transmission, distribution, supply and storage of natural gas.

Article 2

For the purposes of this Directive:

1. 'natural gas undertaking' means any natural or legal person carrying out at least one of the following functions: production, transmission, distribution, supply, purchase or storage of natural gas, including LNG, which is responsible for the commercial, technical and/or maintenance tasks related to those functions, but shall not include final customers;

2. 'upstream pipeline network' means any pipeline or network of pipelines operated and/or constructed as part of an oil or gas production project, or used to convey natural gas from one or more such projects to a processing plant or terminal or final coastal landing terminal;

3. 'transmission' means the transport of natural gas through a high pressure pipeline network other than an upstream pipeline network with a view to its delivery to customers;

4. 'transmission undertaking' means any natural or legal person who carries out the function of transmission;

5. 'distribution' means the transport of natural gas through local or regional pipeline networks with a view to its delivery to customers;

6. 'distribution undertaking' means any natural or legal person who carries out the function of distribution;

7. 'supply' means the delivery and/or sale of natural gas, including LNG, to customers;

8. 'supply undertaking' means any natural or legal person who carries out the function of supply;

9. 'storage facility' means a facility used for the stocking of natural gas and owned and/or operated by a natural gas undertaking, excluding the portion used for production operations;

10. 'storage undertaking' means any natural or legal person who carries out the function of storage;

11. 'LNG facility' means a terminal which is used for the liquefaction of natural gas or the offloading, storage and re-gasification of LNG;

12. 'system' means any transmission networks and/or distribution networks and/or LNG facilities owned and/or operated by a natural gas undertaking, including its facilities supplying ancillary services and those of related undertakings necessary for providing access to transmission and distribution;

13. 'interconnected system' means a number of systems which are linked with each other;

14. 'direct line' means a natural gas pipeline complementary to the interconnected system;

15. 'integrated natural gas undertaking' means a vertically or horizontally integrated undertaking;

16. 'vertically integrated undertaking' means a natural gas undertaking performing two or more of the tasks of production, transmission, distribution, supply or storage of natural gas;

17. 'horizontally integrated undertaking' means an undertaking performing at least one of the functions of production, transmission, distribution, supply or storage of natural gas, and a non-gas activity;

18. 'related undertaking' means affiliated undertakings, within the meaning of Article 41 of the Seventh Council Directive, 83/349/EEC, of 13 June 1983 based on Article 54(3)(g) of the Treaty on consolidated accounts (7), and/or associated undertakings, within the meaning of Article 33(1) thereof, and/or undertakings which belong to the same shareholders;

19. 'system user' means any natural or legal person supplying to, or being supplied by, the system;

20. 'customers' means wholesale or final customers of natural gas and natural gas undertakings which purchase natural gas;

21. 'final customer' means a consumer purchasing natural gas for his own use;

22. 'wholesale customers', where Member States recognise their existence, means any natural or legal persons who purchase and sell natural gas and who do not carry out transmission or distribution functions inside or outside the system where they are established;

23. 'long-term planning' means the planning of supply and transportation capacity of natural gas undertakings on a long-term basis with a view to meeting the demand for natural gas of the system, diversification of sources and securing supplies to customers;

24. 'emergent market' means a Member State in which the first commercial supply of its first long-term natural gas supply contract was made not more than 10 years earlier;

25. 'security' means both security of supply and provision, and technical safety.

CHAPTER II

General Rules for the Organisation of the Sector

Article 3

1. Member States shall ensure, on the basis of their institutional organisation and with due regard for the principle of subsidiarity, that, without prejudice to paragraph 2, natural gas undertakings are operated in accordance with the principles of this Directive with a view to achieving a competitive market in natural gas, and shall not discriminate between such undertakings as regards either rights or obligations.

2. Having full regard to the relevant provisions of the Treaty, in particular Article 90 thereof, Member States may impose on natural gas undertakings, in the general economic interest, public-service obligations which may relate to security, including security of supply, regularity, quality and price of supplies, and to environmental protection. Such obligations shall be clearly defined, transparent, non-discriminatory and verifiable; they, and any revision thereof, shall be published and notified to the Commission by Member States without delay. As a means of carrying out public-service obligations in relation to security of supply, Member States which so wish may introduce the implementation of long-term planning, taking into account the possibility of third parties seeking access to the system.

3. Member States may decide not to apply the provisions of Article 4 with respect to distribution insofar as the application of these provisions would obstruct, in law or in fact, the performance of the obligations imposed on natural gas undertakings in the general economic interest and insofar as the development of trade would not be affected to such an extent as would be contrary to the interests of the Community. The interests of the Community include, inter alia, competition with regard to eligible customers in accordance with this Directive and Article 90 of the Treaty.

Article 4

1. In circumstances where an authorisation (e. g. licence, permission, concession, consent or approval) is required for the construction or operation of natural gas facilities, the Member States or any competent authority they designate shall grant authorisations to build and/or operate such facilities, pipelines and associated equipment on their territory, in accordance

with paragraphs 2 to 4. Member States or any competent authority they designate may also grant authorisations on the same basis for the supply of natural gas and for wholesale customers.

2. Where Member States have a system of authorisation, they shall lay down objective and non-discriminatory criteria which shall be met by an undertaking applying for an authorisation to build and/or operate natural gas facilities or applying for an authorisation to supply natural gas. The non-discriminatory criteria and procedures for the granting of authorisations shall be made public.

3. Member States shall ensure that the reasons for any refusal to grant an authorisation are objective and non-discriminatory and are given to the applicant. Reasons for such refusals shall be forwarded to the Commission for information. Member States shall establish a procedure enabling the applicant to appeal against such refusals.

4. For the development of newly supplied areas and efficient operation generally, and without prejudice to Article 20, Member States may decline to grant a further authorisation to build and operate distribution pipeline systems in any particular area once such pipeline systems have been or are proposed to be built in that area and if existing or proposed capacity is not saturated.

Article 5

Member States shall ensure that technical rules establishing the minimum technical design and operational requirements for the connection to the system of LNG facilities, storage facilities, other transmission or distribution systems, and direct lines, are developed and made available. These technical rules shall ensure the interoperatibility of systems and shall be objective and non-discriminatory. They shall be notified to the Commission in accordance with Article 8 of Council Directive 83/189/EEC of 28 March 1983 laying down a procedure for the provision of information in the field of technical standards and regulations (8).

CHAPTER III

Transmission, Storage and LNG

Article 6

Member States shall take the measures necessary to ensure that transmission, storage and LNG undertakings act in accordance with Articles 7 and 8.

Article 7

1. Each transmission, storage and/or LNG undertaking shall operate, maintain and develop under economic conditions secure, reliable and efficient transmission, storage and/or LNG facilities, with due regard to the environment.

2. In any event, the transmission, storage and/or LNG undertaking shall not discriminate between system users or classes of system users, particularly in favour of its related undertakings.

3. Each transmission, storage and/or LNG undertaking shall provide any other transmission undertaking, any other storage undertaking and/or any distribution undertaking with sufficient information to ensure that the transport and storage of natural gas may take place in a manner compatible with the secure and efficient operation of the interconnected system.

Article 8

1. Without prejudice to Article 12 or any other legal duty to disclose information, each transmission, storage and/or LNG undertaking shall preserve the confidentiality of commercially sensitive information obtained in the course of carrying out its business.

2. Transmission undertakings shall not, in the context of sales or purchases of natural gas by the transmission undertakings or related undertakings, abuse commercially sensitive information obtained from third parties in the context of providing or negotiating access to the system.

CHAPTER IV

Distribution and Supply

Article 9

1. Member States shall ensure that distribution undertakings act in accordance with Articles 10 and 11.

2. Member States may impose on distribution undertakings and/or supply undertakings, an obligation to deliver to customers located in a given area or of a certain class or both. The tariff for such deliveries may be regulated, for instance to ensure equal treatment of the customers concerned.

Article 10

1. Each distribution undertaking shall operate, maintain and develop under economic conditions a secure, reliable and efficient system, with due regard to the environment.

2. In any event, the distribution undertaking must not discriminate between system users or classes of system users, particularly in favour of its related undertakings.

3. Each distribution undertaking shall provide any other distribution undertaking, and/or any transmission and/or storage undertaking with sufficient information to ensure that the transport of gas may take place in a manner compatible with the secure and efficient operation of the interconnected system.

Article 11

1. Without prejudice to Article 12 or any other legal duty to disclose information, each distribution undertaking shall preserve the confidentiality of commercially sensitive information obtained in the course of carrying out its business.

2. Distribution undertakings shall not, in the context of sales or purchases of natural gas by the distribution undertakings or related undertakings, abuse commercially sensitive information obtained from third parties in the context of providing or negotiating access to the system.

CHAPTER V

Unbundling and Transparency of Accounts

Article 12

Member States or any competent authority they designate, including the dispute settlement authorities referred to in Article 21(2) and Article 23(3), shall have right of access to the accounts of natural gas undertakings as set out in Article 13 which they need to consult in carrying out their functions. Member States and any designated competent authority, including the dispute settlement authorities, shall preserve the confidentiality of commercially sensitive information. Member States may introduce exceptions to the principle of confidentiality where this is necessary in order for the competent authorities to carry out their functions.

Article 13

1. Member States shall take the necessary steps to ensure that the accounts of natural gas undertakings are kept in accordance with paragraphs 2 to 5 of this Article.

2. Natural gas undertakings, whatever their system of ownership or legal form, shall draw up, submit to audit and publish their annual accounts in accordance with the rules of national law concerning the annual accounts of limited liability companies adopted pursuant to the Fourth Council Directive 78/660/EEC of 25 July 1978 based on Article 54(3)(g) of the Treaty on the annual accounts of certain types of companies (9).

   Undertakings which are not legally obliged to publish their annual accounts shall keep a copy of these at the disposal of the public at their head office.

3. Integrated natural gas undertakings shall, in their internal accounting, keep separate accounts for their natural gas transmission, distribution and storage activities, and, where appropriate, consolidated accounts for non-gas activities, as they would be required to do if the activities in question were carried out by separate undertakings, with a view to avoiding discrimination, cross-subsidisation and distortion of competition. These internal accounts shall include a balance sheet and a profit and loss account for each activity.

   Where Article 16 applies and access to the system is on the basis of a single charge for both transmission and distribution, the accounts for transmission and distribution activities may be combined.

4. Undertakings shall specify in their internal accounting the rules for the allocation of assets and liabilities, expenditure and income as well as for depreciation, without prejudice to nationally applicable accounting rules, which they follow in drawing up the separate accounts referred to in paragraph 3. These rules may be amended only in exceptional cases. Such amendments shall be mentioned and duly substantiated.

5. The annual accounts shall indicate in notes any transaction of a certain size conducted with related undertakings.

CHAPTER VI

Access to the System

Article 14

For the organisation of access to the system, Member States may choose either or both procedures referred to in Article 15 and in Article 16. These procedures shall operate in accordance with objective, transparent and non-discriminatory criteria.

Article 15

1. In the case of negotiated access, Member States shall take the necessary measures for natural gas undertakings and eligible customers either inside or outside the territory covered by the interconnected system to be able to negotiate access to the system so as to conclude supply contracts with each other on the basis of voluntary commercial agreements. The parties shall be obliged to negotiate access to the system in good faith.

2. The contracts for access to the system shall be negotiated with the relevant natural gas undertakings. Member States shall require natural gas undertakings to publish their main commercial conditions for the use of the system within the first year following implementation of this Directive and on an annual basis every year thereafter.

Article 16

Member States opting for a procedure of regulated access shall take the necessary measures to give natural gas undertakings and eligible customers either inside or outside the territory covered by the interconnected system a right of access to the system, on the basis of published tariffs and/or other terms and obligations for use of that system. This right of access for eligible customers may be given by enabling them to enter into supply contracts with competing natural gas undertakings other than the owner and/or operator of the system or a related undertaking.

Article 17

1. Natural gas undertakings may refuse access to the system on the basis of lack of capacity or where the access to the system would prevent them from carrying out the public-service obligations referred to in Article 3(2) which are assigned to them or on the basis of serious economic and financial difficulties with take-or-pay contracts having regard to the criteria and procedures set out in Article 25 and the alternative chosen by the Member State according to paragraph 1 of that Article. Duly substantiated reasons shall be given for such a refusal.

2. Member States may take the measures necessary to ensure that the natural gas undertaking refusing access to the system on the basis of lack of capacity or a lack of connection shall make the necessary enhancements as far as it is economical to do so or when a potential customer is willing to pay for them. In circumstances where Member States apply Article 4(4), Member States shall take such measures.

Article 18

1. Member States shall specify eligible customers, meaning those customers inside their territory which have the legal capacity to contract for, or to be sold, natural gas in accordance

with Articles 15 and 16, given that all customers mentioned in paragraph 2 of this Article must be included.

2. Member States shall take the necessary measures to ensure that at least the following customers are designated as eligible customers:
  – gas-fired power generators, irrespective of their annual consumption level; however, and in order to safeguard the balance of their electricity market, the Member States may introduce a threshold, which may not exceed the level envisaged for other final customers, for the eligibility of combined heat and power producers. Such thresholds shall be notified to the Commission,
  – other final customers consuming more than 25 million cubic metres of gas per year on a consumption-site basis.

3. Member States shall ensure that the definition of eligible customers referred to in paragraph 1 will result in an opening of the market equal to at least 20 % of the total annual gas consumption of the national gas market.

4. The percentage mentioned in paragraph 3 shall increase to 28 % of the total annual gas consumption of the national gas market five years after the entry into force of this Directive, and to 33 % thereof 20 years after the entry into force of this Directive.

5. If the definition of eligible customers as referred to in paragraph 1 results in a market opening of more than 30 % of the total annual gas consumption of the national gas market, the Member State concerned may modify the definition of eligible customers to the extent that the opening of the market is reduced to no lower than 30 % of such consumption. Member States shall modify the definition of eligible customers in a balanced manner, not creating specific disadvantages for certain types or classes of eligible customers, but taking into account existing market structures.

6. Member States shall take the following measures to ensure that the opening of their natural gas market is increased over a period of 10 years:
  – the threshold set in the second indent of paragraph 2 for eligible customers other than gas-fired power generators, shall be reduced to 15 million cubic metres per year on a consumption-site basis five years after the entry into force of this Directive, and to 5 million cubic metres per year on such basis 10 years after the entry into force of this Directive,
  – the percentage mentioned in paragraph 5 shall increase to 38 % of the total annual gas consumption of the national gas market five years after the entry into force of this Directive, and to 43 % of such consumption 10 years after the entry into force of this Directive.

7. In respect of emergent markets, the gradual market opening provided for by this Article shall start to apply from the expiry of the derogation referred to in Article 26(2).

8. Distribution undertakings, if not already specified as eligible customers under paragraph 1, shall have the legal capacity to contract for natural gas in accordance with Articles 15 and 16 for the volume of natural gas being consumed by their customers designated as eligible within their distribution system, in order to supply those customers.

9. Member States shall publish by 31 January of each year the criteria for the definition of eligible customers referred to in paragraph 1. This information, together with all other appropriate information to justify the fulfilment of market opening under this Article, shall be sent to the Commission to be published in the Official Journal of the European Communities. The Commission may request a Member State to modify its specifications if they create obstacles to the correct application of this Directive as regards the smooth functioning of the internal market in natural gas. If the Member State concerned does not comply with this request within a period of three months, a final decision shall be taken in accordance with procedure I of Article 2 of Council Decision 87/373/EEC of 13 July 1987 laying down the procedures for the exercise of implementing powers conferred on the Commission (10).

Article 19

1. To avoid imbalance in the opening of gas markets during the period referred to in Article 28:

(a) contracts for the supply of gas under the provisions of Articles 15, 16 and 17 with an eligible customer in the system of another Member State shall not be prohibited if the customer is considered as eligible in both systems involved;

(b) in cases where transactions as described in subparagraph (a) are refused because the customer is eligible in only one of the two systems, the Commission may oblige, taking into account the situation in the market and the common interest, the refusing party to execute the requested gas supply, at the request of the Member State where the eligible customer is located.

2. In parallel with the procedure and the timetable provided for in Article 28, and not later than after half of the period provided for in that Article, the Commission shall review the application of paragraph 1(b) of this Article on the basis of market developments taking into account the common interest. In the light of experience, the Commission shall evaluate this situation and report on any possible imbalance in the opening of gas markets with regard to paragraph 1(b).

Article 20

1. Member States shall take the necessary measures to enable:
   – natural gas undertakings established within their territory to supply the customers described in Article 18 of this Directive through a direct line,

– any such eligible customer with their territory to be supplied through a direct line by natural gas undertakings.

2. In circumstances where an authorisation (e. g. licence, permission, concession, consent or approval) is required for the construction or operation of direct lines, the Member States or any competent authority they designate shall lay down the criteria for the grant of authorisations for the construction or operation of such lines in their territory. These criteria shall be objective, transparent and non-discriminatory.

3. Member States may make authorisations to construct a direct line subject either to the refusal of system access on the basis of Article 17 or to the opening of a dispute settlement procedure under Article 21.

Article 21

1. Member States shall ensure that the parties negotiate access to the system in good faith and that none of them abuses its negotiating position to prevent the successful outcome of such negotiations.

2. Member States shall designate a competent authority, which must be independent of the parties, to settle expeditiously disputes relating to the negotiations in question. In particular, this authority shall settle disputes concerning negotiations and refusal of access within the scope of this Directive. The competent authority shall present its conclusions without delay or if possible within 12 weeks of the introduction of the dispute. Recourse to this authority shall be without prejudice to the exercise of rights of appeal under Community law.

3. In the event of cross-border disputes, the dispute settlement authority shall be the dispute settlement authority covering the system of the natural gas undertaking which refuses use of, or access to, the system. Where, in cross-border disputes, more than one such authority covers the system concerned, the authorities shall consult with a view to ensuring that the provisions of this Directive are applied consistently.

Article 22

Member States shall create appropriate and efficient mechanisms for regulation, control and transparency so as to avoid any abuse of a dominant position, in particular to the detriment of consumers, and any predatory behaviour. These mechanisms shall take account of the provisions of the Treaty, and in particular Article 86 thereof.

Article 23

1. Member States shall take the necessary measures to ensure that natural gas undertakings and customers required to be eligible under Article 18, wherever they are located, are able

to obtain access to upstream pipeline networks, including facilities supplying technical services incidental to such access, in accordance with this Article, except for the parts of such networks and facilities which are used for local production operations at the site of a field where the gas is produced. The measures shall be notified to the Commission in accordance with the provisions of Article 29.

2. The access referred to in paragraph 1 shall be provided in a manner determined by the Member State in accordance with the relevant legal instruments. Member States shall apply the objectives of fair and open access, achieving a competitive market in natural gas and avoiding any abuse of a dominant position, taking into account security and regularity of supplies, capacity which is or can reasonably be made available, and environmental protection. The following may be taken into account:

(a) the need to refuse access where there is an incompatibility of technical specifications which cannot be reasonably overcome;

(b) the need to avoid difficulties which cannot be reasonably overcome and could prejudice the efficient, current and planned future production of hydrocarbons, including that from fields of marginal economic viability;

(c) the need to respect the duly substantiated reasonable needs of the owner or operator of the upstream pipeline network for the transport and processing of gas and the interests of all other users of the upstream pipeline network or relevant processing or handling facilities who may be affected; and

(d) the need to apply their laws and administrative procedures, in conformity with Community law, for the grant of authorisation for production or upstream development.

3. Member States shall ensure that they have in place dispute settlement arrangements, including an authority independent of the parties with access to all relevant information, to enable disputes relating to access to upstream pipeline networks to be settled expeditiously, taking into account the criteria in paragraph 2 and the number of parties which may be involved in negotiating access to such networks.

4. In the event of cross-border disputes, the dispute settlement arrangements for the Member State having jurisdiction over the upstream pipeline network which refuses access shall be applied. Where, in cross-border disputes, more than one Member State covers the network concerned, the Member State concerned shall consult with a view to ensuring that the provisions of this Directive are applied consistently.

CHAPTER VII

Final Provisions

Article 24

1. In the event of a sudden crisis in the energy market or where the physical safety or security of persons, apparatus or installations or system integrity is threatened, a Member State may temporarily take the necessary safeguard measures.

2. Such measures shall cause the least possible disturbance to the functioning of the internal market and shall not be wider in scope than is strictly necessary to remedy the sudden difficulties which have arisen.

3. The Member State concerned shall without delay notify these measures to the other Member States, and to the Commission, which may decide that the Member State concerned must amend or abolish such measures, insofar as they distort competition and adversely affect trade in a manner which is at variance with the common interest.

Article 25

1. If a natural gas undertaking encounters, or considers it would encounter, serious economic and financial difficulties because of its take-or-pay commitments accepted in one or more gas-purchase contracts, an application for a temporary derogation from Article 15 and/or Article 16 may be sent to the Member State concerned or the designated competent authority. Applications shall, according to the choice of Member States, be presented on a case-by-case basis either before or after refusal of access to the system. Member States may also give the natural gas undertaking the choice to present an application either before or after refusal of access to the system. Where a natural gas undertaking has refused access, the application shall be presented without delay. The applications shall be accompanied by all relevant information on the nature and extent of the problem and on the efforts undertaken by the gas undertaking to solve the problem.

   If alternative solutions are not reasonably available, and taking into account the provisions of paragraph 3, the Member State or the designated competent authority may decide to grant a derogation.

2. The Member State, or the designated competent authority, shall notify the Commission without delay of its decision to grant a derogation, together with all the relevant information with respect to the derogation. This information may be submitted to the Commission in an aggregated form, enabling the Commission to reach a well-founded decision. Within four weeks of its receipt of this notification, the Commission may request that the Member

State or the designated competent authority concerned amend or withdraw the decision to grant a derogation. If the Member State or the designated competent authority concerned does not comply with this request within a period of four weeks, a final decision shall be taken expeditiously in accordance with procedure I of Article 2 of Decision 87/373/EEC.

The Commission shall preserve the confidentiality of commercially sensitive information.

3. When deciding on the derogations referred to in paragraph 1, the Member State, or the designated competent authority, and the Commission shall take into account, in particular, the following criteria:

(a) the objective to achieve a competitive gas market;

(b) the need to fulfil public-service obligations and to ensure security of supply;

(c) the position of the natural gas undertaking in the gas market and the actual state of competition in this market;

(d) the seriousness of the economic and financial difficulties encountered by natural gas undertakings and transmission undertakings or eligible customers;

(e) the dates of signature and terms of the contract in question, including the extent to which they allow for market changes;

(f) the efforts made to find a solution to the problem;

(g) the extent to which, when accepting the take-or-pay commitments in question, the undertaking could reasonably have foreseen, having regard to the provisions of this Directive, that serious difficulties were likely to arise;

(h) the level of connection of the system with other systems and the degree of interoperability of these systems; and

(i) the effects the granting of a derogation would have on the correct application of this Directive as regards the smooth functioning of the internal natural gas market.

A decision on a request for a derogation concerning take-or-pay contracts concluded before the entry into force of this Directive should not lead to a situation in which it is impossible to find economically viable alternative outlets. Serious difficulties shall in any case be deemed not to exist when the sales of natural gas do not fall below the level of minimum offtake guarantees contained in gas-purchase take-or-pay contracts or in so far as the relevant gas-purchase take-or-pay contract can be adapted or the natural gas undertaking is able to find alternative outlets.

4. Natural gas undertakings which have not been granted a derogation as referred to in paragraph 1 shall not refuse, or shall no longer refuse, access to the system because of take-or-pay commitments accepted in a gas purchase contract. Member States shall ensure that the relevant provisions of Chapter VI are complied with.

5. Any derogation granted under the above provisions shall be duly substantiated. The Commission shall publish the decision in the Official Journal of the European Communities.

6. The Commission shall, within five years of the entry into force of this Directive, submit

a review report on the experience gained from the application of this Article, so as to allow the European Parliament and the Council to consider, in due course, the need to adjust it.

Article 26

1. Member States not directly connected to the interconnected system of any other Member State and having only one main external supplier may derogate from Article 4, Article 18(1), (2), (3), (4) and (6) and/or Article 20 of this Directive. A supplier having a market share of more than 75 % shall be considered to be a main supplier. This derogation shall automatically expire from the moment when at least one of these conditions no longer applies. Any such derogation shall be notified to the Commission.

2. A Member State, qualifying as an emergent market, which because of the implementation of this Directive would experience substantial problems, not associated with the contractual take-or-pay commitments referred to in Article 25, may derogate from Article 4, Article 18(1), (2), (3), (4) and (6) and/or Article 20 of this Directive. This derogation shall automatically expire from the moment when the Member State no longer qualifies as an emergent market. Any such derogation shall be notified to the Commission.

3. Where implementation of this Directive would cause substantial problems in a geographically limited area of a Member State, in particular concerning the development of the transmission infrastructure, and with a view to encouraging investments, the Member State may apply to the Commission for a temporary derogation from Article 4, Article 18(1), (2), (3), (4) and (6) and/or Article 20 for developments within this area.

4. The Commission may grant the derogation referred to in paragraph 3, taking into account, in particular, the following criteria:
   – the need for infrastructure investments, which would not be economical to operate in a competitive market environment,
   – the level and pay-back prospects of investments required,
   – the size and maturity of the gas system in the area concerned,
   – the prospects for the gas market concerned,
   – the geographical size and characteristics of the area or region concerned, and
   – socio-economic and demographic factors.

A derogation may be granted only if no gas infrastructure has been established in this area, or has been so established for less than 10 years. The temporary derogation may not exceed 10 years from the time gas is first supplied in the area.

5. The Commission shall inform the Member States of applications made under paragraphs 3 prior to taking a decision pursuant to paragraph 4, taking into account respect for confidentiality. This decision, as well as the derogations referred to in paragraphs 1 and 2, shall be published in the Official Journal of the European Communities.

Article 27

1. Before the end of the first year following the entry into force of this Directive, the Commission shall submit a report to the European Parliament and the Council on harmonisation requirements which are not linked to the provisions of this Directive. If necessary, the Commission shall attach to the report any harmonisation proposals necessary for the effective operation of the internal natural gas market.

2. The European Parliament and the Council shall give their views on such proposals within two years of their submission.

Article 28

The Commission shall review the application of this Directive and submit a report on the experience gained on the functioning of the internal market in natural gas and the implementation of the general rules mentioned in Article 3 in order to allow the European Parliament and the Council, in the light of experience gained, to consider, in due time, the possibility of provisions for further improving the internal market in natural gas, which would be effective 10 years after the entry into force of the Directive.

Article 29

Member States shall bring into force the laws, regulations and administrative provisions necessary to comply with this Directive no later than two years from the date specified in Article 30. They shall forthwith inform the Commission thereof.

When Member States adopt these provisions, they shall contain a reference to this Directive or shall be accompanied by such reference on the occasion of their official publication. The methods of making such reference shall be laid down by the Member States.

Article 30

This Directive shall enter into force on the 20th day following that of its publication in the Official Journal of the European Communities.

Article 31

This Directive is addressed to the Member States.

Done at Luxembourg, 22 June 1998.

For the European Parliament
The President
J. M. GIL-ROBLES

For the Council
The President
J. CUNNINGHAM

(1) OJ C 65, 14.3.1992, p. 14, and OJ C 123, 4.5.1994, p. 26.

(2) OJ C 73, 15.3.1993, p. 31, and OJ C 195, 18.7.1994, p. 82.

(3) Opinion of the European Parliament of 17 November 1993 (OJ C 329, 6.12.1993, p. 182), Council Common Position (EC) No 17/98 of 12 February 1998 (OJ C 91, 26.3.1998, p. 46) and Decision of the European Parliament of 30 April 1998 (OJ C 152, 18.5.1998). Council Decision of 11 May 1998.

(4) OJ L 147, 12.6.1991, p. 37. Directive as last amended by Directive 95/49/EC (OJ L 233, 30.9.1995, p. 86).

(5) OJ L 185, 17.7.1990, p. 16. Directive as last amended by the 1994 Act of Accession.

(6) OJ L 161, 29.6.1996, p. 147. Decision as last amended by Decision No 1047/97/EC (OJ L 152, 11.6.1997, p. 12).

(7) OJ L 193, 18.7.1983, p. 1. Directive as last amended by the 1994 Act of Accession.

(8) OJ L 109, 26.4.1983, p. 8. Directive as last amended by Directive 96/139/EC (OJ L 32, 10.2.1996, p. 31).

(9) OJ L 222, 14.8.1978, p. 11. Directive as last amended by Directive 94/8/EC (OJ L 82, 25.3.1994, p. 33).

(10) OJ L 197, 18.7.1987, p. 33.

Annex 3

SECOND REPORT FROM THE COMMISSION TO THE COUNCIL AND THE EUROPEAN PARLIAMENT
on the state of liberalisation of the energy markets

1. INTRODUCTION

Energy is a very important element of economic activity and social welfare. The creation of a single energy market based on open and competitive markets represents a great challenge for the Union as it is envisaged to have a direct impact on European industry and consumers welfare.

First, the introduction of competition in the electricity and gas sectors is a means to enhance the competitiveness of the European industry competing in the world markets. One of the critical factors for the international competitiveness of European business is the cost of energy. Compared to USA or Australia, European industry in some cases pays 40% more for electricity and gas due to isolation of national markets and lack of intra-Community trade for these products. The competitive disadvantage of higher prices is particularly marked for the energy intensive industry such as steel, paper, glass and motor vehicle industries. In the most energy-intensive sectors such as chemicals and aluminium, energy can account for 60% of production costs. It is evident that the survival and growth of these industries in the EU depends on their ability to cut productions costs, including energy costs. A single electricity competitive market will also result in an improvement of the standards of service to the benefit of consumers, as the utilities will be exposed to competitive pressure.

Second, the creation of a single market will also strengthen the security of supply across the EU by permitting diversification and flexibility of supplies as a result of the closer integration of the internal energy markets. It will provide for more outlets and better interconnections in the EU.

Third, the internal energy market is likely to have positive effects on the environment. For instance, liberalisation will facilitate in all Member States a switch over to cleaner energy sources for electricity generation such as gas; the operation of a single market will lead to less waste of natural resources as less reserve capacity will be needed in each country, and the single market will offer the possibility to energy consumers to choose cleaner energy sources. To ensure that these positive effects are not mitigated by the impact of more competitive prices on energy consumption, energy saving efforts should be maintained.

Over the last years very important steps have been taken to create a single energy market for the EU. Following the unanimous adoption of the electricity Directive[1] on December 1996, its implementation has been now completed in the majority of the Member States. The Directive lays down rules for allowing real competition between electricity producers while allowing an increasing number of consumers a free choice of their electricity suppliers. While providing for the liberalisation of the electricity markets, it gives special emphasis to public services by providing the mechanisms to pursue public service considerations in the context of a competitive market.

The Directive[2] providing an internal market for natural gas has been adopted on 22 June 1998. Member States should implement it by August 2000. It provides for the gradual opening of the natural gas market to competition over a ten year period to reach 33% of the total gas consumption.

These Directives have provided the foundations for the creation of a single energy market. They have transformed the conditions under which electricity and gas trade will be carried out in the future with a view to lead to significant price reductions across the EU, to enhanced efficiency and to improved security of supply. To appreciate the progress already achieved, one has to look at the picture of the electricity and gas markets some years ago. In the past there was no trade for electricity and gas between the Member States of the EU and often no competition even within the Member States except for certain countries like the UK and the Scandinavian countries, which have started the liberalisation process before the adoption of the Directive. Electricity and gas generation, transmission and distribution were dominated by monopolies. Consumers inevitably had no choice of electricity supplies, and no guarantee for service standards. European energy intensive industry for which electricity represented a considerable cost was put at competitive disadvantage, as electricity prices across Europe were higher than in other areas of the World. Furthermore, the foreclosure of national markets to competition has lead in the past to significant price differences in different countries and even within individual Member States as the following table illustrates:

---

[1] Directive on common rules for the internal market in electricity 96/92/EC OJ L27 of 30.01.1997.

[2] Directive 98/30, OJ L 204 of 21.07.98.

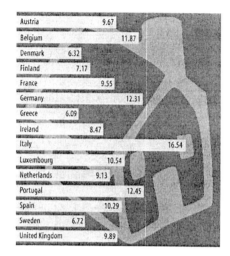
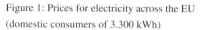
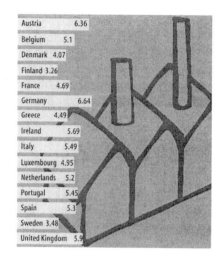

Figure 1: Prices for electricity across the EU	Figure 2: Prices for electricity across the EU
(domestic consumers of 3.300 kWh)	(industrial consumers of 50 GWh)

Source: Eurostat Price level as at July 1997 in ECU x l00/kWh. Prices exclude taxes

The establishment of a single legislative framework applicable to all fifteen national electricity and gas systems was a very delicate task. In the electricity sector, there were highly centralised systems, such as those of France and Italy. There were, furthermore, countries which had already undergone the liberalisation process. In the gas sector, exporting countries such as the UK and the Netherlands have different systems and interests than importing countries and countries such as Portugal and Greece which had introduced gas rather recently. Market structures also varied enormously from country to country. The Directives providing for the liberalisation of the electricity and gas markets have set the framework for the creation of a single market for electricity and gas by allowing, over a period of time, consumers to choose their suppliers, and by providing for competition amongst producers. These Directives were based on three basic principles:

– First, the *introduction of competition* while respecting public service objectives to ensure an adequate and reliable supply of electricity and gas which is of utmost importance to all economic activity and households.

– Second, the *gradual* introduction of competition to the electricity and gas markets to give the necessary time to the industry to adjust to the new environment.

– Third, the Directives do not impose a rigid system to all Member States. They rather provide the *framework* for the creation of a single market while leaving Member States a wide degree of discretion to adopt the system which is best suited to their particular circumstances.

It is evident that this only a start and much remain to be done for the completion of an internal energy market. Ultimately, the success of liberalisation will depend on a series of measures that need to be taken during the coming months which will ensure that intra-Community trade is easily carried out. In this respect the creation of a number of trade facilitating mechanisms is essential together with the supervision of the operation of the markets in practice.

2. ELECTRICITY DIRECTIVE 96/92/EC

2.1 Implementation Throughout the EU – State of Play

2.1.1 Electricity Generation

Generation is one of the main components in the cost of electricity. This cost needs to be significantly reduced if EU prices are to fall to those of some of its main competitors. The Directive introduces full and complete competition across the EU for all new generating capacity. Thus, from February 1999, any producer will be able to build a new power plant and generate electricity anywhere in the Community, either on the basis of an authorisation system or a tendering procedure. The Directive permits Member States to choose between these two procedures when implementing the Directive. Under an authorisation procedure, any company may build and operate a new generation plant, provided that it complies with the planning and energy supply criteria for authorisation specified in the Member State in question. Alternatively, under a tendering procedure, whenever there is a necessity for new generation capacity on the basis of regular long-term planning forecasts, an independent body will draw up an inventory for new means of production and the requisite capacity will be allocated by a tendering procedure. Thus, the monopolies existing until now in many Member States for electricity generation will be exposed to competition.

Whilst the Directive provides the choice for Member States between these two approaches for introducing competition into electricity generation, it is becoming clear that almost all Member States have opted or will opt for the authorisation procedure for the construction of new generation capacity. The reason for this trend developing in the EU is that this procedure represents the most transparent and effective mechanism to open up electricity generation to competition.

2.1.2 Opening up of the markets

In order to create a competitive market that works in practice, sufficient numbers of consumers have to be free to purchase electricity from the supplier of their choice. On the other hand, liberalisation has to take place progressively. The change to competition requires major restructuring, new trading systems and mechanisms to be put into place, and time for companies to adapt to the new competitive environment. The Directive balances these two objectives, requiring Member States to progressively open their markets in three stages: 26% on 19.02.99,28% at 2000 and 33% in 2003.

However, Member States have committed themselves to open up their electricity markets more than this minimum requirement. Countries like the UK, Germany, Sweden and Finland are committed to 100% market opening. Denmark by permitting all distributors to purchase freely is indirectly opening up 90% of its electricity market to competition. Others have also decided to go further than the basic requirements of the Directive, notably the Netherlands and Spain which will open up 33% upon implementation gradually increasing to reach 100% by 2007, Austria 27% upon implementation to reach 50% by 2003, and Italy 30% upon implementation. As a result, more than 60% of total EU electricity demand will be liberalised according to existing plans and more than nearly two thirds of consumers will be able to choose their supplier.

This is illustrated in the following graphic. The first bar gives the opening of the markets on the day the Directive has to be implemented by the Member States. The second gives the situation that according to current plans of the Member States will exist in 2007. Nevertheless it appears highly likely that in reality liberalisation will in fact have progressed even further by this date.

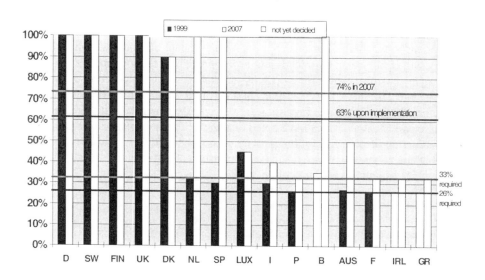

2.1.3 Access to the network

To enable the transport of electricity from producers to eligible customers, the Directive requires the owners and operators of the electricity networks, the Transmission System Operators and the Distribution System Operators, to provide access to their lines to others. The Directive provides three alternative methods of achieving this: regulated third party access, negotiated third party access, or the single buyer model. In fact, all Member States have opted for regulated or negotiated third party access ("TPA"): no country will significantly use the Single Buyer model. Access to transport wires can only be refused when there is not enough capacity to transport the electricity or when transport would make it impossible to carry out public service obligations.

It is generally considered that the system of regulated third party access on the basis of published prices is the method of permitting access to the network that will produce the most effective competitive market. Not only does the system of fixed prices for all ensure that discrimination against competitors cannot take place, it ensures that companies can plan future electricity purchases with advance knowledge of transparent tariffs. To have to renegotiate access prices and conditions at the end of each contract is also an extra burden on the companies. Regulated TPA is the option that most Member States have chosen as the table below illustrates:

Negotiated TPA	Regulated TPA
Greece, Germany Denmark (*)	Belgium, Finland, France Luxembourg, Austria, Netherlands Spain, Sweden, UK, Ireland, Italy Portugal

(*) *Denmark has indicated that it will change to RTPA*

2.1.4 Unbundling

In Europe, the transmission network is largely owned by a vertically integrated electricity company, that generates, transports and sells electricity. These companies own an 'essential service", the transmission network, which, under the new rules, it must offer on equal terms to its own company, and to its competitors. However, there is in reality a clear risk that such companies will be tempted to discriminate in favour of their own group companies when granting access to the network. To prevent discrimination occurring the Directive requires Member States to take three basic measures: (i) ensuring management unbundling of the transmission system operator, (ii) ensuring accounting separation of transmission and distributor activities from other parts of the company and (iii) ensuring that appropriate mechanisms are set up to prevent confidential information being passed by the transmission system operator to other parts of the company.

The management unbundling and confidentiality provisions of the Directive are crucial in preventing the operator of the network from discriminating against potential users of the transmission system.

Management unbundling entails in practice that the day to day management of the network by the TSO must be independent from commercial interests of the vertically integrated company. Thus:

– managers of the transmission system should not sit on the board of directors of the company. The transmission part should act independently from the interests of the vertically integrated company;

– the transmission system operator should have all the necessary means and assets to maintain, develop and manage the network, especially if the ownership of the network remains in the hands of the vertically integrated company;

– the transmission system operator must ensure that it does not disseminate any commercially sensitive information from other companies to other in his own company. Clear, 'Chinese walls" have to be put in place to prevent this flow of information.

The Directive requires vertically integrated undertakings to keep separate accounts for each of the activities of electricity generation, transmission, distribution and any other non-electricity activities.These accounts should be published and be kept according to a standard accounting practice. The objective of these provisions is to ensure the necessary transparency in the operation of electricity undertakings with the view to avoid any cross subsidies between the different activities and thereby distortions of competition. This important obligation will prevent companies disguising their allocation of costs. Transparency is seen in this light as an important precondition for the effective application of competition rules.

All Member States will respect the provisions for separation of accounts in vertically integrated undertakings. Most member States have decided to legally separate the TSO from the vertically integrated company which is the most effective approach to ensure that non-discrimination is taking place. Thus, Spain, the UK (England & Wales), Finland, Sweden, Denmark (west), Austria (east), the Netherlands, Portugal, Greece, Italy and Belgium have decided to appoint a separate legal entity as the transmission system operator. Denmark (east), Germany, France, UK (Scotland & N. Ireland), and Austria (west) will ensure that the TSO is independent in management terms without however appointing a separate legal entity. Member States plans are illustrated in the following table:

2.1.5 Public service obligations

Liberalisation and public policy are not two contrad&tory imperati es. On the contrary, public service will and must play an important role in a liber lised market. This approach is clearly reflected in the electricity Directive, which p ovides for a mechanism enabling Member States to pursue public policy consideratio s without in normal circumstances limiting the liberalisation process. In this light ember States can define public service obligations in the general economic interest within five categories, related to environmental considerations, security, regularity , quality of supply constraints and pricing policy considerations. They can then take e measures necessary to achieve them. What is important is that the measures and mechanisms Member States put in place for the achievement of these objectives should not restrict trade and competition more than necessary.

Therefore, supply of electricity to geographically isolated consumers at reasonable prices, obligations to provide unprofitable services, guaranteed electricity upply to the sick and disabled, limits on the possibility of electricity companies to disconnect customers because of debt, and ensuring continuity of electricity supply are and will remain obligations that can be met in the context of a liberalised market. Governments can still impose on their distribution companies an obligation to supply their customers. Member States have the choice to impose such obligations on all operators in their country. Nevertheless, these obligations should be objective, transparent and imposed on a non-discriminatory basis on all operators equally. There is no single definition of the concept of the public service in the Union. However, there is a common set of provisions existing in almost all Member States designed to regulate the activities of electricity companies, which can listed in three broad categories.

The **first** category relates to the universal service and the overall protection of the consumer. In this line specific provisions exist in most Member States, (such as AUS, D, FIN, DK, UK GR, SP, POR, B and NL), laying down obligations to connect customers, and obligations to supply electricity on a regular basis to consumers. Member States such as Austria also lay down that consumers should be charged at reasonable prices, whereas in other countries such as France and Greece, regulated tariffs apply to captive customers. Furthermore, special provisions are laid down in some countries such as the United Kingdom to protect the elderly and disabled The **second** category concerns the protection of the environment. Specific environmental constrains are provided for electricity generation to ensure environmental friendly electricity production (Germany, Austria, Denmark, Greece).

Support schemes for renewables and combined heat and power are particular in the area of R&TD. Measures are also taken towards internalisation of external costs for instance through fiscal measures[3]. In addition, the role of cost effective mechanisms such as demand side management and energy services are being explored.

The **third** category relates to security of supply considerations, which entail technical specifications for all those connected to the grid, maintenance of reserve capacity, matching supply and demand, availability of capacity to meet demand, securing primary fuels for electricity generation, and maintenance of a secure and reliable system.

The Directive, therefore, gives Member States a wide margin of discretion in deciding how to ensure that public service obligations are met, and which ones to pursue. Nonetheless, the objectives and approaches pursued by the Member States are becoming increasingly similar. Experience to-date indicates that as competition takes hold, Member States require, and the companies meet, increasingly high standards in this area. Not only must companies

---

[3] COM 597°30 of 12.03.97.

meet the minimum standards legally required by Member States, it is often in their commercial interest to exceed them. This continued increase in the quality of public service is one of the basic underlying objectives of the Directive.

2.1.6 Transitional Regimes ("stranded costs")

The introduction of competition in electricity will lead to lower electricity prices.

These lower prices could lead to serious financial difficulties for producers and suppliers who are at present faced with costs based on the situation before competition was introduced.

These costs can take several forms, for instance:
– obligations imposed on electricity companies in he past, for instance for social or environmental reasons leading to extra investments that can not be recuperated;
– fuel and power purchase agreements with a duration beyond 1999, which have been concluded on the basis of the expected price level before liberalisation and would be too expensive under competitive circumstances;

Stranded costs are clearly not the costs that are a result of bad financial management of the company; they have to be clearly caused by the transition to competition. Normally these above market costs are a result of government policy, to favour certain fuels above others for instance. To deal with this issue the Directive provides for Member States to notify **transitional regimes** to the Commission. Such regimes aim to compensate companies for these extra costs, for instance by limiting the market opening to new entrants, to favour dispatch of electricity from certain fuels, or to give financial compensation. Pursuant to the subsidiarity principle it is for each Member States to decide whether, and how much, it wishes to provide for a transitional regime. It is equally for each country to decide how to meet the resultant costs. However, any such decision is subject to Commission control, either pursuant to the Directive, or the state aid rules.

Twelve notifications have been received by the Commission. Individual decisions will have to be adopted for each country during the coming months.

2.2 Second Report on Harmonisation Requirements

According to Article 25 of the Electricity Directive, the Commission had to submit a report to the Council and to the European Parliament on harmonisation requirements in the internal market for electricity. With regard to the ongoing implementation phase the Commission decided to split the report in two parts. The first report, delivered in February 1998, dealt exclusively with the issue of promoting renewables in the competitive internal electricity market. As a consequence of this report and the following discussions, the Commission is now considering the options **to promote increased penetration of renewables in the internal market for electricity.**

The second harmonisation report[4] deals with a broader range of issues. First, it considers **obstacles for cross-border trade**, such as cross-border tarification methodology and settlement, the operation of interconnectors, the management of available transmission capacity, the necessity to reinforce interconnection capacity, and the potential need for a common commercial policy towards 3rd countries. A second set of issues addresses the necessity of **ensuring a level playing field in the European electricity market after liberalisation**. This part discusses, inter alia, standards related to decommissioning of nuclear plants, environmental standards in electricity production[5] and taxation. It raises the question whether the different levels of environmental and other standards amongst Member states, based on EU legislation prior to liberalisation, tend to be too heterogeneous in the light of competition after liberalisation. The taxation chapter focuses on indirect taxes, in particular on energy taxes. It also covers the question of how to treat renewable based electricity and how to treat imported electricity.

The main focus of this second report is cross-border trade. This issue has been extensively discussed during the deliberations of the Electricity Regulation Forum in Florence. At the meeting of 8/9 October cross-border transmission pricing has been recognised as a key issue, and an adequate solution of this issue is the prerequisite for the functioning of a real single market in electricity. It had been agreed to encourage the independent transmission system operators to develop an adequate system of cross-border tarification and settlement. To this end, the Commission invited the representative independent transmission system operators to Brussels on the 21 January 1999. A breakthrough in this difficult issue is needed, and, important steps can already be recognised. Otherwise, or maybe in parallel, there could be a clear need for regulation at the EU level. Thus, the second harmonisation has the function to support the rapid implementation of these industry arrangements, and, if necessary, to prepare the ground for regulatory action.

2.3 Renewable Energy Sources and the Internal Electricity Market

In the White Paper on renewable sources of energy[6] it is stated that renewable energy sources still make an unacceptably modest contribution to the Community's energy balance as compared to the available technical potential. In 1995 the contribution of RES to the Union's overall gross inland energy consumption was somewhat less than 6%. The White Paper sets the indicative ambitious target of a doubling of the share of RES to 12% by

---

[4] COM(99)164, 16.04.1999.

[5] Whilst the entry into force of the Directive will in itself result in environmental benefits due to the introduction of more efficient and cleaner new generating capacity, additional measures to further improve environmental standards in this area can also play an important role in achieving the EU's objectives in this respect.

[6] Energy for the future: renewable sources of energy. White paper for a Community Strategy and action plan, COM(97)599 final, 26.11. 1997.

2010. This percentage is all the more ambitious since the major part of the current 6% RES-share stems from large hydro for which the development perspectives are very limited. The Member States have agreed that there is a need to promote a sustained and substantially increased use of RES throughout the Community level complementary to actions at national level[7].

The share in electricity consumption of electricity from renewable energy sources will increase significantly over the coming years. The International Energy Agency (IEA) has, for example, in its World Energy Outlook for 1998, projected that the increase in RES-E will be far greater than in conventionally generated electricity in the Member States of the European Union.

This is confirmed by indications received by the Commission from the Member States. The following countries[8] have indicated targets for the growth of renewables generated electricity (excluding large hydro, unless otherwise indicated): Austria (3% in 2005), United Kingdom (10% in 2010, incl. large hydro), Denmark (25% increase by 2005, 85 % increase by 2030), Finland (100 MW wind by 2005, 25% increase in bioenergy by 2005), Greece (255-355 MW by 2003), Ireland (19,7% in 2010, incl. large hydro), Portugal (837 MW by 2006), Spain (1200 MW by 2000).

To achieve an increase in the generation of electricity from renewable energy sources, the Member States have adopted different ways of supporting electricity from renewable energy sources. The European Union, with the adoption of Directive 96/92/EC concerning common rules for the internal market in electricity, is in the process of creating a single market for electricity. The integration of the electricity markets implies that the support of RES-E must be seen in the light of the internal market.

In the first report on Harmonisation requirements for the internal electricity market[9], the Commission concluded that:

> *"a clear need for common rules in this area can already be identified. The contemporaneous existence of different support schemes appears likely to result in distortions of trade and competition. The role of renewables in the EU will clearly increase in the coming years, given the Kyoto commitments. Thus, potential market distortions will accordingly increase. Whilst the trade and competition distorting effects of different renewable support schemes is rather limited at present, given the limited EU market share of electricity from renewable sources, this negative effect appears likely to significantly increase in the coming years. In this light, it is appropriate to move towards the definition of some common rules in this area as rapidly as practicable".*

---

[7] Council resolution of 8 June 1998, OJ C 198, 24-6-1998

[8] In replies to a Commission questionniare adressed to all Member States in 1998

[9] Commission report to the Council and the European Parliament on Harmonisation requirements. Directive 96/92 concerning rules for the international market in Electricity. COM (1998), 167, 16.03.1998

It is clear that, at present, the disparate support schemes across the EU do not meet all these requirements. In the light of the above the Commission has adopted on 13 April 1999 a Working Paper[10] on this issue, examining the current support schemes in the Member States and indicating in what way this issue should be dealt with in the light of the internal electricity market.

3. GAS DIRECTIVE 98/3O/EC

The European Parliament and the Council adopted on 22 June 1998 the Directive 98/3O/EC11[11] on common rules for the internal market in natural gas. The directive entered into force on 10 August 1998. Member States must implement it by 10 August 2000.

This Directive forms part of the framework for the internal energy market and represents a parallel of the Directive 96/92/EC.

It establishes some common rules for the transmission, distribution, supply and storage of natural gas. The Directive lays down the rules relating to the organisation and functioning of the natural gas sector, including liquefied natural gas, access to the market, the operation of systems, and the criteria and procedures applicable to the granting of authorisations for transmission, distribution, supply and storage of natural gas.

3.1 Key Issues of the Gas Directive

3.1.1 Market Opening

The Directive ensures that the market will be opened to competition progressively, starting with a first significant step that will guarantee that the high gas consuming industry will be given the possibility to choose freely its supplier. In a ten-year period the market will be liberalised for at least 33% of the total gas consumption during three steps:

1) 10 August 2000

*All gas-fired power generators.

* Final consumers with a minimum 25 million m^3 of annual consumption

This shall lead to at least 20% market opening in each Member State. In case where market opening would exceed 30%, Member State may introduce supplementary thresholds to limit opening to 30%.

---

[10] SEC (99) 470 final of 13 April 1999

[11] Directive 98/30/EC, O.J.E. CL 291 of 21 July 1998

2) 10 August 2003

*All gas-fired power generators

* Final consumers with minimum 15 million m³ of annual consumption

This shall lead to at least 28% market opening in each Member State. In case where market opening would exceed 30%, Member State may introduce supplementary thresholds to limit opening to 30%.

3) 10 August 2008

* All gas-fired power generators

* Final consumers with minimum 5 million m³ of annual consumption

This shall lead to at least 33% market opening in each Member State. In case where market opening would exceed 30%, Member State may introduce supplementary thresholds to limit opening to 30%.

Member States may introduce, in order to safeguard the balance of their electricity market, a threshold for eligibility of combined heat and power producers (CHP), which in any case cannot exceed the threshold for final customers.

3.1.2 Access to the System

Eligible customers will have the possibility to negotiate and conclude supply contracts with any natural gas undertakings, being inside or outside the territory of the Member State. Access to the system for the execution of these contracts will be possible on the basis of two procedures (negotiated access or regulated access), the choice being left to the Member States. Both procedures must operate in accordance with objective, transparent and non-discriminatory criteria.

Where Member States opt for the negotiated Third Party Access the conditions for access to the system are negotiated with the responsible natural gas undertaking. These undertakings are required to publish the main commercial conditions for the use of the system.

Under a negotiated Third Party Access, eligible customers and natural gas undertakings have a right of access to the system, on the basis of published tariffs and/or other terms and obligations for use of that system.

Access to the system may only be refused in case of lack of capacity, when this would impede gas undertakings to carry out some public service obligations, and when this would create some serious economic and financial problems with take-or-pay obligations.

In case where a dispute would arise on the conditions for access to the system, it will be possible to refer the case to a dispute settlement authority that shall be appointed by Member States.

Member States have the possibility to establish different rules for the access to the upstream pipeline network, to take into account the possible specific economic and technical characteristics of this part of the network. Member States must ensure that these rules guarantee a fair and open access and a competitive market in natural gas, avoiding any abuse of a dominant position.

3.1.3 Unbundling

The accounts of all integrated gas undertakings must be as transparent as possible, in particular in order to detect any abuse of a dominant position such as abnormally low or high tariffs or discriminatory practices for equivalent services. To this end, these undertakings must keep in their internal accounting separate accounts for their natural gas transmission, distribution and storage activities, and, where appropriate, consolidated accounts for non-gas activities. These internal accounts will include a balance sheet and a profit and loss account for each activity.

Moreover, to avoid the risk of potential discrimination between users, it is essential that transmission, distribution, storage and LNG undertakings ensure the confidentiality of commercially sensitive information in the course of their business, and thus the Directive requires that they shall not, in the context of sales or purchases of natural gas by the transmission undertakings, distribution undertakings or related undertakings abuse commercially sensitive information obtained in the context of providing or negotiating access to the system.

3.1.4 Public Service Obligations

Member States have the right to impose on natural gas undertakings public service obligations in the general economic interest. These obligations must fall within the framework of five specific areas: security, including security of supply, regularity, quality, price of supply and protection of the environment. Whatever these obligations are, Member States must ensure that they are established under objective, transparent and non-discriminatory criteria. Member States will communicate them to the Commission which will verify the compatibility of these provisions with Community law. In any case, Member States must ensure that these measures represent the least restrictive in terms of competition.

3.1.5 Derogations

Under specific circumstances, the Directive establishes possibilities for Member States to derogate from the application of the main provisions. These derogations, specified under Chapter VII of the Directive, have been introduced in order to take into account potential risks or distortions that could be endangered by the liberalisation of the gas market.

3.1.5.1 TAKE-OR-PAY CONTRACTS

Today, the vast majority of the gas supply in the European Union is contracted under long term take-or-pay contracts concluded between gas supply undertakings and producers. These contracts are characterised by a clause obliging the purchaser to pay for a specific volume of gas regardless of whether the gas is taken or not.

The Directive provides that, if a natural gas undertaking encounters or considers it would encounter serious economic and financial difficulties because of its take-or-pay commitments accepted in one or more gas purchase contracts, it may apply for a temporary derogation from the requirement to grant access to the system, which can be granted by the Member States and then submitted to the final determination of the Commission.

However, a number of conditions must be applied to evaluate if it is necessary to grant a derogation from access or if other alternative measures, less restrictive of competition, can be taken. In any case, a derogation can be presented only when the overall gas sales of the gas undertaking fall below the level of minimum offtake guarantees included in the take-or-pay contract.

3.1.5.2 NON-INTERCONNECTED COUNTRIES

As long as Member States have no connection with the interconnected system of another Member States and have only one main external supplier (with a market share exceeding 75%) they may derogate from the application of some articles of the Directive, including authorisations for gas facilities and direct lines and the obligation in terms of eligible customers. At present, two Member States, Finland and Greece, fall under these conditions, and will have to notify the Commission of the intention to make use of this derogation. However, when these conditions would not be filled, derogations would automatically expire.

3.1.5.3 EMERGENT MARKETS

Countries where gas has been introduced only recently could have substantial problems resulting from the implementation of the Directive and the introduction of competition in a developing market. These countries are considered emergent markets and may therefore benefit from a derogation from the application of the main provisions of the Directive. The conditions under which Member States can be considered emergent is that the first supply of the first long-term gas contract in their market have been made not more than ten years earlier. Greece and Portugal fall at present under these conditions.

3.1.5.4 EMERGENT AREAS WHICH COULD BENEFIT FROM THE ENCOURAGEMENT OF INVESTMENTS

Member States have the possibility to request derogations for geographically limited areas where gas infrastructure has not yet been established or has been in operation for less than 10 years, in a view to encourage new investments and upon the condition that implementation of the Directive would cause substantial problems in such areas.

These derogations, granted by the Commission, cannot be presented in relation to investments in the distribution sector but only to other investments in the gas sector and in particular in relation to transmission infrastructure.

3.2 State of Liberalisation

The gas market will be opened to competition progressively, during a ten-year period, to reach in 2008 at least 33% of the total gas consumption. However, due to the fact that the eligibility of all power generators and of large industrial customers will result in a higher market opening in some Member States, the real level of market opening at EU level will exceed the initial minimum level of 20%. In fact, almost 33% of the total EU gas market will be liberalised from the beginning. Moreover, several Member States will not limit the opening of their gas market to the minimum thresholds established by the Gas directive.

The United Kingdom has already totally liberalised its gas market since May 1998, on the basis of a system of fixed tariffs for access (Regulated TPA). Ireland has opened the market for customers consuming more than 25 million m^3 per year. In Germany, since April 1998 all customers are legally free to choose their supplier on the basis of a Negotiated TPA system. Spain has adopted in October 1998 a new legislative framework that will permit it to progressively liberalise all the market in 2013, with a first 46% of the market already opened since 1998. In Belgium a law should be adopted shortly opening 46,7% of the gas market to competition. The Netherlands is planning to liberalise by 2000 45% of the market and to open it completely in 2007. The other Member States will submit shortly their proposals for implementation, but on the basis of these preliminary figures it is already possible to calculate that, as for electricity, the liberalisation of the gas market is becoming a reality throughout all Europe.

4. CONCLUSIONS

At present there is every reason to be optimistic regarding the creation of a single market for electricity and gas. With respect to the Electricity Directive, most Member States have fully and properly implemented the Directive, and they have chosen structures and approaches that will ensure that competition is effective, while in most cases they liberalise far more rapidly than is required by the Directive. Already, prices in Europe are beginning to fall, as can be seen from the following graphs:

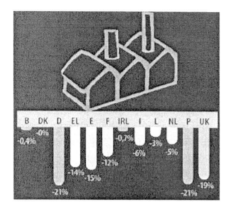

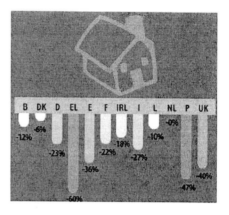

Graph 1
% modification of 1997(2) compared to 1994 electricity prices for industrial consumers (10 GWh annual consumption) prices in national currency/kWh, VAT excluded, prices deflated

Graph 2
% modification of 1998 electricity prices compared to 1994 for household consumers (7500 kWh annual consumption), Prices in national currency/

kWh, tax included, prices deflated

Furthermore, the adoption of the Gas Directive represented another major step for the creation of a single energy market. Member States by August 2000 will have to open up their markets to competition for consumers representing at least 20 % of their gas market. Member States are now in the process of transposing the Directive into their national laws. The Commission is closely following the implementation process of the Gas Directive. At present no major difficulties are likely to arise.

In the future the correct implementation of the Gas Directive by Member States and monitoring the operation of the Electricity Directive in practice will be in the top priorities of the Union. It is vital to ensure that these rules are equally and fairly applied by the establishment of efficient regulatory mechanisms.

This regulatory role will be carried out in partnership between national regulators, competition authorities, and the European Commission. The Electricity Directive itself requires the Member States to set up a dispute settlement authority, independent of electricity companies. However, most Member States have chosen to establish an independent regulator, immediately and on a day-to-day basis independent of, but ultimately responsible to, Government. In any event, it is evident that a clear and increasing understanding across the EU exists of the need for effective regulation in this area, whilst subjecting companies to the minimum red tape possible.

Evidently, the implementation of the Electricity Directive is not the last step towards the creation of a single electricity market. The Directive lays down the groundwork for the *liberalisation* of 15 electricity markets. Nevertheless, much remains to be done to achieve a single market for electricity. In this line the remaining barriers to intra-community trade should be identified and eliminated. Furthermore, the Commission, in close collaboration with the Member States and the electricity industry, should establish more coherent principles concerning a range of unresolved issues that can block cross-border trade. The development of tariff systems and trade facilitating mechanisms to enable the single market to become effective is thus of utmost importance, and will be the principal challenge that the Commission, together with national authorities and Europeg transmission and distribution industries, will be dealing with in the coming months and years.

Furthermore, the Union should take action to promote electricity generated from renewable energy sources with the view to increase green electricity in a substantial and sustainable way, and increasing attention will need to be paid to the environmental dimension of the internal energy market to meet EU environmental objectives.

In addition, the employment effects of the liberalisation of the electricity and gas markets will need to be addressed by Member States and the Union in cooperation with social partners.

The Commission will also examine the consumer dimension of the liberalisation process, especially its impact on residential consumers and how the provisions put in place to guarantee universal service and the protection of consumers are functioning.

Last but not least in the prospect of enlargement of the EU in the coming years the Union should ensure the smooth transition to a wider single market for electricity and gas. In this respect the Commission will implement a specific technical assistance programme vis-à-vis candidate countries for accession to the EU with the view to ensure that the Union seizes all the opportunities from a wider single energy market and that all achievements towards European integration in the energy sector are not endangered.

SUBJECT INDEX